BARREL-AGED STOUT AND SELLING OUT

BARREL-AGED STOUT AND SELLING OUT

★★★★

GOOSE ISLAND, ANHEUSER-BUSCH, AND HOW CRAFT BEER BECAME BIG BUSINESS

JOSH NOEL

First edition
Published by Chicago Review Press Incorporated
814 North Franklin Street
Chicago, Illinois 60610
ISBN 978-1-61373-721-7

Library of Congress Cataloging-in-Publication Data

Names: Noel, Josh, author.
Title: Barrel-aged stout and selling out : Goose Island, Anheuser-Busch, and how craft beer became big business / Josh Noel.
Description: First edition. | Chicago, Illinois : Chicago Review Press, [2018] | Includes bibliographical references and index.
Identifiers: LCCN 2017050648 (print) | LCCN 2017054555 (ebook) | ISBN 9781613737224 (adobe pdf) | ISBN 9781613737231 (kindle) | ISBN 9781613737248 (epub) | ISBN 9781613737217 (trade paper)
Subjects: LCSH: Goose Island Brewery. | Anheuser-Busch, Inc. | Beer industry—United States. | Microbreweries—United States.
Classification: LCC HD9397.U54 (ebook) | LCC HD9397.U54 G6566 2018 (print) |
DDC 338.7/663420973—dc23
LC record available at https://lccn.loc.gov/2017050648

Cover design: John Yates at Stealworks
Cover image: zmurciuk_k/iStock/Thinkstock
Typesetting: Nord Compo

Printed in the United States of America
5 4 3 2 1

For Lauren

Contents

Part II: Selling Out

Prologue

It's November 2012.

Chicago is unseasonably warm, but the leaves have turned and winter approaches. It's barrel-aged beer season.

Beer lovers have flocked to Chicago for one of the nation's signature events: the Festival of Wood and Barrel Aged Beer. FOBAB, to those in the know.

More than sixty breweries from twenty-one states are on hand. They pour 194 beers with colorful names and exotic backstories. Barrel-Aged Snarling Badger, a twice-fermented Berliner Weisse aged in French oak Syrah barrels from a brewery in Idaho. Barrel-Aged Frosted Frog Christmas Ale, a spiced ale from Ohio aged in bourbon barrels. Gnag Reflex, a tart and funky brown ale aged in new oak with cherries from Louisville.

Every beer in the room has spent time in some sort of wood barrel. Bourbon, mostly. But also red wine, white wine, rye whiskey, rum, gin, and virgin oak.

Most breweries are set up at folding tables at the edges of the brick-walled loft, pouring beer in precious two-ounce increments from plastic pitchers. One brewery stands apart, at an elaborate station just inside the entrance. Its tap handles have been drilled into actual barrels to seem as if the beer is flowing straight from the oak. (It is, of course, coming from kegs beyond the barrels.) That brewery is the only one in the room with enough sway, home-court advantage, and budget to construct such an elaborate show: Goose Island Beer Co.

The twenty-four-year-old brewery is a Chicago icon and arguably the reason that so many people stand in the festive, beer-swilling space; back in 1995, Goose Island pioneered the industry's first imperial stout aged in a bourbon barrel. The beer was named Bourbon County Stout. At FOBAB, bourbon barrel–aged stout has become an industry touchstone; it flows in all directions throughout the bright, airy loft.

The room is feeling good.

Craft beer is feeling good.

It is still an underdog. But it is ascendant.

Thirty-five years earlier, the nation was home to fewer than ninety breweries. Now, on this November day, there are nearly twenty-five hundred. More than four hundred have opened during the previous year alone—more than one a day. After decades of Big Beer's bland dominance, American beer is rife with choice. Diversity. Flavor. And rarely is it more diverse and flavorful than at FOBAB.

At the end of the night, thirty-two awards are given: a top-three in ten different categories, plus the top two overall beers poured that day.

The brewery that wins more than any other? The hometown hero.

Goose Island scores five medals, including the coveted Best of Show for its Cherry Rye Bourbon County Stout, an offshoot of the original forged seventeen years earlier. Its brewpub wins two more awards, which gives Goose Island nearly a quarter of the evening's honors—seven of the thirty-two.

Each time Goose Island's name is called, its brewers hug and slap hands and leap to the stage. Their work is elite. Here is proof.

Applause rises from the tightly packed crowd, punctured with a few hoots and hollers. But there is also a curious sound: a smattering of boos. They come from a handful of guys deep in the throng. They're young and lanky and wear T-shirts, hoodies, and baseball caps.

With their third or fourth jeer, I turn to one and ask: Why boo the hometown favorite?

"I don't like Anheuser-Busch," he says.

Many breweries tell the story of craft beer in the United States. Sierra Nevada. Boston Beer. Anchor. Bell's. New Belgium. Dogfish Head. Stone. Lagunitas.

Only one brewery *is* the story of craft beer: Goose Island.

John Hall, a former box company executive, launched the brewery in 1988, when there were just two others in Chicago and fewer than two hundred nationally. Goose Island flourished through the 1990s. Then it struggled. It grew more. It struggled more. It innovated. It took risks. It grew still more.

And then it sold out.

Goose Island's sale in 2011 to Anheuser-Busch wasn't just a sale to the biggest beer company in the world—it was a sale to the company that had spent decades thwarting the American beer industry with confusion, trickery, and dullness. To Anheuser-Busch, less choice was less competition. It was more market share. When American beer was nothing but stadium sponsorships and Super Bowl commercials, Anheuser-Busch was able to account for nearly one of every two beers sold in the United States.

Then came craft beer. American beer drinkers discovered variety. Tastes diversified. Anheuser-Busch could no longer simply suffocate competition. It needed craft beer.

So it bought Goose Island.

The announcement of Goose Island's $38.8 million sale to the world's largest beer company, on March 28, 2011, functionally ended an era for craft beer—an era of collaboration and cooperation, growth and good vibes, and the shared cause of building a lifeboat in a sea of Big Beer banality.

Anheuser-Busch and its parent company, Belgian-Brazilian conglomerate Anheuser-Busch InBev, kept buying breweries, and as they did, divisions grew starker and more rancorous. The classic American success story—nurturing a business that changed an industry, then selling it for millions—became heresy in craft beer.

The beer industry entered an era of revolution—fragmentation, increased competition, and, for the breweries that dared to follow Goose Island's lead with a sale to Anheuser-Busch, searing claims of "sellout."

Selling to the world's largest beer company guaranteed growth for Goose Island and a payday for John Hall. His risk and vision were rewarded. But no matter how good the beer, how many honors or awards, how innovative Goose Island would ever be again, someone deep in the crowd would always boo.

Part I

Barrel-Aged Stout

1

A Brewery Was the Answer

ON A THURSDAY EVENING IN 1986, as a spring storm pounded the Dallas–Ft. Worth airport, John Hall sat in an airplane on the rain-glazed tarmac and did something he would recount for the rest of his life. He reached for a magazine.

John was forty-four and had grown from a low-level sales grunt to one of the senior-most executives at Container Corporation of America, a corrugated box manufacturer housed in a sloping high-rise in downtown Chicago. John had a fine view of the skyline from his fifty-fourth-floor corner office, but he spent much of his time on the road. He was headed home from a few days in Ft. Worth and Houston, visiting two of the plants he managed. But the plane wasn't moving, and the rain wasn't letting up. There was talk of tornadoes. He needed distraction. Tired and ready to be out of his suit, John pulled a magazine from the seatback pocket ahead.

He thumbed through the pages until landing on a story about a tiny brewery one hundred miles north of San Francisco, opened three years earlier by a pair of friends who thought their home brew might be good enough to appeal to a broader audience. It was. Hopland Brewery was California's first brewpub and just the second in the nation since the repeal of Prohibition in 1933. It had become a destination for thirsty travelers headed north on California's fabled Highway 101, with a simple set of directions: "Take the Golden Gate Bridge out of town for two hours; the brewery is on the right." Hopland Brewery made four hundred barrels of beer during its first year—less than what the largest brewers might pour out in a day.

A tiny brewery two thousand miles from home stirred something in John on that Dallas tarmac. He'd loved beer since the age of fifteen, when he and his childhood buddies frequented the Waterloo, Iowa, bars that knew better than to ask the ages of their patrons. Because John's growth spurt didn't come until his later teens, he had to strain to see over the bar as he dropped a quarter and asked for whatever lowbrow midwestern lager was on tap. Old Style. Grain Belt. Gluek's Stite. It didn't much matter. Young John Hall liked beer.

Older John Hall liked beer, too. He'd grown into a stocky man, not quite six feet tall but thickly built from near-daily workouts. He wore an extra layer around the middle from a life of white-collar comfort, and his hair began fleeing in his twenties, which left him bald on top with a fringe of brown circling the back and sides of his head. He believed in respect and clarity and decorum, and though he wasn't the type to close down a bar, he was able to have three or four pints with virtually anyone before heading home to read that day's *Wall Street Journal*. His kids called him "Encyclopedia" because he seemed to know everything.

As a vice president at Container Corporation, he'd traded the cheap lagers of his youth for the beers discovered on the other side of the Atlantic: endlessly drinkable English bitters, deftly layered Belgian ales, and crisp German lagers. European beer looked, smelled, and tasted different from anything John knew at home. A hefeweizen in Bavaria filled his nose with the tang of lemon, the richness of banana and clove, and arrived in gorgeous, sloping half-liter glasses that felt weighty and dignified in his hand. He could never understand why the genius that flowed from the average European tap barely existed in the United States.

Beyond a love of beer, a scrappy, young California brewery resonated with John because of a simple truth after twenty years in the corrugated box industry: he was bored. Corporate finance had been good to him. He'd climbed from a fresh-from-business-school assignment that initially disappointed him—salesman at Container's plant in Sioux City, Iowa—to a lofty perch overseeing a thousand employees at eight plants from the Chicago headquarters. He'd become the $2 billion company's youngest vice president, met Vice President George Bush at the White House, and done well enough to buy his family a condo in Vail. But he couldn't fathom being a cog in someone else's operation for another twenty years. John had already survived one takeover of Container Corporation, when Mobil oil bought the company in the early 1970s; he watched a bunch of executives cash unfathomably large checks on their way out the door. He didn't want to work for an oil company but gritted his teeth and earned his way to the top. A second takeover was ahead, by another box company, and John had no interest in navigating it. Buyouts led to jobs cuts, efficiencies, and changes in culture. He was assured he would survive but was uninterested. He craved a smaller operation where he was the boss and could make the decisions that would lead to success or failure. "If I'm going to work for an asshole, it's going to be me," became his go-to line. The sale would be his chance to cash in his Mobil stock and leave with a seven-figure nest egg.

John had considered a run at acquiring Container Corporation, but he couldn't raise the cash. He weighed buying a label company in Kansas City—it was heavy into digital imaging, which struck him as the future—and a printing company in Mississippi. He hired a firm that brokered sales of small and medium-sized businesses to find a fit. Nothing fit. And then he reached for that magazine. It struck him immediately. A brewery. A brewery was the answer.

Just before John Hall was born in 1942, the United States was home to nearly a thousand breweries. By the time he began drinking in those Waterloo bars in the late 1950s, the number was down to two hundred. As he read that magazine article, in the mid-1980s, there was scarcely more than one hundred.

That plummeting figure, and the creative stagnation of a once-vibrant industry, could be traced to a cultural shift that took root decades earlier.

In the years following World War II, families grew; suburbs did too, and tastes homogenized. The United States became an engine of production and consumption, and that was particularly true for how the nation ate and drank. Fresh and local was traded for processed and prepackaged, cheaper and faster, familiar and ever more abundant. Labels became the language of food and drink. Bread was Wonder. Soup was Campbell's. Breakfast was Kellogg's. Beer was Budweiser.

Like most brands that rose to prominence during the postwar years, the nation's largest beer company had started small. Bavarian Brewery was founded in 1852 by George Schneider on a plot of land just south of downtown St. Louis, a literal stone's throw from the Mississippi River. Before the end of the decade, Schneider had defaulted on a $90,000 loan, which sent control of his brewery to Eberhard Anheuser, a German immigrant and prosperous soap manufacturer. Anheuser soon joined forces with his son-in-law, Adolphus Busch, who owned a wholesale brewing supply store. Before long, the two men renamed the brewery for themselves: Anheuser-Busch. In the 1870s, the partners were approached by Busch's friend Carl Conrad to brew a recipe inspired by a Czech style of pilsner called Budweis, which wowed Conrad during his European travels. He sold the beer, which he called Budweiser, as a premium product in the United States. Between the advent of railroad shipping and Conrad's dogged sales efforts, Budweiser became a national sensation. When Conrad declared bankruptcy in 1883, Anheuser-Busch took control of the prized brand. Touting the beer for its time aged with wood from the beech tree—done not for taste but to aid filtering—Budweiser became the company's engine. Twenty years later, Adolphus Busch created a brand that buoyed Anheuser-Busch even further, a premium beer available only on draft meant to reach a high-end drinker. Busch called it Michelob.

Fueled by its two core brands, Anheuser-Busch became one of the nation's largest breweries, surpassing one million barrels of production in 1901. It doubled that total during the next forty years while cementing its position among America's leading brewers. The growth from there was staggering; fueled by homogenous postwar tastes, Anheuser-Busch churned out thirty-seven million barrels of beer annually by the early 1960s. Once a decidedly local undertaking in neighborhoods from coast to coast, beer drinking became about the brands that looked and tasted the same in Idaho as in Iowa, Flagstaff as in Ft. Lauderdale. Though it continued to tout its St. Louis roots, Anheuser-Busch opened large breweries across the country: Newark in 1951, Los Angeles in 1954, Houston in 1966, Columbus in 1968, and on and on with a regional unfolding that ended with its twelfth brewery, in 1993, in Cartersville, Georgia. Along the way, an ice-cold Budweiser became the American standard. Anheuser-Busch marketers tried to personalize the experience—or make it humorous, or the embodiment of masculinity—while brewers and their automated systems churned endless waves of beer to an airtight distribution network reaching seemingly every corner bar and convenience store. American beer drinkers had been conditioned to believe they were choosing Anheuser-Busch's beer, but that was only half true; Anheuser-Busch had left them few other options.

A handful of other large breweries hung around to battle the St. Louis goliath. One was Schlitz, a Milwaukee brewery that was the nation's top beer maker for much of the first half of the twentieth century. Through the 1950s, it ran neck and neck with Anheuser-Busch for national supremacy. But Anheuser-Busch surged ahead during the 1960s, amid a wave of industry consolidation, and never relented. In a bid to keep up, Schlitz turned to shortcuts during the 1970s: flavor additives, gel to combat haze, and a cheaper, high-temperature fermentation process instead of the traditional time-intensive lagering method. In a matter of years, the reengineered Schlitz destroyed the goodwill it had spent a century building. During the 1970s, Anheuser-Busch accounted for one-sixth of the beer sold in the United States; by the 1980s, due in part to Schlitz's colossal errors, it was up to nearly one-third.

Stepping up as chief rival was Miller Brewing, which had an almost identical origin story: founded in the mid-nineteenth century (1855) by a German immigrant (Friedrich Müller) who took over a failing midwestern (Milwaukee) brewery (Plank Road Brewery), which he renamed for himself and slowly turned into a giant. Owned briefly in the 1960s by a Maryland conglomerate, Miller Brewing landed in the hands of cigarette titan Philip Morris, which turned Miller into a formidable brand with the introduction of its lighter-calorie—or "lite"—beer in the early 1970s, a recipe bought from bankrupt Chicago brewery Meister Brau. Equally important, Miller employed retired sports stars to promote the beer in television spots in which a good-natured argument unfolded: Did the beer "taste great" or was it "less filling"? (The tagline only flaunted its lack of character: "Everything You Always Wanted in a Beer. And Less.") Anheuser-Busch followed in the early 1980s with Bud Light and several iconic advertising campaigns of its own, which usually relied on charming, anthropomorphized animals or women in bikinis. The major brewers tracked each other like sleuths, analyzing competing beers in laboratories and tweaking recipes as necessary. When one dropped the bittering, the other followed. By the mid-1980s, the American beer industry amounted to a war: Which of two companies could make the less-flavorful beer and most effectively advertise that flavorless beer on television? Sales grew wildly, but in every other way, a once-vibrant industry bottomed out: no flavor, no variety, and no competition. In 1950 the nation's top-ten brewers made 38 percent of the beer. By 1980 the top-ten brewers made 93 percent of the beer. Bud and Miller alone accounted for nearly 50 percent of the nation's sales—a figure that would inch toward 70 percent during the decades to come.

John Hall was never a fan of the companies that had stifled American beer. As a young man, he embraced blue-collar midwestern brands, particularly Old Style, brewed amid the bluffs of the upper Mississippi River in La Crosse, Wisconsin, about 130 miles northeast of Waterloo. His friends drank Budweiser, but it never fit him. It was too obvious. The difference between what was inside cans of Budweiser and Old Style might have been negligible, but the difference on the outside felt like everything. Old Style's blue shield, red ribbon, and the words PURE GENUINE meant he was different. Budweiser meant he was like everyone else.

Stirred by that small brewery in California, John knew he was still different. Anheuser-Busch and Miller had slugged their way to the bottom, but that only meant opportunity. The few surviving breweries largely made the same flavorless lager. But not Hopland Brewery. And that meant there was room for more.

As John would learn, there was more. The world of craft beer was small but scrappy. (Most people called it *microbrew* at the time, but the term *craft beer* is widely pegged to 1986—just as John Hall was discovering the industry.)

The nation's forefather craft brewery, Anchor Brewing, belonged to Fritz Maytag, who, like John Hall, was a child of means from small-town Iowa. Maytag had graduated from Stanford in 1959 with a degree in American literature, then studied for a couple years in Japan before dropping out of graduate school to return to San Francisco. On a whim, he bought the faltering Anchor brewery in 1965, which made uneven beer and seemed likely to close in the midst of the national beer malaise. Maytag tweaked the recipe of its trademark steam beer and slowly rehabilitated his investment. More breweries followed: New Albion, in Sonoma, California, started by a former US Navy cadet who discovered the joys of home brewing while stationed in Scotland; Sierra Nevada, of Chico, California, launched by a home brewer who had wrestled with whether to buy a bike shop instead; and Boulder Beer Co., Colorado's first brewery, which was started by a team that included two University of Colorado physics professors. Beer was becoming an industry of second acts. It was what people did for love after staggering around in matters far more practical.

The movement was a slow return to national form. Before Prohibition mostly killed US brewing in 1920, the country had been home to thousands of small breweries. When selling alcohol became legal again, in 1933, the industry recovered quickly: 857 breweries operated within a decade. But for the next thirty-seven years, Anheuser-Busch, Schlitz, and Miller fought it out at the top with a handful of others as the number of American breweries dwindled. The county's entry into World War II killed nearly 40 percent of the beer industry, and homogenizing tastes did the rest. The bottom came in 1978, when the nation was home to just eighty-nine breweries owned by barely forty companies. (Anheuser-Busch owned nine of the breweries.) Big, bland beer was winning, and more than one industry analyst predicted fewer than ten American beer companies would remain by the year 2000.

But then came the worst thing to ever happen to Big Beer: House Resolution 1337, "An Act to amend the Internal Revenue Code of 1954 with respect to excise tax on certain trucks, buses, tractors, et cetera, home production of beer and wine, refunds of the taxes on gasoline and special fuels to aerial applicators, and partial rollovers of lump sum distributions."

Home brewing became legal.

California senator Alan Cranston sponsored the key amendment in 1978 after a group of home brewing constituents lobbied him to overturn an antiquated law that taxed the production of beer brewed at home for personal use, which effectively made it illegal. The resolution took effect February 1, 1979, and allowed a nation to discover fresher, fascinating alternatives to the handful of beers that had strangled generations of taste buds.

As Ken Grossman, founder of Sierra Nevada Brewing Co., wrote in his 2013 book, *Beyond the Pale*, home brewing woke a sleeping giant: "We wanted to share *our beer*, our hoppy, dark flavorful creations. Our friends loved our beers; certainly we could find other people who would as well." Grossman was inspired to go professional by a visit to Anchor Brewing and a tour given by Fritz Maytag. He was taken with Maytag's model of choosing not to compete with cheap light lagers, but instead sell premium products at premium prices. Maytag had embraced innovation and risk, which led Anchor in 1972 to become the first American brewery in decades to brew a porter or, three years later, to release Old Foghorn, a thick, boozy barleywine. In 1981 Grossman followed with his own piece of the revolution, introducing an unlikely flagship: a pale ale that would differentiate him in the market. Sierra Nevada Pale Ale showcased the very ingredient Big Beer had suppressed for decades: earthy, piney, floral hops. What's more, they weren't bitter old-world hops; they were American hops, bright, dank, fruity, and grown in the Pacific Northwest.

Following Sierra Nevada's lead, the US brewing industry slowly chugged to life:

Year	Breweries	Growth
1979	90	
1980	92	2%
1981	92	—
1982	93	1%
1983	93	—
1984	97	4%
1985	110	13%
1986	124	13%
1987	150	21%
1988	199	33%

Brewing, to John Hall, seemed just risky enough to be fun but sensible enough to be practical. Drinking in America had become an increasingly intimate experience. California wine had matured into a force during the 1970s. A Seattle coffee company called Starbucks had just opened its first store in Chicago—its first in the United States beyond its home market. People were becoming more deliberate about how they ate and drank; John figured beer was ready to assume its place in the conversation. Homogeny and facelessness helped Budweiser and Miller become giants, but they had no true relationship with the consumer; it was all image and trickery. John would sell something new. The challenge was no different than when he had been a fresh-faced twenty-three-year-old business school graduate driving the long, flat highways of Iowa and Nebraska. The measure of a man was whether he could sell something. For his second act, John Hall would sell beer to Chicago.

2

"They Serve You a Budweiser, You Take One Sip and Spit It Out and Say, 'Oh My God, I'm Drinking Water'"

John Hall was smart enough to know what he didn't know, and he knew nothing about starting a brewery. So, he tracked down a man from Milwaukee for whom craft beer was also an unlikely second act.

Karl Strauss was literally born into brewing, in 1912, on the second floor of the north German brewery where his father was president and where the Strauss family lived. Strauss, too, learned to brew, and worked at breweries across the country. But as life became increasingly difficult for Jews in Germany, he fled to the United States in 1939. He never saw his mother or brother again; both were captured by Nazis and died in concentration camps.

With designs on eventually reaching San Francisco, Strauss stopped in Milwaukee and landed a low-level job at Pabst Brewing. As his skill became apparent, his responsibilities grew—all the way to vice president of brewing production. Under his watch, Pabst became the nation's third-largest brewery, behind Anheuser-Busch and Schlitz (which was eventually supplanted in second place by Miller).

After retiring in 1983, Strauss set a goal antithetical to his forty-four years at Pabst: he wanted to revitalize American beer. He was dismayed at what the industry had become. "When you visit Germany, you acquire a taste for their beer," Strauss told an interviewer in 1987. "Then when you get on the plane to come home and they serve you a Budweiser, you take one sip and spit it out and say, 'Oh my God, I'm drinking water.'"

Though well into his seventies, he forged a two-pronged attack. First, he accepted a cousin's offer to launch a brewery in San Diego. It was the city's first in fifty years. Strauss helped design the brewery, trained the brewers, and contributed its first recipes. For his troubles, the brewery, which opened in 1989, was christened in his honor: Karl Strauss Brewing Co. Tap handles featured a stately Karl in a blue suit and red tie, hoisting a beer glass. His voice became an icon of San Diego radio, where Strauss narrated commercials ending in his thick, German growl, "or my name isn't Karl Strauss!"

Strauss's second venture was subtler but generated far wider reach: he formed a consulting business with fellow Pabst veteran Arnie Winograd, the company's longtime vice president of public affairs. Between them, Strauss and Winograd had spent a combined seventy-five years at Pabst. Now, they were committed to diversifying American beer. The partners helped launch brewpubs in Oklahoma City; Northampton, Massachusetts; and Adamstown, Pennsylvania—places where the idea of small-batch beer made in a local restaurant was only slightly less absurd than Santa Claus actually showing up with his reindeer on Christmas Eve.

In 1986 the partners got a call from a potential new client. John Hall explained his vision: a brewery that produced the same kind of beer that spilled from Europe's taps and could be bottled and sent to stores across Chicago.

Strauss and Winograd frowned at the idea of a production brewery. If success depended on getting bottles filled and distributed across the city, the battle would be lost before it began; distribution, unlike making beer, was subject to a host of entrenched forces—money, power, and alliances—beyond a small craft brewer's control. Brewpubs, on the other hand, where the beer was made, sold, and consumed on-site, were their specialty, and they suggested John start with one as a simpler entry into the business. Brewpubs had made a slow rise in the States, particularly along the West Coast, during the 1980s. But there were still only twenty or so in the nation, and Strauss and Winograd believed there was potential for hundreds more—and certainly in a city like Chicago. When John said he would be in California for a work trip in the coming weeks, Strauss agreed to meet him so that they could visit a couple of the nation's early brewpubs, in Berkeley and Santa Cruz.

John became a believer. Brewpubs spoke to him as a businessman; they were simple, contained operations without the practical challenges of getting beer into bottles or on shelves. Sales and marketing would mostly be moot. In a brewpub, he could sell his beer by the glass and get all the profit; nothing would be lost to stores or distributors. The downside was that he knew nothing about running a brewery or a restaurant. But hiring the right people would solve that problem. He started by signing on with Strauss and Winograd to help turn his dream into reality.

John's wife of twenty-five years, Pat, was less convinced. A label-making company or a printing company seemed so blandly manageable. What did John know of running a brewery? Or a restaurant? But he had earned the chance. John had worked hard. He'd provided. Pat knew it wouldn't be a starry-eyed labor of love; it would be John's business, and in that sense, his second act didn't matter—printing, labels, beer—because he knew business. And if the brewery faltered, he assured her, he could always return to the corporate world.

The Halls met as students at the State College of Iowa—later renamed University of Northern Iowa—in Cedar Falls, in the early 1960s. John had just untangled himself from a woman who became a bit too marriage minded. He wanted a girlfriend who could stand at his side at the bar, drink beer, and watch University of Iowa football without dreaming of the names of their children. John told a friend that he wanted to meet someone fun and interesting who wouldn't fall in love with him—he actually said that—and the friend knew just the person. Patricia

Hollingsworth was a Des Moines girl majoring in English with a plan to teach high school far from Iowa. She was independent. She was feisty. She was pixie-like pretty with dark eyes, shoulder-length chestnut hair, and a wry smile. She was hard to get. And she wasn't trying to impress John—which, of course, impressed him. She was impressed right back by the fact that the stocky, sandy-haired boy relished getting wobbly on cheap beer but clearly had a plan for himself. It wasn't always so; John was a hard-charging young man who'd flunked out of the University of Notre Dame after his freshman year and, on the night of his sister's wedding the following summer, survived a drunk driving accident that killed the backseat passenger and led to a manslaughter conviction for the driver; both were friends from high school. John, who'd sat in the passenger seat, woke up in the hospital with a dislocated right hip, a broken wrist that never quite healed right, and cuts across his face. On the heels of flunking out of school, the accident provided the proverbial wake-up call. By the time he met Pat, he was sailing though classes with a plan to become a businessman.

John and Pat were engaged in 1965, soon after John graduated, as he worked at a trucking company on the southwest side of Chicago. They married a year later in a small ceremony at St. Margaret Mary Church, a brick behemoth in Chicago's West Rogers Park neighborhood, where John's sister was a parishioner. John was twenty-two and Pat twenty-one. The new Mr. and Mrs. Hall moved to Iowa City so John could pursue a graduate business degree at the University of Iowa. Their first child, a boy named Greg, arrived that November.

In 1966, during his last semester of business school, John took a job with Container Corporation, which assigned the young salesman to Sioux City, Iowa, a town of eighty-seven thousand nestled in a bend of Iowa's western border. Pat didn't mind—a couple of friends from college lived there—but John was disappointed he hadn't been sent to the company headquarters in Chicago. Still, he was pleased to have a steady job at a good company. The Halls bought a small house with a roomy backyard for $16,000 and got down to the business of being a young family. Pat stayed home to raise Greg, and John began traveling the Midwest to convince companies to package their wares in his boxes.

John did well enough to be offered a promotion within two years as controller of the Sioux City plant. He wasn't sure he wanted it; accounting bored him. The real thrill, he thought, was in sales. He consulted his father and a mentor from State College, both of whom said he would be foolish to turn down the job. Do it well, they said, and he could write his ticket to the top. He took the job, and read more accounting books than he thought possible. Two years later, he got the call: Container Corporation promoted him to a plant in suburban Chicago.

The Halls sold their Sioux City house for a $600 profit and headed east. John was ready to spend $30,000 on what he presumed would be a mansion, but suburban Chicago housing prices were steeper than expected; the family landed in the decidedly middle-class suburb of Woodridge. But John was a natural fit for more responsibility, and after three years, he was promoted to controller of a second Chicago-area plant. With that, the Halls finally moved to the fancier suburb where John had wanted to be all along, Hinsdale. It was an easy, homogenous place to raise a family, where dads commuted downtown in suits, wives kept fine homes, kids played Little League, and everyone cleaned up nice for church on Sunday.

John was one of those commuters, catching the 5:30 train every evening, walking the four blocks to his tidy two-story home, then heading upstairs, changing clothes, and eating a dinner Pat had waiting. Other than a job in a card shop after Greg left for college, Pat never worked outside the home, and quite happily; she lived for her family, which, when Greg was ten, came to include a baby girl named Elizabeth. Everyone called her Beth. The days in their tony suburb were safe and predictable. Quitting a six-figure job to open a brewery was anything but safe and predictable.

Convincing investors to buy into a brewery during the 1980s was a slog. Conventional wisdom said that brewing was not the domain of small, independent businesses; it was for massive, faceless companies.

Yet his first major coup was recruiting a fellow Waterloo native, John Burrell, to be a cofounder. Burrell had found success both on the Chicago Board of Trade and as cofounder of Guadalaharry's, a popular Tex-Mex restaurant franchise. The Waterloo Johns were opposites but mostly got along. Burrell could drink late into the night, smoke a joint, and bullshit with the best of them; Hall could drink and bullshit too but knew when to go home and start thinking about the next day. They raised close to $2 million, much of it with the help of a VHS tape recorded at Hall's kitchen table where he explained his vision for a brewpub in the heart of Chicago. As he took on investors with a minimum buy-in of $20,000, Hall's primary condition was unbending: he had to control the business. Twenty years at Container Corporation had shown him the inefficiency of too many decision makers.

With Strauss, Winograd, and Burrell in the fold, John set out to find a building. He made a list of wants and needs, and ranked them. Needs: Central location. Parking. Owning the property. Wants: An outdoor space. A building with history. He zeroed in on Clybourn Avenue, a three-and-a-half-mile corridor running beside the Chicago River in the midst of transition. For decades, the street had been a source of jobs for nearly two thousand workers across thirty factories—steel processing, chemical manufacturing, industrial refrigeration, and custom picture framing. But as those jobs trickled to Mexico and China, Clybourn Avenue became home to condominiums and shopping. Though Edith's Barbecue continued to anchor the street with its peeling walls, worn counter, and sauce recipe that Edith pledged to take to her grave (she did), everything else was quickly fading. A Northwestern University urban development professor told the *Los Angeles Times* that the moment was "a clash of economic cultures—the attractive retail jobs versus the blue-collar, noisy, grimy high-paying jobs. It is a clash between those who make it and those who buy it."

John fell clearly on the side of the new economy: he wanted to summon all the white-collar executives and young professionals he could. He saw inevitable change on that stretch of Clybourn Avenue, and across Chicago, and wanted to be part of it. He believed in progress and that things always moved forward. Either you moved with them, or you slipped back. He found just what he wanted at the southern end of Clybourn Avenue, in an old Turtle Wax factory that had once been a brewing equipment plant—a detail John loved for its potential to resonate with customers. A $23 million effort was underway to convert the seventy-three-year-old loft into a 180,000-square-foot mall that would connect the building's industrial past to the convenience of modern shopping. The *Chicago Tribune* called the project a beacon to "urban sophisticates and affluent suburbanites."

"We want quality merchandise by Chicago people whose display and merchandising techniques are innovative and creative and who place a strong emphasis on personal service," the developer told the newspaper. They wanted exactly what John Hall sought to create. John bought a 10 percent ownership stake in the development and pledged to become the property's anchor tenant.

Even more daunting than finding the right home for his brewery were the two most crucial hires: someone to run the kitchen, and someone to make the beer. Running a restaurant was the part of the business John knew least. He wanted not only a system for the kitchen but also someone experienced to run that system.

He had been an admirer of TGI Fridays, a restaurant chain that launched its breezy vibe in New York City's Upper East Side in 1965 with a model that it replicated from coast to coast. John wanted what they had—crowds of young diners in search of casual fun—and plucked one of their regional Chicago-based managers to make it happen. John offered him a signing bonus to guide the brewpub through the most basic tasks: designing the kitchen, creating job titles, choosing equipment, and doing it all with the budget of a first-time restaurant owner. As for the beer, Karl Strauss gave John three names. Among them was Victor Ecimovich III, a Chicago native who'd been an electrical engineering student at the Illinois Institute of Technology before deciding he was more interested in home brewing. Ecimovich quit IIT and enrolled at the Siebel Institute of Technology, a world-class brewing school in the heart of the Chicago, before landing at Millstream Brewing in eastern Iowa. John was impressed by his experience and hired him straightaway.

Finally, John's brewpub needed a name. He considered something generic, like Chicago Brewing Co. Too predictable. He weighed borrowing a name from history, from one of the city's defunct breweries—Atlas, Lill and Diversey, Schoenhofen, Seipp, Huck. But those felt too backward looking. John wanted to signal a new era in Chicago beer. He wanted to create a story of his own.

He ultimately looked less than half a mile south, at a sliver of land in the north branch of the Chicago River. Beyond sounding a bit curious—Goose Island—the name was uniquely Chicago. Goose Island was 160 acres in the heart of the city, intersected by two prominent thoroughfares, Halsted and Division Streets. It was so well integrated into the grid that few of the thousands of people who crossed it every day realized that they were on an urban island. Even fewer knew its gritty history as a home to Irish immigrants in the 1800s, notorious for beer swilling and bare-knuckled brawls. During industrialization in the late 1800s, Goose Island became home to coal plants and grain elevators and earned the nickname Little Hell for its chugging smokestacks. John spent hours hunched at Chicago's premier public research library looking for the name of his new brewery. It was there, reading about the history of Goose Island, that he found it.

In the 1970s, shopping for beer typically meant reaching for the same six-pack as the time before and the time before that. John Hall had spent the 1970s combing the aisles of obscure stores, shoulder-to-shoulder with that rarest of American creature who wanted flavor and nuance in their beer. John reached for the bottles he discovered during business trips on the other side of the Atlantic. Weihenstephaner Hefeweissbier from Germany. England's Samuel Smith Taddy Porter. Any number of beers from Belgium, where the most adventurous and complex brews in the world were made. Sometimes he bought bottles simply because he'd never heard of them.

John became a frequent patron of the Weinkeller, a beer store in the nearby suburb of Berwyn that was started by a German immigrant in the mid-1970s as a wine shop (hence a name translating to "wine cellar"). But the owner quickly detected an undercurrent of interest in quality beer in suburban Chicago, which led him to stock his shelves with the well-crafted, imported brews impossible to find elsewhere. The Weinkeller would eventually claim the largest selection of beers in the world under one roof, including twenty-four varieties of the weissbier that John Hall came to love during his trips to Germany. At his side for his frequent weekend shopping trips was his quiet, sandy-haired son, Greg.

Young Greg Hall was enthralled with the magnitude of what he saw on those shelves: rows and rows of beer brewed thousands of miles away, across vast oceans and in places he'd only read of in books. Yet here they were in suburban Chicago. Ayinger Celebrator Doppelbock became a particular favorite for the small white plastic goat that hung around its neck, which, of course, John always handed over.

By the middle of high school, Greg's curiosity grew more concrete: What exactly was in those bottles? He developed a system for finding out. The cardinal rule was simple: for each six-pack, never take the first beer and never take the last. If John had whittled a six-pack down to, say, four, he would never notice if Greg quietly trimmed the number to three. When Greg's friends stole beer from their parents, they drank the light, fizzy lagers that John had eschewed. Greg could drink a six-pack of those beers and still walk in a straight line. He figured they couldn't be all that good. He much preferred the weight and heft of what he pulled from his father's basement beer fridge.

As high school went on, Greg and his friends carved out a handful of spaces for their beer consumption—houses, basements, or wooded areas where they wouldn't be bothered—and spent as much time there as possible. Securing beer wasn't much of a challenge. There was John's high-end beer fridge. Several of Greg's friends had fake IDs. One guy's brother worked in a beer store and gladly sold to the high schoolers. Another friend was blessed with a thick beard at the age of fifteen, which led Greg and his buddies to pool their money for a JCPenney sport coat; the boy would walk into a convenience store at 6:00 PM, mutter about the long day he'd had at the office, then buy three cases of a cheap pound-worthy domestic beer, like Natural Light. Decorum among friends dictated that everyone cover the cost for whoever secured that day's brew.

For major events like prom or graduation, Greg bought only the good stuff: Heineken, Beck's, Corona, and Moosehead. Nothing American made. John Hall didn't know it, but he had turned his seventeen-year-old son into a budding beer connoisseur.

In the fall of 1983, Greg headed off to the University of Iowa, back to the college town where he was born. He figured he would either write books for a living or run a bar. Writing was the preference. Thanks to his dad, he'd read every *Best American Essays* and *Best American Short Stories* since the seventh grade. The luminaries who had passed through the Iowa writing school—Kurt Vonnegut, Raymond Carver, Philip Roth—were a North Star to follow. Greg figured that if he would become a writer, it would happen there.

Like most teenagers, he relished breaking away from middle-class suburbia: he could drink and read and write and think important thoughts as he pleased. Beer was of course central to his early college days, and Greg alternated between affordable midwestern brews (six-packs of Augsburger and $5.99 cases of Special Export) and early craft pioneers (Iowa's Millstream Brewing and Wisconsin's Capital Brewery). Just as his father had done twenty years earlier in graduate school, Greg passed evenings at the Airliner, a dim, wood-heavy bar near campus that had barely evolved since opening in 1944.

Greg never took classes too seriously, disappearing from campus for days at a time to see his high school buddies at the University of Illinois. If he didn't travel by Greyhound bus, he hitchhiked, figuring he was gathering experiences for his eventual novel. He would arrive in Champaign with more CDs than clothes and sleep on couches for weeks—so long that his best friend's fraternity brothers thought Greg was a student there. He'd do some reading for class while he was gone, head back for tests, pull Cs, and shrug.

After two years, Greg transferred to Loyola University back in Chicago. He lasted one semester, thanks to a social life that got more attention than his schoolwork. His friends were bartending and going nowhere, and Greg saw the same for himself if he stuck around. He still believed he could write but figured it would only happen in Iowa City. He transferred back happy and recharged and leased a downtown apartment where he forsook telephone and television and enrolled in a writers' workshop class. He passed through the requisite phases, buying every Beat writer at the university bookstore, then doing his best approximation of their spirited, rambling prose. Most of his writing happened during late nights fueled by whiskey and the classic Belgian beer Chimay. Much of it, he'd realize, was crap, except perhaps the long, handwritten letters to friends and his sister, often on pages torn from *Interview* magazine. (It just seemed like something a writer would do.)

Greg was a semester from graduating in the spring of 1988 when he figured there could be no better summer job than working at his dad's new brewpub. He showed up at the gleaming new Goose Island brewery as an assistant brewer on April 30, 1988, two weeks before doors opened. His boss, Victor, swore he wouldn't need a long-term assistant; he just needed someone to help him get started. That was fine—Greg planned to spend the summer drinking beer, flirting with the waitresses, and earning a few bucks before returning to Iowa to finish college and become a proper writer.

But in reality, on that seventy-degree spring day, Greg was beginning a career in the family business. It would last twenty-three years, until the Goose Island Beer Co. was the family business no more.

3

"In Chicago There Are Now No Fewer than Six Breweries, of Which My Favourite Is Goose Island"

A FEW WEEKS BEFORE GOOSE ISLAND opened its doors, on May 13, 1988—a Friday the 13th, as John Hall would wryly note for years to come—Victor Ecimovich III walked into the brewery with a fresh haircut. Buzzed nearly to the sides, a dark shaggy mop was left on top, which gave the brewer the appearance of a bassist from a new wave band from the early part of the decade. John spied the hairdo one afternoon while discussing last-minute details with his partner, John Burrell, and mentor, Karl Strauss. The brain trust did a collective double take.

"Hey," Victor said. "People expect a brewmaster to be a character."

A brief thought flashed in John's mind: *What the hell have I gotten myself into?* But there were bigger issues to face. Like the beer.

Goose Island's opening night would be a fundraiser for a nonprofit agency assisting low-income immigrant families; John wanted to do some good when launching his new business. Plus, it offered exposure as a good neighbor. There hadn't been time for Victor to brew enough beer for the likely packed house, which made a calculation necessary: How could they get the array of beers on tap that people expected from a new brewery? There were just two hundred breweries in the United States at the time, but John had met several prominent players at the Craft Brewers Conference in Boston the previous spring. Among them were Ed and Carol Stoudt, who had just launched Pennsylvania's first craft brewery, Stoudts Brewing Co., an hour west of Philadelphia. (Thirty years later, the state would have more than two hundred breweries.) John called, and sure enough, they agreed to share their equipment for a couple days of brewing and a few weeks of fermentation. Loaded with bags of malt and hops, Victor made the eleven-hour drive to brew Goose Island's first beers seven hundred miles from home: Golden Goose Pilsner and Lincoln Park Lager, both light and approachable and nothing that would befuddle a drinker most comfortable with Bud or Miller. A few weeks later, he made the roundtrip drive again to keg the beers and bring them back to Chicago. Once Goose Island's brewing system was assembled—put together by a young industry hotshot named Dan Carey, who would go on to found New Glarus Brewing in Wisconsin—Victor was able to make two more brews ahead of opening, both slightly more challenging to the American palate: the thick, dark Old Clybourn Porter and a brown-hued English bitter named by Pat Hall. "If the brewery is called Goose Island, there needs to be a Honker's Ale," she told John.

The cool, spring opening night felt something like a wedding. Guests from all eras of John and Pat's lives turned out, jammed shoulder to shoulder across the wood floor and gathered around the hulking bar in the center of the room. John's father, a taciturn man who was no beer drinker, thought his son was nuts to open a brewery. But of course, he made the drive from northwest Iowa. Pat's family was there, also from Iowa. Greg's childhood friends came, and so did John Burrell's trader and restaurant industry buddies. The next Monday came the public opening, word of which was circulated on an invitation doubling as a coaster. The front featured the brewery's pastoral logo of a backward-looking goose treading a grassy hill. On the back, the words: BRING THIS COASTER AND A FRIEND—WE'LL MAKE SURE NEITHER ONE IS HOLDING AN EMPTY MUG! Victor dutifully played the role of brewmaster, laughing off jokes about how easy his job was—he got to drink beer all day! He must have heard the line a hundred times. Still, it was difficult to argue the novelty—a restaurant that made its own beer. Until the previous fall, Chicago hadn't been home to a brewery in more than ten years. Now, within eight months, it had three.

Goose Island's bar was rectangular, made of red-tinged auburn wood. Thick columns sprouted from its corners—along with two more columns on each of the bar's two long sides—to support a loft built of the same dark wood, finished with ornate moldings. There was no reason for the second story or the eight heavy posts to clutter the bar top, but it was what John wanted: less light, less space, and cozier—like those British pubs where he learned to love beer. Beer drinking in America had become formulaic by the 1980s. John wanted it to be intimate again.

John's favorite spots were at the bar's corners, especially the two that faced the front door. There, bartenders were quick to refill his glass, he could hear servers bark their orders, and the cash that affirmed his vision—yes, people wanted beer made down the street, not just anonymous blandness made thousands of miles away—was stuffed into the register. John could see who came and went, chat with his customers, and get to know his employees. A long bar against the wall had merit, but John preferred the community of the rectangle anchoring a room. It was democratic. It made beer a common cause. Guests could talk to each other and smile and wave as bartenders poured frothy pints. John wanted Goose Island to seem as if it had been plucked from an English village where people drank and argued and fell in love and talked the news of the day.

He had succeeded in building the bar of his dreams, and not just because of the bar itself. It was the exposed beams in the ceiling, the seventy-year-old brick walls, and the Chicago beer industry memorabilia tacked to those walls. Two hundred fifty seats were spread across two levels for a menu of hearty pub fare: fried oysters, broiled pork chops, jambalaya, and a hamburger stuffed with tomato, onion, and cheese. Most important, customers knew they were in a brewery from the moment they arrived; one step through Goose Island's front door, to the right and a floor below, sat the brewery, squeezed into a tall, narrow room made even narrower by the brewing tanks lined across the brick floor. Step through another door and there sat the heart of the operation: that big beautiful bar ringed by beer drinkers.

A *Chicago Tribune* dining critic visited after two months and weighed in with a one-star review ("good"), proclaiming the brewpub home to "fine beers, relaxing atmosphere and satisfying, if uneven, food." The review began, of course, by addressing the odd concept of a restaurant that made its own beer: "American mega-breweries and snob-appeal foreign beers had no sooner run the locals out of the market when entrepreneurs began introducing 'boutique beers.' These new, on-premise brewers are not so much bottlers and canners of specialty beers as focal points of restaurants."

And so it was for Goose Island, where the reviewer urged visitors to "graze one's way through the appetizers and not feel obligated to sample the kitchen's other products. In fact, a full-course dinner at Goose Island tends to run straight downhill, the appetizers generally excellent, the entrees mostly mediocre and the desserts universally uninspired."

It was the beer that mattered most, the *Tribune* said, and Goose Island's five drafts scored generally good marks. The pilsner and lager would "appeal to anyone who enjoys common brewing styles." Honker's Ale had "the heartier character of a top-fermented, light English ale." Old Clybourn Porter won particular praise: "Most stouts and porters imported into America taste mostly of caramel. Goose Island's porter exhibits more sophistication, redolent with the full body and pronounced flavor of its toasted grain. Those who ordinarily reject such heavy beers may find themselves converted by this unique experience."

The review didn't note it, but Goose Island's menu talked of beer in bold terms for the late 1980s. While Big Beer duked it out for most memorable commercial, Chicago's tiny new brewpub used sharp, clear language to describe its three core beers: Golden Goose Pilsner ("A fiery golden beer, clean and crisp, with the splendid aroma of imported Czechoslovakian hops that marks a truly great pilsner"), Lincoln Park

Lager ("Our amber lager beer, brewed true to European tradition to be rich and satisfying, using robust roasted malts and just the right touch of European hops"), and Honker's Ale ("A fine pale ale that any Englishman would be proud of: traditional yeast, malt and hops make this ale a classic on both sides of the Atlantic").

Goose Island also touted a series of sporadic releases to match the seasons, a radical thought for the time: "In the interest of variety and fun (for us as well as you!), Goose Island will offer throughout the year a wide range of seasonal and specialty products in addition to our three house brews. We hope you and your friends will return to sample our 'Brewmaster's Specials' and experience some of the fun and custom that is part of the great tradition of brewing." The seasonal offerings included a bock in spring and a hefeweizen in summer, which was served in the proper sloping glassware and called Chicago Vice—a play on *Miami Vice*, the hit television show of the day.

The selection was miles ahead of its customers; 80 to 90 percent of sales were the lighter beers most similar to the nation's major brands. Lincoln Park Lager was the runaway hit, while the slightly more adventurous opted for Golden Goose Pilsner. It was a daunting battle for minds in a Miller Lite town, but the strategy was simple: educate those who wanted to be educated. The most curious customers asked the same question of bartenders: "What's the difference between an ale and a lager?" Those who sneered at such a distinction, who simply wanted a Lincoln Park Lager, would discover better beer in time. "We didn't care that a lot of people didn't like our beer, we cared about the people who did like our beer," John Hall reminisced ten years later. "We spent a lot of time educating people. That's the secret. You're not going to outdo Anheuser-Busch, so you want to do something a little bit different."

But there was one small sign of surrender behind the bar: Miller Lite. As much as he planned to educate his customers, John was also a businessman, and a businessman listened to his customers. The sort of beer made by Goose Island—craft beer, microbrew, boutique beer, whatever—was a mere .01 percent of industry sales. There were essentially two kinds of beer in the United States: large domestic brands and imports. John would never have carried an import; *that* was the competition. But he didn't think someone asking for a Miller Lite in 1988 was so unreasonable, and his business wouldn't be sunk by stubbornness. After Goose Island was open for three months, a bartender told the *Chicago Tribune* that many customers would start with a Lite, "then move on when they see the other beers being served. I sell one bottle for every six large glasses of ours." In the same article, Victor, the brewmaster, put a positive spin on the Miller Lite that sat beside his beer on the bar. "The presence of Lite shows this is not a snob place," he said.

In reality, Victor was unconvinced. He was known to argue with customers who asked for Miller or a Bud, and perhaps even tell someone to get the fuck out if they wanted a beer that they could get at any other bar in the city. He was temperamental, and many of the bartenders—most of whom couldn't care less about where the beer was made and simply wanted bar jobs—were terrified of him. But his point was simple: any customer who wanted a Miller Lite wasn't a real customer. A customer who ordered Golden Goose Pilsner—and liked it—was a customer for life. That customer formed a relationship not with an advertising campaign but with the beer itself, and the idea that it was made under that roof. It was a radical thought in 1988, and each conversion to that way of drinking—and, more important, thinking—counted.

Victor led a steadfast operation Monday through Friday so that he could take weekends off to spend time with his wife and young daughter. He was in his late twenties and, ultimately, brewing to live. It was a job. The generation of brewers who saw their own futures in Victor's beer would live to brew, making beer as creative expression and a means to enter a counterculture. They would identify as artists as much as technicians. But in the late 1980s, brewing was still very much a job.

He brewed three days a week at the fledgling brewpub, kegged and filtered the other two days, then wrapped up by 3:00 PM on Fridays to sip a couple beers with John at the bar before disappearing until Monday morning. The recipes were formulated well, though regulars would detect a slight buttery flavor in some of the beers that they couldn't quite pinpoint; it was diacetyl, a flavor compound excreted by yeast that plagued early American craft brewing. (Years later, Victor would recount that he intended to imbue some diacetyl in his beers, especially Honker's Ale, to evoke traditional British flavors. But early customers were skeptical. Larry Bell, founder of Michigan's Bell's Brewery and an early Goose Island patron, recalled Goose's early diacetyl issues but demurred from criticizing the brewery that would become a rival. "We all had diacetyl problems in those days," he said with a belly laugh.)

Diacetyl or not, Victor's beer built a reputation for Goose Island. It won its first-ever medal at the nation's premier beer festival, Denver's Great American Beer Festival, with a silver among wheat beers for Chicago Vice in 1989. A year later, the world's foremost beer writer, Michael Jackson—a scraggly haired Brit, not the American king of pop—began championing the brewery during his annual visits to the United States. In the British newspaper the *Independent*, Jackson wrote in 1990: "In Chicago, there are now no fewer than six breweries, of which my favourite is Goose Island."

Still, John had concerns about Victor. He thought a brewer who wanted only to brew beer had reached his ceiling. John wanted Victor to want more responsibility: spend time with customers, make the rounds at the bar, put a face to the beer, and lead enthusiastic tours of the brewery. John suspected that small, locally made beer depended on relationships with customers and personal connections with the brewers who made the amber liquid sitting on the bar. That experience was precisely what Bud and Miller couldn't offer. John saw it as an all-important point of differentiation, and no one personified it better than Victor. But Victor mostly wanted to make beer.

The job Victor did take seriously was mentoring Greg Hall. The boss's twenty-two-year-old son was a minimum-wage employee earning $3.35 an hour—John didn't think he was worth more than that—who relished his first job out of college, inglorious as it was. He helped clean the brewery, dumped bags of fresh grain, and shoveled out wet, heavy spent grain. Victor never called Greg his assistant; he was simply his "helper." But Greg relished the job, especially sitting at the bar and drinking the beer he and Victor had made in the next room. He'd nod with a glow as a customer pointed past the broad windows into the brewery and marveled, "You guys made this beer *here*?" It was more exciting than anything he'd done.

Victor told Greg that he expected him to work hard and do whatever was asked of him. In exchange, Victor would teach him what to do and why, plus give him the books that would acquaint Greg with brewing history and beer styles. When Michael Jackson came through Chicago on a late summer night to host a beer tasting at a competing brewpub, it was Victor who bought Greg a ticket. It was a formative experience.

For each attendee, Jackson set out a paper tasting board with circles for ten Midwest-brewed beers. But he put out only nine pours per person. Jackson spent two hours tasting and describing the beers, delving into the ingredients and processes that made each one unique. In a pre-internet era, Jackson's insights were gold; he had established himself as an industry sage with his 1977 *World Guide to Beer* and a follow-up that clued in the world to the genius of Belgian brewing, *The Great Beers of Belgium*. He later gained fame with a short-lived cable television series inspired by his nickname: *The Beer Hunter*. Hearing the man speak was akin to the beer heavens opening. After the tasting, Greg approached the Beer Hunter to sign a book. Greg also asked a question.

"What happened to the last beer?" he said.

"You know what?" Jackson said. "I've had it before, and it's an excellent beer. But I tasted it before it went out, and it just didn't taste right."

"Well, why didn't you pour it anyway and tell everyone what's wrong with it?"

"It's my job to tell people what's good about beer, not what's bad about beer," Jackson said.

Greg didn't get it at first, but as he increasingly became the one in Goose Island's spotlight, the point was made clear: Jackson was a good message guy. He wouldn't hesitate to criticize Big Beer. But when a small brewery released flawed beer, no one knew it from Michael Jackson. In the late 1980s, the nation was home to one hundred small and independently owned breweries that fought the tide of adjunct-heavy, flavorless lagers. They needed all the help they could get.

What 1969 was to rock 'n' roll—*Abbey Road, Let It Bleed, Nashville Skyline, The Velvet Underground*, and both *Led Zeppelin* and *Led Zeppelin II*—1988 was to beer. Rogue Ales opened in southern Oregon. Wynkoop Brewing launched Colorado's first brewpub in downtown Denver. Just south of Lake Erie, Great Lakes Brewing opened Ohio's first brewery in four years. Between San Francisco and the Oregon border, North Coast Brewing sold its first beer. The first Gordon Biersch Brewery appeared in Palo Alto. Deschutes Brewery opened in blue-collar logging town Bend, Oregon. New York City was put on the beer map with the founding of Brooklyn Brewery. And on an industrial corridor north of downtown Chicago, John Hall opened Goose Island. Whatever creativity fueled that year of remarkable growth didn't translate to the nickname ascribed to the group: the Class of '88.

That year was notable not only for its new American breweries—the number climbed to 199, the highest figure since the 1950s—but also due to how many of those breweries would thrive. After starting as brewpubs, Goose Island, Deschutes, Great Lakes, Rogue, and North Coast would all grow to be among the nation's fifty largest craft brewers. Brooklyn Brewery was founded as a beer made under contract—brewed elsewhere, then given the Brooklyn label—and it, too, would eventually become a top-fifty craft brewer. But in 1988, all those breweries were decidedly local pursuits, barely aware of each other's existence.

In Chicago, there was no obvious reason Goose Island should have been more successful than its early local competition. Sieben's. Tap and Growler. The Weinkeller. Golden Prairie. Chicago Brewing Co. O'Grady's Brewery and Pub. Millrose Brewing. Founders Hill. River West. Hopcats. Pavichevich Brewing. All would eventually disappear.

If anything, Chicago Brewing Co., which opened in 1989, earned the early buzz thanks to its Big Shoulders Porter. Golden Prairie found an audience with its fairly wild innovations, including Maple Stout and an ale made with buckwheat. The biggest hit of all was Baderbrau pilsner, made by Pavichevich Brewing in suburban Elmhurst. Baderbrau's lore peaked during the summer of 1990, when an advance man for President George Bush requested a case for the president's suite at the Hyatt Regency. The challenge for them all, just as it was for John Hall, was as broad as it was simple: convincing people to buy the beer. Beer was long ago commoditized as a faceless product made miles away. How could beer made down the street be any good?

"It's somewhat frustrating because we're recognized for making some of the best beers in the country, but 97 percent of Chicago doesn't know we exist," Steve Dinehart, president of Chicago Brewing Co. told the *Chicago Tribune*. Said David Bouhl, of Golden Prairie: "Some people don't think Chicago will ever appreciate microbrewed beers, but that's ridiculous. Chicago is a very sophisticated town. People in Chicago know about fine wines, and it's only a matter of time before they realize there is a category of beer that is much better than domestic mass-market beers and even better than imports, because microbrewed beers are fresh beers."

Nearly every early Goose Island competitor had an undoing. The beer wasn't good enough. The business model wasn't sound. Not enough money. Growing too fast. Despite Baderbrau's cult success, Pavichevich Brewing spent far too much money on branding (gold-lipped tulip glasses and paper stem collars) and marketing (newspaper and radio ads). By 1996, the brewery went bankrupt.

Goose Island ran into what could have been its undoing too—multiple times. The first came three months in, when John had a cold-sweat realization: he was in over his head in the restaurant business. His partner, John Burrell, was more likely to be smoking a joint with Victor than plotting strategy, and the kitchen designed by the former TGI Friday's manager was ill equipped to make anything more than chain food. He had made two cardinal sins of brewpub ownership: an unreliable partner and iffy food. But he had wisely ensured that he had control of the operation, and bought out Burrell. Within a year of opening, he hired a new chef while lurching from menu to menu to keep customers returning for more than just beer.

The other problem was the real estate. John had pledged to own the property where he opened Goose Island, which led him to sink more than $100,000 toward a 10 percent stake in the old Turtle Wax factory. In addition to the upstart brewpub, the building became home to a high-end restaurant, a miniature golf course, a stationery store, a comedy theater, an independent bookstore, and a pool hall. Things went well enough that the developer offered to buy him out at a modest profit after a year. John didn't hesitate to decline. Then the trouble started. In 1991 that developer defaulted on an $18 million loan, which sent the property into receivership and the hands of a decidedly less ambitious owner who planned to raze the historic building and erect a shopping mall of big-box tenants.

Among other business owners, John was served eviction papers. One by one, most folded, and what had been the center of the mall was bulldozed for a parking lot. Clinging to his lease, John took his new landlord to court. Several thousands of dollars later, a judge ruled that Goose Island could stay. But the construction that followed cratered the brewpub's business. During its best years, Goose Island's brewpub grossed $4 million a year. During construction, business was down 25 percent, thanks in part to the demolition of Goose Island's banquet room, which alone had brought in about $700,000 annually. More than once, John was certain his second career would fail. When he returned home to the suburbs, stressed and bedraggled, Pat sometimes offered confidence that he would right the ship, and other times tough love: "This was your dream. Find a way to make it work." He did make it work, by sinking $250,000 into the brewery from his savings. It was ultimately a combination of doing everything well enough and deep pockets that saved Goose Island. Only then could it be remembered as part of a shift in American brewing and a star in the Class of '88.

4

The Fucking With Was On

IN 1990, WHEN HE WAS TWENTY-FIVE YEARS OLD, Greg Hall was struck with a realization. He wanted to be the boss.

He'd had enough of running ideas up the flagpole; he wanted to be the flagpole. He wanted to decide what beer would be made and when. He wanted to craft the vision for Goose Island. The year before, with a letter of recommendation from Victor, Greg enrolled in an eight-week brewing course at the Siebel Institute of Technology. John encouraged him to go and paid for his enrollment, more as a dad than a boss.

When Greg returned with his certificate, John offered a surprising promotion: restaurant manager.

"That doesn't make any sense," Greg said. "I just went to school to be a brewer."

"This is the family business," John said. "If you want to work here, you're going to learn the whole operation."

John offered his son a $25,000 salary—a raise from $6 an hour as assistant brewer (which was a raise from his starting salary of $3.35 an hour)—to close the brewpub five nights a week and report to the general manager. Greg quickly realized that his father was right; he knew nothing about how a restaurant worked. He spent time behind the bar getting to know customers and learning which beers excited them, whether Goose Island's or not. When Victor went on vacation, Greg's workdays were akin to medical school shifts: arriving at 7:00 AM to brew, opening the restaurant for lunch, transitioning to dinner, then cleaning and closing by 3:00 AM. And repeat. Greg eventually just brewed after close; going home at 3:00 AM to return in four hours seemed ridiculous.

The promotion to manager was accompanied by another life-changing event: a Hall family trip to England and Belgium during the fall of 1990. With his father at his side, Greg experienced vibrant European beer culture firsthand. He and John sipped Duvel in dim, wood-heavy pubs and on leafy Belgian verandas—the kinds of moments that would be memorialized in framed photos for decades to come: fresh-faced Greg, sunglasses atop a mop of hair, cradling a chalice of golden suds while John sits across the table in a yellow polo shirt with a glass of his own. When John, Pat, and Greg's sister, Beth, flew home, Greg kept traveling. He took the train to Aachen, Germany, a college town just over the Belgian border where he hung out in bars and slept in a hostel. When he told young Germans he was a brewer in the United States they were bemused. They made beer worth bragging about in America?

On he went to Cologne, where he spent a couple nights drinking the local Kölsch style, then to Odense, Copenhagen, Stockholm, Hamburg, and Munich before meeting a bunch of Americans who asked if he was going to see the Rolling Stones in Prague. Czechoslovakia had just staged its first democratic election since the fall of Communism, and the Stones would mark the occasion with a two-plus-hour show. Greg hopped a train to Prague without a plan and met a German along the way who grilled him about the United States—had he been to Brooklyn? Texas? The Grand Canyon? Then he saw the Stones, packed in with one hundred thousand sweaty Europeans. It amounted to the best three weeks of Greg's life. Everything was so new.

By the time he returned home, the world seemed just a bit smaller and the possibilities a bit broader. He read Michael Jackson's *Pocket Guide to Beer* several times over, memorizing alcohol percentages, bitterness units, and hop bills, just as he had remembered baseball statistics as a boy. If he knew those figures, he presumed, he could make the beers. Ideas coursed through him. He was ready to make decisions.

The only problem: Goose Island already had a brewer. And John wasn't going to throw him overboard for his son.

Greg did what anyone who hit the wall at work would do: he looked elsewhere. He sent a resume to Sierra Nevada Brewing Co., in Northern California, to get on as a grunt brewer. He didn't hear back, but that didn't dissuade him; he decided to move west and knock on the door until he was hired. The industry had so few experienced brewers in the early 1990s that he assumed they would eventually relent. John knew he had a strong asset in his son, but agreed that Greg would benefit from leaving the Midwest and getting out from under the family business. At least for a little while.

But the grind of running a brewpub was wearing on Victor. He'd been making beer—as physically taxing as construction with all the lifting, climbing, ripping, and pouring—five days a week for three years. Even with an assistant, it was grueling work. Victor hadn't intended to quit Goose Island on the day he did. It was a Friday morning during the summer of 1991, and he showed up to pour his beer at a festival across the street from the brewpub. There, he saw a most appalling sight: a Budweiser banner. Didn't John know that Anheuser-Busch would kill Goose Island in a moment if given the chance? Goose Island had built something small and good. John was demeaning it by allowing his brand—*their* brand—to be poured beneath its name. Anger and frustration swelled, and Victor decided right then that he was done.

He called Greg and told him to get down to the brewery. A porter sat in the tank ready to be kegged, but Victor was finished. He had withstood selling Miller Lite against his own beer. Now this.

John was vacationing at his condo in Vail when he got the call. Victor had threatened to quit before, but John talked him back every time. He did it out of necessity; without Victor, he'd be sunk. This time, he had just the replacement in mind.

A few months after ditching his plan to move west, Greg became head brewer of the family business. It was his preferred outcome all along. He soon began looking for a new place to live.

As Victor's minimum-wage assistant, he'd shared a two-bedroom apartment with two other guys, spending $300 per month for the privilege of his own room. He could afford it thanks to half-priced discounts on food and beer at work and a need for little else beyond books, magazines, entry into rock shows, and the occasional beer at Charlie's Ale House, which seemed classy at the time for its import-heavy draft list. But as soon as he took control of Goose Island's brewing operation, Greg was ready for a place of his own. He eventually found a four-story condominium building at the corner of Wisconsin and Fremont Streets, three blocks from the brewpub, in a nicely worn part of the city packed with eighty-year-old brick buildings. Greg was drawn to the cheapest of the three available units. John did a double take when he came by for a look.

"This is the worst one and will be hardest to resell," he told his son. "Why don't you get the one on the first floor?"

The one on the first floor was the most visible unit in the building. It was an old storefront with a door on the corner, right where the old convenience store had left it. The condo cost $140,000—a fortune to Greg, but doable with John's help. So he took his dad's advice. Greg lived there seven years, enduring the occasional knock from someone looking for the old store. But the unit included the good fortune of a dirt-floor cellar down a decrepit flight of wooden stairs. For the store, it had been storage. For Greg, it was a place to keep odd European beers he bought during weekly shopping trips to Chicago's best beer store, which happened to sit across the street from Goose Island.

Under Victor's watch, Goose Island had poured six beers at a time across its twenty-four taps, with one or two rotating based on the season. When Greg took over, he wondered, *Why not pour twelve beers at a time?* Skeptics said he misjudged his customers' appetite for variety. Some choice was good, but no one needed *that* much choice. But with his father's support, he plowed ahead, creating one of Chicago's most ambitious beer menus. Greg began to see it as his brewing laboratory.

The *Chicago Tribune* called the selection "bewildering." There was a dunkelweizen—a German-inspired dark brown wheat ale that boasted rich notes of chocolate and banana. He made a porter accented with smoked cherry wood—but only after a dozen other woods were tried and discarded. He made a rare Finnish style of beer called Sahti flavored with juniper twigs and berries; most customers compared it to drinking a Christmas tree. Greg crafted his own inventions, including a savory update of the hefeweizen that he called Oatzen; it featured the customary herbal-fruity hefeweizen yeast but with the creaminess of oats substituted for wheat. And in Greg's first stab at marketing, Goose Island tapped a Christmas beer the night before Thanksgiving that could be hauled home in sixty-four-ounce clear glass jugs labeled FRESH DRAFT BEER. As the head of the brewing operation—finally!—Greg was driven by a simple, radical thought for 1990s beer drinking: offer the people experience and they would take it.

But it was his very first beer that made perhaps the deepest early impact. It was called PMD Mild Ale, and it was a style of beer that could be found in virtually any pub in England. It was refreshing and easy to drink at a meager 3 percent alcohol, but lushly malt forward, complex, and weighty in the mouth. The mild ale had a rich history. It was the favored drink of coal-stained, sweat-soaked laborers during the Industrial Revolution; it was safe to drink (oftentimes unlike water), offered precious calories, quenched a thirst, and was low enough in alcohol that a laborer could return to work after three of four pints. And, when done right, it was delicious—like a loaf of fresh bread threaded with a wisp of cocoa. Along the Clybourn industrial corridor, Greg would sometimes get to work by driving past the twentieth-century American version of those laborers: Chicago's steel plant workers, sparks flying, steam rising in the blue-collar engine of the city. In their honor, and to honor the history of beer, Greg named his mild ale for the Planned Manufacturing District where Goose Island operated, which was intended to limit residential redevelopment and keep those blue-collar jobs in the city.

In the bar, Greg used PMD Mild Ale as a means to educate or, as he put it, "fuck with people." The people, in this case, were 1990s beer drinkers. Anheuser-Busch and Miller's combined share of the US beer market was 65 percent, which led many customers to issue a simple and mindless request when ordering at the bar: "I'll have your lightest beer."

Greg would inevitably respond with a frothy, chestnut brown pint of PMD Mild. He relished the quizzical looks that followed.

"I don't want this, I want your lightest beer," the customer would say.

"You want the lightest-colored beer, the lowest alcohol, or the fewest calories?" Greg would ask.

The fucking with was on.

"Fewest calories," was the most common answer.

"That's what I gave you."

"But this is dark."

"Do you want a low-calorie beer that's easy to drink?"

"No, I want a light beer."

And there it was, distilled into one sentence: the battle that Goose Island and the nation's band of craft brewers—now up to nearly four hundred—faced during the early 1990s. Anheuser-Busch, Miller, and Coors had zapped the American understanding of beer into one meaningless word: *light*. Or worse, *lite*.

Light beer was more than the absence of color; it was a lack of aroma, taste, and flavor, a reduction of the American palate to the bland center of nothingness. It was a mindless, meaningless handle, and everything that every upstart brewery fought. Greg must have had the conversation a thousand times, and pissed off 998 people along the way. But he didn't care. In 1992 PMD Mild Ale scored a gold medal at the Great American Beer Festival in the English Brown Ale category. The people who needed to get it got it.

Greg gradually trimmed the lineup of flagship beers to Golden Goose Pilsner, Honker's Ale, and Tanzen Gans Kolsch, a light but muscular and vaguely fruity German-style ale he'd learned to love during his European travels. Whenever he dabbled with something new, he would walk across the street to Sam's Wines and Spirits and buy whatever beers it had in the style, especially those he hadn't tried before. It was a technique learned from both Victor and Michael Jackson: you learn by tasting. And as he tasted, he stretched his repertoire, building a stable of more than twenty beers that rotated throughout the year, including Holiday Wassail (a spiced ale available only at the holidays), Special Brown Ale (a favorite of regulars), and a heretofore rarity called India Pale Ale.

For unsuspecting customers, the menu described the beer—called simply "IPA (India Pale Ale)"—as "very strong, very bitter, very pale." It was a style virtually unknown in Chicago but starting to turn heads on the West Coast.

When Greg took over for Victor, John gave him a second and equally important job: face of the brewpub. No one wanted to hear about the future of beer from a balding, fifty-year-old former box company executive. They wanted to hear it from a guy in his twenties who had grown into a handsome, stocky man, with a mop of sandy hair and a goatee. John had long ago recognized an unlikely asset in his son. Even as he was still learning to help Victor brew, Greg had thrown himself into understanding beer—not just how to make it, but how to taste it, talk about it, and make someone else care about it. He knew the history and the science and seemed to intuit what people wanted, usually before they knew they wanted it. He needed to be the face of Goose Island.

Such a step for Greg had once been unlikely. He had been a curious, creative, and occasionally impish child—he got in trouble in second grade for singing the Preparation H jingle in class—but also quiet and shy. And the shy kid, at first, wasn't good in his new role. He was halting and hesitant. The ideas were there, but he lacked a plan to convey them. He couldn't command a room. But then, slowly, he could.

Greg began leading weekly Sunday afternoon tours of the brewery in his button-down flannel, baggy shorts, and steel-toed rubber boots, making clear that Goose Island was the good guy.

"We're brewing beer for our Oktoberfest, and we're using twelve varieties of malt," he told a tour group as a twenty-six-year-old brewmaster during the summer of 1992. "Your big brewers generally only use four similar ones—basically one malt for everything."

He took calls from the media. He preached the merits of small-scale beer from small and independently owned breweries. He championed beer's place beside a fine meal. He was an advocate and a leader. Beer and the family business turned John and Pat's son into an adult before their eyes.

5

"It Started in Chicago as a Brewer Planted an Imaginative Seed in a Garden of Fertile Artists Aching for More Depth of Expression"

THE BREWERY WAS A FIVE-MINUTE walk from Greg's condo—one block south and two blocks west, past a curve in the city's iconic L tracks. As Greg walked below those tracks one morning, something in the air made him worry. At first it seemed to be a bit of smokiness. Then the smell turned sharper and acrid. Like tires burning. It was coming from Goose Island.

A day earlier, he had made a beer more akin to a science experiment. It was the biggest, baddest, darkest, booziest stout he could muster. He poured an obscene amount of malted barley into this beer, so much that it spilled from the mash tun; he and his assistant brewer had to bind the doors shut with towels. Honker's Ale used about 550 pounds of malt. A typical imperial stout, 800 pounds. This concoction, whatever it was, was fueled with 1,550 pounds of churning malted barley. Greg had little idea what he was making. He just wanted the most robust imperial stout imaginable.

There was an occasion to mark, and that occasion was a chance to celebrate the fearlessness of small and independent breweries. Why shouldn't Greg aim for extraordinary with Goose Island's one thousandth batch?

"For a long time, people had the one beer that they drank, and it was the one beer they drank every day," he explained ten years later when reminiscing about that beer. "Nobody eats like that, and people that drink wine don't drink like that. Beer drinkers are starting to catch up. They want to drink different beers for different occasions."

Greg wanted to do something big. And the morning after wrestling the biggest beer he could into his brew house, there it was on the Chicago wind, amid the exhaust, garbage, and waste rising off the Chicago River. If he could smell it a block away, something must have gone horribly wrong.

The beer hadn't gone horribly wrong. It would in fact help define the coming revolution.

It had been born one hundred miles east, in South Bend, Indiana, on October 5, 1994. As brewmaster of Chicago's most ascendant brewpub, Greg had been invited to cohost a beer, bourbon, and cigar dinner at LaSalle Grill, a white tablecloth restaurant two miles south of the Notre Dame campus. He was asked to represent beer for a decadent three-pronged evening: a premeal cigar, multiple courses of food paired with beer and bourbon, then a postdinner cigar. He showed up wearing a black sports jacket with a motley tie of yellow, beige, and brown. A two-inch goatee grew from his chin. Joining him at the head table was a mighty voice of the bourbon industry: Jim Beam master distiller Booker Noe, a sixth-generation whiskey maker and grandson of the actual Jim Beam. The two men, more than thirty years apart in age, took turns leading the room through pairings. Glass in hand, each became increasingly loquacious as the night wore on. Bourbon had been a second fuel for Greg's fiction-writing binges at the University of Iowa, and he was thrilled to have Noe's ear for an evening. Sitting with Noe, he knew he had his chance to make people talk for years about Goose Island's thousandth batch. What about a beer aged in one of Noe's bourbon barrels?

Beer had been housed in wood for thousands of years, whether for fermentation, maturation, or storage. Whatever flavor the beer inherited from the wood was sometimes a bonus (though not always—the inside of a barrel could be rife with bacteria). In post–World War II America, stainless steel and automation became the norm, and the use of wood barrels mostly vanished. But then the legality of home brewing led thirsty adventurers to tear up the rule book in their kitchens, basements, and garages. Though the first example of an imperial stout aged in a bourbon barrel is lost to time, it may well have come from the group of south suburban Chicago home brewers who brought their experiment into Goose Island for a monthly meeting during the early 1990s. One of the home brewers had secured a used whiskey barrel but couldn't make enough stout to fill it himself; he employed his fellow club members to make a similar recipe to blend into the barrel. The result, members of the club would recall years later, was a bit ragged and unrefined. But it made their eyes grow wide.

Whether Greg tasted that beer or even knew of its existence would fade from his memory. One he would not forget came from Boston Beer Co., which had helped spark the craft beer movement with the mainstream appeal of its Boston Lager. But brewery founder Jim Koch was also keen on experimentation. In 1994 his brewery released a thick, boozy bock aged in oak barrels that previously held Jack Daniel's whiskey. At nearly 18 percent alcohol and knee-bucklingly sweet, Sam Adams Triple Bock became an industry sensation. It wasn't that drinkers liked the beer; it was that American beer had been pushed to otherworldly heights. Again and again, Greg heard from amazed customers: "Have you tried Sam Adams Triple Bock?" It tastes like port, they would say. Or brandy. Or liqueur. No one said it tasted like beer. Triple Bock was an impressive feat but had few of the characteristics of great beer—namely, bitterness, balance, or hop character. If Greg ever got his hands on a bourbon barrel, he was determined to put something in—and more importantly, take something out—that was inarguably beer.

And then came that evening with Booker Noe. Over dinner, he leaned in and asked Noe if he could get a few of those used whiskey barrels to age a beer. He caught Noe at a good time. Jim Beam had just taken aim at creating a premium American whiskey market with its Small Batch Bourbon Collection. Knob Creek, Baker's, Booker's, and Basil Hayden's were all nuanced bourbons aged longer than most American whiskeys and at considerably more expense to the customer. Beam was raising the stakes on American whiskey. Greg wanted to do the same for American beer. A couple months later, six four-year-old Beam barrels arrived at the brewpub.

As Greg walked to work that morning with the smell of burning on the air, he wondered if he had created a labor-intensive failure. He wasn't sure whether to be any more optimistic once inside the brewery: the beer was fermenting so aggressively that it had climbed to eighty-eight degrees—almost twenty degrees above normal. The glycol chiller couldn't keep up to suck away the heat. It was an angry locomotive of a beer.

But in the coming days, the pitch-black liquid slowed and then finally stopped bubbling. Greg and his assistant brewer, a recent Siebel graduate, pried the lids off the barrels in a low-ceilinged storage space below the bar and rigged a network of hoses to transfer the beer from the tank. It began with a quick siphon from the mouth. Gravity did the rest. Slowly, the inky stout snaked through the hoses and into Noe's bourbon barrels. A sweet rush of boozy air crept out as the wood filled. Greg smiled.

Imperial stout was a style first brewed in London during the late eighteenth century as an export to Russia, whose long-reigning empress Catherine the Great became an admirer of the pitch-black brew. Initially dubbed Russian imperial stout, the beer was sharply boozy and more aggressively hopped than the average stout, resulting in a hearty blend of roast, malt, and a sweet-bitter mélange of coffee and dark chocolate, with vague notes of stone fruit. At least two British versions—Courage Imperial Russian Stout and Samuel Smith's Imperial Stout—were imported to the United States through the 1980s. (John Hall was a fan.)

There's no evidence of US brewers making the style before Prohibition, which means the first domestic attempt at the beer was likely Bert Grant's Imperial Stout, made by Yakima Brewing and Malting Co. in Yakima, Washington, during the early 1980s. But even into the 1990s, imperial stout mostly remained an outlier in the United States, existing only in limited quantities and on draft at a handful of brewpubs. As Ray Daniels wrote in his 1996 home brewing tome, *Designing Great Beers*, "In the United States you'll find some craft-brewed examples with a good deal of potency, but few are bottled, so they rarely get the aging that yields the most interesting flavor profile."

For Greg, imperial stout was the obvious choice to pour into those Beam barrels. The style is principally defined by three abundant traits: color, flavor, and alcohol. The color leaps out first; it's so impenetrably dark no light passes through. The beer then backs up what the eye sees: miles of aroma, flavor, and boozy weight. Of beer's four principal ingredients—barley, hops, water, and yeast—it is the addition of barley roasted nearly black that imbues imperial stout with both its darkness and roasted char character. That heavy dose of malted barley also produces ample sugars that yeast converts to alcohol, resulting in a beer as boozy as it is dark. When it comes to bourbon barrel aging, a beer too light would be overrun by the wood and whiskey. A beer too sweet might taste brilliant from a barrel, but not enough like beer—like Sam Adams Triple Bock. A deep, dark, silky imperial stout evoking bitter espresso and roasted grain soaked for three months in bourbon-laced oak sounded just about right.

But as Greg would come to learn, the base beer wasn't even the most important element—that was the charred oak inside the barrel. Once harvested from the broad forests where the Midwest meets the South, the guts of a bourbon barrel, doused in flame, are left with a char that caramelizes the oak and creates new layers of flavor. Bourbon enters a barrel crystal clear and spends anywhere from a couple of years to decades mingling with the wood. By the time a used whiskey barrel lands at a brewery—usually via a broker specializing in such connections—the interior is ideally still wet with booze.

Although a barrel-aged beer will take on obvious flavors easily identifiable as bourbon, oak, and char inside a barrel, a complex chemical reaction is also underway, much of which can be traced to when fire met wood. It comes down to one essential factor: extraction. With enough time in a barrel, the charred wood supplies a complex web of flavor compounds that thread gorgeously into imperial stout. Vanillin supplies vanilla. Lactones lend elements of woody coconut. Hemicellulose adds caramel-toffee, which can wind toward notes of cotton candy. As long as the beer is allowed to swim, that barrel is in the midst of extraction, absorbing the liquid and then breathing it back out. The result is a sea of microblending, repeated again and again until the beer is withdrawn. After one hundred days, in the fall of 1995, that beer was Bourbon County Stout.

What Greg pulled from the barrel thrilled and terrified him. He knew it would be a polarizing creation. Chocolate. Vanilla. Caramel. Coconut. Oaky bourbon fierceness. He was proud of the beer. He was eager to serve it. But was the beer drinker of 1995 ready?

Jim Beam's head of sales showed up for the tapping, posing for pictures in a suit while Greg donned his customary outfit of a flannel shirt, cargo pants, and boots. The brewpub charged six dollars for a ten-ounce snifter—more than double the cost of most Goose Island beers. Some customers couldn't believe the gall. Others couldn't believe that their little local brewpub had come up with this sweet, boozy black gold.

Bourbon County Stout's revolutionary status was affirmed that fall, when Goose Island sent the beer a thousand miles west, to the Great American Beer Festival in Denver. For a young brewery that didn't pasteurize its beer—that is, heating it to kill unwanted bacteria, as the big breweries did—getting entries far from home could be a challenge. In 1992 two of its six beers soured during the trip to the GABF. A year later, three of four entries spoiled. A year after that, they didn't even bother competing. In 1995 Goose Island tried again, and among five entries, Bourbon County Stout reached Denver just fine. The challenge was making fest-goers understand it.

For what a stout was supposed to be in 1995, Bourbon County missed style guidelines all over the place: too big, too boozy, too sweet, and far too robust. There were just two categories in which to enter a stout at the time—Dry Stout (low alcohol by definition) and Specialty Stout (such as oatmeal or sweet stouts)—and neither remotely fit the Bourbon County behemoth. At 12 percent alcohol, it was one-third boozier than a contemporary imperial stout. That left Goose Island to enter Bourbon County where the squarest of square pegs competed—the Strong Ale category. Among forty-eight entries, Bourbon County scored one of two honorable mentions. Gold went to a 1990s cult beer called Dog Spit Stout from O'Ryan's Tavern and Brewery in Las Cruces, New Mexico, while silver went to Bell's Expedition Stout. No bronze medal was awarded, which left honorable mentions for Hubscotch Scotch ale from Hubcap Brewery and Kitchen, in Vail, Colorado, and Bourbon County Stout. Greg was convinced that it only took honorable mention because the judges were baffled. They knew it was good. They just didn't know what it was.

It would take another seven years for beers aged in wood barrels to move beyond the "Experimental" or "Specialty" categories at the GABF. In 2002 a Wood- and Barrel-Aged Beer category debuted. That was followed by a Wood- and Barrel-Aged Strong Beer category in 2006. In 2007 came a Wood- and Barrel-Aged Sour Beer category. Finally, in 2010, Greg's seed planted fifteen years earlier sprouted: Wood- and Barrel-Aged Strong Stout became a category. The bronze medal winner that first year, among thirty-four entries, was the one that jump-started the movement: Bourbon County Stout.

A generation of brewers stunned by Bourbon County Stout began experimenting with their own versions. Some of the beers were private reserves never intended to meet customers' lips. Others were bids to learn what worked and what didn't: How long in the barrel? What kind of barrel? What kind of base beer? Brewers gradually learned that any number of styles—barleywine, quad, porter, Scotch ale, brown ale, even a variety of IPAs—could stand up to bourbon and oak. But it was imperial stout that touched a nerve. The offerings proliferated, and the most creative brewers increased their barrel-aging programs year by year. In 2003 the Illinois Craft Brewers Guild launched a festival to celebrate the genre rooted in its backyard: the Festival of Wood and Barrel Aged Beer. Each winter, brewers from farther and farther afield sent kegs of their most ambitious brews to Chicago for a crowd that snapped up tickets within minutes.

As bourbon barrel aging became a necessity for any ambitious brewery, Goose Island's role as forefather became cemented. Nearly two decades after the first keg of Bourbon County Stout was tapped, industry icon Tomme Arthur, cofounder of Southern California breweries Port Brewing and Lost Abbey, would eventually write in *All About Beer* magazine:

> Goose Island Bourbon County Stout proved that big beers could marry the huge flavors of American whiskey with skillful beer production. This statement of fact remains front and center today some 20 years later. Bourbon-barrel-aged beers dot the landscape and have become de facto collectibles for beer enthusiasts everywhere. It started in Chicago as a brewer planted an imaginative seed in a garden of fertile artists aching for more depth of expression. In many ways, bourbon-barrel-aged beers have been nearly reduced to jazz-like standards aspiring brewers must master. So many of them are now regularly executing this barrel-aged standard it's almost become passé.
>
> So, what have we learned about this brewing standard in the past 20 years? Above all, we have learned that few, if any, styles of beers easily handle the rich flavors associated with freshly emptied bourbon barrels as does imperial stout.

In fewer than ten years Goose Island had proved John Hall's initial inkling correct: Americans did crave variety and freshness in their beer.

But he was wrong on one count. Drinkers didn't simply want replications of the beer served on the other side of the Atlantic. It was Greg who proved that drinkers wanted something new and unique. They wanted innovation and experimentation. They wanted revolution.

The revolution was on.

6

St. Louis, We Have a Problem

The suits at Anheuser-Busch had a name for the thousands of people who poured into Denver for the Great American Beer Festival every fall. And the visionaries who had started more than a thousand breweries by the mid-1990s. And the drinkers dazzled by imperial stout aged in bourbon barrels, who helped make "specialty brewing," as it was still called during the mid-1990s, the fastest-growing corner of the industry.

Hop Heads.

In Anheuser-Busch's hallowed St. Louis halls, the term could be applied with derision or faint admiration, but mostly with a sense of wonder. Who were these people? And how could Anheuser-Busch win their affection? Hop Heads didn't care what their neighbors and coworkers drank. They were immune to the charms of a $1 million Super Bowl ad. They didn't care that Bud Light tasted the same in every bar from coast to coast. Hop Heads disdained those things.

Outwardly, Anheuser-Busch was quite healthy. Its fabled Budweiser had been in slow decline since 1988, losing 20 percent of its sales volume in a mere ten years. But thanks to runaway hit Bud Light, the company had crept past 40 percent of the nation's beer sales and eyed the 50 percent mark with no reason to think it couldn't get there. Its gold-plated culture—August Busch III's daily commutes by helicopter, hefty office remodeling budgets with each executive promotion, and first-class plane tickets for even the most junior employee—was quite safe.

But the Hop Heads were a problem.

The disturbance was particularly strong in the Pacific Northwest, where the foundation of a progressive beer culture was laid in 1978 with the arrival of Charles Finkel from New York City. In New York, Finkel imported California and Washington wines as alternatives to the French and Italian staples of the day. In Seattle, he applied that same vision to beer, launching Merchant du Vin to bring some of Europe's most renowned brands to the United States for the first time. Until then, even a style as elemental as pale ale was foreign to the American palate; suddenly, the Pacific Northwest had a front-row seat for what beer could be beyond light lagers.

The region also became a hotbed for making such beers. In 1982 Bert Grant opened Grant's Brewery Pub in Yakima, 150 miles southeast of Seattle; it was not only the Northwest's first craft brewery but also the nation's first brewpub. Grant, a jovial, potbellied Scotsman, was committed to a new and better brand of American beer, all the way down to the REAL ALE license plate on his white Rolls-Royce. About that same time, the cofounder of Starbucks Coffee, Gordon Bowker, teamed up with a wine industry marketing analyst named Paul Shipman to open one of the few small-scale production breweries in the nation. Housed in a former transmission shop just north of downtown Seattle, Redhook Ale Brewery initially baffled drinkers by debuting with a spicy Belgian-inspired ale. But it soon settled into a modern American identity with its Blackhook Porter and Ballard Bitter Pale Ale.

Less than two hundred miles down Interstate 5, in Portland, a similar revolution was underway. By 1984 the city of fewer than four hundred thousand was home to a handful of breweries, including what would briefly become three of the nation's ten largest: Portland Brewing Co., Full Sail Brewing Co., and Widmer Brothers Brewing. Widmer, in particular, generated buzz with its odd choice of a flagship: hefeweizen, a German-style ale showcasing wheat instead of malted barley and exploding with aromatics of banana and clove. A year later, the Oregon legislature became an early craft beer advocate by legalizing breweries' ability to make and sell beer at the same location. With the law on its side, Portland quickly became a brewing epicenter.

By the early 1990s, the problem was laid bare for Anheuser-Busch: something new was unfolding in the Pacific Northwest. Those people wanted Bass or Heineken. Redhook or Widmer Brothers. Not Bud or Bud Light. A war was being fought every day for shelf space and tap handles, and Anheuser-Busch, for once, didn't have the weapons to win.

None other than John Hall summed up Big Beer's dilemma in a 1994 *Chicago Tribune* article:

> Their sales are not growing and some have been forced to change their pricing, which means a decline in profits. Our segment isn't worthy of consideration as real competition, but we have grown significantly over the past eight or nine years and the big guys want to know what's going on, maybe even be part of it.
>
> But how can they do it? The way they operate, their need to please the lowest common denominator tends to exclude them from our segment. Our appeal is to someone looking for something different—not the same thing.

What was Big Beer to do?

In 1994 Anheuser-Busch sent one of its ascendant young brand managers to the Pacific Northwest to find an answer. Tim Schoen was in the midst of a twenty-eight-year career at Anheuser-Busch, where he led some of the company's most iconic brands.

Schoen had recently ended a stint as senior brand manager for Bud Dry, a relic from the nation's brief infatuation with dry beer, a style popular in Japan that boasted bracing flavor, reduced calories, and virtually no aftertaste. Following a strong debut during the late 1980s, the style was mostly gone within five years. The fickle taste buds of the American beer drinker moved on, and so did Schoen, who was tasked with making sense of the Hop Heads.

He was appointed to a recently launched Anheuser-Busch division called the Specialty Brewing Group—code for brands outside the essential core of Bud, Bud Light, and their lower-brow cousins Natural Light and Busch. Schoen's first major project was a one-month whirlwind during the late summer of 1994. Word had leaked that Miller was working on a beer called Red Dog that would get a significant marketing push. August Busch III—known mostly as "the Third" in the halls of Anheuser-Busch—was apoplectic at the thought of his rival outmaneuvering the King of Beers. Damage control was left to Schoen. He holed up with research analysts, brewers, marketers, and copywriters to figure out how to beat Miller's Red Dog launch. He didn't have a name or a beer. Just a directive.

Twenty-eight days later, and after almost as many all-nighters, he had a beer. They spent the month leading hourly taste panels and faxing images across the country to find an identity that would resonate with consumers. Because they didn't want word to leak, they conducted trials not in St. Louis but in Tampa, where Anheuser-Busch operated a theme park. Presuming that Miller's Red Dog would be a malt-forward red lager—a briefly surging style led by Coors's Killian's Red—Schoen's beer was a reddish amber lager built of two preexisting Anheuser-Busch beers, then boosted with caramel malt for a darker tint and richer flavor. More importantly, Schoen launched the beer with an ad on *Monday Night Football.*

To sow confusion with Red Dog—confusion was a common defensive tactic for Anheuser-Busch—the beer was named Red Wolf, even as Anheuser-Busch insisted that the similar names were mere coincidence. Red Wolf got the customary Anheuser-Busch marketing and merchandising push, which included gym bags, sunglasses, key chains, neon signs, coasters, and a $105 black jacket with embroidered logos on the left chest and back. Red Dog turned out not to be a red lager—it was a typical pale yellow light lager—and it performed well initially. But so did Red Wolf, which had done its job. It kept Red Dog in check.

Schoen's reward for a job well done was a plane ticket to the Pacific Northwest to address an even more vexing problem. Word of Anheuser-Busch's predicament was spreading through a mainstream media issuing dire observations of Big Beer's comeuppance:

Popularity of Microbrews Rattles the Beer Giants
Associated Press
July 15, 1993

PORTLAND, Ore.—When retired Scottish policeman Bill Anderson came to America on vacation, he expected to go for weeks without the strong, flavorful beers of his homeland.

Instead, he found Widmer Brewing Co.'s Widmer Hefeweizen, a thick, cloudy brew that is unlike most American beers.

"That's more like a beer," Anderson said, savoring a Hefeweizen by Portland's riverfront. "No disrespect to most American beers, but I find them very light. I enjoy a pint with a bit of body in it. This has got a bit of texture."

A growing number of Americans agree. Increasingly, drinkers are opting for specialty beers produced in "brewpubs" and small breweries that have opened across the country. They're attracted not just by the beers' distinctive taste, but an image that bucks that of mass-produced brands like Miller and Budweiser.

As if being called out by name wasn't bad enough, Anheuser-Busch's competitors were already taking initiative. Back in 1987, Miller agreed to buy Leinenkugel Brewing, a 120-year-old family-owned brewery in the bucolically named Chippewa Falls, Wisconsin. It was a low-stakes but prescient bet: a sizable regional brewery (sixty-one thousand barrels of production a year before the sale), with an appealing brand but no succession plan. In 1995 Miller diversified even further by establishing a subsidiary, American Specialty and Craft Beer Co., to house a wing of craft beer brands. That included Leine's, as it was called; Celis White, launched in Austin, Texas, by Pierre Celis, who had previously created Hoegaarden, a brand he sold to Belgium's biggest beer company, Interbrew; and a 50 percent stake in Maine's Shipyard Brewing Co., which had grown rapidly since opening in 1992. An even more successful incursion into craft had come from Coors, which allowed a young brewer named Keith Villa to develop a bright, spiced witbier in 1995 called Blue Moon.

After clinging to a decades-old belief that it could make all beer to please all people, Anheuser-Busch finally recognized a need to go deeper into specialty beer. Schoen's job was to get an understanding of what was unfolding within craft so that the company's foundation, built on Bud and Bud Light, wouldn't crack. He and a small team split time between Portland and Seattle, visiting bars, quizzing distributors, and talking to drinkers. What did they want? What didn't they want? Would they drink one of these new esoteric beers if it was made by big, bad Anheuser-Busch?

The answers were jarring. These drinkers wanted flavor and character in their beer; the race to the bottom no longer worked. Also, the way these people talked about their beer and the breweries that made it was vastly different from the rest of the country. It was intimate. It was personal. It wasn't so much that they hated Anheuser-Busch and Miller—though some did. They just wanted options. Small and local breweries had proved that variety was possible in American beer.

In October 1994, at an annual meeting of Anheuser-Busch executives and their distributors, Schoen passed out baseball caps with mock ponytails snaking out the back. The hats were inspired by his sojourn to the Pacific Northwest. The room of well-heeled middle-aged men in slacks and dress shirts got a good laugh from the gag—even August Busch III, who dutifully affixed his hat. Then Schoen made his pitch.

"It's funny," he said, "but I'm telling you right now it makes you feel different because it is different."

Schoen explained what he'd seen in the Northwest and the trouble it could cause everyone in that room. If what was happening in Portland and Seattle broke into the mainstream, Anheuser-Busch would need to change. Or else it would be left behind. Big Beer's job was to figure out what people wanted, then give it to them. Light beer? Dry beer? Ice beer? Craft beer? It was ultimately all the same.

A debate began to bubble about how to adapt. Should the company manage its entry into craft as it had with everything else: pivot for swiftness, rather than excellence, and strike—as it had done with Red Wolf? Or was true change afoot? Perhaps it should create a division, as Miller had, with a leader who had the ear of August Busch III, and launch a broad offensive. Or, the most radical option yet: form an entirely new company, spun off from Anheuser-Busch, with its own executives and board of directors. Its mission would be craft innovation and nothing else.

Schoen favored the last approach. He wanted a bold initiative, and he wanted to lead it. He even had a property ready to go. It would be big and autonomous, and with Anheuser-Busch's muscle behind it, it would be unstoppable. It would be called Specialty Brewing Co. All he needed was a yes.

He got a no.

7

St. Louis, We Still Have a Problem

In 1994 it happened.

Craft beer eclipsed 1 percent of US beer sales.

The nation was home to six hundred breweries—up from fewer than one hundred a decade earlier—and the idea of fresh, locally made beer was, like Lazarus of Bethany, back from the dead.

Big Beer's gnat was growing into a fly.

Panicky executives began to wonder if craft might one day reach a galling 10 percent of the market. "We are even looking at things like apricot ales," Miller's director of new business development told *USA Today* in 1994. Apricot ale was traditionally something for Big Beer to mock. Now it was a potential lifeline.

Through 1996, the number of breweries in the United States, along with craft beer's share of the market, steadily grew. Even Disney World opened a 450-seat brewpub. Disney World! If Anheuser-Busch executives couldn't count on tourists to swill the bedrock American beer during the bedrock American vacation, who knew what calamity loomed?

It wasn't as if Anheuser-Busch had no clue how to innovate; in 1988 the company released a decidedly un-Anheuser-Busch-like beer in limited markets and with little fanfare: Anheuser Marzen, which harked back to a traditional European style rather than the cheap American knockoffs in which the company typically traded. But it was killed off quickly, which led an industry analyst to tell the *St. Louis Post-Dispatch* that it was most likely created for research purposes. "I think the idea was to probe the market," Robert Weinberg, a former Anheuser-Busch executive, said. "I think the whole venture was an attempt to buy market information, to buy know-how."

By the mid-1990s, Anheuser-Busch no longer had the luxury of innovating solely as covert inquiry. Amid industry upheaval, it needed to stay relevant. Its Big Beer brethren did too: Coors launched a line of seasonal specialty beers, including Eisbock lager for spring, Weizenbier wheat beer in June, and Oktoberfest Märzen for fall. Miller trotted out Reserve Velvet Stout and Reserve Amber Ale. Detroit's Stroh Brewery, fighting desperately to remain relevant, unfurled a new line of craft beers under the banner of Augsburger, a Wisconsin brand it had acquired in 1989: Augsburger Doppelbock, Augsburger Weiss, and Augsburger Rot, a red lager. "We can't sit by and let our shelf space in stores erode," a Stroh's executive told *USA Today* in 1993. "The way to protect it is to get into the game."

Anheuser-Busch needed to get in the craft game too, and doing it was up to Tim Schoen's Specialty Brewing Group. Schoen started with a publicly stated mission of developing "hand-crafted, small batch beers for the rapidly growing specialty and micro beer segment." *Hand-crafted. Small-batch.* Schoen knew his audience liked those words.

Specialty Brewing Group's first beers appeared in mid-1994 as part of a new brand tied to Anheuser-Busch's Elk Mountain hop farm in northern Idaho. Elk Mountain Amber Ale, stunningly, was the first ale Anheuser-Busch released in its 142-year history. Elk Mountain Red Lager was an attempt to cash in on the malt-forward "red" beer craze. Both beers were released regionally, then nationally. Anheuser-Busch boosted its foray into "specialty brewing" with an advertising campaign that poked fun at its young rivals: "We used to be a microbrewery, too. Then we got better. And better. And better. And, yeah, a bit bigger as well."

A tornado of Anheuser-Busch craft-like brands followed: big brands, small brands, brands to confuse, and brands aimed at specific competitors. ZiegenBock was released in Texas, to take on the locally made hit Shiner Bock; to promote the beer, Anheuser-Busch hauled a goat named "Zigey" around the state. The next year, in Northern California, came Pacific Ridge Pale Ale, which had a laser-like focus of its own: Sierra Nevada Pale Ale. The beer traded heavily on its California roots—BREWED IN NORTHERN CALIFORNIA, read both the label and bottle cap—and was available only in that state. Pacific Ridge was packaged in a similar bottle to Sierra Nevada's flagship and showcased the same Cascade hop. The label said the beer was "inspired by the rugged, natural beauty that surrounds the Northern California brewery"—just like Sierra Nevada's.

The difference: in vintage Anheuser-Busch style, Pacific Ridge was supported by upwards of $3 million for print and billboard ads, plus marketing materials most small breweries could never afford—neon signs, coasters, table tents, banners, and brochures. If Pacific Ridge Pale Ale was a success, the plan was to release two more beers under the banner.

Pacific Ridge was accompanied by American Originals, which Anheuser-Busch touted as the authentic turn-of-the-century recipes from founder Adolphus Busch. The beers debuted in two of the savviest beer markets in the nation, Denver and Seattle. The message behind the brands was so tidy as to be dubious: replications of the company's earliest beers, based on exhaustive research of the original recipes.

"They are as close to the style, taste and look for the original beers as we can discern from our archival records, and I'm sure that my great-great grandfather would be delighted that through the American Originals we are able to honor the rich history he helped create for Anheuser-Busch during our company's early days," August Busch IV, vice president of brand management, said at the time.

The beers included Black and Tan porter, Faust lager, and Muenchener amber ale. In reality, the marketing team behind the idea had little clue how the beers should taste—especially American Hop Ale, which quickly replaced Muenchener. They were just searching for a hit.

The real work was saved for what Anheuser-Busch hoped would be a reignited Michelob line. Once one of the nation's vaunted brands, Michelob had fallen off dramatically through the 1980s. But St. Louis believed the name maintained enough sophistication—and was seen as a step up from Budweiser—that it could support a craft portfolio. Establishing a series of small, new brands would take time; Anheuser-Busch didn't want to take time. Better to dust off a flagging old brand to bring new beers to market, especially when that brand would be celebrating its one hundredth birthday in 1996.

With recipes developed on a pilot brewing system deep in the belly of the St. Louis mother ship, Anheuser-Busch led with Michelob AmberBock in 1995. Michelob HefeWeizen followed in 1996, launching in the sort of developed beer markets—Washington and Oregon—that might actually understand a hefeweizen. Schoen told *Newsday* that Anheuser-Busch's move into craft "legitimized the whole category."

"If Anheuser-Busch is here, it's truly a category," he said.

The presence of Anheuser-Busch also came with a downside for the industry: the market was suddenly rife with $5.99 six-packs. Smaller brewers, who had no ability to blast out the volume that made brewing far less expensive, were stuck charging $7.99 or more per six-pack. John Hall's early ally Carol Stoudt, of Stoudts Brewing, predicted "a major shakeout" not because there were too many breweries but because the small brewers couldn't match the prices of Anheuser-Busch and Miller.

Still, for Anheuser-Busch, it was an odd place to be. The Busch family believed deeply in the power of Budweiser; the broader portfolio always came second. Even its 1990s workhorse, Bud Light, was not the product of quest or experimentation—it was a necessary and relatively late response to the success of Miller Lite. (It was also Anheuser-Busch's third attempt at marketing a light beer; the previous effort, Anheuser-Busch Natural Light, later renamed Natural Light, failed to dazzle when debuting in 1977; Budweiser Light struggled until its name was shortened in 1982.)

But there it was, obvious to all by the mid-1990s: the King of Beers needed to keep up. If things went right with its new line of craft beer, Anheuser-Busch would never lose another tap handle or inch of shelf space to some small upstart. If a drinker was going to transition from Budweiser to craft, well, best to make it Anheuser-Busch's version of craft.

Anheuser-Busch outwardly championed the diversity that had beset beer. "We applaud what is going on with the microbreweries; the explosion in the interest of beer helps raise the excitement level for all beers," a company spokesman told the *Houston Chronicle* in 1995.

In reality, Anheuser-Busch wanted nothing more than to step on the throat of the fledgling craft beer movement, watch it take its last breath, then flood the market with Budweiser once more.

By the mid-1990s, Anheuser-Busch's early dabbling in craft beer became a Big Beer–like flood. Buoyed by the early success of Michelob Amber-Bock, marketing wanted an expanded lineup of four new beers all to be released within a month in 1997. Out came Michelob Golden Pilsner, Michelob Honey Lager, Michelob Pale Ale, and, launched in the Pacific Northwest, Michelob Porter.

To push the beers, the Specialty Brewing Group grabbed the internet domain hopnotes.com and began the unlikely task of championing beer with flavor, albeit with training wheels: "Let's get the pronunciation out of the way first. It's HAY-fuh-VI-sun. . . . Michelob HefeWeizen is cloudy because it's supposed to be. It's not some new-fangled, fad beer—this style is very traditional. It's smooth and thirst-quenching. What more do you want?" Anheuser-Busch used the website to lead live chats with its specialty brewers; the marketing team had learned that personal connection was vital to the growing craft movement.

Like most consumer goods conglomerates, Anheuser-Busch products were not the result of the most creative minds—they came from strategy sessions and focus groups. They were created by marketing people who had so little interest in what was inside their bottles that they simply called beer "the liquid." The liquid was just another box to check, along with a name, a label, an ad campaign, and marketing. The liquid couldn't be bad. But it didn't exactly need to be good. It simply needed to pass taste panels. It was just another part of the brand.

No one was more torn about the bold push behind the Michelob beers than the man making it. Mitch Steele was a brewer who began working for Anheuser-Busch in 1992, as a shift supervisor at the company's Ft. Collins, Colorado, plant. In 1995 he was asked to move to St. Louis to work in new product development. He had previously worked in the wine industry and at a small brewpub in Northern California. If anything, making small-batch beer, even for the world's largest beer company, harked back to his roots. It was also an extended peek under the hood at Anheuser-Busch's business decisions, including a few meetings where August III demanded to know what his company was doing "to keep up with the micro thing."

Steele made the beer, but there was no question who was in charge: the marketing people. They were the ones with access to data, distribution, and sales. They decided what beer would be made when. They seemed to believe in the mission—make credible beer and convince people it was worth drinking—but they had no interest in being part of the growing movement of diversity and choice. That was clear in the beers they sent into the market: the quality was inconsistent and the liquid not always well thought out.

For Steele, Michelob Pale Ale caused particular consternation: between American Hop Ale and Pacific Ridge Pale Ale, how could they differentiate Michelob Pale Ale? They settled on employing German, rather than American, hops. Steele liked the beer well enough, but as he feared, the savviest drinkers noticed the tweak. A beer critic in the *Atlanta Journal-Constitution* wrote, "Inexplicably, Michelob Pale Ale uses classic lager hops, notably Hallertau and Tettnang, with the result that this oddly over-carbonated beer doesn't have the fruity, floral character a pale ale must have. . . . The better pale ales are subtly different from one another—and very different from this one."

Steele was pleased with the honey lager—demanded by marketing after the success of Genesee Brewing's JW Dundee's Original Honey Brown Lager—even if it was nothing he wanted to drink. The pilsner was dumbed down by marketing; less hops, they insisted. The porter was pretty good. But the disappointments that came with innovating for Anheuser-Busch were routine. When Steele and his brewers wowed the Great American Beer Festival with an IPA in 1996, he figured he would be given the green light to make the beer for wide release. Someone corporate—he was never sure who—said no. Too hoppy. Too bitter. Innovation brewers were encouraged to experiment, but few of the beers went anywhere. Even a Scotch ale initially green-lit as a winter seasonal—August Busch III liked it so much he brought a keg home—was dumped when marketing decided that a spiced ale was the safer bet. The Scotch ale was one of the few beers to inspire everyone on the brewing side. But it went down the drain because marketing said so.

By 1998 the Specialty Group abandoned the American Originals and went all in on the Michelob beers. In the company's annual report, August Busch III noted that the specialty segment was still growing faster than the rest of the industry and that it provided higher profit margins. But the category's true use, he said, was propping up the sagging Budweiser: "Eighty percent of the specialty volume is consumed by drinkers who regularly drink mainstream brands. So, the favorable impressions of Anheuser-Busch generated by our specialty portfolio carry over and have a positive impact on our mainstream brands."

In the halls of Anheuser-Busch, the message was clear: craft existed only to defend Bud and Bud Light.

Massive companies like Anheuser-Busch typically face two basic responses when dominance is threatened: develop a homegrown solution or buy their way out. To innovate or to acquire. Anheuser-Busch did both.

While the Specialty Brewing Group developed new brands, the Wholesaler and Business Development unit pursued a quicker fix: entering craft brewing by acquiring an existing brewer.

Wholesaler and Business Development was dedicated to monitoring the brewery's network of distributors and making sure they did their part to push Anheuser-Busch beers from coast to coast. The vast majority of Anheuser-Busch distributors were technically independent businesses and free to carry non-Anheuser-Busch products. However, St. Louis demanded staunch loyalty, often in the form of encouraging its distributors *not* to carry competing brands. (When Tim Schoen was a district sales manager early in his career, he managed relationships with seven Michigan distributors; only one had a portfolio not 100 percent aligned with Anheuser-Busch.) Wholesaler and Business Development was therefore a critical business unit; it was not only a way for Anheuser-Busch to keep tabs on its distributors but also a conduit for distributors to express concerns to St. Louis—such as when the Anheuser-Busch portfolio didn't include the right beers to compete in a home market. With the rise of craft beer during the 1990s, that increasingly became the case, which led Wholesaler and Business Development to go looking for a craft brand that would placate wholesalers. They found it in Seattle, with what had been one of Anheuser-Busch's thorniest competitors: the fast-growing Redhook Ale Brewery.

The two business-driven minds behind Redhook had embraced the rapid growth of a progressive beer market. Just five years after opening, they had launched a larger brewery that could produce seventy-five thousand barrels of beer per year—a staggering figure for an independently owned operation.

Primed for still more growth, Redhook agreed to a deal in 1994 with Anheuser-Busch's Wholesaler and Business Development unit: a reported $17.9 million for a 25 percent stake in the brewery. More importantly, any further expansion of the brand, which was available in just seven Western states at the time, would happen through Anheuser-Busch distributors. Redhook capitalized on the relationship to launch yet another new production brewery, in suburban Seattle, which produced 158,000 barrels in 1995. That was followed by a brewery in New Hampshire with a 250,000-barrel capacity.

The deal barely registered with most beer drinkers—exactly as both parties wanted it. Neither stood to gain from touting the relationship. But within the industry, a dam had been breached. Anheuser-Busch was no longer just copying craft beer—it was invading it. Critics circulated T-shirts that dubbed Redhook, BUDHOOK. At the Craft Brewers Conference, Jerome Chicvara, cofounder of Full Sail Brewing in Hood River, Oregon, compared Anheuser-Busch's wooing of Redhook to Darth Vader's attempts to lure Luke Skywalker to the dark side. Except this time Luke was wooed.

In late 1996, a memo went out on Anheuser-Busch letterhead—bald eagle with wings spread through a gold-rimmed red capital *A* in the upper left corner—to its hundreds of wholesalers and marketing departments under the subject heading SPECIALTY BEER/IMPORT STRATEGY.

Noting that high-end beer—meaning craft and imports—would account for twenty million barrels of sales and 10 percent of the industry when year-end figures were tallied, Anheuser-Busch promised its wholesalers that it planned "to continue competing aggressively for specialty and import volume in 1997. . . . Our experience this year has provided valuable learning. Our plans for '97 are a direct result of this learning and we believe we have a strong plan to increase our mutual share of this important segment."

The basis of the plan, Anheuser-Busch explained, was a "portfolio approach" in which it would "concentrate our national effort against a limited number of brands." The portfolio included Red Wolf ("a safe adventure in terms of price and flavor intensity"), an enhanced Michelob line ("a credible entry point for many specialty drinkers"), and the American Originals. The plan was to undercut competitor pricing (Sam Adams specifically was mentioned) to afford retailers higher profit margins, which would make the beer more attractive to stock. (Although Anheuser-Busch made less money per ounce by selling beer cheaper, it built profits via volume.) Finally, the memo revealed that the Elk Mountain brands would be phased out, along with Muenchener lager and Michelob Centennial, which had been brewed to commemorate that brand's hundredth anniversary. (Anheuser-Busch advised its wholesalers not to let the disappearance of a handful of brands lead to diminished retail presence: "We ask that you manage this transition period to hold and increase your share of available retail shelf and cooler space.")

It touted the advantage of having Redhook in the fold, which offered "the opportunity to compete at the upper-price tier for consumers interested in highly specialized craft beers." The implication was clear: with Redhook, the American Originals, and a handful of fancy Michelob beers, no distributor would need to take on small and local brands, no matter the market: "Our Plan to address the Specialty/Import category is comprehensive and flexible to meet your local market needs."

The next page featured a crude graphic bearing eight targets for Anheuser-Busch's enhanced lineup. Beers at the top of the list were most expensive and least approachable to the average American beer drinker. Beers at the bottom were cheapest and easiest to drink. It was a road map for thwarting the competition.

Competitive Target	Product Portfolio
Micros Regionals Sam Adams Pete's Wicked Ale	American Originals Redhook/Alliances Regionals/Seasonals
Weinhard's Dundee's	Michelob Specialty Brands
Killian's Leinenkugel	Red Wolf

A year later, Anheuser-Busch again reached out to distributors with five pages of questions and answers marked INTERNAL ANHEUSER-BUSCH AND WHOLESALER USE ONLY. The memo made clear that the company's intended craft audience was "the occasional specialty beer drinker. Because they are consistent with the styles of specialty beers, the Michelob Specialty Ales and Lagers will offer these first-time and fringe specialty beer drinkers super-premium beers as a way to enjoy the specialty beer experience. Our secondary target is the core group of beer drinkers who consume specialty and micro brands almost exclusively."

The memo noted that such specialty beers could offer higher margins to wholesalers and retailers and that specialty beer sales had grown 22 percent in 1996, which made it the fastest-growing segment of the beer industry. Though still accounting for less than 4 percent of beer industry sales, Anheuser-Busch made clear it was in the specialty game for as long as it made sense: "While it's impossible to predict what direction the category will go long term, the trends indicate—and we are confident—that the growth rate we are currently experiencing is sustainable for at least the short term." Questions and answers included:

> Q: With the Michelob name, can the public really expect these to be *authentic* specialty beers?
> A: Absolutely. Each of the Michelob Specialty Ales and Lagers was created by our brewmasters, using only the finest, all-natural ingredients. These new recipes have the same commitment to quality that Michelob has had since 1896, and use a variety of yeasts, malts and other flavors to create some truly unique beers.

David Edgar, director of the Institute for Brewing Studies in Boulder, Colorado, had been critical of previous Anheuser-Busch craft efforts but told the *St. Louis Post-Dispatch* that the second wave of brands "have gotten much closer to being competitive as far as flavor and aggressiveness . . . of the malt flavor or hop flavor." However, he said, the beers were also having their intended effect: getting distribution was increasingly difficult for small and independent brewers.

By 1997 the Specialty Brewing Group sent thirteen beers to the market, mostly under the Michelob and American Originals umbrellas. In less than four years, the company had grown from virtually no presence in specialty beer to a top-twelve sales rank among the nation's thirteen hundred–plus craft beer manufacturers. In supermarket sales, the Michelob beers trailed only Boston Beer Co.'s Samuel Adams. Meanwhile Redhook, turbocharged by the power of the Anheuser-Busch distribution network, grew wildly, pushing into forty-seven states. The partnership was so successful that Anheuser-Busch followed by buying a 31 percent stake in another upstart brewery giving it fits: Portland's Widmer Brothers.

Between its own brewing efforts and its stakes in Redhook and Widmer, Anheuser-Busch had scratched out a two-pronged disruption effort against the nation's craft breweries. It was working.

8

"We Have to Look Like We Have Been Here Before"

THE IMAGES WERE SPREAD LOOSELY across the table before John and Greg: half a dozen logos for the new Goose Island production brewery.

After seven years mostly confined to the brewpub's four walls, John's initial dream would finally be realized. Like Sierra Nevada and Samuel Adams—hell, like Bud, Miller, and Coors—Goose Island beer would be brewed, packaged, and sent to taps and shelves as far as Goose Island could send it.

John had found a two-story former woodworking factory two miles west of downtown, on an industrial stretch of Fulton Street even less refined than where he'd opened the brewpub. It was rare to venture to the area without being propositioned by a prostitute. It was the kind of neighborhood where a brewer's car was likely to be stolen (which happened) or another brewer's backpack full of brewing textbooks could be swiped if left near a door propped open to vent a sweltering brewery (which also happened, though the backpack and books were found in a dumpster two blocks away). All that was secondary to John. He was ready to make beer. A lot of beer.

But before there could be a lot of beer, Goose Island needed a look. The logo for the brewpub—a plump, backward-looking goose on a grassy knoll—was pastoral and homey enough for a restaurant. Beside two dozen competitors on a grocery store shelf, it wouldn't stand a chance. A brewpub regular came up with a handful of updated designs to adorn Goose Island's bottles.

Greg, as was his way, favored the boldest look on the table: a highly stylized, angular image of a goose. No one would miss it on a shelf, and the most daring shoppers would be compelled to try it. John favored a clean, classic look: a white-headed, yellow-billed goose angling its neck through an oval with a slight, perhaps welcoming smile. It was framed by the words GOOSE ISLAND and CHICAGO. He thought the most traditional choice was wisest.

"We have to look like we have been here before," he told his son.

The tougher question was what beer to push into the world.

Blonde Ale had become the brewpub's most popular beer, but for the wrong reason: it was the closest thing on tap to easy-drinking, mass-marketed beer. When four friends walked in on a Friday night, odds were good that at least one would ask for "whatever you have that's like Miller Lite," then drink it all night long. If a Miller Lite drinker balked at Blonde Ale, Greg would half-fill a pint glass with the beer, top it with water, then say, "Try that. It still has more flavor than a Miller Lite."

Goose Island was proud of Blonde Ale, and the beer would eventually win a gold medal at the Great American Beer Festival. But its incidental popularity wouldn't translate in bars and supermarkets. The Halls had no interest in trying to convert light lager drinkers into Blonde Ale devotees. The nation's third-largest city was already a cutthroat beer market, as evidenced by the fact that the King of Beers was only its fourth-most popular brand. Miller Lite, Miller Genuine Draft, and Old Style—a throwback regional brand from Wisconsin's G. Heileman Brewing—all outsold it. Pay to play was a well-known way of life in Chicago, as were price wars that led to uncomfortably thin profit margins. Goose Island didn't remotely want to play that game.

That led to an important calculation: Who, exactly, was Goose Island's audience?

The only craft brands with velocity in the city were Sam Adams Boston Lager—a Vienna-style lager offering more body and heft than a Bud or Miller—and Pete's Wicked Ale, an English brown ale contract brewed in Minnesota. Those two brands accounted for nearly a third of the nation's craft beer production during the early part of the '90s, and were even better represented in Chicago. Surely there was room for more fresh, full-flavored, malt-driven beer. Goose Island had just the thing: Honker's Ale. It was smooth, mildly sweet, a touch bready, and a clear difference to macro lagers. But even in its difference, it was approachable. Better still, the beer's name echoed the name of the brewery. Honker's Ale it was.

Goose Island's production brewery whirred to life in November 1995. At its heart sat a fifty-barrel brewing system that was a radical leap from the ten-barrel system Greg manned for eight years at the brewpub. One barrel of production equated to two kegs in the marketplace; the new system would allow Goose Island to grow quickly.

The other key feature of the new brewery was what wasn't there: loads of equipment. Nearly a dozen tanks stood ready to be filled with beer, but the space was otherwise vacant as an airplane hangar. John built his brewery four times larger than needed because growth was the plan, and he didn't intend to fail. It was cheaper to knock out all the construction at once—to pour the floors and add the drains for the tanks that would eventually arrive. John's local beer distributor bragged to media that Goose Island would be the city's second-bestselling specialty brewer within a year, behind only Sam Adams.

John settled in as the brewery's bean counter and chief decision maker while Greg became a roving visionary: what to brew, when to brew it, and how to market it. But the most crucial person in the building might have been Matt Brynildson, an enthusiastic and friendly Minnesotan who was hired six months after the production brewery launched. Brynildson had discovered a love for beer in the early 1990s while attending Kalamazoo College, down the street from Larry Bell's namesake Michigan brewery. It was there, over a pint of porter, that Brynildson's lightbulb moment arrived: maybe beer could be his future. As an undergraduate he had planned to be a doctor, but the combination of science and creativity, leading to such a delightful conclusion, made beer far more enticing. He bought a home brew kit from Bell's store beside the brewery, then brought his beer in for honest assessment. After college, he took a job as a hop chemist at Kalsec (formerly the Kalamazoo Spice Extraction Company) and later enrolled in a two-week brewing course at Chicago's Siebel Institute. Brynildson had been a regular visitor at the Goose Island brewpub since the early 1990s, and marveled at the quality of the beer and experience. He was taken with the intimacy of European beer culture during a college semester in Spain, and how seamlessly it fit into daily life. That's how he felt when stepping into Goose Island's brewpub.

Goose Island's production brewery was similarly impressive. Though drinking at Bell's had been formative, Brynildson had never imagined working there. Its early '90s operation was only slightly more sophisticated than a home brew setup. Sheets of plastic were stretched across the tops of fermenters, which led to as many bad beers as successes. Goose Island was the major leagues. Its heart was an elaborate four-vessel brew house that isolated each step of the brewing process in a way most young breweries did not. John Hall also bought a top-of-the-line, German-made bottle filler. Goose Island was spending big and spending wisely. Brynildson came on as an entry-level cellar man, tending to the beer as it fermented and, arguably the most important job in any brewery, ensuring that the tanks were faultlessly clean. He quickly rose to integrate the lab—crucial for yeast management and quality control—into the daily brewing practice.

On a tight-knit crew of single guys in their twenties, he was equal parts visionary and problem solver. Brynildson was a believer that great beer came from logic, science, and the ability to replicate process. As a good bye present, his old employer had sold him a spectrophotometer for a pittance, which allowed Goose Island to analyze bittering units and color in its beer—insights that few small production breweries were able to glean during the mid-1990s. Brynildson was affable, and people liked him. He was a natural leader.

After six months, Greg pulled him aside and asked if he was ready to be head brewer. It was a stunning offer that came with towering responsibility for a fast-growing brewery with only a modest idea of what it was doing. At the brewpub, Greg had dialed in practices to make the exact beer he wanted before it traveled all of fifty feet to a customer's glass. Fulton Street was a wholly different business. Making Honker's Ale taste the same on that large system, then last for months in a bottle on a shelf, was a riddle. The result had been sending barely passable beer—sometimes deeply flawed beer—into the market. Lucky for them, the American craft beer drinker was learning alongside Goose Island; after decades of light American lager, most people didn't know what a quality ale should taste like.

Brynildson and his team tweaked recipes. They adjusted simple practices, such as using carbon dioxide instead of compressed air to push beer out of tanks, which led to longer shelf life. They tweaked procedures, such as how yeast was pitched into a beer. When Honker's Ale tasted off in 1996, Brynildson and lead brewer Jim Cibak tore fermentation tanks apart until discovering that one had been incorrectly assembled, allowing bacteria to propagate. Every month, practices seemed to improve. So did the beer. It felt like a brewing think tank, with a frequent and fevered exchange of ideas.

The beers kept coming. In addition to the flagship Honker's Ale, they introduced Hex Nut Brown Ale, Oatmeal Stout, and rotating seasonal releases: Kilgubbin Red Ale in spring, an easy-drinking Kölsch in summer called Summertime, and an annual Christmas beer with a rotating recipe. Eventually they added a new beer reflecting a burgeoning late '90s industry trend, which got a simple name to echo its style: India Pale Ale.

Goose Island had dabbled with IPA at the brewpub, but this version was wholly different, intended to define the style for an entire city. Goose Island IPA reflected Greg's belief that a beautifully made beer could be lost behind a wall of bitterness; he wanted it to be unmistakably hop-forward but balanced by sweetness and a malty backbone. The head of Goose Island's lab bought every IPA available on shelves in Chicago—no more than a dozen at the time—to measure their International Bitterness Units. Anchor Brewing's Liberty Ale was king at about 45 IBUs. Goose Island IPA was brewed to be a whopping

70 IBUs. The most essential tweak to the recipe was Brynildson's: adding hop pellets to the beer as a final step after fermentation. It was an unlikely move in American brewing at the time. It spooked Greg. He worried that microbes might infect and ultimately sour the beer. But Brynildson insisted that the addition of pungent pellets to finished beer—called dry hopping, a process not unlike steeping a tea bag in hot water—would lend an assertive aromatic punch. To assuage Greg's concern, Brynildson began by adding the hops to a few gallons of finished beer to create a slurry that was added back into the tank. Finally, as would become industry practice, he simply dumped the pellets into the tank for several days after fermentation. The beer wound up winning six medals at the Great American Beer Festival between 2000 and 2012, making it among the most honored IPAs in the festival's history.

After a robust first year of production in which Goose Island blazed through more than fifteen thousand barrels of beer—a number that most breweries needed at least three years to reach—the industry's primary advocacy and trade group, the Colorado-based Institute for Brewing Studies, bestowed an unexpected honor: "Fastest Start Up Brewery in Craft Beer History."

The people who started breweries as labors of love, who figured out how to run businesses along the way, they were content to stay small. John Hall was a businessman who figured out how to make beer. He even contracted with a soda maker to create a line of Goose Island sodas. He wanted as much shelf space as possible. Staying small wasn't an option.

The person charged with selling all that beer was Bob Collins. He was young enough to be John's son, and in fact was just a few months older than Greg. But John offered him the lofty title of vice president of sales after just a handful of meetings. Collins had previously worked as Boston Beer's one-man Chicago sales force. He spent hours riding around with company founder Jim Koch, an industry star with a Harvard MBA who repeatedly, loudly, pronounced Anheuser-Busch bad for beer. He would fly to Chicago every few months to visit accounts with Collins, spinning wisdom about the need to be in the customer's world. Big Beer worried only about itself, Koch preached; the customer—meaning a bar or a store—was simply a means to accomplish its own goals. The burgeoning world of craft beer was built on relationships and increasingly intimate experiences. Simply selling a tap handle didn't guarantee repeat business. The key was to think from a bar owner's or grocery store manager's perspective. How could Collins make their jobs easier? How could he guarantee their success and in turn guarantee his own? That was the difference between Craft Beer and Big Beer.

When he met John Hall, Collins was working for Union Beverage, a Chicago distributor specializing in spirits but wading into the growing beer market. Collins managed its beer portfolio. Initially he tried to convince John to let Union Beverage distribute Goose Island's beer made on Fulton Street. Instead, John offered him a job. Anxious to get back on the brewery side of the equation, Collins accepted John's offer and became the first employee of Goose Island's production brewery.

John and Collins spent a year sharing an office above the brewpub, a broad room where John's chain-smoking secretary puffed away in the corner. The only bathroom was the same one used by customers three stories below in the brewpub. Even before the brewery was online, John wanted his sales director to have a product to sell and for the brand to carve a presence in Chicago bars. Greg therefore began hauling bags of malt and hops to the G. Heileman brewery in Milwaukee to make the earliest batches of Honker's Ale for broad distribution—nearly a year before Goose Island's production brewery opened. By the time Goose Island was finally making beer, Collins's mandate was clear: sell, sell, sell. John had little interest in curating a boutique sensibility for his brewery. He wanted Goose Island on tap alongside the kings of the mid-1990s tap handles: Bud, Miller, Coors, Heineken, Bass, Harp, Newcastle, and Pabst Blue Ribbon. Collins carved two routes for getting there.

One was to go after light beer handles. If a neighborhood bar or a sports bar carried Bud Light, Miller Lite, and Coors Light on draft, he argued that the bar didn't need three light beers. He backed up his argument with math: though a keg of Honker's cost about thirty-five dollars more than a keg of light beer, the bar could charge an extra dollar or two per pint. A keg that yielded 125 pints could make $250 additional profit. Collins never argued that a bar shouldn't carry light beer. That thought would have gotten him nowhere. But two of the big three? That seemed reasonable, even if it was a hard sell. Light lager was what people knew. A locally made, malt-forward English-style ale was not.

The other option—and the one that was far more successful—was taking aim at imports. Imported beer in the United States was a post–World War II phenomenon, due in part to soldiers who came home with a taste for the more interesting and flavorful beer they discovered on the other side of the Atlantic. Heineken had been imported from the Netherlands since 1933, but its popularity was a .01 percent wisp of the market. It remained a rarified taste, in part because the large domestic companies hatched a "superpremium" category to head off any threat posed by imports—Anheuser-Busch (Michelob), Miller (Löwenbräu), and Coors (Herman Joseph's) among them. The superpremium brands continued to dominate imports into the mid-1980s, at which point American drinkers were struck with a revelation. The same exploratory drinkers who had embraced California wine and coffee beyond Folgers turned toward exotic beers from foreign lands: England (Bass, Newcastle), Ireland (Guinness), Germany (Beck's, St. Pauli Girl), Canada (Molson, Labatt Blue), and Mexico (Corona). By the 1990s, imports became nearly 10 percent of the American beer market, zooming right past craft.

To the savviest craft industry minds, the growth of imports only meant opportunity. One of the first people to recognize it was Jim Koch. He was convinced that growth for his Boston Beer Co.—as well as any other American upstart—lay in stealing drinkers from Heineken, Beck's, or any other middling European lager arriving weeks old in the United States on a warm ship. In advertising and interviews, Koch played a gleeful David to the imports' Goliath. He mocked Heineken as unworthy of its vaunted reputation; it was simply a different version of the same mass-produced lager, just older and staler after its transatlantic journey. "When America asked for Europe's tired and poor, we didn't mean their beer," became his go-to line. Koch chased the same audience as the imports—"white-collar men between the ages of 25 and 50," he said—but insisted his beer was better.

But Koch wasn't above turning on his American craft brethren, and many were put off by his grandstanding. John Hall, however, considered him a cheerleader for them all. If Boston Lager was fresher and tastier than the imports, didn't that reflect well on all American craft beer? When the board of the Institute for Brewing Studies weighed whether to toss Koch from the trade group, John was among his most vocal defenders. Sure, Koch had sharp elbows. He didn't always respect basic decorum. But he had a plan. He had visibility. He went hard after Big Beer and just as hard after imports. Koch had built a tent for the industry. Why not step inside? "The last thing we want is to confuse customers," John told the *New Brewer* magazine at the time. "We have much bigger issues to fight than to squabble among ourselves." John ultimately prevailed; Koch remained a member of the Institute for Brewing Studies.

Though Sam Adams was one of the few craft brands with any traction in Chicago, neither John nor Bob Collins saw it as Goose Island's competition; it was, in fact, a road map. As Collins began to show up in bars armed with beer samples and sales sheets ("The Goose Is Loose in Chicago!" read the title page) the plan wasn't to take Sam Adams handles; it was to get in the same bars as Sam Adams. The goal was to replace European imports. Any bar that carried Sam Adams during the 1990s likely carried the trifecta of Guinness, Bass, and Harp, one of which presented a clear opportunity. It usually wasn't Guinness, which had a loyal following and offered legitimate difference—a low-alcohol, pitch-black stout infused with nitrogen for a thick, creamy mouthfeel. That left Harp or Bass as the target—usually Bass. The English pale ale was everywhere during the 1990s, but not because it had loyalty. Bass was simply the "classy" alternative to major domestics. It had been distributed with Guinness and ridden its esteemed colleague's coattails to prominence. Among vulnerable tap handles, it was the most vulnerable.

Again, Collins had two essential arguments. One was money: a keg of imported beer held 13.2 gallons. An American keg was 15.5 gallons.

Newcastle and Honker's Ale were close enough in price that that extra 2.3 gallons translated to an extra hundred dollars of profit. The second argument was freshness. A beer imported from England could be months old by the time it reached a stateside bar. Goose Island offered beer that was a few weeks old. The brewery stitched together sales materials that underscored the point. It knew it could never win on name recognition, and acknowledged it was starting from behind: "We encourage people to taste Goose Island against their favorite beer. We are confident in the quality and freshness of Goose Island beer." The materials nodded to the fact that the beer was local ("Goose Island beer is brewed and bottled in Chicago; Chicagoans are very loyal to the city, i.e. local sports, local events, etc.") and that it was fresh ("Fact!! Fresh beer is better!").

Chicago was a city known for "pay to play" as a quick route to placing a beer on tap, and Goose Island skated just inside the law with "one-with-ones"—one free keg to pour "samples" for prospective customers when buying a first keg of Honker's Ale. The neighborhood bars were most receptive at first. Then Goose Island pushed into airport hotels and, the particular prize of the day, downtown hotels. There was little local beer available, but visiting business travelers were intrigued at the novel thought of "drinking local," which in turn piqued the interest of the hotels where those business travelers stayed.

Next came the largest grocery and liquor stores, accounts that Collins handled himself. Five years earlier, when he was selling Boston Lager, he had to beg those stores to open their minds. Before the arrival of craft beer, grocery stores were content with a mix of the usual light lagers ($4.99 per six-pack), regional lagers (same), and imports ($6.99). At $7.99 per six-pack, Boston Lager was gallingly expensive. When Collins managed to penetrate Jewel, one of Chicago's biggest grocery chains, it was cause for celebration. By the time Goose Island arrived, mainstream grocery stores were ready. Within months of launching Fulton Street, Goose Island had hundreds of accounts.

Sales efforts were boosted with a heavy investment in spreading the word. John Hall budgeted more than $200,000 for radio ads, print ads, billboards, ads on the sides of city buses, and even a toll-free phone number (800-GOOSE-ME). He sponsored the only local sports teams he could afford: the minor-league baseball Kane County Cougars, forty miles west of the city, and the DePaul University men's basketball team. He spent thousands of dollars to pour beer at Chicago's premier downtown summer festival, Taste of Chicago, where Goose Island got its name on the music stage. Goose Island bought Chicago Cubs season tickets so that John, Greg, or Bob could take their best customers to the occasional afternoon meeting at Wrigley Field. (It also helped Goose Island land Honker's Ale and Summertime at a handful of craft and import kiosks around the ballpark.)

For one radio ad, when the brewery had been open all of eight months, Greg grew a touch overzealous and compared Goose Island to the city's reigning sports star. If Michael Jordan was a brewer, Greg said, he'd be on Goose Island's team. Within days, John received a letter from Jordan's camp, demanding that he "immediately cease and desist from any further use of Mr. Jordan for any purpose whatsoever." Failure to do so would result in taking "the necessary steps to preserve and protect Mr. Jordan's rights." Otherwise, they could pay $2 million to settle. Air Jordan himself was copied on the correspondence. John happily ceased and desisted.

But the ad had done its job, and John believed the job was crucial: getting Goose Island's name everywhere he could. Many corners of the young craft brewing industry disdained marketing and advertising. They saw it as a corrupting influence. The former white-collar executive embraced it and acknowledged as much in early business plans: "Goose Island's approach to marketing and advertising will be as fresh as its beer. Unlike so many craft beers, Goose Island understands the importance of advertising. . . . Consumers all over the city will understand why Goose Island is Chicago's beer."

While Collins pounded the streets and Greg managed an ever-improving team of brewers, John ran the show on Fulton Street. He was quite comfortable with the role, much more so than when starting the brewpub. The restaurant business was a foreign language, full of daily wild cards that forever left chaos on the horizon. On Fulton Street, there was a system. A framework. Something needed to be made and then that something needed to be sold. Cardboard boxes, beer—what was the difference?

John's relief from frenzied weeks came on Friday afternoons, when he walked from his second-floor office to the brew deck, where he grabbed a beer to bullshit and catch up with the crew. He would wander his thirty-seven-thousand-square foot brewery with a Honker's Ale in hand and let his mind wander. What was he building? Where would it go? How would it end? He wouldn't be surprised if he sold the whole thing to Heineken one day. In Chicago, at least, he was planning to steal their business.

9

"They Are One of the Greatest Companies in the World, but Damn—They're Bullies"

Goose Island had been churning out beer from Fulton Street for only a few months when John Hall began to think of sending it beyond Illinois. Opportunity for a company making fresh and flavorful beer wasn't just in Chicago. It was throughout the Midwest. It was everywhere.

He started, naturally, with the states closest to home—Indiana and Wisconsin. Soon he looked to Michigan, where an early conversation gave him unusual hope. An Anheuser-Busch distributor wanted to bring Goose Island to the Wolverine State.

John was thrilled. Anheuser-Busch distributors were the major leagues but also notoriously impenetrable for young breweries. And that was the way Anheuser-Busch liked it. Distribution was a segment of the beer industry largely out of the public view but critical to how beer was sold in the United States. It was particularly crucial to Anheuser-Busch's dominance.

The distribution system traced to the Twenty-First Amendment—the end of Prohibition—which assigned states the responsibility of regulating alcohol sales and consumption and meant the end of once-abundant "tied houses"—bars where breweries could pay to have their beer sold exclusively. Regulators saw two downsides to tied houses: increased consumption due to cheaper and more abundant beer, and the death of competition; entire neighborhoods, or even entire towns, could be dominated by one brewery.

The post-Prohibition response was breaking alcohol sales into three tiers, two of which were plainly visible to consumers: the first (the brewery that made the beer) and the third (the retailer, whether a bar, restaurant, or grocery, liquor, or convenience store). The tier hovering in between, just out of view, was the distribution tier, which did exactly as its name implied: distribute beer from point A (brewers) to point C (retailers). The establishment of a second tier—an independent, professional tier solely to move alcohol through the system—was intended to create a buffer between the companies that made beer and the retailers who sold it.

In reality, the middle tier wasn't always so independent. Instead of the pre-Prohibition practice of breweries sweetening the pot to guarantee taps or shelf space, distributors often did it. And instead of breweries forging close and questionable ties to retailers, breweries simply forged close and questionable ties with distributors—who then did the same with retailers. It was a system with little oversight, and Anheuser-Busch manipulated it to turn its powerful distribution network into a band of coast-to-coast loyalists. Miller did the same.

Distributors—also called wholesalers—were not merely intermediaries getting beer into restaurants, stores, and bars—they were the boots on the ground. In all corners of all fifty states, Anheuser-Busch's hundreds of distributors allowed the goliath to seem as if it were everywhere, sponsoring softball teams, bowling leagues, festivals, and rodeos. In reality, that was the work of the distributors. August Busch III forever repeated during his thirty years at the helm that Anheuser-Busch's most essential customers weren't its drinkers but its distributors. They were the soldiers who kept the company on its lofty perch. As *Fortune* magazine reported in 1987, distributors often acted more like subordinates than partners:

> Each year every wholesaler is asked to suggest a special local promotion for each brand. Anheuser-Busch often covers half the cost, and it almost always outdoes its rivals. Example: Last

> summer Robert Montana, 47, president of Clare Rose Inc., a distributorship on Long Island, New York, and Michael LaBroad, 30, then the Michelob Light product manager, launched Michelob Light Concentration Day to boost flat sales.
>
> On June 4, all 30 of Clare Rose's trucks delivered only Michelob Light. The Michelob Light brand team from Anheuser-Busch's corporate headquarters donned tuxedos and rode the trucks with two Playboy Playmates, who handed out photographs of themselves to retailers. The tally: 21,000 cases sold (the amount typically sold over 20 days) and placements in 400 new accounts. Now Clare Rose's Michelob Light volume is running 7.4 percent ahead of last year, and Anheuser-Busch is holding Concentration Days in other markets.

If distributors were loyal to Anheuser-Busch, drinkers would follow, and the nation's largest beer company would be able to maintain if not grow its stranglehold on American taste buds.

John had learned of that loyalty when shopping for distribution in Chicago before the Fulton Street brewery had opened; neither the local Anheuser-Busch nor Miller distributors would even take his call. Instead, Goose Island was forced to go with Union Beverage, a Chicago spirits distributor that had taken advantage of Anheuser-Busch and Miller's disinterest in new brands to carry the nation's upstarts—Samuel Adams from the East Coast and Sierra Nevada from the West. It was quite happy to take on locally made Goose Island. John would have preferred to be with a beer distributor, but that just wasn't going to happen during the mid-1990s.

But now, after just one year of bottling Goose Island beer, he was primed to breach Anheuser-Busch's fortress—at least in Michigan.

And then—*poof.*

Before a contract could be signed, that Anheuser-Busch distributor backed out. John had little doubt about the cause. It was an initiative that had elicited little awareness among the beer drinking public but sent shockwaves through the industry.

It was 100 Percent Share of Mind.

During the spring of 1996, thousands of Anheuser-Busch distributors gathered for the company's annual sales and marketing meeting. The event usually amounted to Anheuser-Busch coddling its distributors—the company was known to fly in big-name entertainers and dole out endless food and drink—while unspooling marching orders for the coming year. This time the niceties were tamped down. August Busch III had a mandate and it would be famously quoted for years to come: "You have 100 percent share of our mind—we must have yours. Each of you [must] exert your undivided attention and total efforts on Anheuser-Busch products. . . . If you sell our competitors' products, can you give us your best efforts? I don't think so." With that utterance came the birth of 100 Percent Share of Mind, an effort by Anheuser-Busch to grab 100 percent of their distributors' minds and, more importantly, delivery trucks.

The program was born out of August Busch III's mid-1990s realization that his once-loyal distribution army was increasingly carrying non-Anheuser-Busch brands. Choice was proliferating for American beer drinkers, and distributors embraced it, if for no other reason than the financial advantage; craft beer generated higher profit margins than domestic lagers. Their customers wanted these beers, especially in forward-thinking markets such as Seattle, Portland, San Francisco, and Denver, where craft beer could account for a whopping 25 percent of gross industry revenues. Concern spiraled to disgust as August III increasingly spied small, fledgling brands at the warehouses of Anheuser Busch distributors.

"They want more attention that the craft beers are taking away," an industry consultant told *Beverage World* magazine in 1996. "A-B distributors carry some regionals, some waters and imports, but that's never seemed to have concerned St. Louis as much as the whole craft beer phenomenon."

The remedy was 100 Hundred Percent Share of Mind. The program incentivized Anheuser-Busch distributors to sell Anheuser-Busch products and nothing else. The way to do that, of course, was money. Anheuser-Busch tied discounts (cash payments of two cents per case), marketing assistance (a $1,500 per-truck "painting allowance"), and favorable terms (four days of extended credit) for exclusively selling Anheuser-Busch products.

Anheuser-Busch graded its distributors' portfolios from A to E. "A" distributors carried only Anheuser-Busch products and were eligible for incentives. "E" distributors carried competing brands—most likely Sam Adams, Sierra Nevada, or Heineken—and got nothing. In some cases, "E" distributors got worse than nothing: Anheuser-Busch might threaten to withdraw its contract, effectively putting a distributor out of business. Of its nearly one thousand distributors, Anheuser-Busch already had exclusivity with about 40 percent, particularly those close to home (the Midwest) and in the regions with the least adventurous consumers (the South). With 100 Percent Share of Mind, Anheuser-Busch hoped to push that figure toward 70 percent. For anyone unclear about the new mandate, Anheuser-Busch president Pat Stokes said, "We strongly object to the premise that a wholesaler's sales personnel can adequately service both competing brands and our brands. You owe us the same commitment we gave you."

Distributors were doggedly monitored from St. Louis and made to enter into so-called "equity agreements," which afforded Anheuser-Busch outsized control of what were in theory independent businesses—all the way down to granting Anheuser-Busch the ability to veto the sale of a distributor to another distributor. The agreements also set sales goals that the juggernaut could wield when it was unhappy with performance or decisions—such as carrying a brand that St. Louis saw as a threat. When it was unhappy, Anheuser-Busch was known to deploy a team to visit a distributor's accounts, comb through its contracts, and highlight every last failure. As the vast majority of its wholesalers' businesses, Anheuser-Busch's threats echoed loudly. Losing Bud and Bud Light from a portfolio could put a wholesaler out of business.

The most loyal distributors were just fine with the mandate. To others, it sounded backward. Anheuser-Busch alone hadn't turned itself into a giant; distributors had played key roles in getting it there. Through the 1960s and '70s, when American beer still had regional variability, Anheuser-Busch brands—Bud, Busch, and Michelob, mostly—were lucky to get 20 percent of some trucks. Distributors had dutifully nursed the brands along and helped Anheuser-Busch become ascendant. They were partners, not puppets.

Yet, for those who didn't cooperate, pressure mounted. Anheuser-Busch's local market managers hammered the message: exclusivity, exclusivity, exclusivity. At every meeting, during every call, and at every event, they nudged. Then they nudged more. It wasn't hostile. But it wasn't comfortable. When the holdouts put a pencil to the numbers—would the rebates and expanded marketing budget actually put them ahead?—the answer was clear: not even close. As independent businessmen, they were best served by offering customers options. It wasn't the '70s anymore. Beer drinkers wanted choice.

August Busch III even got on the case, meeting privately with small groups of wholesalers around the nation. When he met resistance, he relented slightly. Existing brands were fine, he said. Just don't pick up any new brands.

Despite a handful of holdouts, plenty of Anheuser-Busch distributors took their medicine as prescribed. The result: hundreds of small and independently owned breweries frozen out of a large share of the country's most powerful distribution network. The president of Old Dominion Brewing Co., in Ashburn, Virginia, told the *Washington Post* in 1997 that three Anheuser-Busch distributors dropped him due to 100 Percent Share of Mind. Though he was able to replace them, he said, "The guys that are now selling our beer are not as good as distributors as the guys we had before. You go from the first tier to somewhat below that." On the other side of the country, reports emerged of distributors dropping two major regional West Coast brands: Sierra Nevada and Oregon's Full Sail Brewing.

Three other brewers, all in Northern California, finally filed federal class-action lawsuits claiming that 100 Percent Share of Mind unfairly eroded their businesses: St. Stan's Brewing Co., in Modesto, which claimed business was cut in half in some territories after being dropped by five Anheuser-Busch wholesalers; El Toro Brewing Co., in Morgan Hill, which said it lost $100,000 after switching to a less effective distributor; and Anderson Valley Brewing Co., in Boonville, whose owner, Ken Allen, claimed six Anheuser-Busch distributors in California and

Nevada dropped his brand, setting the company back "for a year or two." He told the *Los Angeles Times* that the lawsuit was "a true David and Goliath story," but later updated the analogy for the *Santa Rosa Press Democrat*: "David and Goliath is no comparison. They are so much bigger than Goliath, and I am so much smaller than David. It's like the ant and the elephant."

Allen tried to drop out of the lawsuit after Anheuser-Busch demanded that he turn over internal financial figures, but when the behemoth would not relent, he resolved to continue his fight. "They are one of the greatest companies in the world," he said. "But damn—they're bullies."

If nothing else, the lawsuit caught the attention of the Justice Department, which faxed a letter to Anheuser-Busch's St. Louis headquarters on a Thursday morning in October 1997 announcing that it was investigating the brewery's sales and distribution practices.

Distributor incentive programs were nothing new, but with 100 Percent Share of Mind, Anheuser-Busch's goal was clear: reining in a large swath of the nation's beer distributors while facing its heartiest competition in decades. And it worked: as its wholesalers shed craft brands, Anheuser-Busch's 48 percent share of the market inched toward 50 percent. The company eyed a goal of 60 percent by 2005. For those on the right side of it, 100 Percent Share of Mind was an effective weapon. Distributor loyalty was among the factors that attracted Redhook to its deal with Anheuser-Busch in 1994: "The Anheuser-Busch wholesalers have always been very selective about the products they carry," Redhook cofounder Paul Shipman said in 1997 as news of the Justice Department investigation broke. "That means if you are carried by an Anheuser-Busch wholesaler, you tend to be able to get more access to that wholesaler in terms of working on your brand."

Inspired by 100 Percent Share of Mind, Miller Brewing instituted its own version of the program, with what it called "Fair Share" provisions, mandating that sales commissions for Miller products be greater than or equal to brands outside the Miller family. It also required distributors to seek Miller's approval before acquiring or divesting brands, as well as give Miller a degree of control over both hiring and the amount of debt a wholesaler could take on.

The Brewers' Association of America, one of the craft industry's prime advocacy groups, saw a full-on assault on consumer choice. In 1998 it issued a position paper expressing concern about the contracts Anheuser-Busch and Miller used to control their distributors: "Both contracts would inevitably interfere with the independent wholesaler's ability to distribute the products of small brewers. These contracts bode ill for competition in the beer industry and ultimately for the American beer drinker."

Noting that Anheuser-Busch and Miller wholesalers accounted for nearly 80 percent of beer deliveries in the country—"often the best means of beer distribution in most states"—the Brewers' Association of America argued that both companies used their distribution networks to "[restrict] growth possibilities for all other brewers and especially small brewers. Ultimately, they will reduce consumer choice." The three-tier system separating breweries, distributors, and retailers had largely worked to foster "a relatively level playing field which has given Americans the widest variety of competitively priced beers in the world," the Brewers' Association of America said. But incentive programs and so-called "equity contracts" threatened not only that equanimity but also the supposed independence of the distribution tier. The Brewers' Association of America concluded:

> If all the Miller wholesalers sign this contract as their Anheuser-Busch brethren did, small brewers will be further restricted from growing their brands and giving their customers what they have clearly demonstrated they want: variety. In the past 20 years, the number of breweries in this country has grown from less than 40 to more than 1,200. If these contracts are enforced, they may doom the American beer drinker to only a few brands from a few brewers.

Of course, longtime rivals Anheuser-Busch and Miller argued that they were merely upholding a cornerstone of American enterprise. "If 90 percent of their house is Miller, we expect 90 percent of their resources to go towards supporting Miller brands," a company spokeswoman said. "We think that's a reasonable standard." Miller's vice president of sales added: "You have to live up to these standards or you're not going to be a Miller distributor."

An Anheuser-Busch vice president of corporate law told the *Chicago Tribune* in 1997 that a program such as 100 Percent Share of Mind was nothing for craft brewers to worry about. It was merely "common business practice," he said.

John read that in the morning paper and shook his head. That Michigan distributor that backed out of a deal with Goose Island? John was quite sure that 100 Percent Share of Mind played a role. And, in that same article, he said as much to the *Chicago Tribune*.

"No question it had something to do with it," he said.

10

Shrinking but Free

WITHIN A YEAR OF OPENING its production brewery, in 1995, Goose Island ran into its first ground war.

Entrepreneurs and speculators had noted craft beer's annual double-digit growth and wanted their share. One of the most popular methods was developing a snazzy name, a memorable label and a decent-enough recipe, then paying someone to make the beer. The industry called it contract brewing, and two of its most famous start-ups began life that way: Boston Beer and Brooklyn Brewery, both of which thrived through the 1990s predominantly as brands and marketing. It was a model that provided Goose Island unexpected early competition.

Launched one month before Goose Island's Fulton Street brewery whirred to life, State Street Brewing Co. invoked one of Chicago's most legendary thoroughfares with a swaggering slogan: "Chicago really deserves a good beer, and this is a great beer." Greg Hall took note of the implication that Chicago had been without a "great beer"—or even a "good beer."

"We've been here since 1988," he told the *Chicago Tribune*.

The key difference between the breweries was that Goose Island actually was one. State Street beer was made three hundred miles south, at Evansville Brewing Co. in Evansville, Indiana. It was part of a wave of hundreds of contract brands that emerged during the early '90s. The year Goose Island's brewpub was founded, most of America's craft beer was made by what the Association of Brewers deemed microbreweries:

breweries producing fewer than fifteen thousand barrels of beer per year. But as craft beer soared, contract breweries became affordable points of entry for brands like State Street. From 1991 to 1994, contract brands became the greatest share of the craft segment.

Though breweries producing more than fifteen thousand barrels of beer per year ("regional craft brewers") would soon become the industry's engine, contract brewers continued to outpace microbrewers for decades, which led to an early moment of craft beer industry reckoning: Was contract brewing authentic? Was it honest with customers? Was it simply an exercise in marketing, and no better than the strategy that fueled Big Beer? The media began to take note of the battle in which industry voices advocated for one of two positions: "All that matters is what's in the glass" versus "Where beer comes from is crucial."

In the unlikely role of defending all things good and pure was Anheuser-Busch. In a seminal moment for the burgeoning craft beer industry, television news program *Dateline* aired what it fashioned an exposé about contract brewing in October 1996: "But do you know where some of those exotic and expensive specialty beers are really being made?" intoned host Stone Phillips. Anheuser-Busch's vice president of consumer awareness, Francine Katz, told the television program that contract brewing "comes down to honesty and truth in labeling. . . . All we're saying is, 'Hey guys, let's agree on some basic rules of honesty, let's be truthful on our labels.'" She directed particular ire at Pete's Brewing, whose Wicked Ale was manufactured at Stroh's Brewing in St. Paul, Minnesota.

When it wasn't needling Pete's, Anheuser-Busch battled Boston Beer. Just before Halloween 1996, the company launched a radio ad in which the ghost of Samuel Adams—a Founding Father and political philosopher—berated Jim Koch for misleading drinkers about where his beer was made. The ads aired in fourteen markets, mostly on classic and alternative rock stations. A print ad followed, showing bottles of Sam Adams and Michelob Light beside the question, WHICH BEER IS BREWED AND BOTTLED IN NEW ENGLAND? (Anheuser-Busch operated a brewery in Merrimack, New Hampshire; most Sam Adams was made in Cincinnati.)

State Street Brewing was a drop in the beer bucket compared to Boston Beer and Pete's Brewing, but it gave Goose Island headaches.

The "brewery" was founded by Steve Cahillane, a thirty-year-old graduate of Harvard Business School (like Jim Koch), who sounded as if he was reading from his business plan when explaining his business to the *Chicago Tribune* in 1995: "Specialty or microbrews have been showing fantastic growth, as consumers have sought different tasting brews. I want to give Chicago an ale that's as rich in character as the city itself."

For close to a year, Goose Island and State Street stood toe-to-toe, fighting for the mantle of Chicago's beer. When Bob Collins scored a twenty-five-case display at the local supermarket chain, right next to it, inevitably, was a twenty-five-case display of State Street. Even more concerning for Collins was that State Street seemed to have the stronger brand, marketing, and sales. John fumed in closed-door meetings about his unexpected foe parading itself as a Chicago beer. Staying the course proved to be the only option. And it worked. Like many contract brands doubling as quick economic opportunities, State Street had a crucial flaw: the beer was OK at best. The brand, highlighted by a turn-of-the-century photo on its label of "that great street," played well among impulse shoppers. But it rarely got the all-important second purchases. Cahillane, who later became president of Coca-Cola's North and Latin American operations, sold State Street in 1997 to the Indiana brewery that had been making the beer.

Left alone as the undisputed king of Chicago brewing, John was able to take a modest victory lap in the press. "It takes more than a good beer to get by," he told the *Chicago Tribune* in 1997. "You need a good deal of planning and marketing know-how. Too many people got into this business without knowing an awful lot about it, and didn't know how to compete."

With State Street vanquished, Goose Island was able to steadily grow:

Year	Goose Island production (barrels)	Annual growth
1996	15,359	—
1997	28,581	86%
1998	35,779	25%
1999	43,037	20%

The growth was all the more remarkable against the backdrop of a craft industry where torrid progress had skidded to a near halt. Not only had craft beer's veil been pierced with the "revelations" about contract brewing; dozens of breweries that had been in planning during the can't-miss years of 1993 to 1996 finally opened, sending fresh beer into a market that couldn't support it. Many of those new brewery owners also failed to understand what a tricky, multifaceted business they had entered: operating with tight profit margins, training and managing sales forces, picking distributors, educating consumers—owning a brewery was far more complex than simply making beer your friends thought was good. An industry correction followed, as volume growth slowed as the number of new breweries surged:

Year	Breweries	Brewery openings	Brewery closings	Industry sales growth
1995	858	287	27	50%
1996	1,149	333	36	25%
1997	1,396	309	92	5%
1998	1,514	206	124	0%
1999	1,564	169	119	2%
2000	1,566	107	113	4%

The crucial year, when the wires crossed, was 1997: 309 new breweries opened while growth slowed to 5 percent. The trend continued in 1998 as 206 breweries opened amid *zero* growth. Craft beer had grown too large for its foundation.

By 1999, Charlie Papazian, president of the Association of Brewers, sounded positively dejected in his organization's annual industry report in *New Brewer* magazine. Though craft beer was up to 3 percent of beer industry sales, it seemed poised to stay there—if not regress. Papazian blamed "fractious grumbling" within the industry and a lack of a unified front. He looked to, of all things, milk, pork, and the Wendy's fast-food chain for inspiration—not the products themselves, but their abilities to capture the imagination with simple, memorable taglines. "Got Milk?" "The other white meat." "Where's the beef?"

> I think it's time for "Got Beer?" "The Other White Beer." "Where's the Beer?" It's time to develop a strong, clean, crisp, easy to "get" positive image for American craft brewers.
>
> Will over 1,300 American craft brewers agree on the theme?
>
> Never.
>
> Should 1,300 American craft brewers get on board and move the 3 percent forward?
>
> Yes.
>
> Will it take some humility for the positive move forward and future growth and stability of the American craft-brewing community? Do I really have to answer that last question?

Papazian concluded by asking, "Have we simply become satisfied with 3 percent? If not, then what will our message be? We need one. And I'm absolutely certain that it can be done. I can't imagine stopping at 3 percent. I simply cannot accept that."

In the same issue of *New Brewer*, David Edgar, executive director for the Institute for Brewing Studies (a wing of the Association of Brewers), summed up the previous year: "What happened to the craft brewing industry in 1998? Everything. Buyouts, mergers, brand sell-offs, closings, openings, breweries growing by double digits, breweries declining by double digits, new products launched by the dozen and older brands quietly discontinued by the dozen. It varied by region and by state, but no geographic area was immune to the changes and volatility."

Goose Island managed to keep growing by double digits during the regression due to aggressive sales and marketing, (mostly) quality beer, and the size of its home market. Beer, sales, marketing—Goose Island had developed into the complete package within just a few years. The brewery was such a source of optimism that a Honker's Ale tap handle appeared on the cover of the *New Brewer* issue in which Papazian despaired about the state of the industry, beside the headline "Bucking the Trend: Strong Regionals, Brewpub Groups Keep Growing in Flat Year." In a year of bad news, Goose Island was the good news.

It had even been a steadying force during the initial consolidation. Goose Island plucked one brewery from the ash heap, turning the shuttered Weeghman Park brewpub, one block south of Wrigley Field, into its second brewpub. It also bought the once-ascendant Baderbrau brand out of bankruptcy, revived its flagship pilsner, and won a silver medal with it at the GABF in 1998. John believed such consolidation was necessary for a healthy industry—like a controlled burn in an overgrown forest.

As competitors struggled, Goose Island surged into some of Chicago's most visible accounts. The Holiday Inn at O'Hare International Airport was draining two kegs of Honker's Ale each week. Every year, the Fulton Street brewery grew, whether by taking on more space, more equipment, or both. Goose Island became the nation's eighteenth-largest craft brewery, just behind California's Mendocino Brewing. Mendocino had begun life as Hopland Brewing—the very brewery that John Hall read about on the airplane all those years ago.

Now he owned a brewery too. It was nearly just as big.

And then it stopped.

Like the rest of the industry, Goose Island's growth hit a wall. It had reached forty-three thousand barrels of production in a swift four years, but wouldn't reach fifty thousand for another seven years.

To John and Greg, the problem was obvious: their distributor. When launching Fulton Street in 1995, when no beer distributor would even bother to pick up the phone, they were stuck with one option: Union Beverage. After four years, the cracks in Union's approach had grown plain. It was a wine and liquor distributor that acted like a wine and liquor distributor. You couldn't blame it. But it didn't work for beer. Vodka, as a liquid in a bottle, was resilient. It was 40 percent alcohol and could sit on a shelf for months without degrading. It could withstand light and heat. Freshness was not an issue. Honker's Ale was less than 5 percent alcohol. It oxidized relatively quickly in a bottle, especially at room temperature. Union's delivery schedule called for fewer, larger deliveries; beer needed more frequent, smaller deliveries. Union also didn't deliver during weekends—a grave problem when a Honker's Ale keg kicked on a Friday night. Working together, Goose Island and Union had cherry-picked accounts that led to quick, broad growth. But after four years, when twice the effort was needed to win over reluctant customers, progress stalled. Growth in a city of eight million people shouldn't have flamed out at forty-three thousand barrels of annual production. But Union seemed content to further its beer business by acquiring more brands rather than growing the brands it had.

To make up for the stagnation at home, Goose Island expanded its distribution footprint: from six midwestern states in 2001 (when it made 42,145 barrels of beer) to thirteen, plus Texas, in 2002 (when it made 47,351). From the outside, it looked like solid growth and the establishment of a regional footprint. But if he could have, John would have sold every last barrel at home. Local growth was smart growth. Fanning out to neighboring states was borderline desperation. Selling beer a thousand miles from home was more expensive and filled with unpredictability; there was no telling how a far-flung distributor would care for the beer or how long it might sit on a shelf. Selling a fresh six-pack to a local, loyal customer was ostensibly the same as selling six bottles to a curious first-timer in Louisville. But the local shopper was far more likely to buy a Goose Island six-pack again.

The good news was that Goose Island's fast growth had caught the attention of another distributor: River North, in Chicago.

The Anheuser-Busch distributor.

Five years earlier, when it was run by Anheuser-Busch loyalists, River North wouldn't talk to John. Now, the operation had new ownership, landing in the lap of politically connected twenty-eight-year-old Yusef Jackson, the son of civil rights advocate Jesse Jackson.

Yusef Jackson had been a third-year associate at a Chicago law firm when August Busch IV handpicked him, with an assist from Yusef's famous father, to become River North's majority owner. The irony was inescapable: sixteen years earlier, Jesse Jackson had led a high-profile boycott of Anheuser-Busch behind a rallying cry of "Bud's a Dud" due to what he claimed were discriminatory hiring and business practices. Anheuser-Busch pumped a reported $10 million into a minority distributorship ownership program, but few changes were as symbolically important as steering control of a major urban distributor to one of the most prominent black families in the nation. Jesse Jackson denied playing a role in the deal, but *Chicago Tribune* reporters concluded in 2001 that the elder Jackson had "indirectly helped" his son through high-powered connections. When the deal was completed, Yusef had 67 percent ownership; his brother, Jonathan, owned 23 percent; and Donald Niestrom Jr., a beer industry veteran who would go on to become a retail sales director for Anheuser-Busch, had 10 percent.

Yusef Jackson said all the right things when taking over—"We intend to make Bud and Bud Light the No. 1 brand here; we want to be in the position to match Chicago's market share with Busch's market share nationally"—but the situation was dire. Anheuser-Busch dominated nationally, but Chicago was an odd outlier where Miller commanded 41.4 percent of the market. Anheuser-Busch ran a very distant and tenuous second, at 18.4 percent, barely ahead of Stroh/G. Heileman Brewing Co., which merged in 1996, at 16.3 percent. If River North was to close the gap, it needed to think beyond Bud. Goose Island was that opportunity—a local, ascendant brand. If it had reached forty-three thousand barrels of production in four years, who knew what could be ahead? Goose Island might be the next Boston Beer or Sierra Nevada.

John was flattered by the interest, but even more so, intrigued. If River North was interested, so might be the local Miller distributor, Chicago Beverage Systems. John reached out. Sure enough, it was. So was the entire local network of Miller distributors—more than ten in all. The same could not be said of the Anheuser-Busch network. Due to their cozy relationships with Anheuser-Busch, few of its Chicago-area distributors felt the same urgency as River North to diversify. Which meant John had his suitor. It was the Miller network.

There was one hurdle between Goose Island and a union with Miller distributors. It was, without a hint of irony, called the Beer Industry Fair Dealing Act. Passed in 1982, the Illinois law gave distributors near-monopolistic locks on a brewery's sales once the sides entered into a contract. Though a distributor could exit a deal at any time, a brewery could only withdraw after proving "good cause" in court or if the distributor agreed to accept "reasonable compensation for the fair market value of the wholesaler's business with relation to the affected brand or brands." If a brewery accounted for less than 10 percent of a distributor's sales, it was slightly easier to end the arrangement—but only slightly. If above 10 percent, a brewery had no recourse whatsoever; a move to a new distributor was wholly dependent on the original distributor agreeing to sell the rights. If it didn't want to, it didn't need to.

Such was the case for Goose Island. Though John saw stalling out at forty-three thousand barrels as a problem, it was just fine with Union Beverage. Goose Island remained its crown jewel. It didn't *want* to handle more beer. It also had no interest in selling the brand to Miller. When Miller made its offer for the rights to Goose Island, it got a flat no. How dare John try to leave?

In an attempt to smooth things over, John soon heard from Jim LaCrosse, the president of National Wine & Spirits, Union Beverage's Indianapolis-based parent company. LaCrosse was a small investor in Goose Island's Fulton Street brewery and a more significant investor in a recently launched operation called US Beverage.

US Beverage was another business that emerged as craft beer began to catch fire. In 1997, just as the tide seemed to be forever mounting against Big Beer (when, in fact, the bubble was starting to burst), the former president of Seagram Beverage Co., Joseph Fisch, launched US Beverage to handle sales and marketing for breweries and alcohol brands across the nation.

LaCrosse pitched John on what he described as a "win-win"—stay with Union Beverage, but with US Beverage as its new "master distributor." US Beverage would handle sales, marketing, and distributor relationships across the country; the existing Goose Island sales and marketing force would become employees of US Beverage. In exchange,

Goose Island would be paid $1 million to grow and add new equipment. John liked the sound of that cash infusion; margins were tight and Goose Island sorely needed capital. US Beverage would also provide Goose Island with the contract and equipment to produce Hooper's Hooch, a lemonade-flavored malt beverage that US Beverage introduced after Coors Brewing's success with Zima in 1993.

Done right, John envisioned US Beverage boosting growth by solidifying sales at home while supporting a growing regional footprint. Plus, he could use the Hooper's Hooch equipment to bring Goose Island's soda production in-house. In March 2000, the sides signed a deal expiring on December 31, 2009. Goose Island built in a little protection for itself: if US Beverage didn't grow sales to keep pace with select competitors—Boston Beer, Sierra Nevada, Great Lakes, Bell's, Boulevard, and Summit—Goose Island could opt out with ninety days of notice. John proclaimed optimism when the deal was announced a month later: "United States Beverage offers the marketing expertise and well-established distribution network to strengthen Goose Island's position as the Midwest's leading craft brewer. This alliance will strengthen our brand building and improve our distribution throughout the Midwest."

But it didn't take long for things to sour. Like Union Beverage, US Beverage brought a mindset befitting the spirits industry. Goose Island's packaging slowly shifted from a slight majority of draft to the vast majority in bottles. Those on the front lines had learned that craft beer was built on draft, where the profit margins were higher, the customer experience more intimate, and the bar lower for a first sale; US Beverage was oblivious to those realities. Worse, US Beverage was unconcerned about old beer degrading in the market. One Goose Island brewer made a habit of buying year-old six-packs of Honker's Ale at Walgreens when visiting his wife's family in Northwest Indiana just to get them off shelves. Goose Island came to believe that US Beverage had almost single-handedly doomed its short-lived pilsner, simply called Goose Pils. At US Beverage's insistence, the beer had been unfurled in twelve-packs of twelve-ounce bottles at supermarkets—a classic Big Beer approach to sales, but a disaster for craft. Within four years, Goose Pils was gone.

While Goose Island stagnated, midwestern competitors surged past: Summit (Minnesota), Boulevard (Kansas City), and August Schell (Minnesota) all grew larger than Goose Island while old rival Bell's was hot on its trail. Fellow Class of '88 member Deschutes had long blown by Goose Island and was nearly three times the size while establishing itself as the exact thing John Hall had wanted to be—a regional powerhouse. Goose Island, by contrast, was growing and shrinking, healthy and then sick. It realized that the break-even point was producing forty-eight thousand barrels of beer per year—four thousand per month—but struggled to get there. Contract brewing private label brands for Whole Foods and Trader Joe's helped keep the brewery afloat but still couldn't make it profitable.

Year	Goose Island production (barrels)	Growth
2000	41,050	–5%
2001	42,145	3%
2002	47,351	12%
2003	44,752	–5%

The real problem was happening at home: a sales decline of more than 11 percent in supermarkets and drugstores. Overall, local sales slipped 7.4 percent, to $2.15 million, with market share down more than 3 percent. Hooper's Hooch wasn't helping as promised. In addition to demoralizing brewers—making that sugary stuff wasn't why they went into brewing—the Zima-fueled alcopop fad was flickering away, and instead of a projected 500,000 cases of sales per year, Goose Island was making less and less of the brand: 157,000 cases in 2001, 110,000 cases in 2002, and 76,000 cases in 2003. In the face of declining sales, Goose Island lost its line of credit with LaSalle Bank and met with a bankruptcy counselor—a sobering day if for no other reason than the symbolism. They had cracked open the door to the question: What if they didn't make it?

Finally, on April 2, 2004, after four years with US Beverage, Goose Island saw hope: it faxed a letter to US Beverage's Connecticut headquarters announcing that it would abandon its contract. An opt-out clause mandated that US Beverage order at least 675,000 cases of beer in a given year. In a three-paragraph letter, John explained that US Beverage had failed to order 675,000 cases of Goose Island beer in 2003, which allowed it to void the deal. John said he appreciated US Beverage's efforts and that he looked forward to working with the company on "a smooth transition and the orderly performance of the parties' remaining obligations."

US Beverage executives were incensed. A week before the ninety-day window came due, they sued Goose Island in the Illinois Circuit Court of Cook County, claiming that the brewery was bound to its agreement by the Beer Industry Fair Dealing Act. US Beverage claimed Goose Island was in deep financial straits, and blamed falling sales on the very goal John had craved: building a committed local audience.

> While USB could have pursued the goal of "chasing volume" (i.e., attempting to sell as many cases of beer as possible, regardless of the price and overall well-being of the product line), the USB plans sought to carefully grow the Goose Island brand while maintaining gross margin and providing for the long-term health of the brand by developing brand loyalty and reputation in the marketplace. Goose Island consented to and encouraged these plans and strategies, knowing full well that sales volume might suffer as a result and that the realities of the market rendered the parties' initial expectations about sales volume unsound.
>
> Indeed, despite the impact this strategy would have on sales volume, John Hall, Goose Island's founder and president, informed USB on multiple occasions that, if not for USB, Goose Island would have been out of business.

The problem, Goose Island replied in the lawsuit, was that USB simply failed to meet sales goals each of the four years that the companies were aligned: a 9 percent shortfall in 2001, 8.8 percent in 2002, 11.4 percent in 2003, and 11.7 percent in 2004. Hooper's Hooch, Goose

Island said, was an "abysmal failure." Things got ugly and then uglier: Goose Island claimed that US Beverage told distributors that Goose Island was going out of business or that US Beverage would be buying the brewery. John came to believe that US Beverage did in fact want to buy the brewery, especially when its lawyers asked for a list of shareholders, presumably to stage a hostile takeover.

However, that September, US Beverage offered to settle the case for $339,557.30. After two months of haggling, the sides finally settled. Goose Island was free.

It was shrinking and gasping for life. But it was free.

11

"They're Ready to Take It to the Next Level"

By 2003, Goose Island's sales were slumping. Production was down 5 percent from the previous year. It was barely making more beer than it had five years earlier. The breweries that couldn't withstand the industry downturn were closing—nearly seven hundred during the previous six years—and John Hall began to wonder if his might be among them. Goose Island needed a jolt.

The good news, as far as Greg Hall was concerned, was that the war had been won: since Goose Island's brewpub opened fifteen years earlier, American taste buds had been converted. During the early days, lagers—that is, the beers most similar to Bud and Miller—comprised 90 percent of sales. Now ales were 90 percent of sales.

"When we introduced Honker's Ale in 1988, it was considered pretty hoppy and esoteric," Greg told the *Chicago Tribune* in 2003. "Now that generation has grown accustomed to higher-quality beer and has made beers like Honker's their everyday beer. They're ready to take it to the next level."

The next level was Greg's attempt at jump-starting the flagging brewery. It was also Goose Island's most ambitious bottled beers to date. There were four of them, pioneered on Clybourn Avenue for what was initially called the FOAM series ("Fucking Outstanding Ales of the Month"), then handpicked by Greg to be replicated on Fulton Street for a larger audience. They were far enough outliers that media took to calling them "extreme" beers. Eventually, they became the Reserve series: Imperial IPA (crammed with eight pounds of hops per barrel), Demolition 1800 Ale (commemorating the construction that almost doomed the brewpub during the early 1990s), Pere Jacques (a Belgian dubbel inspired by Chimay Blue), and the legendary Bourbon County Stout (later officially renamed Bourbon County *Brand* Stout for legal reasons), which had been pioneered at the brewpub eight years earlier. All were at least 8 percent alcohol. None were the easy drinking that defined Honker's Ale.

The initial plan was to brew one hundred barrels of each, and when they were gone, they were gone until the next year. That idea lasted all of a month. The beers were so popular that Goose Island had no choice but to brew them in ever-larger amounts, especially Bourbon County Stout. Four hundred barrels of the boozy stout in 2004 became a thousand barrels in 2005, then twelve hundred barrels in 2006. (The brewery inadvertently misrepresented Bourbon County Stout as tracing to 1992 on the beer's earliest labels and marketing materials. That continued for fourteen years, until the true date—1995—was unearthed during the reporting of this book.) Bourbon County Stout wasn't without sacrifice; the beer was costly, time consuming, and labor intensive. Brewing one batch took four times as long as a batch of Honker's Ale; then came the three months of barrel aging. But Greg argued it was how Goose Island could differentiate itself. The Reserve series created a halo around the rest of the portfolio, and that elevated everything else coming out of the brewery. Honker's Ale alone wouldn't support the agenda anymore.

The Reserve series would soon include one more beer that forever changed Goose Island's mission: Matilda. Greg had wanted to release the beer in 2003, but the brewery couldn't figure out how to tame the oddball yeast at its heart: *Brettanomyces*. Brett for short.

Brettanomyces was a naturally abundant yeast, present in beer as long as beer had been made. It had largely been considered a spoiling agent—an enemy of "clean" beer—but Belgian brewers embraced it with their spontaneously fermented lambics, which depended on the "wild" yeast riding the air for depth and character. *Brettanomyces* had only been identified during the early part of the twentieth century and had been featured by only one major brewery, Orval, which was housed at a monastery in south Belgium. Since its founding in 1931, Orval became one of the world's renowned breweries while making exactly two beers: Orval, a 6.2 percent alcohol Belgian pale ale showcasing Brett, and Petite Orval, a 3.5 percent alcohol version of the same beer available only at the brewery. Orval was one of Greg's favorite beers, if not his very favorite. What made it special, he knew, was *Brettanomyces.*

Beer writer Michael Jackson had famously compared the persnickety yeast to a cat. *Brettanomyces*, he was widely quoted, would "do its own thing; it's not going to come when you call it and sit when you say 'sit.' If you can respect its individuality and suggest rather than dictate what it does in your fermentation, it can reward the brewer and the drinker." In other words, the volatility and unpredictably of *Brettanomyces* was part of its charm; the Belgians had made some of the world's most beautiful beer by letting its magic unfurl. Used right, it imbued stunning layers of flavor—sweaty barnyard funk, wet leather, adhesive bandage, horse blanket, green apple, vanilla, and roses—that transformed beer from a refreshing afterthought to profound as the greatest wine. For the thousands of years that beer was made and stored in wood barrels, little could be done to keep *Brettanomyces* at bay. But during the twentieth century, stainless steel and automation made *Brettanomyces* easier to evade; Big Beer came to see Brett as a literal plague. The new era of American brewers, however, looked beyond replication and consistency. They were intrigued by this catlike yeast.

Inspired by the handful of American breweries experimenting with Brett yeast—Russian River and New Belgium among them—Greg walked into the Goose Island lab one afternoon and told its manager, Mary Pellettieri, that he wanted to make the American version of Orval. It was a classic, he said, but he wanted to pioneer something a touch richer, with a little more weight, more residual sweetness, and more Brett character—something that would thrive beside a hearty meal. Pellettieri could scarcely believe what she was hearing; Greg wanted her to not only introduce an untamable yeast that threatened to infect every other beer in the brewery but also improve on one of the world's great beers.

Greg had handpicked Pellettieri to run Goose Island's lab in 2001. She was there months later when hijacked jetliners crashed into the World Trade Center, the Pentagon, and a field in western Pennsylvania. She spent the day listening to news unfurl on public radio and shared updates with the brewers, who continued to make beer as if nothing had happened. She eventually sneaked up to the brewery's roof to look east, just to be sure the Sears Tower was still standing.

Pellettieri was a home brewer who had worked at the Siebel Institute of Technology and a food lab on the South Side of Chicago. She had withstood the lean years at Goose Island, including her maternity leave in 2003, when Greg asked her to take a few extra weeks because the company was having a hard time making payroll. Now she was being charged with Goose Island's biggest innovation since Bourbon County Stout.

The job took nearly a year. Pellettieri could find little literature about managing *Brettanomyces* in beer—only how to avoid it. Instead, she combed journals from the wine industry, which had long wrestled with Brett. She ordered a vial of Brett from one of the industry's foremost yeast sources, White Labs in San Diego, and fed it into a pale ale already fermented with Belgian yeast. Every week for three months, they fed the beer fresh wort—or unfermented beer—full of sugars on which it could feast. Brett proved to be an opportunistic yeast, just as finicky as Michael Jackson said; treated right, with proper levels of alcohol and enough warmth, it thrived, creating a large gelatinous pellicle. No one would ever drink the beer if they saw the process; it looked like mucus. The beer required an obscene amount of work—at least three unique fermentations—but Greg was sure there was no other way that it would succeed.

Matilda inched into existence during the second half of 2004, at the Midwest's preeminent beer festival, Great Taste of the Midwest in Madison, Wisconsin, where it was poured alongside Pere Jacques, Imperial IPA, and Demolition. Two months later, it debuted at the Great American Beer Festival, where it achieved an honor even greater than a medal.

Michael Jackson, who was already well acquainted with Greg's work, stopped by Goose Island's table to affirm rumors of an Orval-inspired beer. He stayed an hour, commandeering a chair behind the brewers to sip and sniff Matilda and scribble in his journal. Then he sipped and sniffed and scribbled more. He couldn't believe that a brewery in Chicago had made a beer so beautiful, so adventurous, so complex. Jackson generally opposed the idea of picking a "best" beer from a field of hundreds or thousands; amid such variety, it was a fool's errand. But after the festival, he wrote, "Were there a best in show award, I would have been tempted to pin it on Matilda's chest." Goose Island's brewers—especially Pellettieri and Greg—were aglow. Not only had they learned to make elite beer; they were also true innovators. The next year, Matilda got its GABF medal: gold, among nineteen entries in the Belgian and French-Style Ale category.

With Matilda in the fold, Goose Island debuted a sharp new campaign in 2005 for its Reserve series: luminous images of the five beers, each a distinct shade, in sloping, long-stemmed Goose Island–branded goblets and bathed in evocative language: Imperial IPA ("You'll smell the hops from a yard away"), Demolition 1800 (a "strong, intense golden ale with a grassy citrus aroma and 'honey' malt middle"), Pere Jacques ("a fruity aroma, notes of banana, apricot and plum balanced against a strong whiff of caramel and chocolate"), Matilda ("fruity and spicy flavor . . . complex maltiness balanced with a profuse amount of hops"), and the legendary Bourbon County Stout ("an intense mix of charred oak, chocolate, vanilla, caramel and smoke").

Marketed with a tagline of "Huge beer—tiny batches," all were packaged in twelve-ounce bottles, with black-and-white labels crammed with words telling the story of each beer. The stories spoke directly to the person holding the bottle, illuminating the inspiration (Pere Jacques was named for the priest who gave Greg a tour of his abbey's brewery, culminating with a feast of roast duck, wild boar, and beer) and what was inside the bottle (Imperial IPA was "strong enough to wake the dead and filled with more bitterness than a woman scorned"—words that presumably would not have been chosen a few years later). Each story was attributed to "Greg Hall, Brewmaster." It was a revolutionary way to sell beer. Each beer had a story, and the story became essential to the beer.

The Reserve beers became an annual calendar of releases: Pere Jacques on January 15, Demolition on May 15, Matilda on August 15, Imperial IPA on November 15, and Bourbon County Stout on December 15.

Greg admired artists who made beautiful things accessible to an urban lifestyle—the food of Paul Kahan, the music of Jeff Tweedy. Greg began to see himself in that vein. Wilco was Chicago's music. Goose Island was Chicago's beer. And it was Greg's playground. The proof was right there on the bottles.

Whatever was left to prove, Greg had proved it. He was, without a doubt, as John told the *Chicago Tribune* in 2009, "the creative engine for the company."

He had read the same books as his father—bestselling marketing tomes such as *Good to Great* and *Positioning: The Battle for Your Mind*—about how companies communicate to skeptical, media-saturated audiences. Greg was intrigued by branding, marketing, and strategy. How do you differentiate your product? Speak to an audience? Price. Design. Exclusivity. Story. He came to think of beer like anything else that stirred an audience. No one cared about their brand of washing machine. But jewelry? A cell phone? A car? Everyone knew a Cadillac was better than a Chevy, even people with no idea about the technical merits beneath the hood. Why? A Cadillac cost more.

The same thought could apply to beer.

When it was still in the picture, US Beverage had wanted to sell the Reserve beers at the same price as Honker's Ale. Charging too much would alienate the customer, it said. Greg argued the opposite; charging more would intrigue the customer. It would instill value in the beer. This beer was a Cadillac, and they charged like it: $8.99 for a four-pack of the Reserve beers versus $6.99 six-packs of Honker's. They charged even more for Bourbon County Stout.

As the legend of Greg Hall grew, no one seemed to believe it more than Greg himself. Many of his meetings happened in bars, over beers, as he expounded on the history of beer, the future of the beer, and his vision for Goose Island. He ordered course after course of food and beer and explained the intricacies of what was unfolding on the table. He could talk for half an hour uninterrupted. He was good at it. He spoke of beer like poetry, using words like *craggy* to describe a beer's foamy head. He never seemed to doubt himself.

His audiences included family, friends, and Goose Island brewers, whom he would treat to three-hour dinners at the hip restaurants popping up around Chicago inspired by fresh ingredients and rustic European cuisine. Finally, Chicago wasn't just a city of steak houses, pizza places, and Italian restaurants; it was home to visionary chefs redefining the American palate.

Greg would order every dish on the menu to share family style and pair with Pere Jacques, Matilda, Demolition, and experimental beers hauled in from the brewery. If he arrived empty-handed, the kitchen might rush someone out to buy the best Goose Island beers available to pair with his meal. They might even make a few dishes incorporating the beers as ingredients—just for him. He never waited for tables. Dishes arrived free of charge. Often, when he asked for the check, he was waved off; an industry icon didn't need to pay. (Though he was always a generous tipper.)

Greg drank a lot. *A lot.* It was his job.

On the road—whether in New York or Portland or St. Louis—he would spend a typical day traveling with the local Goose Island rep from account to account, visiting the bars that reliably carried the Reserve beers and clamored for Bourbon County Stout's arrival every winter. He had one or two beers at every stop—sometimes his own, sometimes whatever the bartender recommended. Then that night he would host a beer dinner at one of the cool, modern-type restaurants he favored back home and savor each course of beer and food right along with his audience. He was a good drunk. Loquacious, if not quite boisterous, and full of the knowledge people wanted to hear. He would tell the story of how Matilda came to be across twenty winding minutes. A rep might wonder if he should be cut off. But ultimately everyone had a good time. The beer was good. The food was good. Greg was genial. He had a kingly presence.

His narrow inner circle knew him to be generous, loyal, and intensely emotional. But much of the world found him aloof and difficult to read. He had an uncanny ability to avoid looking someone in the eye for an entire conversation. He'd glance around the room, seemingly wondering if there was someone else he should be talking to. Answers could be short and lacking the social cues most people shared to encourage conversation. Then he could grill you, as if the quality of your entire existence depended on the answer. *Are you cool? Smart? Knowledgeable?* Every Goose Island employee knew who he was, of course, but when one of them finally met Greg for the first time, sometimes after months on the job, there could be long silences, then a peppering of questions: *How do you spend your time when you're not at the brewery? What beers do you drink when you're not drinking Goose Island? Have you read Michael Jackson?* It could feel like a job interview after already being on the job. The answers were important, but so was the ability not to become flustered.

Anyone confused by a terse character without use for pleasantries could be confused by Greg. Some people found him arrogant. He *was* arrogant. To his admirers, though, it was an earned arrogance. And usually good-natured. He was smart and well read, brimming with ideas and in the process of defining a city's beer culture. His detractors saw someone who could operate outside the rules of decorum and civility. Even true believers would sometimes question the depth of their friendship with Greg Hall. He could seem unknowable—the opposite of his father, who walked through the brewery slapping backs and asking everyone how things were. *Work? The family? Catch that game last night?* Greg wasn't that person. He could be thirty minutes late to a meeting with his brewers, then step out to take a phone call for twenty minutes. Other times he blew off meetings altogether. John was gentlemanly, thoughtful, and focused. Greg usually seemed ready to move on to the next conversation.

But he commanded the subject of beer. He knew it. He'd even done a string of radio commercials, all of which began, "Here's Greg Hall, brewmaster of Goose Island beer." Then, over a soundtrack of bar chatter, clinking bottles, and a peppy guitar-drum beat, he spun a one-minute tale about the merits of Honker's Ale.

> These days everybody wants to get more out of life. It's amazing how far some people will go. Climbing mountains in the Himalayas. Skydiving. Or even bungee jumping. If you want to get more out of your life, start by getting more out of your beer. Honker's Ale is one of the first beers we made at Goose Island and now it's the one we've brewed the longest. We've made close to 100 different beers and learned a lot about brewing. First off we learned to leave Honker's alone. When you hit the first pitch out of the park, you don't change your swing. . . . I've dedicated a lot of my life to this beer. If you're looking to get more, you may find it in a pint of Honker's Ale. Cheers.

Greg Hall was literally the voice of Chicago beer.

12

ITS4U

TITILLATING THE GEEKIEST BEER GEEKS generated credibility among the elite, but Goose Island had a more urgent problem: volume. It didn't make beer that people wanted to slam through on a Friday night.

Honker's Ale was respectable, if slightly staid. Matilda and Pere Jacque were for sipping. Bourbon County Stout was an event unto itself. The most successful breweries had something in their portfolio that the average beer drinker could drink on repeat. New Glarus's Spotted Cow. Summit's Hefeweizen. Harpoon's UFO White. Goose Island needed one of those.

It had released a pilsner in 2001, Goose Pils, which was good enough to win silver at the Great American Beer Festival. But the idea of a "craft" pilsner was alien to most drinkers. Budweiser was pilsner. Craft was a retort to pilsner. Goose Island salespeople struggled to articulate a case for the beer, and drinkers didn't buy it.

Summertime Kölsch had always been popular. The question was not so unreasonably raised: Why not make Summertime the year-round easy-drinking beer? But the answer was obvious: This was Chicago. A beer called Summertime wouldn't fly during a ten-degree February day. And they didn't want to kill a successful brand to try reinventing it.

The easy-drinking beer also had to appeal to an increasingly necessary demographic: youth. The original craft beer audience—home brewers and those who had John Hall–like epiphanies in the bars of

Europe—was solidified: white male professionals between thirty and sixty. It was time to aim younger, to appeal to a new and more diverse generation. Goose Island hired a marketing firm to strategize on the project, which called the audience for this new beer "a young, trendy club and bar crowd who sought excitement in the big city of Chicago." The product would be "a new ultra-urban beer targeting the mainstream beer drinker."

Goose Island's sales team wanted it to be a wheat beer. "Gimme your pale ale" had become the default order on the West Coast, but in Chicago, it was, "Gimme your wheat beer." Greg had only a mild desire to make a wheat beer. But he suspected it could be good business. Just as he had done with Matilda—issuing a broad edict to figure it out—he did the same for this mystery wheat ale. He asked Goose Island's head brewer, John J. Hall, who was no relation, to figure it out: something unfiltered, with light citrus notes. And then John J., as he was called, was set loose to come up with a recipe.

Just as important as what was in the bottle was how to position the beer. By the early 2000s, craft beer was splintering into identities. It was cool, it was hip, it was counterculture, it was "you're not worthy," as San Diego's Stone Brewing had made the tagline for its intensely bitter and standoffish Arrogant Bastard strong ale. For its new wheat beer, Goose Island wanted everyone to be worthy. Want an easy-going beer on a Friday night without a ton of calories or challenging flavor? Yes, you. Happening upon this beer instead of Miller Lite? Yes, you. A seasoned beer drinker who needs something refreshing? You too. It needed to be a beer for everybody. And in that way, Goose Island was beginning to think strategically—and not unlike Big Beer.

Goose Island's agency, called Torque, came up with a twenty-six-page presentation, titled "Sprucing the New Goose," that detailed its vision for the beer. The wheat beer needed to blend seemingly competing agendas: Goose Island's heritage, Chicago's iconic sturdiness, the emerging edginess of craft beer, and the accessibility of a "great new everyday beer." Proposed names were a mix of silly puns and insider Chicago references: Haymarket Ale, Elevated Ale, Skyscraper Ale, Ale Capone, Lake Shore Draft, and Backwards River Ale (a reference to the early twentieth-century engineering feat of reversing the flow of the Chicago River). Torque favored calling the beer Backwards River Wheat Ale with a tagline of "Go Against the Flow." It was a nod to both the actual Goose Island, which sat in the Chicago River, and the beer's countercultural nature. "This beer is about taking a different course of action," Torque wrote in a presentation for the Halls. "It's about thinking and drinking differently." Different from what?

"Pilsner beers."

"Milwaukee and St. Louis."

"Mainstream expectation and the establishment."

The Backwards River name came with five potential logos, from light to dark and from literal (an image of a flowing river) to metaphorical (an arrow twisting left). Greg was unsure. "Backwards River Wheat" stumbled off the tongue. He favored calling the beer Ceres Wheat Ale—named for the goddess of agriculture—but few people could figure out how to pronounce it. Plus, a Danish brewery already laid claim to the name.

The name of the new beer ultimately came from Greg, though not without debate and consternation: 312 Urban Wheat Ale. The Torque team loved it. John Hall thought it was ridiculous.

312 referenced Chicago's area code and reflected the brand they all wanted to create: urban, hip, and young. Greg had been known to rail against "the fucking 708ers"—the people who entered the city from the suburban area code, Chicago's version of New York's bridge-and-tunnel crowd. A beer called 312 was his love letter to the city and a sneer toward the fucking 708ers (even though he had grown up in the 708). When the question was raised of alienating suburban beer drinkers, Greg tapped the knowledge he'd gleaned from marketing books: it was aspirational, he said. Corona didn't sell beer. It sold beach. Coors sold mountains. 312 would sell city: the churning, gritty, rock 'n' roll heart of Chicago. That's why the beer wouldn't just be 312 Wheat Ale but 312 *Urban* Wheat Ale. US Beverage, whose tenure with Goose Island was winding down, insisted that the word *urban* connoted something Goose Island didn't intend—*gasp*—black America. Greg drove around Chicago, snapping photos of the word *urban* in its many uses: banks,

clothing stores, salons, record shops. The word was everywhere when you looked. It had power. Most people under the age of thirty wanted to be in a city, Greg figured. They didn't want to be in the mountains. The mountains were boring! The city teemed with life. Name the beer for the city.

Greg also insisted that the beer should be steered away from an overt Goose Island affiliation. From late nights of beer tastings on Southport Avenue—*the* spot at the time for recent Big Ten graduates to drink on weekends—Greg deduced that Goose Island was an old person's brand. It was the restaurant where the grads' parents took them. The young person's affection was for a midwestern brand that had raced right past Goose Island: Bell's, of Kalamazoo, Michigan, which had matured during the 1990s into a regional icon. It had an entry-level Amber Ale. A world-class IPA called Two Hearted. Several lauded specialty beers. And, particularly powerful in Chicago, a seasonal wheat ale called Oberon, whose release every summer was treated as a beer-drinking holiday. Oberon was back? Summer had arrived. Goose Island needed one of those. 312 Urban Wheat Ale would be it—except it would be available all year.

John thought Greg's ideas for the brand were ludicrous. Why position the beer away from Goose Island? They had spent nearly twenty years building equity with local drinkers. They were the wrong drinkers, Greg argued—at least for this beer. John was thinking of the past. Greg thought of the future.

OK, fine, John said. But you don't name a beer for an area code! Again, Greg argued: it was a beer for a new generation. John tested the idea with mock-ups of the brand to friends at the Wrigleyville brewpub. They proved both John and Greg right: anyone over the age of forty didn't get it. Anyone under the age of forty—the target audience—loved it.

312 Urban Wheat Ale it would be.

Torque sketched out a brand intended to be unique, irreverent, and eye-catching, but unlikely to immediately register as Goose Island. They employed a yellow scheme—bright, memorable, and evoking the wheat within 312—anchored by heavy black lines. They wrote punchy taglines ("ITS4U") and crafted a playful sensibility, such as coasters with dotted-line outlines for one peanut, quarters for the jukebox, a phone number, and, of course, a pint of 312. Another coaster laid out Chicago urban myths with a wink: "Myth: After killing John Dillinger outside the Biograph Theater, the Feds put his penis in a jar that's now at FBI headquarters. Reality: Dillinger's penis is in penis heaven, and it just beat Capone's penis in a mean game of Texas hold 'em. Give 'em hell, Johnny!"

312's sell sheet, handed out to prospective accounts, practically mocked Goose Island's own early existence: "Why does every craft beer on tap have to be an imitation of some 'old world' beer? Chicago beer drinkers are a highly evolved species. Serve them a pint that reflects the distinctive character of the city and it'll move faster than a speeding El train." It also appealed directly to 312's prospective audience with a series of radio ads that mined Big Beer's playbook. They talked to the youth in its own language:

> 312 is a domestic beer. It's not imported. It's easy to say and easier to drink. Some people drink beer they can't pronounce to make them appear sophisticated. They don't hear the bartender laughing as they walk away. But you, you're confident. You're just being you. You drink 312 made right here in the new world. Not the old world. If you wanted to appear sophisticated, you'd wear an ascot. 312 Urban Wheat Ale isn't about sophistication. It's about the simple enjoyment of beer. It's unfiltered. Nothing went into it that needs to come out. 312 is OK with who it is, with that spicy aroma and crisp fruit-like flavor and creamy body. Who wouldn't be? Foreign beers have their place: foreign countries. You're in Chicago. Drink native. Ask for 312. If the bartender laughs, he's laughing with you, not at you. Unless you're wearing an ascot.

Most important, the beer delivered. It was a lean 4.3 percent alcohol, accomplishing the goal of pleasing the "Gimme your wheat beer" crowd, but nuanced enough for seasoned beer drinkers. That was due in part to a fluke: a nightshift brewer threw the wrong hop in one of the earliest batches of 312, but everyone agreed it made the beer better. 312 Urban

Wheat Ale would go on to win four medals in five years at the Great American Beer Festival.

But for a brewery looking to push volume through the taps of Chicago, the greatest genius of 312 was its tap handle. Goose Island's standard tap handle—a white goose head—was iconic in the city, but a bar would only carry so many of them. Goose Island had learned as much a few years earlier with a beer that was a passion project for Greg: an IPA infused with nitrogen rather than the classic carbon dioxide. It was the same method used to pour Guinness's thick, cascading body and amplified flavor. Goose Island's nitro IPA got a strong sales and marketing push but was a tough sell due to the time, attention, and specialized equipment that a pour required. The bigger problem was that placing it on draft usually meant the company was cannibalizing itself; a nitro IPA handle often replaced a Honker's Ale handle. And when it did replace Honker's, the IPA did far less business. Nitro IPA flamed out, and the sales team scrambled to get Honker's back on those taps. The episode taught a key lesson at a time when most bars had no more than a dozen taps: Getting more than one was difficult. More than two was impossible. Therefore, the new tap handle couldn't be yet another white goose head.

A retro black telephone tap handle, however, was irresistible. Salespeople found astonishing success, driving from account to account and leading with that tap handle at every stop. They'd pour a sample of the beer for a bar manager, then whip out the black telephone tap handle: "It's 312—get it?" The most ambitious salespeople were scoring eight or nine 312 placements per day—a best-ever day became routine.

312 was an irresistible brand. It was local, well made, easy to drink, and had an eye-catching tap handle. It was exactly the beer that Chicago wanted. After the ill-fated Goose Pils, almost exclusively available in supermarket twelve-packs, 312 was available only on draft for the first six months. The idea was to build excitement and demand. It worked. Within weeks, one hundred bars had the beer on tap. Sales shot 20 percent beyond expectation.

Goose Island was officially shaking off the rust of five stagnant years.

13

"They Are the King of Beers"

John Hall was feeling good.

312 Urban Wheat Ale had jump-started growth, and for the first time, Goose Island was consistently profitable. Honker's Ale had been the brewery's top-selling beer for a decade, but 312 surpassed it within three years. After another five years, 312 had *doubled* Honker's. In supermarkets and convenience stores, 312 was the second-bestselling craft beer in Chicago, behind only Samuel Adams Boston Lager. When factoring in bar sales, 312 was likely the city's top-selling craft beer.

Goose Island finally had its volume beer. It had a lineup of classic styles, anchored by John's beloved Honker's Ale. It helped pioneer the use of *Brettanomyces* in the United States. It introduced the world to the joys of imperial stout aged in bourbon barrels.

So, yes. John was feeling good.

"The variety of beers we now have kind of covers the spectrum," he told an interviewer in 2005. "But there are enough beers in our portfolio to keep beer drinkers interested and develop loyalty to our products. That's important. How much choice do you really get from Anheuser-Busch, for instance?"

Anheuser-Busch was asking itself the same question. The answer wasn't good.

The company had appeared to dodge craft beer's bullet during the 1990s with minority stakes in Redhook and Widmer, fairly inexpensive insurance policies that Anheuser-Busch hoped never to redeem. Ideally, its own brands—Elk Mountain, American Originals, and the Michelob line—would prosper while craft would cease to be a threat. Though Anheuser-Busch's brands mostly sputtered, it didn't matter; from 1997 to 2003, craft's growth slowed to an average of less than 3 percent per year. The threat had receded. But now, a consumer shift made beers like 312 Urban Wheat Ale everyday occasions for a new generation of drinkers. Craft was ascendant once more.

Anheuser-Busch's pilot brewery once again began to churn out faux craft brands: Michelob Hop Hound, Michelob Ginger Wheat, and, in a nod to Bourbon County Stout, Michelob Winter's Bourbon Cask Ale (promoted as "rich with barrel-aged flavor"). Among the efforts sprouted—finally—one hit: Spring Heat Spiced Wheat, an unfiltered Belgian-style wheat ale introduced as a spring draft-only release in 2006. It was, at heart, a knockoff of Coors's hugely successful Blue Moon Belgian White. Two years later, Spring Heat Spiced Wheat was rebranded as a year-round beer called Shock Top, and became the company's lead craft brand. Otherwise, Anheuser-Busch's latest incursion into craft beer was once again met with a consumer shrug. It offered no story. No resonance. "Consumers want romance," Anheuser-Busch brewmaster George Reisch acknowledged to the *San Diego Union-Tribune*. "They are sick and tired of branding without the story."

It was time for Tony Short to dust off his old strategy. Short was a vice president in Anheuser-Busch's Wholesaler Development division, managing relationships with St. Louis's prized distribution network. Mostly his job was to be sure that distributors were supporting the interests of Anheuser-Busch. But occasionally the concern flowed the other way. Such was the case during the 1990s with the initial rise of craft beer. Short's response had been the Redhook and Widmer deals. Now he needed to strike again. And for the right brewery, Anheuser-Busch had plenty to offer: gobs of cash, some of the industry's premier brewers and lab technology, and access to that mighty distribution network.

Short talked with dozens of breweries about deals similar to what he'd hatched with Redhook and Widmer a decade earlier. The iconic Sierra Nevada. The fast-rising New Belgium. Abita Brewing in Louisiana.

Long Trail Brewing in Vermont. Boulevard Brewing in Kansas City. Many, including Boulevard, backed away after one meeting. "We didn't feel the need to take the conversation to the next level," the brewery's chief marketing officer told the *St. Louis Post-Dispatch* in 2006. "It just didn't fit into our plans."

Then there was Goose Island. The Chicago brewery was attractive not just for its portfolio but also for its location. Chicago was notoriously difficult for Anheuser-Busch to penetrate; the city had been a fortress of Miller products for decades. Having an ascendant local brand on its trucks would allow Budweiser and Bud Light an entry point. Yes—things were so grave in Chicago that Anheuser-Busch actually *needed* craft beer.

And John Hall needed Anheuser-Busch right back. Though his brewery was finally growing again, he was certain that better distribution would launch Goose Island into the big time. He had been shopping for a new distributor, and unlike ten years earlier, interest was unanimous. Goose Island had scrapped its way to becoming a significant regional player, dueling with Bell's (Michigan), Boulevard (Kansas City), and Summit (Twin Cities). The Miller network was still appealing; it had a strong array of craft brands, which meant its salespeople knew how to sell John's beer. But now Tony Short was interested too.

In October 2005, Anheuser-Busch sent a brewer and engineer to dig in to Goose Island's production brewery. The verdict, in a five-page memo sent to a team of executives in St. Louis, was that Goose Island could stand to improve shelf stability so that its bottles were good for the six months promised on the label. Yeast management practices needed to be tweaked, but Goose Island knew as much; it wanted help developing tests to optimize fermentation. Goose Island would need to run far more efficiently to reach the 50 percent sales growth it targeted in 2006. But Anheuser-Busch could assist with all those things; running a brewery at peak form was its expertise. Though there was one small concern noted in the memo—Greg Hall appeared "somewhat skeptical and concerned with A-B involvement"—Goose Island, they concluded, was "an acceptable investment from a technical standpoint."

John was thrilled. Craft beer had been largely built by a band of iconoclasts and radicals, but he was neither. He was the business guy who once sold corrugated boxes. He saw no victory in staying small or independently owned. He'd wanted to build a powerful beer company from the start and to attract the interest of a major player. He thought the suitor might be foreign—Heineken, perhaps—but here it was: the pitch was coming from St. Louis. They needed him. He needed them. And he liked what they offered: expertise, distribution, and the promise of growth.

But negotiations were difficult. More than one Anheuser-Busch veteran, even those who had worked on the Redhook and Widmer deals, would describe talks with Goose Island as some of the most contentious of their careers. Anheuser-Busch offered to buy the entirety of Goose Island; John said the entire brewery wasn't for sale. Anheuser-Busch tried to guarantee itself a path to majority ownership. John said no to that too. For months, he haggled with Tony Short over price and parameters. Finally, they settled on a sale of just under 42 percent of the brewery: the minority shareholders. John and Greg would keep their stakes and continue to run operations, but the minority shareholders would be bought out as Goose Island was folded in with Redhook and Widmer as Anheuser-Busch's craft wing.

Yet the deal dragged on. And on. Yusef Jackson, who owned Anheuser-Busch's Chicago distributorship, River North, called John for periodic updates. He couldn't get Goose Island beer on his trucks fast enough. John gradually ran out of answers. He didn't know the reason for the holdup. Then Jackson offered a tip: August Busch IV would be in town the next week for dinner at Gibsons, a downtown steakhouse. He urged John to happen to show up.

August IV was the great-great-grandson of company founder Adolphus Busch and carried a checkered past of drugs, fast cars, and the privilege that accompanied an iconic last name. As a nineteen-year-old student at the University of Arizona in the early 1980s, news reports said, he crashed his black Corvette after leaving a bar, killing a woman who sat in the passenger seat. Busch, who reportedly left the woman at the scene, was found at his townhouse four miles away, lying in bed and caked in dried blood. A semiautomatic rifle was at the foot of the bed, and a loaded sawed-off shotgun sat on the kitchen table. Busch claimed no memory of the wreck, and the blood and urine samples he provided were mysteriously compromised at a Tucson hospital. He was never charged.

A year later, Busch was arrested in his native St. Louis after a chase that ended with undercover narcotics officers shooting out the tires of his Mercedes-Benz. Busch, who had just left a strip club, claimed he thought officers were trying to kidnap him. Police accused him of trying to run over two cops. A St. Louis jury acquitted Busch of assault after three days of testimony, which led many in his hometown to presume that the prince of the Busch family hovered above the law. He was a handsome, dark-haired playboy, reckless and untouchable.

After dutifully taking his place in the family company, he began to rise, and displayed a knack for marketing. He worked on the initial launch of Bud Dry and later took aim at refreshing Budweiser, working on the iconic campaign of three frogs chirping "*Bud-wei-ser.*"

"Industry rivals are surprised at how the boss's rebellious, risk-loving 32-year-old son has recharged Anheuser-Busch," *Fortune* magazine reported in 1997. "Profits, disappointing for several years, are increasing at a double-digit pace again, and the company's stock price is up 27 percent from a year ago." Budweiser might have been the king of beers, but at Anheuser-Busch, shareholder return was king. For August IV, all was forgiven.

By the evening of the steakhouse dinner, he had become president of Anheuser-Busch's beer division. He was still something of an odd figure in the company, continuing his playboy ways and spending ample time at his compound in Lake of the Ozarks. (Another girlfriend was found dead, in 2011, this time at his St. Louis mansion, from an oxycodone overdose; August IV settled a lawsuit with the woman's family for $1.75 million.)

John and Greg arrived at Gibsons at the appointed hour and arranged to sit one table from August IV, his bodyguard, Yusef Jackson, and their crew. The Halls had brought two employees from the brewpub who knew nothing of the covert operation about to unfold. In walked Yusef and August IV in a party of six. The Halls feigned surprised that the Anheuser-Busch bigwigs were a table away and sent over a round of Goose Island beer. The Fourth sent a round of Budweiser in return.

Greg scrutinized the label, leaned in, and said, "Our beer is fresher than yours." Jackson was only vaguely amused.

But it got the Fourth's attention. After the meal, he came over and asked about the status of their deal. John said he would sign the paperwork as soon as he had it. The Fourth whipped out his phone and barked orders. The Halls were never sure who that call went to. But the deal was done within sixty days with Goose Island's valuation pegged at $8.3 million—nearly $3.5 million for the 42 percent stake.

The element far from the public eye but most crucial for everyone involved was Yusef Jackson acquiring Goose Island's Chicago-area distribution rights from Union Beverage. The wholesalers were left to negotiate the price, and they settled at a whopping $9.1 million for both Goose Island and Grolsch, a Dutch import. The president of Union Beverage said in a statement that the company was "disappointed" to surrender Goose Island but that it "could not pass up the opportunity to sell the distribution rights for an unprecedented amount that represents a tremendous valuation for the brands."

Goose Island's distribution rights in its hometown were worth about as much as the brewery itself. Even John Hall was stunned by the figure.

When news of the deal broke, in June 2006, it was structured to sound like something it wasn't: an agreement between Goose Island and Widmer Brothers, a brewery almost 40 percent owned by Anheuser-Busch. Widmer was four years older than Goose Island, four times as large, and from Portland, Oregon, the breadbasket of the American craft beer movement.

"Like Goose Island, the Widmers are leaders in craft brewing and share our passion for craft beer," John Hall was quoted in a press release. "When it came time to create a partnership, Widmer and Goose Island were a natural fit. Both companies are run by the original family members and share a passion for creating truly remarkable beers."

Partly for the optics of remaining "craft," but also to manage its investments under one umbrella, Anheuser-Busch's minority acquisition of Goose Island was funneled to Widmer. The media least familiar with beer industry machinations dutifully reported the press release, describing the deal as a meeting between two like-minded craft brewers.

Those with a sharper understanding and clearer eyes weren't sure what to make of it. What was the goal? The endgame? It was difficult to divine Anheuser-Busch's motives; the St. Louis juggernaut had bought a 31 percent stake in Widmer in 1997 but slowly nudged the investment to 39.5 percent. Its stake in Redhook had similarly grown, from 25 percent in 1994 to 33.7 percent. What was ahead for Goose Island? Most industry voices presumed the deal didn't mean anything good for craft beer.

Dan Kopman, president and chief operating officer of the Saint Louis Brewery's Schlafly brand, saw the deal as "a Chicago play." While the deal, he said, made sense for both sides—access to Anheuser-Busch distribution could only help Goose Island—it didn't sit right: "It's like David selling out to Goliath." Jay Brooks, a Northern California beer blogger who knew and liked the Widmer brothers, couldn't pinpoint his unease but also couldn't shake it: "I can't put my finger on what bothers me about this, perhaps it is just simple paranoia on my part. For now, I'll try to concentrate on the positive aspects of this and try to silence that voice in the back of my head and wish Kurt, Rob and John and Greg Hall all the best."

Sam Calagione, founder of Delaware's Dogfish Head brewery, was unapologetic about his skepticism. "In five years, if AB really gives a shit about craft beer, then I'll stand corrected," he told the *Philadelphia Daily News* a week after the deal was announced. "But every early indication is that their motivation is no different than it was in the 1990s, the last time we were experiencing big growth."

Did Anheuser-Busch care about craft beer? Well, yes. But more accurately, it cared about craft beer because of what craft beer could do for it. Which of course Calagione understood: "We are market share. They want to buy us, then indoctrinate us."

John and Greg paid the skeptics no mind.

"It's going to be huge," John told the *St. Louis Post-Dispatch*. "They are the king of beers."

Within a year, Anheuser Busch's two Pacific Northwest craft investments merged into one company: the Craft Brewers Alliance (later renamed the Craft Brew Alliance), a company 36.4 percent owned by Anheuser-Busch. The 42 percent stake in Goose Island owned by Widmer became property of the CBA, which also had minority ownership in Hawaii's Kona Brewing. (Kona would be wholly absorbed by the CBA in 2010 for $13.9 million.) Widmer had denied that the strings for its merger with Redhook were pulled from St. Louis, but Anheuser-Busch lobbied heavily for the deal. In addition to its minority ownership, it maintained two seats on the CBA's board of directors.

Life as part of the Craft Brewers Alliance—and in the Anheuser-Busch distribution network—was good for Goose Island. Sales spiked 60 percent within the first year. Within five years, the number of cases it sold in downstate Illinois surged from eight thousand to one hundred thousand. Entire counties that had never been exposed to craft beer had Honker's Ale and 312 Urban Wheat rolling into town on the same trucks as Bud and Bud Light. If Greg had been skeptical of the deal—as the memo to Anheuser-Busch executives suggested—he put it aside for the public. He even began joking about how Goose Island's beer was better with a little "beechwood aging."

"Walk into any bar, they probably have Bud and Bud Light," Greg told the *Chicago Sun-Times* a year after the sale. "It gives us a lot more opportunity to get into those places."

OK, so Anheuser-Busch had stepped on craft beer's throat once or twice. Wasn't that business? And being on the same team as Anheuser-Busch was good for Goose Island's business.

"We've got more brewers, we pay the brewers better and give them better benefits because we're selling more beer," Greg told *All About Beer* magazine in 2010. "I don't see how that's a bad thing."

The Brewers Association disagreed.

The trade group had been formed in 2005, the year before Goose Island's minority sale, as a unification of the event-driven Association of Brewers and policy-driven Brewers' Association of America. The Brewers Association's inaugural board of directors was a cast of industry all-stars, including Ken Grossman of Sierra Nevada, Kim Jordan of New Belgium, Sam Calagione of Dogfish Head, Vinnie Cilurzo of Russian River, and Dick Cantwell of Elysian. Among their first major undertakings was answering a seemingly unanswerable question: What is craft beer?

The question was at once simple—it wasn't Bud, Miller, or Coors—and deeply vexing. Everyone seemed to have an internal compass on the matter, but there was no clear answer. Legendary beer writer Fred Eckhardt had taken up the subject in *All About Beer* magazine nine years earlier, with an article titled "What Is 'Craft Beer'?" He suggested that the term was born with Vince Cottone's 1986 book *Good Beer Guide: Breweries and Pubs of the Pacific Northwest.* The terms *boutique brewery, cottage brewery*, and especially *microbrewery* were in fashion, but Cottone suggested that *craft* was the most apt description, marked by "a small brewery using traditional methods and ingredients to produce a handcrafted, uncompromised beer that is marketed locally."

More than ten years later, Eckhardt took the conversation a step further by asking brewers to weigh in from companies both large and small. One of the most searing answers was from Tom Schmidt, an Anheuser-Busch brewmaster and director of brewing education. He rejected the premise of the question:

> I don't believe there is anything such as "craft beer." The use of the term may lead consumers to believe that beer made in some small, quaint place is much better than beer that is produced in a large, efficient brewery, where quality and consistency are the hallmarks. We all fight the same battle using the same raw materials. These supposedly "craft breweries" are finding that, to produce consistent products, they require process controls much the same as the larger breweries. Our brewmasters are (dedicated) "craftsmen," not just brewing "engineers" who monitor the process from afar. Just because we are successful should not detract from the fact that we are also quality "craftsmen."

Yet, the Brewers Association's inaugural board was determined to draw the lines that established who was in and who was out. Was it size? Was it beer? Was it business? The answer was yes to all three.

After a year of debate, they pegged a craft brewer as "small" (manufacturing fewer than two million barrels per year), "independent" (less than 25 percent could be owned by a company that itself was not a craft brewer), and "traditional" (beers could only be made by traditional brewing methods with adjuncts that enhanced rather than lightened flavor). Craft beer, the Brewers Association said, could only be made by a craft brewer. (In a bid to seem less strident, the organization would later drop any effort to define "craft beer" and use its definition only to define a "craft brewer.")

With the first rigid definition of "craft" in American beer, boundaries were formed and alliances severed. Redhook, Widmer, and Goose Island, whose deal had been consummated just months earlier, were immediately on the outside. All three were prominent in the Brewers Association's 2006 ranking of the nation's fifty largest domestic craft breweries: Redhook in fifth place (234,200 barrels), Widmer in sixth (225,492 barrels), and Goose Island in twenty-first (52,879 barrels). When the rankings were updated in 2007, all three were scrubbed as if they never existed. Advocates for the definition said there hadn't been an attempt to exclude anyone; they were simply trying to create a clean data set to understand how craft beer performed in the market. As Big Beer waded into the industry, they also wanted to limit voting rights to the companies that most needed the unified muscle of the nation's small and independently owned breweries.

It was a painful time that tested decades-long friendships. The issue of ownership was particularly thorny. But the board decided it was meaningful both within the industry and to consumers. Depending on the industry, the concept of "beneficial ownership" typically sat well below 50 percent; often it was 10 or 25 percent. The board went with the latter. And out went Redhook, Widmer, and Goose Island.

Paul Shipman of Redhook didn't have many fans within the industry, but the Widmer brothers did; Kurt and Rob were two of its best-liked people. Gary Fish, who sat on the Brewers Association board and had grown his Deschutes Brewery into a national power 150 miles from the Widmers, was a vocal skeptic of the definition; the Widmers had been industry pioneers and didn't deserve excommunication, he said. Still, they were out, and the brothers would nurse a grudge for decades.

A different excommunication gnawed at Ray Daniels, who handled marketing and messaging for the Brewers Association. Daniels had been among Goose Island's earliest champions. As a Brewers Association staff member and not a board member, he wasn't privy to discussions in which the definition was hatched. But his job would include advocating for the new definition. Daniels, who would go on to start the Cicerone Certification Program, knew John. He knew Greg. He knew they still controlled the brewery, innovated, and sought to push beer forward. Booting Goose Island from the club for a 42 percent ownership stake by Anheuser-Busch seemed arbitrary to Daniels. Fifty-one percent? Fine. But he couldn't reconcile 25. The inability to defend a definition he didn't believe in helped spur him out the door the following January.

Greg called Goose Island's excommunication from craft beer "extraordinarily goofy," insisting the move had nothing to do with what was inside the bottles. Goose Island's minority sale was simply about distribution. About business. Not beer. And wasn't beer what mattered? Wasn't that what defined the idea of "craft"?

The Brewers Association didn't think so. It suspected a war was brewing.

Goose Island was out of the club, but no matter. Aligned with Anheuser-Busch, it enjoyed rare power for a brewery of its size.

Shortly after the sale, the main bearing on Goose Island's bottle filler failed on a Thursday afternoon. The manufacturer, Krones, said it would be there in three weeks to assist. Goose Island called its patron to the south. Anheuser-Busch sent a technician and two engineers to Goose Island that afternoon and informed Krones that it had no choice but to do the same. Sure enough, engineers from both companies spent the weekend toiling so that Goose Island could again be filling bottles by Tuesday morning. Without a minority sale to Anheuser-Busch, Goose Island would likely have had to shut down production for a couple of weeks. It was good to ride with the king.

More important, with Anheuser-Busch's distribution muscle, Goose Island launched into growth it hadn't seen since Fulton Street's early years. Fueled by 312 Urban Wheat Ale, the brewery was making and selling beer at a radical clip.

Not only had Goose Island's production gone up, but also the amount of beer stored at the brewery went down by half. The well-oiled machine that was Anheuser-Busch distribution pushed beer into the marketplace with relentless efficiency. Across its relatively tiny footprint of sixty square miles in the heart of the city, Yusef Jackson's River North distributorship sold more volume than Goose Island had sent to all of Illinois the previous year. Before the deal, Goose Island would get irate calls from retailers and customers saying they couldn't find the beer. Now it was cruising and took on the sheen of a major force—so major that leaders of the free world debated its merit.

In 2010, President Barack Obama sent 312 Urban Wheat to British prime minister David Cameron as payment for a World Cup bet. Obama even started their joint news conference the next month at the White House by joking about the warmer temperature at which Brits drank their beer: "We have just concluded some excellent discussions—including whether the beers from our hometowns that we exchanged are best served warm or cold. My understanding is that the prime minister enjoyed our 312 beer, and we may send him some more. I thought the beer we got was excellent—but I did drink it cold."

Cameron replied: "I did enjoy drinking the 312 beer—cold—during the World Cup. I enjoyed it so much that when I watched Germany beat Argentina I actually cheered for Germany. That's something that's a big admission for a British person to make. So, the beer is obviously very effective."

A widely circulated photo illustrated the moment: President Obama, sitting with legs crossed before an American flag, wearing a dark suit and holding a bottle of 312 in his left hand, its yellow label popping amid the red, white, and blue. (Greg would eventually make the photo his Facebook profile photo.)

What could John Hall do but laugh? The naysayers grumbled, but with Anheuser-Busch's help, he had created the beer company of his dreams.

14

"If You Tell Me I'm-a Pay Forty-Five Dollars for a Beer, I'm-a Tell You Kiss My *Beep* and to Get *Beep* Out of My Face Before I Beat *Beep*"

The first sip of the first Goose Island beer aged in a wine barrel came in late 2007, in the same cool cave beneath the Clybourn Avenue bar where Bourbon County Stout was born twelve years earlier.

Matt Lincoln, a long-limbed, bearded brewer who joined Goose Island in 2005 after tiring of a chef's life in Seattle, hunched beneath the low ceiling and dipped into the Cabernet Sauvignon barrel for the first few ounces.

The beer was OK. Just not quite tart enough.

His second taste, a few weeks later, began to take shape. It was even better after another month. Depth and complexity were unfurling.

Finally, after the beer had rested in its oaky home for six months, swimming in and out of the wood, Lincoln had something. Goose Island had something.

Its color sat at the intersection of copper and ruddy amber. Just a long sniff—funky and tart, a cross between fruity vinegar and sweet jam—could send the taste buds careening. The flavor began robust and earthy, grassy and leathery, then gave way to a blast of berry tartness that seemed as if it might go on forever. Then an oaky, under-ripe fruitiness crept in. Finally, a bright, chalky finish. It was masterful. Especially beside a hearty meal, whether duck breast, one of the city's trademark deep-dish sausage pizzas, or stinky cheese.

What would come to be called Juliet was based on Lincoln's old home brew recipe, when he'd churned out far more beer in his Seattle basement than he and his roommates could drink. The original version was an ale featuring rye in the grain bill (for light spiciness) and marionberries (for jam-like sweetness). The Goose Island version added *Brettanomyces* and was aged in Napa Valley wine barrels that Lincoln sourced himself.

It was an approach to beer almost as radical in 2007 as aging a stout in bourbon barrels was fifteen years earlier. A handful of American breweries already dabbled in such layered, wood-aged fruit sours—New Belgium in Ft. Collins, Russian River in Northern California, and the Lost Abbey in Southern California. But American craft brewing remained built on the foundation of Boston Lager, Sierra Nevada Pale Ale, and a fan base learning to love IPAs.

Greg was rarely at the brewery by that time; he had become one of the industry's leading voices, and forever seemed to host beer dinners in New York or Portland. But he had made clear that Goose Island should be at the forefront of what was next. The result was an "innovation team," headed by Mary Pellettieri, open to any brewer who wanted relief from making endless waves of 312. All they had to do was fill out a short questionnaire about their interests and ideas. Lincoln raised his hand.

Joining the innovation team didn't spare anyone the grind of making the beers that fueled Goose Island's growth. But it did offer the chance to think broadly and like a home brewer again. Greg wanted expensive, time-consuming beers that were labors of art and love. He had Matilda, a few classic Belgian-inspired beers, and the behemoth that was Bourbon County Stout. But he wanted to elevate the Goose Island portfolio higher still. While the brewery had one of the nation's most ambitious bourbon barrel–aging programs, there wasn't a single wine barrel under its roof. He had to explain the added risk and expense to his father, but John Hall had never wavered on investing in beer. Good beer was good business. His mantra was simple: Always make more beer. Don't get distracted.

Each member of the innovation team was asked to arrive at the first meeting with three ideas. It was Lincoln's amplified home brew that lit up the room. He sketched out an updated recipe over beers with two fellow innovation brewers, Brian Taylor, who would go on to start Whiner Beer Co. in Chicago, and Phil Wymore, who would launch Perennial Artisan Ales in St. Louis. When it finally came time for the pilot batch, Lincoln did it at the brewpub, where the ten-barrel system was a more ideal playground than Fulton Street's fifty-barrel workhorse. It was an obscenely long day. Raw materials arrived five hours late, and the brew didn't finish until nearly 10:00 PM. When the beer was done fermenting in stainless steel after two weeks, Lincoln jammed one hundred pounds of plump, ripe marionberries into each Cabernet barrel. Then he transferred the beer. And he waited.

Once that first version was a success, Goose Island scaled up a batch at Fulton Street, replacing marionberries (which had to be sourced from the Pacific Northwest) with blackberries (prevalent in the Midwest). The brewery filled eight more wine barrels with its exotic concoction and let them sit. By the time the second round of Juliet was finished after nearly a year of aging, Lincoln was preparing to leave Goose Island and move back to Seattle. But he made a point to be on the packaging line for the day his beer was poured into tall twenty-two-ounce bottles, ready to be sent into the world. Greg decided to name the beer after the daughter of Jean-Pierre Van Roy and Claude Cantillon, owners of the Belgian brewery that had pioneered this sort of beautiful beer. Her name was Julie. Greg thought "Juliet" looked and sounded better as a beer name.

Bottles of Juliet finally reached stores during the spring of 2009 at a cost of $15.99—about six times the per-ounce cost of a six-pack of 312 Urban Wheat Ale. No matter. The future had arrived. The beers sold out in ten days.

As he lorded over more beer-pairing dinners, amplifying the message of good beer, Greg came to think of Goose Island's expanding Reserve line like a constellation of wines. Matilda was a nice second beer, he would say—a big Chardonnay. It wasn't quite a red but certainly not a soft white. Sofie (named for Greg's daughter, born in 1999), a saison released about the same time as Juliet, was akin to that lighter white; it was fruity and effervescent, meant to start a meal. Brian Taylor had come up with half a dozen variations of the beer, tweaking the yeast and hops with each batch. All were tasty, but none quite threaded the needle. The two best versions were dry hopped with spicy, fruity Amarillo hops and one brewed with orange zest. They couldn't decide which to pick. Then the answer became so very clear, and reflected the burgeoning ethos of craft beer: blend them.

Greg had been right about Bourbon County Stout and he'd been right about 312. He'd gotten out of the way to let Matt Brynildson create an IPA that would win six medals at the Great American Beer Festival. His approach with the innovation team was a hybrid of the previous efforts: he gave them the goal, then let them chart the path to get there. He vetoed little—though any recipe featuring chamomile was a nonstarter—and usually didn't even want to talk about a beer until there was something to taste. He'd try anything, and if he liked it, they'd figure out how to make more. It was that simple. The approach led to plenty of wasted time and money on failed projects, but he didn't care. He convinced John not to care, either. Because it also yielded some of the most exciting beer in the United States.

The innovation kept coming, with a common thread of fruit, wild yeast, and aging in oak barrels. Juliet and Sofie were followed by Madame Rose, a fruity, oaky Belgian-style brown ale aged with cherries that was inspired by the Belgian classic Rodenbach. Lolita was a Belgian-style pale ale aged with raspberries. Together, the new roster of beers was known as "the Sisters."

John Laffler, a former addiction counselor who decided his home brewing hobby made for a less stressful career, was promoted from the sanitation crew to manage the ever-growing barrel program. Laffler used different types of *Brettanomyces* in different concentrations, blended beer from various barrels, and played with different aging techniques. The program grew so wildly that fellow brewers kidded Laffler: Did he have some kind of wheel to spin to decide the type of barrel, fruit, and yeast to use? Within the brewery, he took on a nickname: the Barrel Whisperer. His beers often sold briskly, even in the teeth of a global financial crisis. When Laffler started at the brewery, Goose Island had had two hundred bourbon and forty wine barrels. Within three years, the figure had grown to nearly five thousand combined—slightly more bourbon than wine.

"A number of restaurants have craft beers, but what they don't have is the right beers to go with their foods," Greg told the *Chicago Tribune* while promoting the release of Juliet and Sofie. "Once chefs try drinking a sour beer with their food, you'll start to see sour beers on their menus."

Chefs were always on Greg's mind. His culinary worship was in full swing, and two-hour four-course lunches were the norm. The few beers that sneaked onto the menus of those restaurants looked more appropriate for dive bars than white tablecloths. Wine looked elegant. Beer looked juvenile. Goose Island was making elegant beer. It needed elegant packaging.

Greg and a Goose Island designer spent hours browsing wine and champagne labels, weighing what worked and what didn't. The best ones looked so wildly different than what appeared on beer bottles. They were clean and elegant, sophisticated even, as if popping the cork wasn't just about drinking well; it was the start of an occasion. That was the feeling Greg wanted to evoke with Goose Island's Reserve line.

The Matilda label was redesigned to look like a Chardonnay—white canvas with the beer's name in tall, elegant black cursive. Pere Jacques mimicked port with its squat serif black letters on a white label. Sofie took after champagne, with a shade of apple green picked by Sofie herself. Greg believed craft beer was entering a new realm, where the feeling it evoked was as important as what was in the bottle. Craft beer drinkers didn't just buy beer, and they didn't just buy authenticity. They bought experience.

Of the entire Reserve line, Matilda became the unlikely star. Greg thought Pere Jacques—intended to be an American approximation of

Chimay Blue—would break out. But Matilda quickly surpassed it. His explanation betrayed his increasing belief in the power of the brand: the name. Ma-*TIL*-da. It rolled off the tongue. Anyone could say it. It had cadence. Elegance, even. Pere Jacques—Pair-*ZHOCK*—did not. It was hard sounds and difficult to pronounce. In an increasingly crowded beer market, Greg had come to believe that the beer had to be good but the marketing even better. Names, labels, colors, fonts, and bottle shape all merged into one burst of feeling. The bridge between brewing great beer and selling great beer was the brand. Had Pere Jacques been named Matilda, and Matilda named Pere Jacques, they might have traveled opposite paths. Matilda's success convinced Greg that brand was behind any beer's first sale. If the beer was good, the drinker would come back. But the name, the label, the story, and the feeling it evoked in the very first moment of recognition—that's what got people to try it.

By 2010, Bourbon County Stout was a sensation among beer's early adopters but an obscurity to the public at large. It was released once a year and could reliably be found on shelves for months to those in the know. Greg was ready to change that.

It was time for Bourbon County to become more than a beer. It had to be a brand. Bourbon County Vanilla Stout. Bourbon County Coffee Stout. And the biggest curveball of all, Rare Bourbon County Stout. "Rare," as the beer nerds would come to call it, was aged two years instead of one year in the pinnacle of hype-worthy oak: barrels that had held one of the world's most revered bourbons, twenty-three-year-old Pappy Van Winkle's Family Reserve.

As for the marketing, the Bourbon County family of beers got nearly identical labels, the twist being a different bright color for each: red for Coffee, pale yellow for Vanilla, and deep emerald for Rare, which was given the added splendor of a cardboard box printed with 250 words of story attributed to Greg. It was the history of Goose Island, of Bourbon County Stout, and the barrels used to age the beer: "Extremely rare, the barrels were filled with Bourbon County Stout, aged for two years, and have resulted in a beer that I believe to be the finest Goose Island has ever produced in its eighteen years of barrel-aging stout."

Few of the breweries aging beer in bourbon barrels in 2010—and by then there were many—talked of vintage and the source of the barrels. With Rare, Goose Island aimed to create an experience not with just the beer but with its story. The beer had to be good, but the words—"revolution" and "experimentation" and, most of all, "rare"—created value. And with that value came the boldest decision of all: $42.99 for a twenty-two-ounce bottle.

Rare Bourbon County Stout would be among the most expensive American craft beers ever. But with the right story and message, Greg was sure that not only would people pay it—they would *gladly* pay it. Goose Island would enter beer drinkers' lives in a new way. It wouldn't just accompany an occasion; it would *be* the occasion.

It all came down to an understanding of value, which Greg had read of in marketing books but learned firsthand over lunch at one of his favorite restaurants. He noticed one day that the tea menu had been reinvented. The old menu featured a handful of teas in the $8 to $15 range. No one ever ordered a $15 tea—who in their sound mind would order the most expensive tea, especially at $15? But one day, the menu was updated with an eye-opening range of prices: $8, $15, $35, and $150. Greg asked the chef about the change. He was told that the new context had made the $15 tea the most popular. Ordering the $8 tea made you look—and feel—cheap, especially when trying to impress a client or a date. But the second-least expensive tea made you seem worldly. And it was a pittance compared to a $150 tea. The prices barely mattered. The context mattered. The lesson was clear: give people a context to buy a premium product, and they would. Sofie and Matilda cost more than Honker's Ale and 312 Urban Wheat. Now, Rare Bourbon County Stout cost more than all of them.

Rare.

What implied a premium product more than *rare*?

Finally came the question of how to sell the beer. Just shooting Rare into the market like any other beer didn't seem worthy of asking people to pay forty-three dollars for it. Neighboring Three Floyds Brewing, in the border town of Munster, Indiana, had proven that beer fanatics prized beer as an event; its annual Dark Lord Day festival had brought the faithful to Three Floyds' suburban office park every year since 2005. The weather didn't matter: people showed up, waited in line, and paid a premium for twenty-two-ounce bottles of Dark Lord, an imperial stout brewed with coffee, Mexican vanilla, and Indian sugar. Why shouldn't Goose Island have an event of its own?

Goose Island decided to release half the bottles at once at the vast liquor store across the street from the brewpub, where Greg had been a customer for more than twenty years. Back in the 1990s, when he needed to taste all dozen IPAs on the shelf, he'd cross Marcey Street, walk into the old Sam's Wines and Spirits, and scour the fluorescent-lit aisles. Now the store was part of a local chain called Binny's Beverage Depot, and Binny's was one of Goose Island's most essential customers.

The release would happen the day after Thanksgiving. People would be feeling festive and extravagant, so Goose Island would simply name the event for what it was: Black Friday. Goose Island sent two pallets—about a thousand twenty-two-ounce bottles—while assuaging nervous Binny's staff that they wouldn't be stuck with a bunch of unsellable $42.99 beer; Goose Island promised to buy it back if needed. It wasn't an unreasonable concern. A year earlier, Goose Island had to buy back several cases of Bourbon County Stout from an Indiana distributor that just couldn't figure out how to make customers understand it. A beer four times the price might be an even steeper climb.

During the windup to the release, the price became the major talking point—just as Greg intended. News outlets that rarely thought beyond Budweiser and Miller couldn't resist the bait. Television resorted to the classic man-on-the-street interview and reaped the rewards. Amid the clink of bottles in a buzzing bar, a well-coifed reporter from the local Fox affiliate approached a man nursing a pint of beer:

"Our question is: Would you pay forty-five dollars for a bottle of beer?"

The man on the street paused a full stunned second before answering.

"Hell no," the man on the street said. "Get the hell out of here. If you tell me I'm-a pay forty-five dollars for a beer, I'm-a tell you kiss my *beep* and to get *beep* out of my face before I beat *beep*."

"My sentiments exactly," the reporter concluded.

Goose Island loved it. *Of course* those guys said that.

Rare wasn't for them.

"You may like it, you may love it and you may not get it, but you'll never forget it," Greg told the *Chicago Tribune* days before the release. "It has more flavor intensity than any beer—and I'd add wine and maybe some spirits—than you've ever had."

By 6:00 AM on Black Friday, in twenty-degree weather, the line snaked around the store. When doors opened at 9:00 AM, tall displays of Rare, Vanilla, Coffee, and the classic regular Bourbon County Stout stood waiting. By 12:30 PM, every bottle was gone.

The next day, Goose Island staff visited the eBay website to look for signs of Rare. Sure enough, it was there.

Already posted for resale at $150 per bottle.

15

"We Have to Do Something, and We've Looked at All the Possibilities"

Ryan Tucker was a burly delivery driver at the Wrigleyville brewpub who looked every bit the former Division II offensive lineman that he was. With shoulders wide as a refrigerator, he spent two years as number 64 for the Northern State University football team in Aberdeen, South Dakota. Then he gave up football and transferred back home, to a school in suburban Chicago.

After college, he started working at Goose Island's pub as a bouncer, then graduated to delivery driver. On a peak-of-summer Sunday afternoon before the Cubs hosted the rival St. Louis Cardinals, he was pressed into service as a bar back. Soon came a crisis: the bar ran out of plastic cups. Bartenders pleaded with Tucker. *We need more cups!* He drove to Fulton Street but didn't have a key to the storeroom where sleeves were filled with thousands of Goose Island–emblazoned cups. And he couldn't find someone who did. So Tucker did what any enterprising former offensive lineman facing an agitated pack of bartenders would do: he grabbed a keg and snapped the hinges off the door. Crisis averted—but only until a manager heard what Tucker had done and wrote him up for destroying company property.

When word filtered back to John, his reaction was swift, and broadcast to the entire management team: "No one should be breaking doors down, but why doesn't this guy have a key to the storeroom? *Goddamn it, get this guy a fucking key!*" A door was easier to replace than a loyal, hardworking employee. Before long, Tucker was on the marketing team. Soon he was helping coordinate Goose Island's role at the highest-profile festivals and fundraisers in Chicago.

Tucker embodied a reality at Goose Island: loyal and diligent employees could always rise. It didn't matter if they started as bouncers, hosts, bartenders, or sales grunts. The lazy or self-serving ones, John never forgave. Anyone who did their best could ascend. Anyone who did their best, then struck out on their own, got a pat on the back on the way out the door. When Phil Wymore—the brewer behind Madame Rose—announced he was leaving to start his own brewery, John called him into his office for a five-minute chat. Wymore was stunned and a little nervous. The founder of the company wanted to talk to *him*? He had no idea what to expect. But John shook his hand, thanked him for his service, and offered a piece of advice: choose your distributors very carefully. John was universally cherished in the brewery. Sure, he had a hell of a temper and could get in someone's face with a string of expletives. But he was always quick to acknowledge when he'd been too harsh and usually suggested they talk it out over a beer. He was zealous but fair. And genuinely nice. Everyone knew he couldn't stand to fire anyone.

Even more than owning a brewery, John prided himself on owning a business and building a foundation to make that business hum. He had started at the bottom of a massive company and worked his way up. There was little he admired more than others doing the same, and he relished creating the opportunity. He knew that successful organizations weren't built top-down. They were bottom-up. They were based on problem solving and the right people in the right places.

His most important hire had fallen into his lap: his son. The rest came together over time. He hired Tony Bowker in 2000 to be Goose Island's chief financial officer. The affable blue-eyed Brit with a taste for sailing had held the same position at one of Chicago's largest parking lot companies. When it was sold, Bowker got a financial cushion that made him affordable to an upstart brewery that sorely needed his expertise. Mark Kamarauskas came over to head operations after growing weary of the corporate life at Coca-Cola. Bob Kenney came on as vice president of sales after twenty-three years at Heineken. Though Kenney initially had little understanding of how to sell craft beer—at Heineken, the approach had nothing to do with story, education, or food pairings; it was simply *sell, sell, sell*—John saw Kenney's Big Beer experience as the ability to get things done.

Under the new regime, growth was relentless. Brewing leaped from five twenty-four-hour days to a constant churn in 2007 that didn't slow even for holidays. The sales staff grew from two people to fourteen. Four three-hundred-barrel fermentation tanks arrived, which nearly doubled brewing capacity in a matter of months. When the business to the west of the Fulton Street brewery shut down, John leased the space, blasted through the wall, and built a ten-thousand-square-foot cooler. Before then, pallets of beer awaiting distributor pickup had sat exposed to the summer heat and winter chill.

Matilda, Sofie, and Bourbon County Stout gave Goose Island credibility, but 312 gave it volume, and volume was the engine of any growing beer company. Early in 2010, a second volume beer was released: Green Line Pale Ale. With a solid wood block tap handle that read GREEN LINE in clean sans serif font, it was only moderately identifiable as a Goose Island brand. Much as the phone handle had given 312 a unique identity, the block of wood did the same and allowed Goose Island to argue for a whopping three or four tap handles in one bar—a white goose head for Honker's Ale or IPA, a telephone for 312, a wood block for Green Line, and a gold goose head for one of the Reserve beers. For a brewery growing increasingly savvy about marketing, Green Line offered a fresh twist: it was available only in Chicago and only on draft. It was instantly a special occasion beer—you could only have it while socializing in a bar or restaurant.

Green Line quickly became one of the most popular draft beers in the city, cannibalizing whatever power Honker's Ale had retained after the emergence of 312. Within months, Green Line had nearly one thousand

Chicago accounts; Honker's had fewer than fifty. Tastes had changed. In upper-middle-class ZIP codes, where craft beer was thriving, Green Line became *the* most popular draft beer—ahead of even mighty Miller Lite. The brewery had built an enviable and diverse portfolio: the approachable (312), the buzz worthy (Green Line), the collectible (Bourbon County Stout), and the elevated (Matilda, which was the sales department's "wildly important goal"—WIG for short—due to a profit margin almost double that of 312). The numbers evinced a brewery on the move:

Year	Barrels produced	Growth
2004	49,212	10%
2005	52,879	7%
2006	61,152	16%
2007	88,998	46%
2008	99,946	12%
2009	110,648	11%
2010	126,213	14%
2011	149,788	19%

Goose Island was no longer a craft brewer according to the Brewers Association, but it undeniably made craft beer. By that standard, it had grown to become the eleventh largest maker of craft beer in the nation—right behind Kansas City's Boulevard Brewing and just ahead of Stone Brewing, near San Diego. One Friday afternoon on the brew deck—a small space beside the brew house, where a handful of beers were always on tap for employees—Bob Kenney asked John if he had imagined Goose Island growing so large.

"Absolutely," John told him. "But not this quickly."

By 2009, when Goose Island production had almost doubled in a mere three years, it became clear to John and his executive team that things were changing. There was no going back. The brewery was profitable and more was expected. It was time to grow up.

The shift was subtle but unmistakable. Some brewers saw it as a drift from prioritizing beer production to sales and marketing. The coveted assignments that once went to the brewers—particularly attending beer conferences and festivals—were increasingly spread to other departments. A freewheeling culture inched toward professionalism. In what baffled some and inspired others, staff was sent one by one to Rapport Leadership International outside of Las Vegas, a two-day character-building seminar heavy on self-affirmation: *You're bigger, you're stronger, you're better!* One scenario involved role-playing as if you'd won the lottery—literally won the lottery. Others were made to walk on actual hot coals. The goal was to unleash the unfettered you. John had been to Rapport at the recommendation of one of his consultants, and there he was moved to craft a mission statement that he tucked into the leather-bound organizer he carried throughout the workweek: "I am committed to building an executive management team that encourages teamwork and trust, defines roles and creates a climate of innovation and excellence through the company."

Some criticized Rapport as cultlike or brainwashing, but John was taken with the concept. For a workforce grappling with wild growth and rapid change, he wanted to establish a culture of strong leaders and independence. He thought Rapport's rah-rah tactics could get him there. Goose Island sent thirty-seven employees from across the company to the training, including brewers, salespeople, marketers, and the executive team. At the end of the two days, a coworker who had already been through Rapport would fly out for graduation. Some returned home hoarse from so much yelling, exhilarated and forever changed. Others thought it was silly bullshit, evidence of a craft brewery straying from its roots.

Karen King, fair skinned and wide eyed, managed a St. Louis gymnastics academy when she decided to work in the beer industry. She scoured beer websites, sent her résumé in all directions, and, to increase her odds of meeting people in the industry, took a job at the most prolific chain of craft beer bars in St. Louis, the International Tap House.

She'd been there a few months when Goose Island's Iowa-based sales rep, Paul DeVries, walked in. He was meeting with his St. Louis distributor. Goose Island had been growing at such a rapid clip that it was swiftly adding regional representatives to be the face of the brewery at far-flung beer festivals, supermarket samplings, and beer dinners. DeVries was based in Ames, Iowa, but handled sales and distribution for seven Midwest states. With a thick gold watch, tucked-in button-down shirt, and pinkie ring, DeVries looked more like an insurance agent than the face of one of the nation's ascendant craft breweries. But he and King quickly bonded over a love of beer. She impressed him with her knowledge of Goose Island in particular. Her brother lived in Chicago, and each visit led her to the Clybourn brewpub. She had marveled at its brilliantly inventive beer menu—Matilda in particular. Most craft beer lovers experience a moment of conversion, and for King, the moment was her first sip of Matilda. It was spicy and layered and complex, but approachable and satisfying. It was the first time she'd tasted *Brettanomyces* in a beer. She became such a fan that her brother gave her a case as a wedding present. DeVries liked King's pluck and passion, and said he needed a St. Louis rep. Would she be interested? Of course she would.

King had no sales experience, beer industry or otherwise, but was exactly the kind of person a wildly growing Goose Island liked to hire: an affable beer lover prepared to learn, work hard, and be part of the company's culture. The last round of six interviews was a flight to Chicago, where King met sales director Bob Kenney, Illinois sales manager Ken Stout, and John Hall. She was most nervous to meet John, but that chat proved surprisingly easy; he had a way of putting people at ease.

On her first day as a Goose Island employee, King was handed a list of wholesalers in and around St. Louis and given a mission of pushing 312 Urban Wheat Ale, Matilda, and the seasonal beers—Summertime, Harvest Ale, or Mild Winter—which typically drove volume as impulse buys for supermarket shoppers. King had her foothold in the industry. She would be selling not only Goose Island's portfolio but also the idea of fresh beer made in Chicago. The nation was home to eighteen hundred breweries—the most in more than one hundred years—and craft brewing seemed poised to keep growing. For the first time in ten years, bar and restaurant managers were asking the Bud distributors about craft beer. There were the relics from Anheuser-Busch's previous dalliance with craft—Widmer and Redhook—but now those distributors also had Goose Island to offer. King was the boots on the ground. She cold-called across St. Louis with a cooler full of samples and a daily route sketched out on MapQuest.

King found fast success, gathering 312 handles with almost as much speed as her counterparts in Chicago. But then she ran into a problem: the beer stopped coming. King would sell twenty-five kegs almost immediately—twenty-five new tap handles pouring Goose Island in St. Louis! All because of her! And then, no more beer. There wasn't enough to send her, she was told. She and other remote salespeople sprinkled around the country would order five cases of Matilda and get one. They would order a dozen kegs of 312 and get none.

King's distributors would call in a panic—*If we don't get more beer, we're going to lose those lines to Schlafly or New Belgium!* King would push the message up the chain. Sometimes she could get bottles of the beer with less velocity—Pere Jacques and Sofie, mostly—but very few kegs. Other times she couldn't get beer at all; in a crunch, Goose Island could never short its home market. Instead, places like St. Louis, Iowa City, and Cleveland could do without.

By 2010, the ethos at Goose Island had changed. The steady growth fueled by love for Chicago, beer, and innovation was subsumed by urgency: *work hard, work fast, all this needs to get done, and GO GO GO.* The brewery built of cinder block and brick walls, cement floors and fluorescent lights, had grown into a maze of tubes, pipes, and hoses, jammed to the hilt. There was a constant churn of new tanks arriving. Equipment rumbling. Things changing. Economic and strategic goals transforming.

More.

Now.

The growth was frenzied and unparalleled. People shifted in and out of jobs. Communication could be spotty. Frustrations grew. Brewers felt pressure from sales. Sales felt let down by marketing. It wasn't uncommon to have five different bosses in two years. In 2010 alone, twenty new people were hired into newly created jobs. The new hires who had perceived Goose Island as a large, well-run regional brewery quickly realized that internal structure was charted on the fly. Ever more young salespeople were running around, with marching orders that amounted to a list of wholesalers and volume goals. *And good luck to you!* At its best, craft beer was a creative, progressive, and nurturing industry, in which brewery owners talked about "smart growth" and "building culture." By 2010, it was simply full speed ahead at Goose Island.

It was selling through its seasonal lineup so quickly that the biggest beer-buying weekend of the year—Fourth of July—would clean out the entire supply of Summertime. Fueled by 312 Urban Wheat Ale, which was as much as 70 percent of production during summer, Goose Island was selling ever-more beer. When sales at the local chain of Jewel grocery stores eclipsed one hundred thousand cases, the brewery's management team treated the Jewel beer buyers to a beer-pairing dinner at the brewpub, culminating with the chef's take on a dark chocolate Nestlé Crunch bar, topped with bacon bits and paired with Pere Jacques.

The ever-growing sales staff begged John to brew more IPA; if that beer could be packaged in twelve-packs, instead of just sixers, they could sell *even more beer*. Twelve-packs were the format that drove volume and, ultimately, sales. John said no; sure, IPA twelve-packs would have been popular, but IPA was Goose Island's most expensive core brand to produce. Why make more of the more expensive beer when they already couldn't make enough 312—a cheaper, faster beer?

Times were good at Goose Island. They couldn't make enough beer! But they were also dire. *They couldn't make enough beer.* Casualties abounded. Production of the vaunted Bourbon County Stout dropped by more than one-third—from fifteen hundred barrels to less than a thousand—in 2010 and 2011 because the equipment was so busy churning out 312. Goose Island could have made *only* 312, and it still wouldn't have met demand. So they trimmed where they could. Brewing and fermentation of 312 had typically taken twelve days—eight days to ferment, then four days to "crash" the beer as yeast dropped out and flavor was locked in. Suddenly, brewers were given one day to crash the beer. Bourbon County Stout saw similar trims. The best versions of the beer were always a blend of older and younger beers, but they started making so much that the timeline was diminished, and all the beer was mostly the same age by the time it was bottled. Brewers grumbled, wondering if quantity was valued over quality.

With wild growth, and the sheer volume of beer churning out of Fulton Street, came missteps. In 2010, the brewery recalled six hundred barrels of Matilda—the equivalent of twelve hundred kegs—due to a *Lactobacillus* infection that added an unwanted layer of sourness.

However, the innovation brewers turned the proverbial lemons into lemonade—or, in this case, Matilda into Dominique. The last two hundred barrels of infected Matilda were diverted into bourbon barrels as an experiment. Voilà: a new sister was born. Some people said Dominique was Goose Island's best beer yet. "That's the really exciting thing with craft beer: people want what is new and exciting," Greg said of Dominique upon its release in early 2011. "It shows how far the beer drinkers have come and that it is an exciting time to be a brewer." Months later, Goose Island recalled six thousand cases of Sofie for a similar reason.

In a bid to keep up with production, the brewery announced on a Friday during the spring of 2010 that it would stop making Nut Brown and Oatmeal Stout, two well-made beers that appealed to the original Goose Island audience but not the new generation of drinkers who sought the easy-drinking mainstream (312) or adventure (Bourbon County Stout). The next night, Nut Brown won its second World Beer Cup gold medal. There it was: Goose Island was winning medals for beers it killed off to keep up with demand. Something had to give.

Still, it was an undeniably exciting place to work during an exciting time. The secret of variety, choice, and innovation was out; everyone wanted a piece of craft beer. Breweries were opening at the rate of one a day. Chicago had gone from one production brewery—Goose Island—to nearly a dozen. Goose Island was in the midst of a sixteen-year run of winning twenty-five medals at the Great American Beer Festival—at least one every year. (Twelve came during the particularly fertile five-year period between 2007 and 2011.) But there were endless questions and no right answers. How do you grow when there's nowhere left to grow? When there is no money to grow? Goose Island opened its doors when John Hall was forty-five. Now he was staring at seventy.

In December 2010, John assembled his management team for its regular Friday meeting. As always, they gathered in the conference room off the long hallway between John's and Greg's offices: chief operating officer Tony Bowker, sales director Bob Kenney, head of operations Mark Kamarauskas, Illinois sales director Ken Stout, John, and Greg.

John didn't waste time.

"We have to do something," he said. "And we've looked at all the possibilities."

Half the table already knew what John would say. The other half wouldn't believe what they were about to hear.

Part II

Selling Out

16

"No Matter What Happens Monday, We'll Still Clean the Kettle"

THE MEETING WAS CALLED FOR 9:00 AM on Monday morning. Every employee was summoned.

Sales reps from a half dozen states were ordered to fly in. Overnight brewers who'd just finished their shifts were told to return. The receptionist's orders were simple: only buzz in employees. No outside sales people. No drop-in visitors. And for the love of god, no media. The meeting had been announced late the previous week, and with conspicuously little context. Just be there, they were told.

There would be no sleeping in for the handful of brewers who had just flown back from the Craft Brewers Conference in San Francisco. The four-day gathering had been an industry celebration: craft beer was back. In his annual address, the head of the Brewers Association announced that craft was up to nearly 5 percent of the nation's beer sales, and the ceiling wasn't in sight. "We've got share growth, the idea of 'local' is now mainstream, millennials identify with craft, and nearly everyone believes craft will double or triple its share," he told a ballroom packed with brewers, salespeople, and brewery owners.

The keynote address was given by Sierra Nevada's Ken Grossman and Anchor's Fritz Maytag, two iconic elder statesmen. Both men had survived decades of industry ebbs and flows and Big Beer's occasional blitzkrieg. Their address came in the form of a conversation while seated in thickly upholstered chairs, each with his own bottle of Fritz and Ken's Ale, a collaborative imperial stout made to celebrate Sierra Nevada's thirtieth anniversary. Maytag recalled mixed feelings about snatching up used equipment from the regional breweries that faltered throughout the 1970s, as Anheuser-Busch and Miller tightened their grips on the nation's taste buds.

"A lot of these regional breweries were closing, and in many cases, the closing was a family tragedy," Maytag told the room. "They were heartbroken, I'm sure, and they would close down without cleaning up. But I recall going to the Erie Brewing Company, which had closed, and I looked in the kettle, and it was spotless. Spotless! They were a family brewery that went way back, and you could just tell the pride was still there."

After the address, everyone filtered into the Hilton's expansive hallway. Keith Gabbett, a brewer at Goose Island for two years, turned to two of his coworkers.

"No matter what happens Monday, we'll still clean the kettle," he said.

March 28, 2011, was unseasonably cold in Chicago. Temperatures barely nudged above freezing.

In coats and hats and gloves, close to one hundred Goose Island employees filed into the warehouse behind the brewery's loading dock. It was a gritty and unceremonious space, but large enough to accommodate so many people.

In small clusters, they huddled and tried to stay warm. Sales and marketing had been told the previous Thursday of a mandatory conference call on Friday. During the call, the head of sales, Bob Kenney, said there would be a "mandatory training program" at the brewery on

Monday. He pleaded ignorance when anyone pushed for details; it was a human resources initiative, he said. Goose Island spent thousands of dollars getting sales staff to the brewery on last-minute airfares from Columbus, Minneapolis, Des Moines, St. Louis, and New York City. Others drove in from Milwaukee. Now, gathered in the warehouse, everyone tried to piece together the clues.

Some swore that John was retiring.

Others suspected that the long-rumored sparkling-new Goose Island brewery would finally be built along the Chicago River.

Or maybe it was a 100 percent sale to the Craft Brewers Alliance. That would be an unpleasant outcome. After all, the CBA was 32 percent owned by Anheuser-Busch. But Widmer, Redhook, and newly acquired Kona were solid enough brands. It wouldn't be a disaster.

The most hopeful among them had noticed John's bright spirits in recent weeks. The news had to be good. One veteran brewer even brought in Belgian lambics from home that he had been cellaring to celebrate the mystery news. Even if John was retiring, well, it would be sad, but handing the reins to Greg would be cause for celebration. How could the company *not* be passed to Greg? Goose Island was practically his birthright.

The staff milled about the loading dock, keeping warm and waiting for John to arrive. The previous week, a woman who worked in marketing was told to be sure that the company's audiovisual equipment was fully charged. She thought it was an odd request; the brewery didn't have any events planned. But now, standing in a corner with video camera in hand, she understood. Her job was to capture whatever was about to unfold.

John and his inner circle had quietly spent months working toward this moment. There had been code names and secret meetings far from the brewery. John had worked with a public relations consultant specializing in crisis management. Speak in images, she said. Be concrete. Tell the story that would be repeated over dinner tables that night. Employees would be scared. They wouldn't be able to visualize the future. Create the future that would put them at ease. Be confident and sincere. Strong body language would follow. They practiced his delivery on camera. John winced when he watched it back.

Goose Island's chief operating officer, Tony Bowker, had drafted a chart of when to reveal the news to whom. The previous Wednesday, he'd sat down with eight top managers—heads of brewing, sales, marketing, operations, wholesaler services, supply chain, design, and the controller—to reveal the news and to plan the day. Bowker implored everyone in attendance: not a word was to be shared before Monday. But a day later, a salesperson caused a minor stir with a text message to a marketing colleague:

> hey, do y'all have a conference call tomorrow about the big news?

The message had been passed on to Bowker, who immediately emailed Bob Kenney. Did he know anything about this? Kenney said speculation was obviously underway; he figured his salesperson was just fishing. Two *Chicago Tribune* reporters had reached out to confirm rumors. Both were shooed away. Word was clearly filtering out.

The secrecy had built tension and adrenaline for months, and as Bowker stepped into the warehouse on that Monday morning, there finally was relief. Some letting go. No one would want to hear the news, but Bowker was ready to send it into the world. Ready to move on and to live in the new reality. During Goose Island's lean years, he was fond of telling his marketing staff that they were making history—they just couldn't see it yet. They were about to see it.

John returned home that morning from Tobago, where his daughter, Beth, lived with her family. John and Pat's trip had already been booked when the negotiations turned to an agreement, so the announcement would have to wait. John would return March 27. It was decided: the news would be delivered first thing on March 28, a Monday morning.

But the plane was late, landing in Chicago Monday at 2:00 AM. John crawled into bed an hour later. Nerves kept him awake. The day had arrived.

Finally, he drifted off for a couple of hours.

John arrived at the brewery early that Monday morning. He and Bowker needed to talk to the trade press before Wall Street opened. Then would come the staff. He and his executive team brainstormed dozens of likely questions, whether from employees or media:

> Will there be job losses?
> Will production be moved?
> Who will be in charge?
> Will the Goose Island name go away?
> Will the brewery stay open?
> What's the timeline for this transaction?
> Will Goose Island expand capacity?
> What will my business card now read?

Nothing could surprise him. Or that was the idea.

Just before 9:00 AM, John walked into the warehouse and small-talked a bit. He took his spot at the front of the room, gathered his breath, and then said the words he'd spent months practicing.

Everyone knew the challenges Goose Island faced. They couldn't make enough beer. They needed to grow. After surveying the options, he found the answer.

A sale.

A 100 percent sale to Anheuser-Busch. To the biggest beer company in the world.

John would stay on as chief executive officer and retain ownership of the original Clybourn Avenue brewpub. Bowker would remain chief operating officer. Then came the bombshell: Greg was done. Anheuser-Busch had wanted him to stay on. His father had wanted him to stay on. Initially *he* had wanted to stay on. But Greg said it was time to create something for himself. He would consult a few days per month on Goose Island's beers, branding, and strategy, but after twenty years, his last day as brewmaster would be April 30—the day before the deal closed. Then the reins would be passed to head brewer Brett Porter. Greg was in the room but didn't say a word.

Otherwise, John told to a stunned crowd, nothing would change. Goose Island would stay in Chicago. No one would lose a job. They would be able to make more beer. This was solving a problem.

He talked for only a few minutes, extemporaneously, about how it had been his dream to travel anywhere in the United States and order a Goose Island beer. With Anheuser-Busch, that would be possible. He said he loved the company and the employees, and that of all the options, this was the best.

He wanted to underscore that point: this was best for both the company and everyone in that room. He said he was surprised that such a large company had met his terms, but it had. The business cards would not say Anheuser-Busch. Neither would the paychecks. Anheuser-Busch would sink $1.3 million in immediate upgrades, including additional brewing equipment. The deal was happening on his terms, he said.

Shock stared back at him. Anger. Betrayal. Didn't he understand that these people loved the thing he had built? It was theirs as much as his. He was corrupting it.

Then the questions came. He couldn't help growing annoyed when someone asked if Anheuser-Busch might shut down the brewery. Or lay everyone off and move production to St. Louis. Of course they would still have jobs, he said. He wouldn't have made the deal otherwise. A handful of good soldiers applauded. But mostly there was confusion and disbelief.

John mingled briefly. A longtime member of the marketing team, Suzanne Wolcott, wouldn't talk to him. Wouldn't even look at him. She was the head of education for Goose Island, a face of the company preaching the gospel of good beer at bars, restaurants, and beer festivals across the country. She'd sat through countless meetings with Anheuser-Busch distributors and heard them mock craft beer. They saw it as the oddball stepchild to the beer that real Americans drank. And John was joining that team? John saw Wolcott's tears and rage—everyone saw it—and he tried to talk to her. She walked away.

What he wanted people to know, but what few of them could hear, was that he knew how they felt. Or at least he thought he did. He'd been through two takeovers of Container Corporation, including one by a global oil company. But they couldn't hear him. He came from the world of boxes. This was beer. How could he know? He was the one cashing out. They were the ones left behind.

John went off to work the phones and make sense of the deal for the press. It was the first time the King of Beers had bought 100 percent of an American craft brewery. On its website, Goose Island posted a letter to customers. Beside a photo of a smiling John Hall in a brown sport coat bearing a Goose Island lapel pin, it read:

> March 28, 2011
>
> Dear Friends,
>
> When I first started Goose Island Clybourn in 1988, drinkers were just beginning to explore new beer styles and "craft beer" was a term that no one had even thought of. I couldn't imagine the explosive growth that craft beer has had in the last few years, or the amazing creativity of so many new brewers, and the discovery of the amazing possibilities of beer by a whole generation of drinkers.
>
> I am very proud of Goose Island's contribution to this craft beer movement, of the many awards won by our brewers, our growing number of employees, our support of the communities and life of Chicago, and the friendship of so many beer lovers in Chicago and elsewhere.
>
> Over the past five years our partnerships with Craft Brewers Alliance and Anheuser-Busch have enabled Goose Island to reach a growing number of beer drinkers. This has fueled our growth to the point that demand for our beers has outgrown the capacity of our brewery. Recently, we've even had to limit production of some classic and medal-winning styles. To keep up with growing demand from drinkers we've explored a variety of paths to secure new capital to support our growth.

> Today's agreement to consolidate ownership of Goose Island under Anheuser-Busch will provide us with the best resources available to continue along our path of growth and innovation.
>
> I am more excited than ever about Goose Island's future. With the support and financial backing of our new partner, we will continue to brew our authentic classic styles, develop new amazing beers, and serve our drinkers.
>
> Cheers!
>
> John Hall

At 12:03 PM, John emailed a word-for-word copy to every Goose Island employee—with the exception of the sunny "Cheers!" signoff.

John J. Hall—the brewer behind 312 Urban Wheat Ale—started making beer at the age of thirty, after getting a home brew kit for his birthday. Brewing remained no more than a hobby until the fateful day that he thumbed through a newspaper during a break from his job as audiovisual supervisor at a Marriott hotel in downtown Chicago. He landed on an article about a California winery wading into beer by sending its employees to a brewing school in Chicago. The article didn't name the school, so Hall asked the guy at his local home brew store: What is this school that teaches you to make beer in Chicago? The Siebel Institute, he was told. Hall had to wait more than a year to be admitted, but he spent the time—especially those breaks at the Marriott—studying brewing textbooks. Finally, the day came. He saved all his vacation time so that he could continue to draw a paycheck while enrolled in brewing school. When he graduated two months later, he traded his red polyester blazer for an entry-level job at his hometown brewery. He was equal parts thrilled and proud.

During the next fourteen years, John J. rose to become Goose Island's lead brewer. He was proud to be part of the daily grind. The innovation brewers got to create wild experiments and try new things. John J.

churned out the beer that was the company's backbone. There was no better example than his own creation, which had propelled Goose Island into the stratosphere: 312 Urban Wheat Ale.

March 28, 2011, was the second day of a weeklong family trip to Ireland. A relative who could scarcely stand not to have her cell phone in hand was scanning Facebook when she screamed—"Oh my God!"

John J. went cold. He wondered who back home had died.

His sister-in-law told him what she'd read: Goose Island had been sold to Anheuser-Busch. He didn't believe it. She must have seen an old story about the minority sale from five years earlier. No, she said. This was new. John J. didn't have an international calling plan, but he powered up his cell phone. Sure enough, a message awaited from the head of operations, Mark Kamarauskas.

Employees were shuttled by department to a series of smaller meetings. Brett Porter, the round-bellied head brewer who was about to be promoted to brewmaster, handled the brewers. His primary concern was how to answer questions about the inevitable drug testing that came with life as part of a conglomerate. But the brewers had few questions. Most just wanted to get out of there and start pondering their futures. Mark Kamarauskas drifted between operations and warehouse staff, packaging and sanitation, the lab and maintenance. Concern centered mostly on who would continue to have jobs.

Sales and marketing was taken to the Wrigleyville brewpub, where they headed up the stairs with disbelief. They sat in a room overlooking Clark Street usually reserved for private parties. Bob Kenney spoke. Ken Stout, the head of sales in Illinois, spoke. Tony Bowker eventually showed up. They reinforced the point: this was good for everyone in the room. Under Anheuser-Busch, the brewery would grow and everyone would have a chance to rise.

A woman with graying hair came to the front of the room. No one recognized her. She was Ellen Malloy, a Greg Hall ally specializing in restaurant industry public relations. She echoed the theme of the day:

nothing would change. She compared the sale to the $360 million deal between McDonald's and Chipotle in 1988, when the Denver-based burrito chain totaled just fourteen stores. McDonald's helped grow the brand to nearly five hundred restaurants across the country before selling its stake in 2006. And look at Chipotle now, Malloy said; it was a restaurant industry giant. No one who walked into a Chipotle knew McDonald's had a hand in its growth. All McDonald's did was let it grow.

Chipotle? They weren't fucking Chipotle! Who was this woman?

Most important, Malloy told them, was how they talked about the deal. Distributors and bar managers would be asking questions. So would family and friends. Stick to the basics, she said.

Nothing will change.

This will allow us to make more beer.

This will allow us to make better beer.

Nothing will change.

We'll finally be able to keep up with demand.

We'll be able to make even more Bourbon County!

Nothing will change.

Say it with confidence, she said. Enthusiasm.

And don't talk to reporters. They would be reaching out. Offer a polite "no comment," and urge them to contact the brewery.

Suzanne Wolcott was bawling.

Someone whispered that she wouldn't last a week.

But through the shock and disappointment, some of it made sense. There wasn't enough beer. No one knew it better than the salespeople in that room. If Goose Island would finally be able to keep up with demand and grow, well, maybe this deal wasn't all bad? It was the American dream to build something and sell it for millions. Good for John Hall.

Then again, Anheuser-Busch was the very thing they had been fighting all these years.

Oh, and one other thing, they were told. In a few months, everyone would be subject to a hair follicle drug test.

A handful of employees sneaked to a top-floor room and smoked marijuana from a pipe. If they were going to be drug tested, they might as well get high while they could. Then they went back down and pondered their futures over hamburgers, fries, and pitchers of beer.

At 3:00 PM, everyone reconvened at the brewery. John said Anheuser-Busch had bought Goose Island because it couldn't create such a thing—the beer, the people, the culture. It had tried. It had failed.

Craft beer had won, he said.

Goose Island had won.

Through puffy eyes, Suzanne Wolcott drove to a taco, beer, and whiskey joint called Big Star, in the trendy Wicker Park neighborhood, to meet up with John Laffler and Tom Korder, the brewers in charge of Goose Island's barrel-aging program. The three of them sat there for hours, commiserating, drinking bourbon and Three Floyds' Gumballhead. Three Floyds would never have sold out, damn it.

Laffler pledged never to work on another batch of Goose Island beer. That morning, while John Hall was still speaking, he had texted a friend at Chicago's upstart Revolution Brewing to see if he could work there for a few months; Laffler planned to start his own brewery anyway. Korder, who was also planning to start a new brewery, posted something salty enough on social media—about how this was far blacker than Black Friday—that everyone urged him to take it down.

Greg Hall came by to reassure them, but his visit was awkward and brief. When he left, Wolcott ripped the Matilda case off her iPhone and hurled it across the bar. Right into the garbage.

17

"Not Fuck It Up"

In October 2010, six months before the company-wide meeting at the loading dock, John Hall's phone rang. It was Tony Short calling.

Short was the Anheuser-Busch veteran who had executed the company's initial minority-stake deal with Goose Island five years earlier. After starting in the beer giant's internal auditing department, he ascended to Wholesaler Development, the small, powerful group dedicated to monitoring the company's vast network of distributors.

Short wanted to know if John had a few minutes for a private chat at Anheuser-Busch's upcoming sales and marketing conference in New Orleans.

Of course, John said, and hung up.

John had recently hired Chicago investment banker Livingstone Partners to find the money that would solve the brewery's vexing crossroad: it couldn't make enough beer and didn't have the money to grow—but needed to grow. Goose Island had broadcast its partnership with Livingstone loudly, intending to make clear that it was open for business. It was 42 percent owned by the Craft Brewers Alliance. Now it was ready to sell the other 58 percent.

Tony Short heard them. If he was willing to solve Goose Island's problems, John Hall was ready to listen.

Two weeks later, John stood in the cavernous Ernest N. Morial Convention Center in downtown New Orleans, pouring Goose Island samples for the nation's Anheuser-Busch wholesalers. He had flown down with Greg, chief operating officer Tony Bowker, and vice president of sales Bob Kenney with a goal of convincing distributors to put 312, Honker's Ale, and IPA on their trucks. The ones from North Dakota or Arkansas or West Virginia would take one sip of IPA and frown.

"No one's going to buy your beer where I live," they'd say.

A few minutes before 4:00 PM, John headed up to the third floor of the sprawling convention center. Tony Short had reserved a small room, two floors above the bustling conference floor, where he could churn through dozens of covert meetings. Most lasted just ten or fifteen minutes.

They shook hands and John took a seat. Short asked if John was interested in selling the remaining 58 percent of Goose Island to Anheuser-Busch. What didn't need to be said was the crucial difference between this version of Anheuser-Busch and the one to which John had sold 42 percent of his company five years earlier.

In 2005 Anheuser-Busch was not only the largest beer company in the nation but also a global business icon. In 2010 it was merely a piece on a chess board: a subsidiary of Anheuser-Busch InBev, the world's new largest beer company. Anheuser-Busch had become but a division of a Belgium-based beer conglomerate run by Brazilians. Its development was one of the astounding business stories of the industrialized era.

It began in 1989, when three of Brazil's most successful investment bankers—Jorge Paulo Lemann, Carlos Alberto Sicupira, and Marcel Herrmann Telles—bought the hundred-year-old Brazilian brewery Companhia Cervejaria Brahma for a reported $50 million. It was a fairly pedestrian company at the time, barely returning dividends while pumping out the same sort of bland light lager as most other breweries. But a ruthless banker's approach tightened business practices and squeezed profits. That included shifting some beer production from Brazil to Venezuela, which, ironically, made the Brazilian brand Brazil's biggest import. "It was just cheaper to do," Telles told media at the time. In 1995 alone, Brahma sales grew 73 percent.

In 1999 Brahma took control of its chief Brazilian rival, Companhia Antarctica Paulista, in a $7 billion deal. The resulting company, Ambev, became the world's third-largest beer company, and the largest in South America. The deal was approved by Brazilian regulators despite fears that Ambev would stifle consumer choice, and the fact that Ambev would account for 70 percent of the nation's beer market. Three years later, Ambev fortified its power by adding Quinsa, brewer of Argentina's top-selling beer, Quilmes.

Then came the biggest move yet for Lemann, Sicupira, and Telles. In 2004 Ambev merged with Europe's largest brewery, Interbrew, of Belgium, which itself was the product of a 1987 merger between Brouwerij Artois—brewer of Stella Artois—and Piedboeuf, which produced Belgium's top-selling beer, Jupiler. The deal made billionaires of Lemann, Sicupira, and Telles and resulted in InBev, which supplanted Anheuser-Busch as the world's largest beer company. The creation of InBev was framed as a merger but was in fact a takeover; the Brazilian oligarchs were in command, and Lemann's protégé, fellow Brazilian Carlos Brito, was soon installed as CEO.

The Brazilians next turned their sights on the biggest prize of all. Led at the time by August Busch IV, Anheuser-Busch had no interest in being acquired when InBev's first bid came in at $46 billion during the summer of 2008. Busch and his board scrambled to fight off the takeover and attempted to make the deal too costly by roping Mexico's Grupo Modelo, maker of Corona, into the deal. Anheuser-Busch filed a lawsuit claiming that InBev had misled investors. It cited InBev's Cuban businesses as a reason for shareholders to reject the bid. But years of failing to anticipate the consolidating global beer industry weakened Anheuser-Busch's hand, and when InBev upped its offer to $52 billion, the deal was done.

A tremor rippled through St. Louis. The billionaire Brazilians were ruthless cost cutters across their companies, which came to include Heinz, Kraft, Burger King, and Canadian coffee-and-doughnut chain Tim Hortons. They were known to sell private jets (and then fly coach), close factories, lay off countless employees, and even limit color printing.

To soothe nerves, the world's new largest beer company incorporated the name of its American conquest and pledged to keep its North American headquarters in St. Louis (though it was gradually moved to New York City). The inevitable purge soon followed in the gilded, old-guard halls of Anheuser-Busch, starting with August Busch IV. A handful of the savviest veterans stayed to help integrate cultures, including veteran marketing executive Dave Peacock, a second-generation Anheuser-Busch employee who met his wife on his first day at the company. Peacock was named president of the new Anheuser-Busch—the one that was a subsidiary of Anheuser-Busch InBev—but there was no question who ran things: the Brazilians. The extraordinarily savvy, wealthy, well-educated, and aggressive Brazilians, for whom beer was simply a financial bet.

But the deal that had roiled St. Louis raised barely an eyebrow in Chicago. The advantages of Anheuser-Busch's distribution network remained the same after the InBev takeover. So was the speed-dial access to St. Louis and some of the industry's best technicians. No Brazilian ever showed up to look around or kick the tires on their little investment. As far as anyone at Goose Island could tell, the Brazilians didn't even know they existed.

So it was little wonder that it wasn't a Brazilian reaching out in New Orleans. It was Anheuser-Busch veteran Tony Short. And his question was simple: Was John Hall interested in selling his brewery to the world's largest beer company?

John said yes.

Pat Hall didn't like it. Goose Island had been built by the Hall family. It was difficult to fathom as anything else. And she worried about Greg.

Greg didn't like it either. He understood it. But he didn't like it. John was the risk taker and the businessman. Greg made Goose Island what it was. He had worked for the company since the age of twenty-two, when he was thin and had a head full of thick sandy hair. Now he was forty-five and carrying the weight of all those beer dinners. He had two bad knees and walked with a limp. He was divorced with two kids. He'd have liked to keep the business in the family and make the decisions that took Goose Island into the next generation. Maybe even pass the business to his kids one day. But he understood. That wasn't an option. John had never promised it.

Yet Greg was essential during the process of shopping the company. John and Tony Bowker led the effort, but when it came time to tell the story of Goose Island with bankers and beer executives, it was Greg who spoke. He *was* the story. Without the story, Goose Island was nothing but liquid in a bottle.

John and Tony had looked at several potential routes for the company. A sale to private equity was an option. John was impressed with Cincinnati-based DeWitt Capital Group, which would have bought the brewery and left Greg in charge. It likely would have meant a new Goose Island brewery. There was nothing John and Greg wanted more, though they envisioned it in two different places. Greg wanted the site of the old Finkl Steel plant, just north of a bend in the Chicago River, two blocks from where hundreds of thousands of cars cruised by every day on Interstate 90/94. He envisioned a gleaming urban brewery in the middle of the city, built to look like it had been there for a hundred years. On its roof, a Goose Island logo would glow, just like the iconic red GENESEE BEER sign lighting up downtown Auburn, New York. John preferred a spot one mile south, along a gritty stretch of Elston Avenue opposite the actual Goose Island, where a brewery could be built with a roof deck overlooking the river and the city's majestic skyline.

But even if a new brewery resulted from a sale to private equity, and Greg stayed in charge, there was one daunting risk: the endgame. Odds were good that a private equity firm would look to boost the value of Goose Island, then score a profit within five or ten years by selling it to the highest bidder. And who knew who that might be?

MillerCoors had invited John to lunch to see if there might be a fit. In early 2011, he spent a couple of hours over a white tablecloth at a Michelin-starred restaurant in downtown Chicago with two members of Tenth and Blake, MillerCoors's craft wing formed six months earlier: senior director of strategy and operations Jeff White (in the midst of a Big Beer diversion between stints at Boston Beer and Sierra Nevada) and Dick Leinenkugel (who had transitioned into mergers and acquisitions after twenty years running sales and marketing for the brewery started by his great-great-grandfather in 1867). It was a cordial meeting among industry veterans. Like Anheuser-Busch, Tenth and Blake was beginning to devise a response to the return of craft. John nodded with appreciation as White and Leinenkugel discussed a possible fit with MillerCoors, but he kept quiet about his meeting with Anheuser-Busch. Had he been able to enter Miller's distribution network ten years earlier, as he'd wanted, a sale to MillerCoors would have made sense. But now he was wound deeply into the Anheuser-Busch network. And that made Anheuser-Busch seem like the best option.

There was only one true alternative to Anheuser-Busch: selling the remaining 58 percent to the Craft Brewers Alliance. Even though it was partly owned by Anheuser-Busch, the CBA was an independent publicly traded entity and eager to bring Goose Island into the fold with Redhook, Widmer, and Kona.

Discussions began in early October—before John even met with Tony Short in New Orleans—when CBA CEO Terry Michaelson, a longtime Widmer executive, flew to Chicago to make his pitch. Flanked by investment bankers from both sides, Michaelson laid out his vision of Goose Island's growth into a dominant midwestern player, battling Kansas City's Boulevard Brewing and Kalamazoo's Bell's Brewery for regional supremacy. Meanwhile, higher-end brands like Bourbon County Stout and Matilda would be funneled nationally to the savviest beer markets. While he couldn't promise a new Goose Island brewery, that would be the goal—a facility large enough to also produce Redhook, Widmer, and Kona for the Midwest. In the meantime, Goose Island's volume beers would continue to be made at CBA breweries on the East and West Coasts for those markets. As numbers were tossed around, it was clear that Goose Island valued itself far higher than the CBA did. No one was happy with the meeting.

Still, the next week, Michaelson followed up with an email thanking John for the discussion, saying he wanted to be "a partner that helps you solve strategic obstacles that may prevent you from accomplishing your growth goals." John replied the next day that he was open to further talks and wanted their bankers to hammer out a valuation. If there was going to be an offer, John wanted to know what it would be.

Michaelson was back in touch three weeks later, saying he looked forward to continuing negotiations while trying to bond over a common adversary: Anheuser-Busch.

"We value our partnership with you and appreciate how you have worked with us over time—even when AB has made it difficult for all of us," Michaelson wrote. "It is exciting to finally be at a place in our companies' development where we have clarity in how we will manage AB going forward and to have a strong vision for the future."

John was in no hurry to get back to him.

He preferred the common adversary.

What Michaelson didn't know was that since his trip to Chicago, John had met with Tony Short in New Orleans. Now, Goose Island and Anheuser-Busch were planning another meeting to hammer out details of a potential sale. That meeting happened December 10, 2010, a day that began with Dave Peacock flying to Chicago's Midway International Airport.

Goose Island had been on Peacock's radar since well before he had an ounce of power at Anheuser-Busch. His wife was a former Chicago resident and still had friends there. The Peacocks visited a couple of times a year through the 1990s, and trips to the Goose Island brewpub were usually in order. Peacock even threw his wife a birthday party at the Wrigleyville pub. He came to admire the company. He saw it as willing to stretch boundaries while understanding the importance of process and responsible business.

John, Greg, and Tony Bowker hosted Peacock at the University Club, a 125-year-old private club built of dark wood and gray stone in the heart of downtown Chicago. John had joined less than a year earlier precisely for this reason; he needed a quiet place to meet with bankers, advisors, and prospective buyers.

Peacock said he was there primarily to listen. He knew they were interested. They knew he was interested. But he wanted to hear their goals and understand how they could be met as part of the world's largest beer company. John and Tony launched into a four-page presentation that was part vision statement ("Continue expanding Goose Island's market leading position in craft beer within Chicago and the Midwest"), part sales pitch ("Demand-pull for Goose Island products among consumers is difficult to replicate, providing significant scarcity value"), and part mandate. They handed Peacock a list of demands:

Remain an autonomous, Chicago-headquartered company

- CEO (John Hall) located in Chicago, reporting to a senior executive within the Anheuser-Busch organization
- Brewing, sales, and marketing functions report to John Hall
- Stationery, cards, phones, email, vendor checks, paychecks, and 401k plan should all be identified as Goose Island
- Maintain an independent culture (e.g., Leinenkugel)
- Maintain support for local brewing and cultural communities

Brewing Operations

- Based in Chicago
- Supervised by Goose Island Brewmaster (Greg Hall)
- Transitional outsourcing of 312 (in cans) and Classic and Seasonal brews to fulfill near term growth opportunities
- Plan to add capacity in existing or new brewery in Chicago to meet demand for regional, alternatively fermented and barrel-aged beers
- Continued focus on improving sustainability and reducing environmental impact of brewery

Peacock was amenable to every point, and for a simple reason: Goose Island was an ideal acquisition. It was based in a city where Anheuser-Busch had unusually low market share. Chicago drinkers—like drinkers in the Rocky Mountains, the Northeast, and the Pacific Northwest—disproportionally favored craft beer. And most crucially, consumers liked Goose Island. It performed well on preference tests, where panels were given a beer, its label, and a few details about the brewery—"story," as the marketing folks called it. Goose Island scored even better than Sierra Nevada. Much of the appeal, Peacock concluded, was the story. Being "Chicago's craft beer" resonated. Chicago was a city of sports, crime, politics, architecture, and big shoulders. It was a cosmopolitan streak in a working-class ethic. People wanted its beer. So did Anheuser-Busch.

Yes, Peacock agreed. John would report to him, and him alone. Goose Island would be left alone to do what it had always done, but with additional resources. Production of 312 Urban Wheat Ale and other beers would be shipped off to Anheuser-Busch plants so that Goose Island could grow its higher-end beers. And, of course: the brewery would remain based in Chicago. (All the promises were made on a handshake basis, with the exception of a pledge in the purchase agreement to invest at least $1 million "to acquire additional brewing assets for installation at [Goose Island's] Chicago brewery as soon as practicable.")

John left the meeting convinced. Anheuser-Busch was the answer.

The business would grow and its spirit remain intact. He had worked for a big company and ascended its ranks. He knew how takeovers worked. Some acquisitions were rooted in cutting costs, slashing staff, and ratcheting up profits. Others were quite the opposite: a bigger company needing to absorb a culture and a product that it couldn't create on its own. John was certain that a Goose Island sale would be the latter scenario. Sure, some things would be lost. Far more would be gained. Blowback was inevitable. But, ultimately, he believed he would be validated.

In January 2011, Anheuser-Busch sent its director of global brands and a packaging manager for a one-day sweep of the Fulton Street brewery to sketch out future capacity plans, followed by lunch with John and Greg at the brewpub. (The old Anheuser-Busch would have flown them up first-class; as part of InBev, they delayed the visit by a day to save $130 on airfare.) Goose Island weighed whether to devise a cover story to explain the presence of two Anheuser-Busch workers poking around the brewery, but they decided no curiosity would be raised due to the existing Craft Brewers Alliance relationship. The fact that St. Louis had any interest about what was happening at Goose Island was generally taken as a badge of honor.

Eventually, the bankers reached a number: $22.5 million for the 58 percent stake owned by John, Greg, Bowker, and a small group of investors. (John had the largest single stake—24 percent—which would have netted him $5.4 million; Greg's 7 percent stake would equate to nearly $1.6 million.) They signed a term sheet on February 18, 2011. However, secrecy remained paramount; they were still five weeks from an announcement. Goose Island adopted Anheuser-Busch's code name for the deal: Giant. Anheuser-Busch was "the Giant." Traveling to St. Louis was "going up the beanstalk." The few people aware of the deal called its inevitable announcement "G-Day."

But there was one hurdle before that announcement, and it was significant: the Craft Brewers Alliance had a right to match any offer for Goose Island's majority stake. To everyone's surprise, it announced it would exercise that right.

At first, Terry Michaelson wasn't sure that his company would be able to match. News of Goose Island and Anheuser-Busch negotiations had stunned him; he learned of the agreement while visiting Kona's brewery in Hawaii, during a conference call with Peacock. Michaelson had no idea what they would be discussing when Peacock requested the call. But after hanging up, and overcoming his shock, he called his bank to find out if it would finance matching the offer. It did. The irony was lost on no one: the CBA, which was 32.2 percent owned by Anheuser-Busch, and which had two Anheuser-Busch representatives on its board, was now its primary competition for Goose Island. The CBA was a publicly traded company unto itself, and Michaelson's obligation was to its shareholders—not Anheuser-Busch.

But John remained committed to the idea that Anheuser-Busch was the smarter move, even if it would be a tougher sell both to his employees and beer drinkers. With the CBA, he believed, Goose Island would never be more than a regional player, forever a stepchild in the Portland-based family. With Anheuser-Busch, the possibilities were almost literally limitless. His right-hand man, Tony Bowker, agreed; you didn't get into the ring with Anheuser-Busch without intending to make a deal.

Invoking Goose Island's legal name, John told Michaelson by email that he was unequivocally opposed to an acquisition by the CBA: "We endorse and are excited about the acquisition of Fulton Street by AB based on several factors, including AB's express support of Goose Island's culture of independent innovation in the upper echelon of craft beer, their commitment to invest in the growth of Goose Island's strategic brands, their recognition of the importance of continued investment in brewing capacity in Chicago and their commitment to the continued leadership of Goose Island's current management."

If the CBA held firm, John said, it would have his brewery, but not him. He would resign.

Yet it pushed ahead. Michaelson made the case that Anheuser-Busch could hardly be trusted; who knew where things could go as part of the evil empire? He recruited Kona's president, Mattson Davis, to appeal to John. The CBA even drafted a press release dated March 31, 2011: "Craft Brewers Alliance and Goose Island Beer Company Expand Relationship," with a secondary headline that threw a little shade in the direction of St. Louis and, arguably, John: "Chicago-based Goose Island Enhances Distribution, Marketing and Production Capabilities as Part of Group Dedicated to Craft Brewing." The CBA mapped out a plan for announcing the deal, which included Michaelson in Chicago to break the news at John's side.

But in reality, Michaelson had little belief that his company would come away with Goose Island. Though the initial interest was sincere—especially at a price far lower than what Anheuser-Busch agreed to pay—its right to match was a chess piece to extract what it could from St. Louis. Everyone knew the deal would get done; it was just a matter of when and how. And what the CBA could get out of it.

Finally, on March 25, Anheuser-Busch offered $16.3 million for the 42 percent stake in Goose Island—a 368 percent appreciation in five years—plus a reduction in distribution fees worth another $14.7 million for CBA brands in Anheuser-Busch's wholesaler network. Anheuser-Busch was prepared to announce its acquisition of a majority stake in Goose Island on March 28, with or without the CBA on board; a draft of the press release said the fate of the 42 percent stake was "currently in negotiations." But on the evening of March 27, as John Hall was flying back from Tobago, the CBA accepted Anheuser-Busch's offer. John learned of the agreement by email.

"Great news for sure!" he replied.

Goose Island's $38.8 million sale to Anheuser-Busch InBev was announced March 28, 2011:

> Goose Island selects current partner Anheuser-Busch for growth strategy
>
> CHICAGO (March 28, 2011) – Chicago-based Goose Island, one of the nation's most-respected and fastest-growing small brewers with sales concentrated throughout the Midwest, today announced it had agreed to be acquired by Anheuser-Busch, its current distribution partner, in a move that will bring additional capital into Goose Island's operations to meet growing consumer demand for its brands and deepen its Chicago and Midwest distribution. . . .
>
> Goose Island sold approximately 127,000 barrels of Honkers Ale, 312 Urban Wheat Ale, Matilda and other brands in 2010. To help meet immediate demand, an additional $1.3 million will be invested to increase Goose Island's Chicago Fulton Street brewery's production as early as this summer.
>
> "Demand for our beers has grown beyond our capacity to serve our wholesale partners, retailers, and beer lovers," said Goose Island founder and president John Hall, who will continue as Goose Island chief executive officer. "This partnership between our extraordinary artisanal brewing team and one of the best brewers in the world in Anheuser-Busch will bring resources to brew more beer here in Chicago to reach more beer drinkers, while continuing our development of new beer styles. This agreement helps us achieve our goals with an ideal partner who helped fuel our growth, appreciates our products and supports their success."

> Hall will continue to be responsible for Goose Island beer production and the expansion of Goose Island's Chicago brewery, where production will continue and its business will still be based.
>
> "The new structure will preserve the qualities that make Goose Island's beers unique, strictly maintain our recipes and brewing processes," Hall said. "We had several options, but we decided to go with Anheuser-Busch because it was the best. The transaction is good for our stakeholders, employees and customers." . . .
>
> "These critically acclaimed beers are the hometown pride of Chicagoans," said Dave Peacock, president of Anheuser-Busch, Inc. "We are very committed to expanding in the high-end beer segment, and this deal expands our portfolio of brands with high-quality, regional beers. As we share ideas and bring our different strengths and experiences together, we can accelerate the growth of these brands."

A month after the deal was announced, Peacock visited Goose Island with Marcel Telles, one-third of the billionaire power trio that had grown Brazil's second-largest brewery into Anheuser-Busch InBev. Telles—described in the South American press as a "ferociously competitive Brazilian wheeler and dealer"—stood with Peacock on the deck overlooking the brewery, where John and his staff had passed countless Friday afternoons for the last twenty years. Peacock swelled with satisfaction. Goose Island was theirs.

As they climbed into their car, Telles continued the conversation. It was important not to overintegrate Goose Island into the broader company, he said. It needed to be leveraged for what it was: a hub of innovation. The world's largest beer company couldn't achieve that innovation on its own.

"There's one thing we need to do," Telles said.

"What's that?" Peacock said.

"Not fuck it up."

18

"It Doesn't Count as a Sell Out Until You Hit $40 Million"

THE FIRST TWEET POPPED UP within ten hours.

> Hi Everyone—I'll be fielding questions about the upcoming takeover of Goose Island Brewery by Anheuser-Busch InBev. (March 28, 2011, 6:20 PM)

Two minutes later, for anyone fooled by the first tweet, the mockery was made clear.

> The sale of Goose Island was not a sell-out; it doesn't count as a sell out until you hit $40 million. $38 million is really nothing. (March 28, 2011, 6:22 PM)

Five years earlier, Twitter didn't even exist. By 2011, it was a playground for the cynical and the savvy. Any vaguely controversial development could be worth a parody account, and so it was for @Goose_Island_PR, which aimed daggers in all directions.

> To those complaining, now our Belgian beers might actually be brewed IN Belgium. Or Hoboken New Jersey. Not sure yet. (March 28, 2011, 6:28 PM)

> Revamping our beers: Demolition will no longer mark demolition of old building but of the rest of the craft brewing industry. (March 28, 2011, 7:35 PM)
>
> Don't worry, nothing will change. Except the beer. And brewmaster. And who signs the checks. And gets the $$$. (March 28, 2011, 7:44 PM)
>
> Successful purchases with share of $38mil: Trampoline. It helps me cannonball into the piles of money. #BestPurchaseEver (March 28, 2011, 7:55 PM)
>
> Aside from the changes, nothing will change. We will follow in footsteps of other great breweries, like RollingRock #DontGoogleIt (March 28, 2011, 7:59 PM)

The mystery author of @Goose_Island_PR knew history.

In March 2006, rumors began to spread that the Rolling Rock beer brand, made in Latrobe, Pennsylvania, forty miles southeast of Pittsburgh, was for sale. Golfer Arnold Palmer and Fred ("Mister") Rogers both hailed from the town of eighty-five hundred, but Latrobe was best known for its beer. Brewed at Latrobe Brewing Co. since 1939, Rolling Rock remained a community pillar in the mountainous sliver of the Rust Belt long after many businesses shuttered amid the rise of free trade and big-box stores. Anheuser-Busch emerged as Rolling Rock's likely suitor, which generated cautious optimism: "We're keeping our fingers crossed and hoping and praying that whoever buys it keeps it here," Latrobe's mayor told the *Pittsburgh Tribune-Review*. Sure enough, Anheuser-Busch was confirmed as the buyer days later, paying $82 million, but only for Rolling Rock's brands and recipes—not the Latrobe brewery itself. Production of Rolling Rock would be shipped to Anheuser-Busch's second-oldest plant, in Newark, New Jersey. Unless a new owner could be found for the brewery, all 250 employees would be laid off. The mayor called the plan "an injustice for the city." Union organizers called for a nationwide boycott of all Anheuser-Busch products.

Bringing production in-house was an obvious step toward Anheuser-Busch recouping its investment, but also cast the beer giant as a Grim Reaper: cutting costs, cutting jobs, and a questionable commitment to its acquisitions. By the end of 2006, Rolling Rock sales were down 14 percent. Three years later, reports emerged of Anheuser-Busch looking to sell its struggling brand.

That outcome was not lost on the keenest industry observers, including @Goose_Island_PR, who crafted an apocalyptic vision of Goose Island under Anheuser-Busch ownership. Pepe Nero, a dark saison pioneered just a year earlier, became diet beer "Pepe Zero." Bourbon County Stout would henceforth be aged in rain and oil barrels because they were cheaper. An energy-infused version of Pere Jacques would be called Pere Jacked. 312 Urban Wheat was transformed to 31.2 Urban Wheat, an "exciting 31.2 calorie beer." And in a mixed metaphor of sorts, Matilda became "MaCHILLda" and "MaCHILLada"—lime and tomato variants of the Goose Island classic made with *Brettanomyces*. (It was in fact a reference to Miller Chill, a light lager with lime that was discontinued, ironically enough, after losing a market battle with Bud Light Lime.)

The Twitter account slowed to a halt after less than a month, but the point was made. And it was made again and again across the internet during the weeks and months after the sale: Goose Island was a sellout. Anheuser-Busch was out to destroy craft beer.

For twenty years, craft beer and Big Beer had been mostly parallel lines.

The lines had intersected.

Within hours, the rush began to explain what it meant. Because it *had* to mean something.

Yes, there had been Widmer and Redhook. But those were minority stakes, and as far as anyone could tell, the companies had been left alone. Same for Old Dominion Brewing, just outside of Washington, DC, in which Anheuser-Busch bought a 49 percent stake in 2007. Miller bought Wisconsin's iconic Leinenkugel in 1988, but that was a lifetime ago, when craft was 0.1 percent of the entire industry. It was an oddly prescient, though isolated move.

A spate of minor deals had rippled through the industry in 2010: Independent Brewers United (maker of the Pyramid and Magic Hat brands) was bought by a New York City private equity firm. The Craft Brewers Alliance bought Kona. A former executive vice president at US Beverage bought Anderson Valley, a Northern California craft brewery that dated to 1987. And the most iconic craft brewer of all, Anchor, was bought by a San Francisco beverage industry investment and consulting firm.

But this was something different: a full-blown sale of an established American craft brewery to the biggest beer company in the world. The company that created brands solely to disrupt and confuse. The one behind 100 Percent Share of Mind. The one that had commandeered nearly half of the nation's beer distributors. The one that would condescend to any combination of words, flavors, or marketing to boost its stock price. The one that prized shareholders over beer. Goose Island sold to *them.*

A seismic shift had occurred.

But what was it?

John Hall jumped into spin mode, working the phones with media and tastemakers. He told the *Chicago Tribune* that Anheuser-Busch "didn't buy us to change what we're doing." He insisted that he wouldn't have sold the company if St. Louis planned to take a hatchet to the beer or the brewery. "I wouldn't have worked 23 years to build what I have to piss it away in five minutes," he said.

Dave Peacock echoed the point in the *St. Louis Business Journal*, insisting that Goose Island was an attractive target because "they have excellent brands with interesting stories; they are innovative."

"It would be crazy to change the taste of their products," he said.

Still, scores of beer drinkers vowed to abandon Goose Island, much to the amusement of a longtime fan who launched a blog he called *Goose Island Meltdown*. It was a collection of outraged comments plucked mostly from Facebook:

> You truely broke my heart Goose Island. R.I.P.

> Welcome to goose-wieser

> I have purchased my last 6 from Goose, I don't put money in the pockets of AB.
>
> I feel as if someone in my family has died! RIP Goose Island :(

An onslaught was unleashed upon Goose Island's social media channels, which were ordered to go silent. Don't respond. Don't defend. Don't argue. Don't edit or delete angry Facebook comments; they didn't want to be accused of making a fraught situation worse with censorship. But at computers across the brewery, Goose Island employees tracked every vicious word, constantly refreshing feeds and screens.

"I wasn't prepared for the things that I've heard and seen people saying," Brett Porter told Chicago's *RedEye* on the day the deal was announced. "It seems to be the biggest story in Chicago today."

Beer writers were a bit more measured—but only a bit. Many weighed in within hours of the announcement, including a blog called *The Pint Glass*, which stitched together a crude image of Darth Vader hoisting a glass emblazoned with Goose Island's logo. The deal "opens the possibility of the new ownership to disastrously alter the make-up of the craft brew," *The Pint Glass* wrote. "Cheaper ingredients, processes streamlined for mass and massive production to meet demand have the potential to take finely tuned beers and make them nothing more than 'fancified' macros. Therefore removing the essence of the original beer."

Michigan blogger Stu Stuart foresaw disaster:

> This purchase will likely have an eventual ripple effect, in the form of cost cutting, layoffs, dumbing down of recipes, the large muscle of the AB InBev taking up even more shelf space and tap handles at retail outlets. But the largest effect, in my opinion, is the resentment felt by loyal Goose Island customers, who had what they felt was an intimate relationship with an independent brewing company, an unspoken agreement, a hometown hero they could believe in and stand behind.

Stephen Beaumont, a Canadian beer writer, was also skeptical:

> On the one hand, I would personally welcome the arrival of many millions of dollars and the freedom it would entail, while on the other, I question very strongly the honourability of Anheuser-Busch InBev when it comes to protecting the jobs of Goose Island workers, the involvement of Goose Island in the Chicago community—always a matter of importance for the Halls—and, ultimately, the character of the beer over time.

On his blog, *Top Fermented*, Erik Lars Myers, founder of North Carolina's Mystery Brewing Co., presumed that Goose Island's "technically brilliant" beers would endure, but what loomed concerned him:

> What really terrifies me is the thought that this is the first A-B-I takeover, but I am positive it will not be the last. In the coming years we are sure to see a lot of larger craft breweries get gobbled up by the big players in the market. It's been happening in Europe for years. Why should America be exempt?
>
> Once that starts happening, what does that mean for the small craft market? We cannot compete, on any level, with the international marketing machines that are the world's largest breweries.

Jim Vorel, a central Illinois newspaper entertainment writer who blogged about beer on the side as Kid Carboy Jr. for the *Aleheads* blog, was borderline apoplectic:

> Ask yourself—if you're a craft beer fan and don't drink AB products, what is your reason for not doing so? Is it only because they produce products that taste like piss? If that's the case, then this move really doesn't mean that much to you. Now AB will likely be producing products that *don't* taste like piss, under the Goose Island name.
>
> But if your beef with AB goes deeper—if you abhor their business practices and ideology, and view them as the Evil Empire that so many of us do, well then, this is a blow if you also like Goose Island products. Because if you feel that AB is

> the enemy, you can't rationally keep purchasing Goose Island beers. Realize what this buyout means—as majority shareholders, that means Anheuser Busch "owns" Goose Island—they will be the ones profiting from future success, not the people who built Goose Island into what it is today. You know, the people who gave up on their business to take the buyout. They allowed AB to go from only partial to majority ownership, effectively taking the future of the brewery out of their hands. Currently, AB has no announced plans for sweeping changes, but they now have [the] power to do just that on a whim.
>
> I personally can't see myself buying more Goose Island, knowing that AB will be pulling the strings.

(Vorel, who went on to become a beer writer for *Paste* magazine, would regret saying Anheuser-Busch beers "taste like piss" but did follow through on his pledge to avoid Goose Island—and other Anheuser-Busch products—for personal, though not professional purposes.)

Others used the sale as a means to turn contemplative about where the industry stood. Jeff Alworth, a longtime beer blogger in Portland, Oregon, wrote on his *Beervana* blog two days after the announcement:

> I happened to re-post an item on Sunday about the difference between craft beer and craft breweries. For thirty years, Americans acknowledged no distinction between the two: first you described a craft brewery (small and independent) and then you could point to craft beer (the product of a craft brewery). It's a facile definition, but a durable one. What I find most interesting about the sale of Goose Island is a tacit acknowledgement that the two are indeed separate. To the extent people are bothered about it, it's because they worry Goose Island's beer will change. It's a watershed in the way we think about beer. Americans are becoming more sophisticated in their understanding of good beer, and as a consequence, they have a more subtle understanding of the business behind it.

One of the few outright cheerleaders was Andy Crouch, a Boston criminal defense attorney whose side gig was beer blogging and a monthly column for *BeerAdvocate* magazine. Beneath an irresistible headline—"Why the Anheuser Busch InBev–Goose Island Deal Is Good for Craft Beer"—Crouch, a suburban Chicago native, admitted on his blog that he had "been accused of being a Goose Island-apologist and even a touch sycophantic when it comes to my hometown brewer." But he went on to salute the deal as a positive sign for American beer:

> The Goose Island sale to AB-InBev in one sense must be seen as a victory for craft brewers. Instead of simply trying to knock-off or belittle their efforts, the world's largest brewery clearly appreciates some of the nuances of the American marketplace. And it is certainly vindication for the hard work and efforts of the Goose Island family.
>
> I also expect that this will signal the end of the half-hearted, Budweiser American Ale stabs at flavorful beer that we have seen in the past. Better to have the behemoth support, promote, and deliver flavorful craft beer than to crowd tap handles with flavorless and embarrassing knock-off brands (beyond the handful that will remain, such as Shock Top).
>
> The deal also gives us hope that AB-InBev will finally take baby steps towards getting serious about supporting better beer. I expect Goose Island will receive a helpful infusion of cash and greater access to more markets as the division grows. As the industry continues to gray, it's inevitable that many other craft brewers will find a buyer in AB-InBev, which will in turn lead to craft brewers comprising a greater percentage (however negligible globally) of the AB-InBev brewery portfolio. Assuming craft beer drinkers do not abandon their favorite but now-sold craft brewers, AB-InBev will experience pressures to continue to brew brands and keep local breweries in operation that they have not before faced in places around the world, including in Belgium.

And then there was the wait-and-see crowd. Maureen Ogle, author of *Ambitious Brew: The Story of American Beer*, published in 2006, insisted there was no reason to be surprised by the deal; an audience had been firmly established for the imported and craft beers that offered higher profit margins (the very same argument Goose Island had used to convince wary bar owners to buy Honker's Ale during the mid-1990s). The big brewers *had* to get involved in craft, she argued. Ogle saw two options for where the Goose Island–Anheuser-Busch marriage might go:

> One, it can leave the beer makers alone to keep making what they make (premium beers).
>
> Or two, it can tell the beer makers to cease and desist and start making Budweiser knock-offs.
>
> Smart money says they opt for Door Number One. Why? Because ABIB isn't looking for Bud knockoffs. It's hunting for premium beers. (Remember those: the ones that yield more profit per bottle than Bud?) Why screw with the goose that's laying the golden egg?

Stan Hieronymus, one of the foremost voices in beer journalism, kept it simple: "Since everybody else has an opinion about what the Goose Island sale means I'll be honest and type, *I don't know*. And unless you're drinking beer with Dave Peacock and Carlos Brito right now there's every chance you don't know either. Instead, meet me for the Goose Island tour in 2014. We'll see what's available in the tasting room after the tour ends."

19

"I'm Never Going to Buy It Now, Because I Don't Consider It a Craft Brewery"

A FEW WEEKS AFTER THE SALE, a Goose Island sales rep walked into the Grafton, a bar in Chicago's Lincoln Square neighborhood. It was an area in transition, segueing from the vanguard of Chicago's German population to a home for young families and professionals. The Grafton was part of the shift. Since opening in 2002, it had served hearty Irish comfort food amid a cozy landscape of dark wood, dim lighting, and a roaring fireplace where students from the next-door music school jammed between frothy pints of craft beer. The Grafton was among the first Chicago bars to tap Lagunitas and New Belgium, and had been a frequent supporter of Goose Island. It was therefore a regular stop for Jeff Peterson.

Peterson had worked for Goose Island for two years, undertaking an endless effort to score new draft handles while maintaining his longtime accounts. Drinkers couldn't get enough 312 Urban Wheat Ale. Matilda and Sofie had elevated Chicago's understanding of beer's elegance. Bourbon County Stout's release had become an annual celebration. Peterson's job was simple. His job was fun. Then came the sale.

As a face of Goose Island, he suddenly lurched from crisis to crisis. Seemingly every bar manager and beer buyer wanted to know why they should keep Goose Island on draft. Others didn't even bother with a conversation. They just said they were done. Such was the case at the Grafton, where the beer buyer told Peterson that the bar would no longer carry the hometown favorite. Peterson shook his head. And then he surveyed the taps and saw something odd: Leffe, a Belgian brand owned by Anheuser-Busch InBev, on draft.

He was having some form of this conversation almost every day, encountering visceral reactions that echoed a theme: Goose Island had been something special. It gave meaning to the words *local* and *craft*. Now it was lining the pockets of the biggest beer company in the world. Peterson began losing tap handles to the breweries that most bar managers considered authentic craft beer—local upstarts such as Revolution and Half Acre and national brands making hard pushes into Chicago, like Lagunitas and New Belgium. It didn't happen immediately. Most of the bars that regularly poured Goose Island had plenty of kegs stashed in the cooler or more on order. But after a month or two, when the repeat orders didn't come, the losses kicked in.

Peterson had little ammunition with skeptical bar managers, but he used what he had. His bosses urged a simple response: "We needed to make more beer. Who cares who's signing the checks?" But to anyone immune to the "All that matters is what's in the glass" argument, and who vowed to drop 312, Honker's, or IPA, Peterson said, fine—but don't expect Bourbon County Stout kegs in November. It was a powerful chip in the bars of Chicago. It saved dozens of handles.

The blowback wasn't only close to home. The owner of the Birch, a craft beer bar in Norfolk, Virginia, told the local *Virginian-Pilot* that he was abandoning his longtime goal of pouring Goose Island: "I'm never going to buy it now, because I don't consider it a craft brewery." A bar manager in Burlington, Vermont, openly wrestled in his twice-monthly newspaper column whether to carry Goose Island. (He dropped it after customers stopped ordering it.) The chain of HopCat bars, founded in Grand Rapids, Michigan, not only stopped selling Goose Island—it dropped any brands owned by Anheuser-Busch InBev or MillerCoors.

The *Washington Post* posted a correction a week after the sale was announced for mistakenly calling Pere Jacques "craft."

But the fallout was most intense in Chicago, where longtime supporters dropped the beer and the brewery was uninvited from local beer events and festivals. Goose Island brewers heard it from other brewers in the industry: "Oh, you work for Anheuser-Busch now." The newer breweries, so proud to be part of the craft beer club, were often the most malicious. The veterans who had survived the industry's first downturn, during the 1990s, were the most understanding.

Jeff Peterson began to feel squeezed between the accounts distancing themselves from his beer and the bosses that wanted an explanation for his lost sales. The job had turned from joyously trumpeting the hometown brew to desperately trying to save business. It was an unceremonious grind for a salesman with a suburban mortgage, an infant son at home, and a $35,000 salary. Within days, Peterson went from wowing new customers to justifying his existence. He even got heckled in line at Starbucks. A joker behind him took note of his Goose Island shirt and called him "Budweiser." Peterson wasn't the type to get into a fight while waiting for coffee, but unloading months of frustration seemed awfully appealing in the moment.

He began to take it all personally. He even defended the company on an internet comment thread decrying the sale. His boss told him not to do that again. Marketing would handle that. Peterson eventually realized that he needed to stop taking it personally. It had nothing to do with him.

In a storm of negativity, Goose Island's most valuable advocate wasn't an employee. It was a bar owner.

Michael Roper was a Detroit native who began working in bars at the age of eighteen. His eyes were opened when his boss returned from a trip to San Francisco with an exotic beer called Anchor Steam. It was difficult to know what to make of the malty, full-bodied lager. It was so nuanced. Roper began visiting Chicago in 1972, and always made a point to visit the ethnic neighborhood grocery stores, where authentic imported German Weissbier and Kölsch could be found. They were probably months older than they should have been, but Roper was happy to haul them back to Detroit.

Roper finally moved to Chicago in 1982. He hung out at the few bars that made the effort to serve European imports and the beer from America's nascent craft brewing industry. In 1992 he started his own bar, the Hopleaf, in a former dive on a dicey stretch of Clark Street. A handful of bars served imported, local, or the rare craft beer, but none served those beers exclusively. Roper decided to open that bar. In a city where virtually every bar had an Old Style sign hanging out front, better beer seemed like a healthy point of differentiation.

Hopleaf took over a liquor store doubling as a bar with two beers on draft: Old Style and Special Export, both from G. Heileman Brewing in La Crosse, Wisconsin. Roper initially ran the bar just as it had been, opening at 7:00 AM for the night shift workers and the alcoholics. He sold through the stocks of cheap vodka and weird ethnic liquors and slowly built the bar of his dreams. Two taps became eight—no one else in the neighborhood had more than two—one of which was set aside for Roper's favorite brewery: Bell's. He carried a permanent handle of Bell's Amber and even had a Bell's neon made for Hopleaf's front window. (Bell's kicked in a keg to cover the cost.) Michigan expats heading north on the Clark Street bus would see that glowing sign, pull the cord to signal a stop, and then beeline to one of the few places where the iconic midwestern brew could be found in Chicago. Throughout the 1990s, Bell's Amber was by far Hopleaf's top-selling beer. Roper saw Goose Island as just another brewery struggling to impress locals. The beer was passable but unexciting.

Then came his first sip of Bourbon County Stout. And Roper was converted. He thought it could be the industry's biggest development since the advent of light beer. With the addition of Goose Island's Reserve series and its wine barrel–aged sour beers, Roper was convinced that world-class beer was being made in Chicago. He was never a fan of Goose Island's volume beers—and never carried 312 Urban Wheat Ale—but became a ceaseless cheerleader for the brewery's specialty beers. Especially Bourbon County Stout.

As Hopleaf grew into one of the city's most revered bars, Roper became friendly with Greg Hall. Hopleaf, in turn, became Greg's favorite haunt away from the brewery. For Goose Island marketing staff trying to entice an increasingly busy Greg to speak at their beer dinners, a joke developed: the easiest way to ensure his attendance was to hold it at Hopleaf.

A day or two before the sale was announced, Greg called Roper and asked to come by for a chat. He seemed deflated when he arrived. He took a seat at the bar and told Roper that Goose Island would be announcing in the coming days that it was selling to Anheuser-Busch InBev. Greg insisted that Anheuser-Busch InBev understood the good work Goose Island was doing and that production of the high-end beers that Roper had championed would inevitably be ramped up. Plus, it was deeply invested in quality control; for what they were, Bud and Bud Light were made with stunning consistency. But Roper sensed that Greg's enthusiasm was half-hearted. He even seemed a little embarrassed.

Roper wasn't happy. When the news broke, neither were his customers. They sat at Hopleaf's bar and jawed about how the "good" Goose Island beers would disappear as Anheuser-Busch doubled down on production of 312. But Roper also knew the backstory: capacity was maxed out, John Hall was approaching retirement, and something had to give. The new brewmaster, Brett Porter, had built a fine reputation at Oregon's Deschutes Brewery and insisted he'd stay on along with any current Goose Island brewer who would join him. Roper had been assured that Anheuser-Busch InBev would be taking over in name only. Little would change. And odds seemed good that Goose Island would get a new brewery. So Roper sat at his computer and hammered out a 1,158-word Facebook post:

> My Thoughts on Goose Island/AB Inbev
> By Michael Roper, proprietor, Hopleaf, Chicago
>
> There is a lot of buzz about the purchase of our hometown Chicago brewery, Goose Island by AB/InBev. Some are wishing them well, but more are not. I believe that is unfair and I would like to tell our customers why I think it is unfair.

It is hard to overestimate the positive effect that Goose Island has had on Chicago's craft beer scene. After the failures of Chicago Brewing Company, Golden Prairie, River West, Pavichevich/Baderbrau and others, it seemed that there was a curse on home grown beer in Chicago. One brewery proved otherwise. A combination of prudent growth, good products, shrewd business practices and smart marketing made Goose Island the first successful craft brewery in Chicago. For many years, they were the only one.

With the crowd pleasing flagship Honkers Ale and in later years 312 paying the bills, Goose Island was able to give us the many great Reserve Series beers that were and are world class brews. We at Hopleaf have been proud to serve them for years. Goose has been a pioneer in American oak aged beers and aging in whiskey barrels. Great beer has brought great success and many honors.

AB/Inbev knows what they are getting with Goose Island and what they are getting is a brewery that does what they can't do. They can't make beers like Matilda, Sofie, Juliet, Bourbon County Stout, Pere Jacques or Madame Rose. They can't even make anything like Goose Island IPA or Oatmeal Stout. They have given up trying and purchasing a brewery like Goose is more a symbol of surrender than might be obvious. This is the only way that they can bring good beer into their portfolio. It is a smart move for them. The last thing that they will want to do is to screw up a good thing. . . .

I know that these takeovers don't always work out. Sapporo's takeover of Unibroue has not been good for their beer. On the other hand, Duvel/Mortgaat's purchase of Ommegang, Chouffe and Liefman's has been a good fit; in fact in the case of Liefman's it probably saved them from extinction. If I detect that Goose Island is not the beer that it has been, I will drop them like a rock. I don't expect that to happen. It could even get better. I am going to give them a chance and I hope that others will too. If they brew great beer with quality ingredients in a new brewery in Chicago that employs our fellow Chicago residents, they stay involved in the community, and continue to innovate

> while brewing the beers we have already embraced, what is so bad about that? It is good. If they make AB/Inbev a better company, how can that be bad? It means that we have won. . . .
>
> Finally, this was a tough decision for the Halls to make. I don't envy what Greg will face when he goes out in public over the coming months. After a spell consulting with the new owners and brewers, Greg Hall is going to move on. I predict that we will see him in a role somewhere in Chicago doing something to further our craft beer scene. Whatever he does, I wish him the best. I also want to thank him for his inestimable contributions to craft beer in Chicago. We would be so much the poorer if there had not been a Goose Island and a Greg Hall here. I am full of hope that Goose Island will continue to prosper in Chicago brewing great beer and making us proud. I hope that everyone will be fair and give them a chance. If the liquid in the glass changes for the worse, we can all vote with our next purchase of another brand of beer.

An authoritative voice had spoken; the piece was quoted widely by reporters and bloggers. Peterson printed out Roper's post and in yellow highlighter amplified the last three sentences: *I am full of hope that Goose Island will continue to prosper in Chicago brewing great beer and making us proud. I hope that everyone will be fair and give them a chance. If the liquid in the glass changes for the worse, we can all vote with our next purchase of another brand of beer.* To the most cynical bar owners and beer buyers, Peterson handed over his highlighted copy of the Facebook post and said, "If the owner of the best beer bar in Chicago is giving us a chance, why won't you?"

Three weeks after the sale, a dozen Goose Island employees gathered at Bangers & Lace, a new craft beer bar in the Wicker Park neighborhood. If Hopleaf helped pioneer craft beer service in Chicago, Bangers & Lace was the next generation. It had opened six months earlier, during the fall of 2010, taking Roper's European-style motif—brick walls, wood floors, dim lighting, broad windows to the street—and giving it an updated sheen, highlighted by taps that poured some of the world's best beer.

Goose Island employees had gathered on a Friday night to celebrate John Laffler's birthday; he was the brewer who managed the barrel-aging program. Brewers were on hand. Sales and marketing staff too. Greg was there. The crew spent the evening drinking Goose Island's loftiest beers—Juliet, Lolita, Rare Bourbon County Stout—and a half-dozen rounds of Malört shots, the intensely bitter Swedish spirit that had become a barroom sacrament among Chicago drinkers.

Toward the end of the night, Greg sidled up to the bar and leaned against it, looking down. One bartender joked to another that it looked like Greg was "taking a leak"—which he was, into two separate beer glasses. As he and his group began to leave, Greg told his colleagues, "Don't drink that." The bartender pressed his finger against the glasses, and the warmth told him what had just unfolded.

"Hey, what's this?" the bartender said.

"Beer," Greg said.

"Perfect," the bartender said. "Let's have a toast before you go."

Greg, who was clearly drunk, declined and moved the glasses to a ledge near the door.

Minutes later, as the bartender stepped outside to throw out the glasses, he spied Greg sitting in the passenger seat of a parked car. The bartender tapped on the glass and said he wanted to introduce himself as the guy who had to clean Greg Hall's piss off the bar.

"Enjoy your newfound fortune and have a great night," he said.

The next day, Greg tried to repair the damage. He sent the bartender a private message via Facebook: "I apologize for my outlandish behavior last night. I enjoyed myself at Bangers and Lace very much, the beer selection is tops as was our service. . . . I'm very sorry to have ruined the night as I did. No excuses, just sincere apology." He also sent a case of Goose Island's latest innovation release—Big John, an imperial stout made with cacao nibs—as a peace offering. On Facebook, he wrote a two-word public post: "My bad."

His apology tour included a call to Roper. "You might be hearing some bad things about me," he said. "I did something really, really stupid." Three weeks after Roper spent an hour crafting a defense of Goose Island on Facebook, Greg Hall did *this*. The incident was gaining enough chatter that Greg sat down his kids to tell them what he had done and underscore how foolish it was. He called another half-dozen colleagues and friends in the industry.

He told the *Chicago Tribune* that he "fucked up big time." He was so drunk at the time, he said, he couldn't remember the incident: "I feel awful. I wouldn't stand it if someone did it at my place or if one of my people did something like that."

It was a galling incident, but few people who knew Greg could claim surprise. He was a brilliant tastemaker and marketer, and had influenced craft beer like few others. But he had also long operated in a universe of handlers who constantly steered him back within the boundaries of standard decorum, often to save him from himself. A good chunk of the sales and marketing staff had seen him overserved at an event or a beer dinner. Usually things never pushed beyond discomfort and the hope that things wouldn't get worse. But sometimes they did get worse. It was a hazard of the job: an outsized persona surrounded by alcohol and admirers. (To his credit, colleagues would later recall, he always left his car behind and took a $100 parking ticket rather than drive drunk.) Friends and colleagues were horrified after the Bangers & Lace incident; why had no one stopped him? By Sunday morning, word began to circulate among Goose Island's top executives, followed by one question: *Does John know?*

Not only had Goose Island sold out—its newly rich brewmaster was extending a middle finger to the industry on his way out the door. Goose Island brewers mostly thought it was funny; if anything, it added to the outsized legend of Greg Hall. Sales and marketing, though, was furious. They were already dousing fires. Greg's piss-filled beer glasses were fresh gasoline. Whatever sales bonuses they were already unlikely to get were assuredly gone. Marketing was baffled. How the hell could they spin this?

A mix of amusement, horror, and schadenfreude trickled through the industry. At least one bar, in Chicago's north suburbs, taped the *Tribune* article to its wall. Others that had previously heeded Michael Roper's advice and given the brewery a chance said that this time, they were done. A day after the incident became public, and less than three weeks before he was to leave the company, Greg sent an email to the staff.

Goose Island Family,

As my time as an employee with the brewery is coming to an end, I find that I've put myself in a position that is an embarrassment to the brewery and our employees.

Last Friday night, I behaved badly at a local account. The behavior is reprehensible and would not be tolerated if it were any employee, including myself. I admit I had over-consumed, but that is not an excuse. The fact that I was with a handful of fellow employees adds to my shame.

We all work in an industry where we are expected to be responsible with the product we are so proud to brew and serve. I apologize to all Goose Island employees for my irresponsibility and hope that I haven't compromised the relationships with any accounts. If there is any account that would benefit from a call, please let me know.

It's been a great ride for me at Goose Island. I appreciate all the support all of you have given me over the last 23 years.

Sincerely,

Gregory Hall

A week later, the @Goose_Island_PR Twitter account sprang back into action:

Sorry I've been off the twitter a bit—I've been too busy trying to fine tune the flavor of Greg Hall's piss into a fine beer. (April 18, 2011, 5:48 PM)

Seriously, though—Greg Hall is a millionaire. You should be begging to drink his piss. Do you not understand he's better than you? (April 18, 2011, 5:48 PM)

But, in the spirit of fairness (and helping me do my job), why don't you give me the best uses for #GregHallPiss MAKE IT TREND, PEOPLE. (April 18, 2011, 5:49 PM)

Over the coming days, the author behind the account couldn't resist a few more jabs.

> I'm drawing up blueprints now for the Greg Hall bronze statue beer machine to serve the new Greg Hall's Special Hand Pull Golden Ale. (April 20, 2011, 3:26 PM)

> Had Greg sit down over weekend to fill an oak barrel with Greg Hall's Special Golden Ale. Now to let it age. What will it taste like? (April 27, 2011, 1:42 PM)

An impossible situation had become just a bit more impossible.

20

"People Are Looking for Us to Fuck It Up"

Shortly after the deal closed, in May 2011, a Goose Island operations employee did what she'd done most days before the sale.

She rose from her desk, walked the long hallway to the brewery, and filled a bottle from a stainless-steel tank that held cool water used for brewing. Like most days, she didn't think twice about it, or what was on her feet. Flip-flops.

It was noted.

As one of its first initiatives as the new boss, Anheuser-Busch sent technicians and engineers from its Quality Assurance division to evaluate Goose Island's operation. One of those engineers happened to be standing at the brew house when the woman filled her water bottle. The technicians and engineers also noted that brewers wore shorts to work. And that people and forklifts shared the same pathways. And that no one wore safety glasses.

By the time they were finished, Quality Assurance had found 120 flaws in Goose Island's operation, 100 of which were safety related. Most were minor, but to some in the brewery, a laundry list of shortcomings was a sign of despotic things to come—especially when paired with the looming drug testing. But Goose Island's head of operations, Mark Kamarauskas, craved the direction. Kams, as he was called around the brewery, was a hulking buzz-cut of a man: beefy, tall, and looking the part of an excellent prison guard. He'd been with Goose Island for nearly ten years, back when it was still learning to grow and struggling to be profitable. He'd previously spent eight years managing operations at an independently owned Coca-Cola plant in suburban Chicago, where the sugary elixir was made, bottled, and distributed within a small, regional footprint. Kamarauskas envisioned himself as a Coke lifer, but only until the plant was sold to Coke itself in July 2001. Directives began to arrive from Atlanta, including decisions about equipment, packaging, and supply. He became less of a manager, more of puppet controlled from afar. Within a year, and without a plan for what was next, he gave his two-week notice.

Kamarauskas was only marginally aware of the local brewery when asked to consult for three months on Goose Island's sputtering bottling line; it was the same equipment he had operated at Coke. The then operations manager had advocated for buying a new bottling line a mere seven years after John Hall invested in a top-flight German model. Within a couple of weeks, Kamarauskas reported back to John: *You don't have a machine problem. You have a people problem.* Kamarauskas didn't know it, but he'd hit John squarely in a soft spot. John relished building an operation of the right people in the right places—bottom to top. Kamarauskas made a case that he had failed. The evidence was a poorly operated bottle filler. John accepted Kamarauskas's recommendations, then offered him a job as the brewery's head of brewing operations. Kamarauskas accepted.

Kams quickly saw the ocean of difference between Coca-Cola and a scrappy 2002-era craft brewery. For all the high-level planning required at his old job, Goose Island was casting about with barely a plan. It was keeping up by the week. Then came the churning volume of 312 Urban Wheat Ale, and Kamarauskas was plunged into a new batch of problems: *How do we keep up with insatiable demand? How do we add more equipment? Where do we put it?* There was little long-term vision. Just endless short-term problems.

So when Anheuser-Busch's Quality Assurance division handed Kamarauskas a log of 120 mostly minor problems and the recommendation to improve practices, he smiled—especially if St. Louis would pay

John Hall (right) and Goose Island's original brewer, Victor Ecimovich III, at the brewpub on May 14, 1988—a day after Goose Island first opened its doors on Chicago's Clybourn Avenue. *Courtesy of John Hall*

Greg, John, and Beth Hall in Belgium during a family trip in 1990. *Courtesy of John Hall*

(from left) Goose Island salesman Ashley Bowersox, John Hall, Chicago mayor Richard M. Daley, and Greg Hall at Chicago's annual summer food and music festival, Taste of Chicago, in 1998. Unlike many of his early craft beer contemporaries, John Hall was a believer in the value of marketing; as soon as it could afford to do so, Goose Island became a Taste of Chicago sponsor. *Courtesy of John Hall*

(from left) Greg Hall, Emmanuelle Marti of La Diva cigars, and LaSalle Grill owner Mark McDonnell at LaSalle Grill, in South Bend, Indiana, on October 5, 1994. Greg and Goose Island represented beer in a beer, bourbon, and cigar dinner hosted by the restaurant. Representing bourbon was Jim Beam master distiller Booker Noe, whom Greg asked for used bourbon barrels to age beer. That beer, released a year later, was the iconic Bourbon County Stout. *Courtesy of Mark McDonnell*

Greg Hall (left) and Booker Noe (center, rear) in a group photo at LaSalle Grill on October 5, 1994. *Courtesy of Mark McDonnell*

John Hall launched Goose Island's Fulton Street production facility in 1995 with the intention of growing the company quickly. Above are the brew deck (upper left), brewing console (upper right), bottling line (lower left), and brewer Jim Cibak at the lauter tun (lower right). All are circa the late 1990s. *All courtesy of Jason Neton*

The Goose Island staff holiday photo in 1997, including Greg Hall (lower right), head brewer Matt Brynildson (front row, second from left), and John Hall (back left, holding beer bottle). Note the Buddha statute beside Brynildson—it wears Goose Island's recently awarded Great American Beer Festival gold medal (for Honker's Ale), the first for the Fulton Street brewery.
Courtesy of Jason Neton

Head brewer Matt Brynildson scheduling brewing production at the Fulton Street brewery (above) and in the Goose Island lab (right). Brynildson would go on to acclaim as brewmaster at Firestone Walker Brewing in Paso Robles, California.
Courtesy of Jason Neton

(Left) Six-packs of Oatmeal Stout, Honker's Ale, India Pale Ale, and Nut Brown Ale, circa 2005. It was the second generation of Goose Island packaging. (Right) The original packaging for 312 Urban Wheat Ale when it debuted in 2005. *Courtesy of Torque Digital Media*

(Left) Many brands were tested for what ultimately became 312 Urban Wheat Ale. Among them: Backwards River Ale, with a tagline of "Go against the flow." (Right) The original packaging for Matilda, when first released in bottles in 2004. Like the rest of Goose Island's Reserve beers, it subsequently got a far sleeker look to mimic a wine label. *Courtesy of Torque Digital Media*

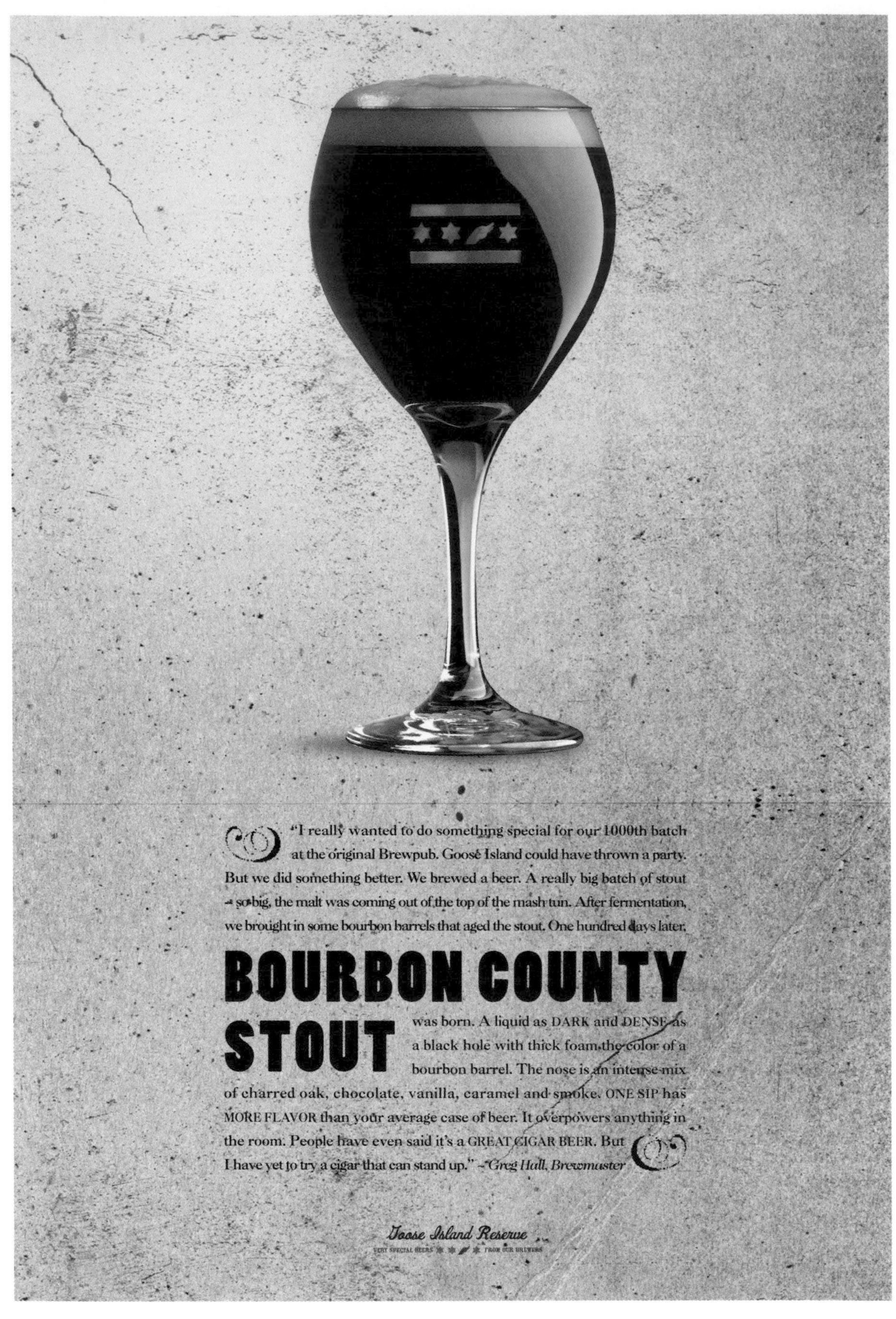

A promotional poster for Bourbon County Stout when first packaged in bottles, in 2003. It would become one of the most influential beers in the history of the industry. *Courtesy of Torque Digital Media*

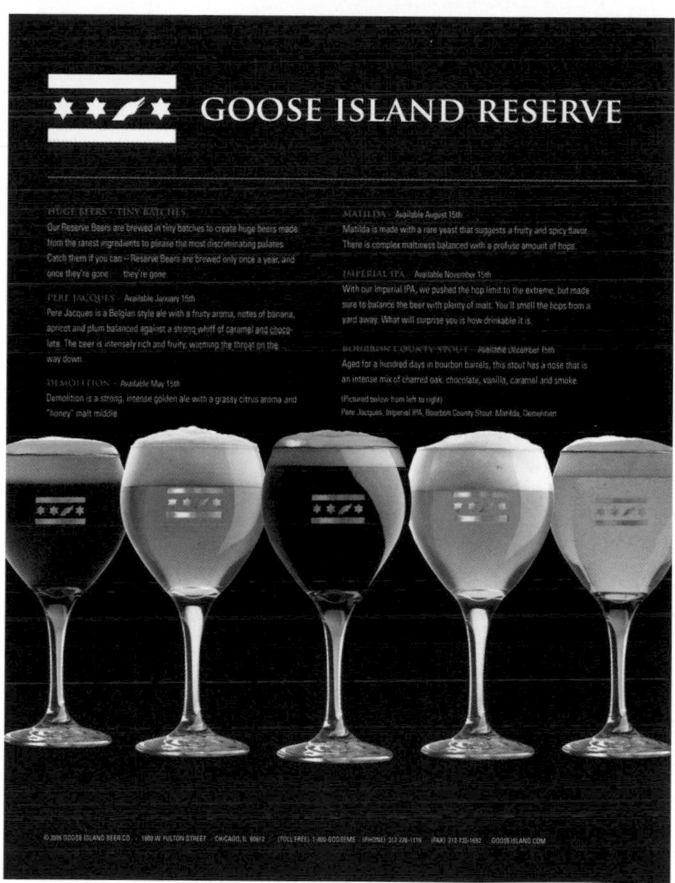

A sales sheet for the Reserve family of Goose Island beers—(from left) Pere Jacques, Imperial IPA, Bourbon County Stout, Matilda, and Demolition—in 2005. *Courtesy of Torque Digital Media*

(Left) The original bar at Goose Island's Clybourn Avenue brewpub on its last night, in January 2017, before a major renovation that closed the restaurant for ten months. Parent company Anheuser-Busch InBev thought a more modern, sleeker look would make the pub more competitive with a new generation of beer drinkers. (Right) John Hall wears a sweatshirt bearing the original Goose Island logo on the last night of service at the Clybourn Avenue brewpub he opened twenty-nine years earlier. *Courtesy of Josh Noel*

(Left) Greg Hall (standing at right) tells the story of Bourbon County Stout for a crowd at Goose Island's Clybourn Avenue pub in November 2017. Though Greg left Goose Island's daily operations after its sale to Anheuser-Busch InBev in 2011, he stayed active with the brewery and with Anheuser-Busch, to whom he later sold Virtue Cider. *Courtesy of Josh Noel.* (Right) John Hall at the opening of the Goose Island pub in London in late 2016, as Anheuser-Busch InBev took the brand it bought in 2011 global. *Courtesy of John Hall*

for the improvements. An Anheuser-Busch InBev global management system was adopted to standardized procedures—meetings, reports, and logistics—at the company's breweries across the globe. For a company that liked to shuffle people in and out of jobs, it simplified transitions. There were more meetings—far more meetings—but Kamarauskas relished the order. He could sketch out goals, plans. There were resources.

Hundreds of thousands of dollars were poured into safety: handrails, guardrails, yellow lines to designate machinery-free walkways. Bonuses were tied to safety, and incentives were implemented. Whichever department identified the most infractions won a pizza party. (Maintenance won.) Some grumbled. Kamarauskas didn't care. A year before the sale there had been six injuries on the job, four of which were lost-time. With the sale, that ended.

The new overlords were also surprisingly open minded. When Anheuser-Busch engineers expressed concern that Goose Island appeared to have at least two more brewers than necessary for the amount of beer it produced, Kamarauskas explained that things worked differently in craft. St. Louis viewed brewers as widgets in the supply chain; they made a product that was largely an outgrowth of marketing. The act of making beer was an efficiency waiting to happen—no different than negotiating the price of raw goods.

In craft breweries, Kamarauskas said, brewers were more than cogs in an operation—they *were* the operation. They explored ingredients and process. They consulted chefs and farmers, distillers and barrel makers. They collaborated with other breweries. They went into the market and told the story of the beer. Anheuser-Busch asked: Wasn't that the job of marketing?

Goose Island looked at things differently, Kamarauskas said. Marketing supported brewing. Not the other way around.

St. Louis was skeptical. But the two "extra" brewers stayed.

The brewery and everyone inside it held their collective breath for the first six months. They waited for *the change*. Not just the minor tweaks but the immutable change, when nothing would ever be the same. Everyone would be replaced by robots in red polo shirts and safety glasses. Or the brewery would be torn from its foundation, loaded onto the back of a truck, and dropped in St. Louis. Something. Anything that matched the heat and the bluster.

Instead, the change came in a million little ways. There was drug testing, and some people left because of it. They were going to smoke weed after work, and the largest beer company in the world would not tell them otherwise. There was increased safety, and some brewers grumbled. No longer being able to wear shorts at work was a loss; brewing got hot, even during the depth of Chicago winter. The pizza party incentive to identify safety lapses seemed like a vast snitching campaign to some.

It wasn't that it no longer felt like Goose Island—it was that it also felt like Anheuser-Busch. Who could argue with safety? But they didn't want to work at a brewery where they were ordered to wear safety glasses, boots, gloves, back harnesses, hard hats, and neon vests; they might as well have been at a construction site. Something was lost. Sales and marketing increasingly referred to beers as "brands." The word came up so often that a veteran brewer joked about branding the marketing team with a bucket of hot coals and a Goose Island logo. Individually, the changes were small; together, they became something significant. Employees eventually clocked in with an identification code and fingerprint. A fingerprint to make beer. What could be less craft?

But the single major shift never arrived during those earliest months. John Hall was still there. And Tony Bowker. And Mark Kamarauskas. There were even reassuring signs. In early 2012, the brewery launched the Fulton & Wood project—named for the location of the brewery—of new and experimental draft-only beers available only in Chicago. The results were fairly high quality and true to the spirit of what Goose Island had always been.

Sure, St. Louis folks showed up now and then, and Goose Island people sometimes had to head south. But it all just became part of the culture. The most cynical took to calling Anheuser-Busch "the Antichrist." The rest called it "the Mothership." No one ever said they were going to Anheuser-Busch. They were "going to St. Louis." The meaning was understood.

Many of the employees who swore they would leave stuck around, including the trio that headed to Big Star in a haze of fury on the day of the announcement. It was that exact trio—John Laffler, Tom Korder, and Suzanne Wolcott—that led presentations on Goose Island's behalf the next summer at the Great Taste of the Midwest, the region's preeminent beer festival. In a hilltop pavilion overlooking downtown Madison, Wisconsin, Wolcott demonstrated techniques for cooking with beer. Korder and Laffler lectured about Goose Island's barrel-aging program.

Meanwhile, Anheuser-Busch had pledged to pump $1.3 million into boosting Goose Island's operations, and it began almost immediately. It bought fermentation tanks. It bought a yeast propagator. It bought a bigger centrifuge. The Anheuser-Busch employees who visited—engineers, technicians, and brewers—seemed genuinely excited about what was happening at Goose Island. Budgets ballooned. When brewers started getting poached by Revolution and Lagunitas (which announced plans in 2012 to launch a Chicago brewery), Kamarauskas asked St. Louis to authorize raises. The bosses readily complied, creating three tiers of brewer that paid at different levels. Everyone got a company American Express credit card. Quality control improved.

Goose Island used its access to Anheuser-Busch's lab to optimize production of Matilda; every day it sent a sample of the beer as it fermented, in a bid to understand exactly how *Brettanomyces* worked. Anheuser-Busch lab techs were able to explain what compounds were unfolding and when. It was remarkable to have a world-class laboratory validate what they had understood only through taste and smell for a decade.

Dave Peacock walked through the brewery and handed out business cards with instructions to contact him directly if anything seemed amiss. He assured employees that money and resources would flow to Chicago, while little would be demanded in return other than making good beer, innovating, and growing. Efficiencies were encouraged but not required. Goose Island experimented with new raw materials—hops and grain directly from Anheuser-Busch's production facilities, or at least their preferred suppliers—but if a new ingredient didn't work, they were free to change direction.

Anheuser-Busch had access to resources that brewers never could have imagined. When Brett Porter, the brewmaster who replaced Greg Hall, wanted a rare hop from Poland, he simply "picked up the phone," he told *Crain's Chicago Business*.

"There's nothing like having a little clout," he said.

The truth was that things weren't all bad as part of the world's largest beer company.

But the world didn't know that. What the world knew was what happened to 312 Urban Wheat Ale.

On July 30, four months after the sale, Goose Island announced that its flagship beer would no longer be made in Chicago. It would be brewed at an Anheuser-Busch plant in Baldwinsville, New York. Six days earlier, Anheuser-Busch had quietly filed paperwork with the Onondaga County Clerk's Office to operate as Goose Island Beer Co. in upstate New York.

Reaction was fierce. *Modern Brewery Age* magazine called it "the kind of tone-deaf move that inevitably follows the acquisition of small brewers by large ones."

"To the logisticians, it doesn't matter where you brew it, as long as it meets the spec," the magazine wrote. "InBev celebrates efficiency, and spurns sentimentality. But to craft beer consumers, issues of authenticity, locality and differentiation rank right up there with the taste profile and price point. And InBev spurns those values at their peril."

Reporters in all directions scrambled to look up Baldwinsville's area code for an irresistible headline: "312 to Be Brewed in the 315." Some observers couldn't even bother to get their facts right before spiking the ball: "Three months after the deal, AB InBev started brewing Goose Island signature 312 Imperial Pale Ale—named after a Chicago area code—in Baldwinsville, N.Y., where the area code is 315," wrote *Bloomberg* magazine beneath the headline "The Plot to Destroy America's Beer." (Never mind that 312 was a wheat ale and not an "imperial pale ale," a style that barely exists, if it does at all.)

In fact, anything less than off-loading the burden of 312 would have been a nonstarter for Goose Island during negotiations. Mark Kamarauskas was ready to hand 312 to Anheuser-Busch from the day the deal closed. 312 had strangled production since 2006 and plunged the brewery into the eternal crisis of not being able to make enough beer.

Kamarauskas's only concern was who would decide when Anheuser-Busch's version of 312 was acceptable. He knew his brewers could get there and that Anheuser-Busch's brewers could get there. But where would the bar be set?

In June, Kamarauskas and Brett Porter flew to Syracuse, then drove fifteen miles to one of the smallest of Anheuser-Busch's twelve breweries. The Baldwinsville plant was unique within the company for not being built by Anheuser-Busch; Schlitz built it during the mid-1970s as a last desperate gasp to remain relevant. But it was too late for Schlitz, and the faltering company sold the Baldwinsville brewery to Anheuser-Busch in late 1979 for $100 million. With the 1.1 million square foot Baldwinsville plant—its eleventh brewery—Anheuser-Busch planned to grow even more dominant with production of its new Budweiser Light (a name later shortened).

Anheuser-Busch spent three years modernizing the Baldwinsville operation before finally brewing there in 1983. It was designed to be among the nimblest in the company's brewery fleet and took on years of innovation projects: LA, a low-alcohol, reduced-calorie beer launched in 1984; tequila-and-lime flavored Tequiza in 1999; Bacardí Silver, a line of rum-and-citrus flavored malt beverages introduced in 2002; Johnny Appleseed hard cider; the line of Bud Light Mixxtails cocktail-like malt beverages; the family of sugary Bud Light Lime margarita-inspired "Rita" drinks. And 312 Urban Wheat Ale.

For all its muscle and might, the nation's largest brewer was forever catching up to evolving consumer tastes; Baldwinsville was tabbed as its staging ground for innovation. (In 1989, Anheuser-Busch paid $1 million for unlawfully dumping phosphorus-contaminated water from the Baldwinsville brewery into the nearby Seneca River. Lawyers said three employees acted without the knowledge of the company; two were fired and one was allowed to resign.)

When it came time to bring Goose Island's ales into the fold, Baldwinsville was the natural destination despite the obvious challenges: in Chicago, Goose Island worked in fifty-barrel batches. Baldwinsville brewed thousand-barrel batches. Equipment was different in not only size but also shape. Like most small breweries, Goose Island's fermentation tanks were vertical. Baldwinsville was full of massive horizontal tanks—easier for its iconic beechwood aging, a process that helps filter the beer but imparts no flavor.

Tank geometry made scaling up 312 more difficult than anyone imagined. The broader surface area led to different head pressure on the beer, which resulted in more intense and fruitier esters than what came from taller, skinnier tanks. The result was a version of 312 that was too robust—an imperial version of 312. It tasted OK. It just wasn't 312.

Anheuser-Busch brewers were pleased with their version, but to Chicago, changing the profile wasn't an option. The beer was established in the market as Goose Island's signature brand. Any noticeable change would lead the critics to pounce. "People are looking for us to fuck it up," Kamarauskas told his team. The batch was dumped.

They attempted a second batch of 312 in Baldwinsville. Goose Island ordered that one dumped too.

Same for the third batch.

"We ended up dumping more beer than every frat house in America could have drunk in a single year when we started making 312," Brett Porter later told the *Chicago Tribune*. "We dumped batch after batch after batch after batch after batch."

Finally, St. Louis became worried. Where was this headed? They had dumped three thousand barrels of 312 Urban Wheat Ale—more beer than most US breweries made in a year. Was Goose Island sufficiently open minded? Were they tasting blind? Of course, they replied.

For the fourth tasting, St. Louis sent the big guns up north: Pete Kraemer, Anheuser-Busch's head of brewing operations, and Jane Killebrew, the director of brewing, quality, and innovation. Both were among the few Anheuser-Busch veterans who had survived the takeover three years earlier.

With a small Anheuser-Busch brewing team, they filed into Goose Island's conference room and sat opposite Mark Kamarauskas, Brett

Porter, Tony Bowker, and John. Each had four samples of 312 set out before them. Quietly, they sipped and jotted notes.

Then everyone shared their conclusions. Goose Island let their guests go first. There was little consistency between the samples favored by Kraemer and Killebrew; Kraemer liked samples Killebrew didn't, and vice versa. Then the four Goose Island veterans shared their thoughts, revealing identical conclusions: the first two samples were spot on, the third was a mess, and the fourth was not quite right but passable. Then the big reveal: the first two were Goose Island brews. The third was the rejected third batch from Baldwinsville. The fourth was the fourth batch from Baldwinsville, which they were all tasting for the first time.

Kraemer was taken aback; how did all four of them land on identical results? Especially when he couldn't see it? The Goose Island team took turns explaining. The beer needed a yeasty doughlike quality. Elements of lemon peel. Notes of citrus and hops. The light bulb went off. Kraemer tasted the samples again and concluded they were right. He turned to his team of brewers and told them to listen up. Where was the hop aroma? And the lemon peel? What had they tried? What hadn't they tried?

A heated discussion followed about how to claim the beer. The words ANHEUSER-BUSCH would appear nowhere on the label. But how far should they go in disavowing the parent company? The brain trust in St. Louis wanted to maintain Goose Island's Chicago identity on the label and nothing more. Technically, Goose Island was "making" the beer, so no further clarity was required about its origins. But John, Tony, and Greg (who was still consulting) were united that there could not be a hint of Goose Island hiding the source of 312 Urban Wheat Ale. It would affirm every skeptic. When the first labels were approved for the first version of Anheuser-Busch's 312, in November 2011, there, squarely on the front of the bottle, on a mustard yellow label retaining an image of the Chicago skyline, was the compromise: BREWED AND BOTTLED BY GOOSE ISLAND BEER CO. IN BALDWINSVILLE, NY.

They soon scaled up Honker's Ale and IPA at Baldwinsville too. The tank geometry remained a challenge, especially in the case of IPA, which required double the ratio of hops to achieve the same aroma. They did it by aping the approach to making Budweiser: instead of flooding beer into a tank laid with beechwood, the beer was flooded into a tank full of dried hops, shoveled in by hand.

The Anheuser-Busch versions of Goose Island beers were close enough to the originals to pass taste panels. But brewers back in Chicago nursed mixed feelings. Though relieved to be free of churning out 312, they were disappointed on principle. It was their beer. It was Chicago's beer. Now it was sharing tanks with Bud, Bud Light, and who knew what else. Honker's Ale had been a tough beer to brew with consistency in Chicago, and initially seemed to fare well on Anheuser-Busch equipment. But then, to some, it started to seem thinner and to lack nuance. And IPA—how were they supposed to explain that? It was perfectly fine but wholly different. The beers weren't necessarily *bad*; they were just different.

But off-loading the brands was ultimately an unqualified conquest. It allowed Goose Island to grow wildly under Anheuser-Busch ownership while retaining its Chicago identity. When a New Jersey newspaper recommended ten "refreshing spring brews" the next year, among them were Shock Top Lemon Shandy, credited to "Anheuser-Busch Inc., Missouri," and 312 Urban Wheat Ale, credited to "Goose Island, Illinois." It was a small but notable win: both beers were made on the same equipment at the same brewery in upstate New York. Yet the message was spreading: Goose Island was a Chicago beer. Ten breweries on the list were actually nine.

The ink was barely dry on the contracts when Anheuser-Busch did something baffling.

It trademarked area codes for fifteen cities: 215 (Philadelphia), 412 (Pittsburgh), 305 (Miami), 619 (San Diego), 202 (Washington, DC), 602 (Phoenix), 704 (Charlotte, North Carolina), 702 (Las Vegas), 214 (Dallas), 415 (San Francisco), 216 (Cleveland), 303 (Denver), 615 (Nashville), 713 (Houston), and, of course, 314 (St. Louis). The news broke in mid-July that the US Patent and Trademark Office received the applications from Anheuser-Busch on May 20—three weeks after the deal with Goose Island had closed.

Questions raced. Now that Anheuser-Busch owned 312, would the beer become nothing but a marketing trope, adjusted city by city as a faux local offering? Observers were left to guess. Many assumed the worst.

"We're being attacked," Bill Covaleski, cofounder of Victory Brewing Co., told the *Philadelphia Inquirer*. "Philadelphia's craft brewers are going to be forced to defend our status, but I'd rather be in this position than be the attacker."

He told the newspaper to expect a local "215" beer on tap within six to eight months. It wasn't an unreasonable thought. Anheuser-Busch had spent decades trying to confuse consumers and crush competition. A string of area code beers was straight out of the old playbook.

Agitated Goose Island employees wondered what the hell was happening to their brand. Don't worry, they were told. It was just an offensive maneuver by overzealous intellectual property lawyers. Anheuser-Busch didn't want anyone copying the idea.

Sure enough, none of the additional area code beers ever emerged. But the trademarking frenzy did produce an odd outcome on the West Coast. The dreadful thought of Anheuser-Busch swooping in to grab the local 805 area code motivated central California's Firestone Walker Brewing to create a new beer as a defensive tactic. None other than former Goose Island visionary Matt Brynildson, who had been Firestone Walker brewmaster for more than ten years, rushed out a draft beer invoking 805. A trademark lawyer told the brewery that as soon as it had an 805 product in the market, it was safe. One of Firestone Walker's founders urged Brynildson to make the beer hopped up and aggressively "craft." Brynildson disagreed; he said the beer should be as accessible as possible—much like 312 Urban Wheat Ale.

Brynildson's vision won out, and the result—the easy-drinking, low-alcohol 805 Blonde Ale—wound up succeeding as far more than defense. Once packaged in an eye-catching black-and-white can, 805 Blonde became Firestone Walker's biggest-selling beer. The irony was acute: amid its rarified tastes, California was a land where Anheuser-Busch struggled mightily against craft and imports. The surging 805 Blonde Ale only made its problems worse.

Karen King went back to St. Louis and tried to make a go of it.

In the year since Goose Island had taken a chance on the former manager of a gymnastics academy with little beer industry experience, she had become a favorite within the brewery, and for John Hall personally. It was impossible not to be won over by King's amiability and enthusiasm. She was just *nice*. She worked hard. She believed in Goose Island.

She was a longtime St. Louis resident who considered herself a fan of Anheuser-Busch and its role in the community. She and her husband, Cory, were passionate home brewers. They weren't above keeping Budweiser in the fridge at home. But working for Anheuser-Busch—especially now that it was part of Anheuser-Busch InBev—was something else entirely. Like most Goose Island employees, she was a believer in craft beer and independence and working for a family-run business. If she had wanted to work for the world's largest beer company, she would have applied to work for the world's largest beer company.

Now, she worked for the world's largest beer company.

Just after the sale was announced, Dave Peacock emailed her from Chile, welcoming her to the team. He said he looked forward to meeting Goose Island's lone St. Louis employee. She was impressed enough to forward the email to her father.

A few months later, for St. Louis Craft Beer Week, King hosted her first major Goose Island event. It was at the Stable, a suburban bar that catered to the mainstream (dollar bottles of Stag) while also embracing craft. King was thrilled to secure ten taps for Goose Island beer, including the previous year's Bourbon County Stout, Dominique, and an array of rare bottles. The line stretched out the door, including a gaggle of her new Anheuser-Busch colleagues, wearing jeans and polo shirts. They came out to support her, filling two large tables, then proceeded to slug down Bud Light after Bud Light. Couldn't they have at least ordered rounds of 312?

King was invited to Anheuser-Busch, where two higher-ups took her into a small conference room to grill her about selling Goose Island in Bud's backyard. They were curious about her sales numbers, which were astronomical for no other reason than Goose Island's negligible presence in the city before she was hired. With success like that, they joked, they couldn't wait to get her on the Budweiser team. At least, she hoped it was a joke.

Gradually people started falling away. A half-dozen Goose Island employees quit, citing the sale as the reason. Many of the defections came from the sales team, and among them was Karen King, who left in October 2011. It was a difficult decision. But as Goose Island's lone employee in Anheuser-Busch's backyard, she figured there was no way they would keep her on board. She wasn't going to wait to be laid off. Instead, she would get back to her roots: she and her husband would start a brewery of their own, called Side Project.

The most jarring departure, however, wasn't a Goose Island employee. It happened January 23, 2012, and there was no phone call, no email, no warning. John learned with the rest of the world: Dave Peacock resigned.

Pundits saw the move as the battleship's final turn from old Anheuser-Busch to new Anheuser-Busch InBev. The *St. Louis Post-Dispatch* reported that Peacock was walking away from stock options worth close to $28 million. "I didn't really mind leaving that money on the table," Peacock told the newspaper. "It was just the right time for me."

John had no idea what it meant. Peacock had been the guy sitting across the table as Goose Island's brain trust hammered out details of the sale. Most of those details had been affirmed on a handshake. Peacock's was the hand he shook. He was the guy John trusted, the buffer between Goose Island and the sprawling universe of Big Beer above. The buffer was gone.

21

"Trust Us a Little Bit"

As long as Anheuser-Busch wooed him, it traveled to Chicago to meet with John Hall. Now, two weeks short of the first anniversary of the announcement of the sale, Dave Peacock was gone and John was summoned to St. Louis.

It was time to meet the new boss.

John was already growing unhappy. The integration between Goose Island and Anheuser-Busch had been tedious and one-sided. The young Brazilian assigned to the task, who flew to Chicago from St. Louis every week to roam the halls of the Fulton Street brewery and report back, seemed only to be working for the bosses down south. John initially assumed that the kid was operating in the interest of both sides, that they were all one big happy family. Not so much. The kid endlessly pressed John for information but rarely shared anything in return. John was a big believer in trust. The kid had violated it quickly. Dave Peacock was good for his word and got the kid out of there when John complained. But trust had been eroded.

Peacock's surprise resignation was the bigger issue, and not just because John had been left to absorb the news from media reports like anyone else. He was losing his lifeline to the company. When he'd agreed to sell, John figured he would be tethered to, and protected by, Peacock. It was as if John had sold his company to *him*—not these faceless Brazilians. But now Peacock was out as president of Anheuser-Busch, and the company hadn't even bothered to replace him. John was left to report to Peacock's old boss—Luiz Edmond, the head of Anheuser-Busch InBev's North American operation.

The fair-skinned, forty-six-year-old Brazilian was a trusted soldier who had been in the fold since 1990. He started with the company at the age of twenty-three, through Brahma's immersive and intensive management trainee program, designed to identify the brightest young talent. It was a program that the company retained as it grew larger, pitting top MBA graduates against each other in group interviews to gauge how they operated when challenged in social settings. The company was known to be in an endless loop of identifying and nurturing its young, hardworking talent, setting those people on track for rapid promotions. Edmond was a classic example; in a mere six years, he was the company's chief sales officer. He ascended to CEO of Ambev, the South American operation, before transferring into the same role at the company's American conquest. Edmond's initial concerns at Anheuser-Busch were far bigger than measly Goose Island—they were jump-starting Bud Light, reversing Budweiser's years of decline, and pulling one of the most iconic companies in the United States into line with a radically modernized and global corporate culture.

But now, the agitated founder of Goose Island sat across his desk trying to assert whatever power remained a year after selling his company. John arrived with a typed list of points. Some were identical to his demands during negotiations with Peacock. Others were a reaction to what had bothered him most about the fledgling relationship between the companies.

> Goose Island will continue as an independent company with headquarters in Chicago; brewing, sales and marketing reporting to me. I will report to a senior executive in St. Louis.
>
> AB's business model needs to be modified for Goose Island to be successful. I believe it is critical for Goose Island's brand health to be viewed as an independent company by consumers and employees.
>
> Expansion plans are not collaborative.

That last issue was the most distressing. After amicably exporting production to Baldwinsville the previous summer—everyone agreed it needed to be done—Anheuser-Busch had unilaterally ordered 312, IPA, Honker's Ale, and Goose Island's seasonal beers to also be made at its plants in Ft. Collins, Colorado (for the western half of the country), and Montreal (for Canada).

It wasn't the most crucial issue, but it symbolized how John felt his grip slipping on the company. He was Goose Island's CEO, but it was starting to seem like a vanity title. He typed up nine names of former employees who had quit since the sale—Karen King among them—and cited the new ownership as a factor.

Edmond listened patiently. Then he said that he would do what he thought was best for Goose Island. He made clear that there was one decision maker in the room. It was not John Hall.

John had prided himself on running Goose Island as a bottom-up organization; many of the most important decisions started in the brew house. Once John peeked behind the curtain in St. Louis, it was clear that things at Anheuser-Busch began at the top and trickled down. Now they were trickling into Goose Island.

Though many of his worst fears were unfounded, small disagreements festered from the start. Like Goose Island's plan to roll out a lager—namely, a pilsner. The pushback from St. Louis was swift: no pilsner. That would compete with Budweiser. Goose Island's job was to stick to ales. John and his team argued that Goose Island and Budweiser appealed to vastly different drinkers. A Goose Island pilsner would compete only against other craft pilsners. Nearly every decision maker at Goose Island believed that introducing a pilsner was imperative. John expected the style to overtake IPA one day as the industry's bedrock. It was the most popular type of beer across the globe for a reason. The craft industry would not be immune to its easy charms.

No way, St. Louis said.

Another issue was sales. Since parting with US Beverage, Goose Island had slowly built a modest national sales force: Columbus, Ohio; suburban Detroit; the Twin Cities; St. Louis; Ames, Iowa; Milwaukee; New York City. To Anheuser-Busch, it was a luxury. In early 2012, Goose Island's national salespeople were told their jobs were eliminated, but they had the chance to interview for positions selling Anheuser-Busch's high-end portfolio: Shock Top, Hoegaarden, Leffe, Beck's, Stella Artois—and Goose Island. Some interviewed and were hired. Some interviewed and were not hired. Some didn't even bother.

In an effort to bridge the culture gap, Anheuser-Busch brought a star Goose Island salesman to manage the high-end portfolio in its Midwest regional office, which accounted for 80 percent of Goose Island's sales. Eric Hobbs had been hired by Goose Island four years earlier after a chance meeting with Tony Bowker at a bar. Hobbs was just breaking into the industry; if Goose was a beer industry Triple A affiliate, he was toiling in the rookie league—Huber Brewing, in Wisconsin, selling afterthought regional brands.

He was passionate and knowledgeable enough that Bowker left their chance meeting determined to hire him. The next day a midlevel sales manager called Hobbs in for an interview. He was thrilled to land at Goose Island and proud to work there. When he picked up his employee allotment of beer—a case per week of the core or seasonal brands—he made a point of lingering to chat with brewers. After the sale, John and Tony pulled him aside and asked him to apply for a job on the dark side. He could help ease the transition with the old-school Bud guys.

Hobbs's time at Anheuser-Busch was good to him. He applied the craft playbook to Big Beer, and soared. He won a trip to the Super Bowl for his rollout of Beck's Sapphire (though he sent a subordinate in his place). He was flown first-class to the Cannes Film Festival—where Stella Artois was a sponsor—with his fellow high-end managers. Then they hopped in a gleaming black SUV stocked with Stella to ride to their hotel overlooking the Mediterranean, walked the red carpet in tuxes for opening night of the Wes Anderson film *Moonrise Kingdom*, headed to a casino after-party, watched the sunrise, and then climbed aboard a puddle jumper to Belgium to visit the Stella and Hoegaarden breweries. Big Beer was fun when you did it well.

Back in the office, things were stranger. The office had already been through post–Anheuser-Busch InBev culture shock when he arrived. Offices were gone and no one tucked shirts into slacks anymore. Jeans were in. So were common work spaces. When Hobbs sat down his colleagues to introduce them to Bourbon County Stout, Juliet, and Sofie, they laughed. It wasn't outright mockery but edgier than purely good-natured. His boss had asked him to lead a tasting for these old-school Bud guys, so he did what he had done a hundred times before when working at Goose Island; he told the backstory of each beer—inspired largely by how he had heard Greg talk about the beers—and described the unique flavors and aromas of each. The Anheuser-Busch guys were baffled. They gave him a little shit, as if Hobbs was some pinkie-up beer snob. They'd never heard beer talked about like that.

Getting them to understand craft beer and to sell it effectively was a slog, but Hobbs figured they would come around. It was inevitable. John was glad to have him as a link between Goose Island and Big Beer. Otherwise the thought of these Bud guys trying to sell his beer was laughable—just as losing his national sales staff was a small betrayal. You couldn't have people who didn't understand craft beer trying to sell it.

But the most polarizing issue was expanding Goose Island's footprint. Everyone wanted Goose Island to grow. The question was how. And when. Opinions diverged wildly between Chicago and St. Louis.

When the Goose Island sale closed, Anheuser-Busch wholesalers were again clamoring for craft brands as they had during the mid-1990s. St. Louis wanted to supply them. Otherwise, those distributors might do the unthinkable: take on brands outside the Anheuser-Busch family. An average of 1.2 new breweries were opening *every day* by 2012. Anheuser-Busch distributors were encountering a flood of new options, and if St. Louis couldn't provide an IPA, well, some upstart could. Anheuser-Busch executives were ready to blast Goose Island as far as anyone wanted it.

John and his team were united that any rollout ending at the nation's sports bars, convenience stores, and Applebee's restaurants needed to unfurl deliberately. The Anheuser-Busch distribution network was powerful but mostly clueless about selling craft beer. It needed time to learn. Flooding the market with Goose Island, as if it were the latest incarnation of flavored Budweiser, just wouldn't work—even if flooding was Anheuser-Busch's specialty. Earlier that year, brand-new Bud Light Platinum had reached 95 percent of the company's five hundred plus distributors within weeks. A sugary Bud Light line extension—Cran-Brrr-Rita—reached 80 percent of distributors in a mere *four days*. Anheuser-Busch's skill was scale and speed. It wielded a powerful cudgel. Goose Island didn't want to be a cudgel. That wasn't craft beer.

John and Tony Bowker made their initial pitch about how to grow Goose Island at Anheuser-Busch's legendary Wholesaler Sales and Marketing Communication Meeting—SAMCOM in industry circles—in Dallas, in 2011. Speakers included company CEO Carlos Brito, baseball manager Tony La Russa, race car driver Kevin Harvick, rapper Pitbull, and Dallas Mavericks owner Mark Cuban. The signature event, after a day of updating wholesalers about the company's new products, packaging, and branding for 2012, was a "Bud Light Party." The crowd took over American Airlines Arena—home court of the Dallas Mavericks and Dallas Stars hockey team—for live music, *Monday Night Football*, food, and endless Bud Light.

John and Greg had attended SAMCOM since their minority stake deal with Anheuser-Busch in 2006, when they were tucked into a corner pouring samples alongside Widmer and Redhook. It was the same annual conference where John first covertly discussed a possible sale with Tony Short, in New Orleans, in 2010. By 2011, as an Anheuser-Busch property, they had graduated to the big time: John, along with Bowker and head of sales Bob Kenney, gave a breakout lecture to the hundreds of wholesalers whose regions stood to be among the first to get Goose Island.

The forty-five minutes touched on the brewery's mission and brand values before diving into a methodical plan hinging on building awareness via draft beer. They needed to "gain trial"—industry speak for getting people to try the beer—before sending it to supermarket shelves. Salespeople needed to do more than simply *sellsellsell* and aim for sales quotas; they needed to develop knowledge and expertise and understand "where to take the right brands." For every new Goose Island market, John and his team proposed appointing a brand manager—someone whose credentials were affirmed either by the Cicerone Certification Program or the Master Brewers Association of the Americas who would "have craft knowledge, decision making ability and act as point person" for all things Goose Island. That person would be required to spend time in Chicago learning about the brewery, its brands, and its culture.

They wanted to begin by expanding in markets where Goose Island was already successful. They wanted to "grow, but not at the expense of brand health," reaching consumers methodically, by focusing on local events and getting the beer into "influencer accounts"—top beer bars in a given market—to engage a local craft beer community and generate buzz. In every new market, they proposed launching exclusively on draft for two months, followed by packaged beer. Classic and vintage brands would take the lead, supported by 312 as an "active lifestyle" brand and Bourbon County Stout as an "extreme specialty brand." The rollout would begin with the full portfolio reaching the Northeast by early 2012, followed by the vintage portfolio in higher-end markets—San Francisco, Dallas, Atlanta, and Denver.

Peacock had been on board with the plan. He figured the craft guys knew best. But now the decision was Edmond's, and he was less sure. After their rocky introduction, John and his new boss settled into an amicable relationship. Edmond gradually convinced John that he understood the brand better than most of his contemporaries, not with words but with actions. At a meeting in St. Louis, Edmond surprised John by agreeing that Bourbon County Stout needed a better package than a standard twenty-two- or twelve-ounce bottle. It was one of the world's iconic beers and needed to be seen as such. Edmond approved a costly plan to get Bourbon County into its own branded five-hundred-milliliter bottle. It was the kind of move John never could have afforded when he owned the company. It was a heartening development.

Less heartening was the next meeting with Edmond, in March 2012. John and Tony Bowker headed to St. Louis to pitch the idea of the gradual rollout they outlined at SAMCOM. It was a meeting of a dozen Anheuser-Busch executives gathered around a conference table; Bowker began by playing a video from his laptop that Goose Island's marketing staff made on a twenty-dollar budget to promote the launch of the Baldwinsville-made 312 cans. Set to the tune of Hall and Oates's "You Make My Dreams," the two-and-a-half-minute video showed young, hip marketers launching 312 cans from the roof of the brewery to people at iconic locations around Chicago—Wrigley Field, the United Center, the lakefront. In place of the iconic lyrics "You make my dreams come true," the brewery's media director, who produced the video, belted out, "You're drinking a 3-1-2!" (They made the video in February, including the scene at the beach; they had to break ice atop Lake Michigan so a brand manager could tumble into the water while catching a can in shorts and a T-shirt while a woman from the marketing department lay on the beach in a bikini.)

Bowker started with the video hoping for a dose of levity, and to show the St. Louis executives that Goose Island could handle this. They understood craft beer messaging far better than anyone else in the room. Edmond, like every other executive at the table, chuckled at the video. But his conclusion was steadfast: the plan must be accelerated. Bud and Bud Light were struggling. The company wasn't selling enough beer. It was losing shelf space and tap handles. The distribution network had a slot for a new brand. Goose Island needed to be it. Anheuser-Busch and its parent company forever thought in terms of "gaps": What were its weaknesses? What holes could be filled? When there were no obvious gaps, it looked to create them; there was always opportunity for improvement, always share to be taken from competitors. Goose Island filled a gap, and a big one: in a world where Bud and Bud Light were fading by the month, it would be Anheuser-Busch's national craft beer brand.

John and Bowker went back to Chicago and continued to plead their case along with Bob Kenney and Mark Hegedus, Goose Island's senior marketing director. The rollout would be the first major test of whether Anheuser-Busch was as soullessly focused on the bottom line as the naysayers insisted. In April, they got one more chance to make their case, when Michael Taylor, an Anheuser-Busch veteran working in mergers and acquisitions, visited Goose Island's new office on Ashland Avenue, with two members of the marketing team. Edmond didn't even bother traveling for the meeting.

During a couple of hours in Goose Island's conference room, Bowker and Hegedus made their argument yet again across a whiteboard for a slow, measured rollout—starting with full distribution through the East, then to the South, and then inching West, ending with a slow crawl across California. Along the way, Anheuser-Busch distributors and their sales forces would need to be educated about the brewery, the brand, and the nuances that distinguished a wheat ale from a pale ale, a Guinness from a Bourbon County Stout. As things stood, the distributors didn't understand the brand and lacked the tools to make it succeed. Pushing distribution ahead of awareness might lead to a short-term boost, but it wasn't sustainable. It was about building momentum and understanding that some markets were more difficult to penetrate than others. Ever the Brit, Tony Bowker described Goose Island's proposal as a colonial model, rather than Anheuser-Busch's typical invasion. Done right, it would take as long as two years. Trust us, they said. You do Big Beer. We do craft beer.

Nope.

Rollout would begin in the fall.

John was demoralized by officially losing control of his company. But he and the rest of Goose Island's executives figured they would at least have a hand in the launch. They would get to mold brand managers in major markets. They would be able to lead with the classic and vintage portfolios, as they had envisioned. They would have a seat at the table.

Again: nope.

Goose Island never even got the courtesy of a call to learn that it was relegated to bit player for its own rollout. During the early afternoon of June 27, 2012, an email was forwarded to Bob Kenney that had been sent that morning from Andy Goeler, Anheuser-Busch's vice president of import, craft, and specialty, to the company's head of retail sales. It revealed that Goose Island would be going national at the end of October. The plan was to release 312 Urban Wheat Ale, Honker's Ale, India Pale Ale, and the Mild Winter seasonal on draft in a mere four months with six- and twelve-packs to follow in March 2013. The big push would be behind 312.

"As you know, this is aggressive!!" Goeler wrote.

The email was forwarded four times through the company before reaching Kenney. He couldn't believe it. No one on Fulton Street could believe it. Anheuser-Busch was orchestrating the rollout behind their backs. The timing wasn't meant to suit Goose Island; it was meant to fire up Anheuser-Busch wholesalers, who would hear details at that fall's SAMCOM (ironically, to be held in Chicago).

Goose Island's small consolation was that they had at least been heard about the importance of staggering the rollout: draft first, then packaged beer. At least awareness of the brands could be built one pint glass at a time for a few months before asking people to buy twelve-packs in grocery stores. It was consolation, but small consolation. A rollout that should have taken years would happen in months.

So, John did the only thing he could do. He resigned.

He had planned to stay at Goose Island for at least three years after the sale. Maybe even four or five. He was sixty-eight when the deal closed, and he imagined himself leading the company into his early seventies. Then he would hand the reins to Tony Bowker.

But here he was, barely a year later, typing a letter of resignation. He didn't need St. Louis to gut the company and the culture he had built. He'd had one knee surgery in July and was due for another in October. He was getting older. So was Pat. He'd built something. He'd been paid well for it. He didn't need the aggravation.

He kept the letter for a week. He weighed whether to send it. He didn't want to be rash. Goose Island was his creation. Was he ready to abandon it?

He was. He sent it. And he wondered if the naysayers had been right. Maybe he never should have trusted Anheuser-Busch. Maybe it had all been a colossal mistake.

He never heard back from Edmond.

Instead, the response came from the company's "chief people officer," James Brickey, who simply acknowledged receipt of John's letter. On September 21, John replied, laying out his gripes anew:

> While technically I continue to have the title of president and CEO, my role has been diminished to something much less than that of the most senior executive of the business. The announcement and communication of the Goose Island national expansion and route to market strategy are prime examples of major decisions that a CEO should be heavily involved in as opposed to learning of these decisions after they had been made. To compound the issue, I learned of the decisions indirectly through the Goose Island sales organization, not from my superior. With that understanding, ABI has not cured the circumstances constituting the basis for my resignation for good reason.

Finally, Edmond got the message.

He flew to Midway International Airport with David Almeida, another Brazilian who was vice president of sales for Anheuser-Busch InBev, for a face-to-face meeting.

"You've built a great company," Edmond said. "Be proud of it. We'll listen to you. But trust us a little bit."

John found Edmond far more personable than in their early showdowns. But the outcome was the same. Edmond said they planned to go forward with the national rollout. Distributors needed a legitimate craft beer, he said. Goose Island was what they had.

They shook hands and John agreed to stay on until December 31. Then he would retire.

He would be a good solider during the transition, spinning the "everything is fine" company line. He didn't want to do anything that would hurt the brand. He even agreed to soothe the cynics by joining, with Bowker, a newly formed Anheuser-Busch craft advisory board that in reality was an excuse to sit around and drink a few beers. Mostly, it was cover.

In a lengthy cover story that November, a reporter working on behalf of an American Marketing Association magazine knew nothing of John's resignation letters or the fact that the brand had been taken national against its wishes. It quoted a company spokesman who said John was "here and he's still running the show."

> In fact, according to both AB InBev and Goose Island, the Goose Island team does, and will continue to, drive the branding and marketing campaigns—and many of the business decisions—for the brand. "We're not going to make any changes to what the brand is," says Andy Goeler, vice president of craft, specialty and import beers at AB InBev. "It's gotten to where it is based on what it stands for and its association with the local Chicago community, and we think that's a powerful platform as it starts to roll into other markets."

In reality, Anheuser-Busch was having its way. John had wanted Bowker to take over the company, and Bowker wanted the job. But Anheuser-Busch went its own way on that matter too. As John's replacement, it appointed none other than Andy Goeler, one of the few St. Louis veterans to thrive after the merger.

John couldn't believe it. The guy who had championed an irrationally swift rollout for Goose Island would be taking over the company. He'd met Goeler. He liked him well enough. Certainly he respected him. But he couldn't fathom him running Goose Island. Goeler was Big Beer in jeans and a polo shirt.

The next time they saw each other, as John's tenure at Goose Island was winding down, he looked Goeler in the eye and told him he was the wrong guy for the job.

22

St. Louis—and Belgium and Brazil—We Have a Problem

LUIZ EDMOND WAS FEELING GOOD. Mostly.

Five years after InBev's takeover of Anheuser-Busch, the deal had been more than a coup—it created a giant. What began as Brazil's second-biggest beer company gobbled its way across the globe: through South America, into Europe and China, then to North America. The formation of Anheuser-Busch InBev had been the largest all-cash transaction in history. The deal upped the company's brands worth at least $1 billion from nine to fourteen. It meant millions in bonuses for top executives, Edmond included. Anheuser-Busch gave the Brazilians not only a new global flagship—Budweiser—but also six of the top ten brands in the United States, the world's most profitable beer market.

But Anheuser-Busch InBev was also facing more headwinds than expected. The first problem was a recession that dented the American beer industry, causing sales to drop precipitously beginning in 2009—a year after InBev took over Anheuser-Busch. The financial crisis was paired with Americans' growing fondness for wine and spirits, especially among the people drinking in bars and clubs. But most challenging was an increasingly fragmented market. Budweiser had been hemorrhaging sales for years and even suffered the indignity of slipping behind Coors Light as the nation's second-biggest-selling beer. Bud Light remained on top but receded each year. Worse, the company's core audience wasn't spending more money—it was spending less. When buying Anheuser-Busch, the Brazilians liked the company's dominance but not its reliance on budget brands such as Busch Light and Natural Light. Those sorts of beers, which made up 30 percent of the portfolio, carried lower profit margins. The Brazilians wanted to give consumers incentive to trade up, toward higher profit margins, not down, as the old Anheuser-Busch had been content to do. But the troubles were most apparent in the numbers: When InBev took over Anheuser-Busch, the company commanded 48.8 percent of the US market. Five years later, it was 45.7 percent—and falling.

Still, they were in an enviable position. Anheuser-Busch led almost every segment of American beer: value (Natural Light, Busch, and Busch Light), premium (Bud and Bud Light), and premium plus (surprise hit Michelob Ultra, initially aimed at baby boomers but which resonated as an "active lifestyle" brand). Though the company was losing overall share, Edmond stood before a room packed with investors in New York City in late 2013 and offered a reason for optimism: the company had identified the segment where it had plenty of runway to grow.

"A-B leads every single segment except the high-end," Edmond said. "Which, by the way, is a great opportunity for us."

The fact that Anheuser-Busch hadn't been well positioned in the high end was clear from the moment the Brazilians landed in St. Louis. But first, they had other concerns to address: integrating cultures, cutting costs, and slashing debt. They did so, and to great reward. For cutting debt to less than two and a half times the company's EBITDA—earnings before interest, tax, depreciation, and amortization—about forty executives were awarded stock options worth $1.57 billion during the spring of 2012.

Their windfall secured, the executives began to eye holes in the portfolio. There were plenty, and for a simple reason: Anheuser-Busch InBev was strong in the segments of American beer that were losing share. In areas of growth—craft and imports—it was barely represented.

Top leadership was united that the company needed to act forcefully. If it stayed still, Anheuser-Busch InBev would continue to be large, but in the United States, it wouldn't be relevant. It wouldn't attract new customers. The questions rained from as high as the board of directors: *What can we do to keep up?*

The issue was particularly urgent because, like Anheuser-Busch before them, Anheuser-Busch InBev saw crumbling distributor loyalty. As had happened during craft beer's mid-1990s boom, once-loyal wholesalers were increasingly taking on brands from outside the Anheuser-Busch portfolio. They'd been burned by their fidelity.

"We have made the competition stronger by basically forfeiting these brands to them," a Memphis distributor told the *Wall Street Journal* after ending Anheuser-Busch exclusivity by taking on Pennsylvania's Yuengling Lager, along with ten other Tennessee wholesalers. "We saw a brand with some very strong potential, and we didn't want that brand to fall into competitive hands in the state."

All Anheuser-Busch had been able to do in response was pledge optimism about a high-end portfolio of fairly low-end brands. Imports, at least, were looking up. Before the merger, Anheuser-Busch had less than 1 percent of the US import market. As a global beer company, it had new clout and a robust lineup. It lacked credible Mexican brands at a time when Americans were embracing Corona and Modelo—that was a legitimate problem—but it did bring a core of European brands to stand up to Heineken. Chief among them: Belgium's Stella Artois, which the company assigned a goal of being "recognized by the affluent consumer as the superior premium beer in the world." In the United States, it was beginning to work: starting in 2008, Heineken's share dropped while Stella's climbed.

The craft lineup, however, was in borderline crisis. When InBev took over, it amounted to two beers: Shock Top and Landshark Lager. Shock Top, born as Spring Heat Spiced Wheat and the lone success under the Michelob craft initiative, did respectable business battling MillerCoors's Blue Moon Belgian White. But it did little to win over adventurous drinkers. Landshark Lager, a vague attempt at battling Corona, inspired no one. The question was what to do.

The principal options were what the industry called "line extensions"—outgrowths of existing brands, like what had been tried with Michelob. That was a proven failure. There was the possibility of creating wholly new brands, like Shock Top, but those were costly, time intensive, and not an Anheuser-Busch strength; it was far better at following than leading. Just as Bud Light followed Miller Lite, Michelob Golden Draft followed Miller Genuine Draft, and Bud Light Lime followed Miller Chill, Shock Top had followed Blue Moon. The odds of innovating the next great craft beer were not on Anheuser-Busch's side.

The answer, the Brazilians, concluded, was what they did best: acquisitions.

At the 2010 Consumer and Retail Conference in New York City, Dave Peacock pledged optimism about Anheuser-Busch's meager portfolio of craft and imports brands, saying they possessed great "upside" and amounted to a "credible portfolio of high end options to achieve our goal."

However, Tony Short had quietly gauged John Hall's interest in selling Goose Island a month earlier. And, in three weeks, Peacock would fly to Chicago to bring the deal across the finish line.

With Goose Island in the fold, Anheuser-Busch had an important weapon in its arsenal. It was a small weapon in an unfathomably large arsenal. But an important weapon all the same.

"We believe it is not a matter of if, but when growth returns in the U.S. beer market, and we want to be properly positioned with consumers when that turnaround occurs," Peacock told *Supermarket News* months after acquiring Goose Island. "We have room to grow in the high-end category, which will allow us to capture occasions from other beverages."

Occasions. That's how Big Beer thought.

Each time a beer was bought, it was as part of an "occasion." It could be to unwind after work. Or to accompany mowing the lawn. Or to get ready for a night out. Or as part of that night out. Or while watching the Super Bowl. To a drinker, buying beer was buying beer. To the biggest beer company in the world, it was a moment to dissect, to understand, and to own. As recently as the 1990s, Americans were likely to drink two or three different beers for every ten occasions, led by a dominant brand cracked seven or eight of those times. By the time of the Goose Island deal in 2011, many Americans were drinking seven to ten different beers for those ten occasions. Consumer tastes had fragmented. Nearly one-fifth of the beer sold was craft or imported.

Shortly after acquiring Goose Island, Anheuser-Busch mapped out six primary "shopper occasions" and slotted the Chicago brewery as beer for "savoring":

Everyday food occasions (Budweiser, Bud Light, Busch, Busch Light)
Hanging out occasions (Bud Light, Budweiser, Natural Light, Rolling Rock)
Indulging occasions (Bud Light Lime, Rita beers, Shock Top, Stella Artois)
Partying occasions (Bud Light Platinum, Budweiser Black Crown, Beck's, Rita beers)
Relaxing occasions (Budweiser, Bud Light, Busch, Busch Light)
Savoring occasions (Stella Artois, Shock Top, Goose Island, Leffe)

The same point of sale material that had been the stuff of Big Beer—sidewalk chalkboards, umbrellas, and vinyl banners hung inside bars—were deployed nationally bearing the Goose Island logo. They were available at the password-protected website wholesalers used to order promotional tools for Bud and Bud Light: ABmarketing.com.

The same "retail labs"—mock shopping environments that Anheuser-Busch staged in St. Louis—began to include 312 Urban Wheat Ale in their calculations. Big Beer was invested in not only making and distributing beer but also infiltrating the sales tier by employing "category space analysts," which arranged shelf displays for willing grocery and convenience stores. One mock convenience store scene included cases of Bud Light flanked by bags of Ruffles (blue beside blue), Budweiser with Doritos (red-red), and 312 Urban Wheat Ale beside Lay's (yellow-yellow). Ideas were prototyped and obsessively tweaked before they were taken into the market. For every new priority—usually, unfurling a new brand—teams spent hours brainstorming, unable to leave until they devised one hundred ideas for how to bring a beer to market. Suddenly that included Goose Island.

Anheuser-Busch InBev's annual report to shareholders typically clocked in at close to two hundred pages. Somewhere near page 60 came an innocuous heading: "Risks relating to AB InBev and the Beer and Beverage Industry." It was the kind of small print among tens of thousands of words not meant to elicit a second glance; the risks were typically copied from the previous year's report. They amounted to the things that could send the stock price tumbling. Like the need for reduced pricing in a tight marketplace. Or making capital investments. Or spending more on marketing.

But in 2012—a year after Anheuser-Busch InBev bought Goose Island—the risks included a new wrinkle: "Also, innovation faces inherent risks, and the new products AB InBev introduces may not be successful, while competitors may be able to respond quicker to the emerging trends, such as the increasing consumer preference for 'craft beers' produced by smaller microbreweries."

The moment of craft beer's arrival can be endlessly debated. It could be when Sierra Nevada first brewed its pale ale. Or when that pale ale was distributed east of the Rocky Mountains. Or when Greg Hall first sipped Bourbon County Stout. Or when craft passed 5 percent of the nation's beer sales (in 2011). Or 10 percent (2014). But quite likely, it was the moment that the words *craft beers* infiltrated the annual report of the biggest beer company in the world.

Craft was officially a threat.

Anheuser-Busch categorized its new audience into two groups: "Accessible" and "Discovery" craft drinkers. Anheuser-Busch's head of high-end beers at the time, Adam Oakley, spelled out the difference for investors in 2013:

> "Accessible" craft consumers are influenced by advertising. They're image-driven, price sensitive, typically younger adults and often new to craft.
>
> In comparison, "Discovery" craft drinkers are more interested in brewers' backstories. They seek bolder beer styles and are more discerning about the beers they purchase and share with their friends.
>
> "Accessible" craft consumers drink brands like Blue Moon, Leinenkugel and Redd's.
>
> "Discovery" craft consumers drink Sam Adams, Sierra Nevada and Fat Tire.
>
> And most importantly, "Accessible" craft accounts for 60 percent of craft volume, "Discovery" craft 40 percent.

Oakley summarized: "Our 2014 craft strategy is very simple; Shock Top targets 'Accessible' craft, while Goose Island targets 'Discovery' craft."

This was why Luiz Edmond overruled the pleas coming from Chicago to roll out Goose Island in a measured stream. Anheuser-Busch needed a flood of "Discovery" craft beer.

In a 2012 *Harvard Business Review* article, James Allen, a senior partner in the London office of consulting firm Bain & Company, noted that the Brazilians had been wildly successful at every step in their beer business—not as brewers but as financial and cultural engineers. The creation of each new company was followed by a marked rise in earnings:

> The consistent, dramatic increases in profitability after each of these combinations—in AmBev, then in InBev, then in AB InBev—are evidence of a repeatable model at work.
>
> AB InBev's repeatable model is built around 10 nonnegotiable beliefs. Only one of them talks about cost cutting. The majority focus on the kind of people, culture and ways of working that AB InBev believes are required to win. And it is not

> enough that top management believe in these ideas: What makes a repeatable model so powerful is that the employees on the front line believe in them too. Management and front-line employees dream the same dreams.
>
> I've witnessed the power of these dreams on a number of occasions. While working in Brazil, we invited an AB InBev team (from the original AmBev) to talk to a client of ours about how they compete. Our client was amazed by their passion for winning. They spoke about how they "owned each city, each store and each shelf" and battled every day to beat the competition.

But it was Jorge Paulo Lemann himself who best underscored his own motives, with a quote dating to the late 1980s, just as he and his partners were entering the beer business: "I was looking at Latin America and who was the richest guy in Venezuela: a brewer. The richest guy in Colombia: a brewer. The richest in Argentina: a brewer. These guys couldn't all be geniuses. It's the business that must be good."

Skeptics often wielded the quote as a criticism and evidence of his lack of sentimentality about the beer business. But economists Ina Verstl and Ernst Faltermeier argued in their 2016 book *The Beer Monopoly: How Brewers Bought and Built for World Domination* that turning beer into a string of efficiencies to reward top executives with millions in bonuses was "the whole point of the exercise." While other large beer companies obsessed over the amount of beer they produced—volume—the Brazilians focused only on profitability. Dig an inch beneath the surface, Verstl and Faltermeier argued, and it was obvious: The Brazilians didn't care about beer as beer. They cared about beer as business.

> What critics fail to see is that the Brazilians adhere to a different view of human nature. Whereas in post-materialist societies the notion of "homo reciprocans"—the bearded tree-hugger who altruistically wants to make the world a better place—prevails, the Brazilians favor "homo oeconomicus," a tough cookie, who is exclusively motivated by self-interest. Their reliance on clear metrics to steer and measure staff performance not only matches this view, it also functions as a safeguard against key knowledge

> leaving the company through the revolving doors. As we see it, their reducing of work/labor to a set of metrics was merely another component of their ultimate scheme to design an all-encompassing numbers-based model for running the best beer company. This model was not just applied to Brazil. It would have been Mr. Lemann's intention to develop a genuine one-fits-all blueprint, whose fundamentals could be put to work anywhere. Once they felt confident of that, Mr. Lemann decided that Brahma should start playing beer monopoly.

Beer monopoly was good to Lemann; he became Brazil's richest person. But with American craft beer, he and his partners had run into unusual doubts. The Brazilians were brilliant and disciplined financiers, but could they build brands? And could they build them in a craft realm that had repeatedly thwarted its predecessor company? Experts were skeptical.

During a question-and-answer session with analysts in 2013, a Belgian banker asked Anheuser-Busch InBev executives why they hadn't been more forceful in American craft beer to date: "Why haven't you shifted gears by inorganic growth in the high end yet—except for Goose of course?" In other words: Why hadn't they bought more craft breweries?

"We get this question from our wholesalers all the time—why are we not buying more cases?" Luiz Edmond said, invoking industry slang for growth through acquisitions. "Why we are not buying more cases: we are in the business of building brands, and we believe our brands can compete in the high-end segment. So, we acquired Goose, and Goose is growing, so why would we dilute that effort with something else, and put dollars into two brands as opposed to putting dollars into one brand?

"So, we have an amazing opportunity to take this brand to the next level. It has been growing phenomenally well, but we need to guarantee that we are not just gaining distribution by using our national scale, but that we are also supporting the gains in distribution with increased awareness and consideration. We believe we have enough portfolios inside Goose that we can bet with one bigger brand as opposed to betting on a lot of different things. Having said that, if we find something that is unique, that can add value to our portfolio, we are happy to discuss. But the focus now is to grow with the brands that we have."

Then the most powerful beer executive on the planet jumped in.

"It's interesting," Anheuser-Busch InBev chief executive officer Carlos Brito said, "because a couple of years ago when we came here to the U.S. and then a year later when the so-called 'craft beer phenomenon' started happening, I was asked time and again in quarterly calls and meetings like this: 'Well, how do you see the so-called craft segment evolving?'"

(Brito had a habit of calling craft beer "so-called craft beer." He rejected the implication that brewing macro brands wasn't also a craft.)

"And I always said, I think—because we believe that we can shape the industry together with some other players—if we could shape the craft segment as the import segment was shaped by accident, or by plan, in that five brands or five manufacturers have 80 percent of the action, and then you have a long tail, and we said, 'Well, maybe that could happen with craft as well—why not?'"

He noted that during the previous three years, 81 percent of growth within craft "came from national brands, supported by national companies, and not from the every-ten-block type brand, the regional brands."

"Now, I'm not discounting (the smaller and regional brands), I'm not discounting them," Brito said. "I think they have a very important role to play to bring interest to the category. But I'm just saying that yes, I think that it can be shaped in a way that most growth will be commanded by few brands—and by a few national brands."

23

"Anheuser-Busch Is Letting Us Do Our Own Thing"

"Anheuser-Busch is letting us do our own thing," Andy Goeler told *Crain's Chicago Business* in May 2013, five months after taking over for John Hall at the helm of Goose Island.

"I'm not getting directives."

Goeler wasn't getting directives from St. Louis for a simple reason: he *was* the directive.

For as little as Anheuser-Busch had incorporated Goose Island into its broader agenda for the first year after the sale, it compensated quickly with the appointment of Goeler.

Goeler was fifty-six at the time and the epitome of the Anheuser-Busch company man. He'd come on as a salesman in rough-and-tumble Jersey City in 1980, at twenty-three, after graduating Fairleigh Dickinson University with a marketing degree. He was a staunch believer in Anheuser-Busch and its culture, traveling from bar to bar with a bottle of Windex so that he could clean the Budweiser globes hanging from the smoky ceilings of North Jersey's bars. In 1995 he was named director of marketing for Bud Light. It displaced Budweiser as America's top-selling beer under his watch. Then Goeler took over Budweiser to try reversing the early days of that brand's decline.

Goeler, a thickset, brown-haired man who seemed to be perpetually squinting, was extraordinarily driven. If tasked with presenting a marketing strategy, he had his team build two hundred slides. Then he whittled it to one hundred. Then fifty. The he whittled it more. He was one of the most legendary performers at SAMCOM, Anheuser-Busch's annual wholesaler conference. He relished inspiring the troops and creating believers almost as true as himself. He thought of it, he would say, as "a business rallying cry." He famously never used a script before a crowd and never stood still. He paced with a wireless microphone. Back and forth, back and forth across the stage, unspooling a message he'd practiced relentlessly so that it would seem organic in the moment.

Goeler was running Budweiser when approached in 2004 about managing a high-end portfolio for Anheuser-Busch. Like leading any beer unit at Anheuser-Busch, it was in reality a marketing job. At first it seemed like a demotion; the company didn't *have* any high-end brands. But, of course, that was the problem.

As vice president of imports, craft, and specialty beer, Goeler traveled through Europe and Asia looking for brands to import to the United States. But most of the good ones, he concluded, were spoken for. He struck a deal to bring in Grolsch, a Dutch lager that did little to improve the company's fortunes. Instead he focused efforts on relaunching the Michelob craft unit. When introduced in the late 1800s, Michelob was a draft-only beer that required its own draft system and glassware. It seemed to Goeler like "the original craft beer," as he would tell any and every audience. He cleaned up Anheuser-Busch's pilot brewery and, to give the brewers a sense of purpose, informally rechristened it the Michelob Brewing Co.

As the head of craft and imports, Goeler was the natural if unimaginative choice to take control of Goose Island once John Hall had had enough. It was time to blast Goose Island from Anheuser-Busch's cannon; Goeler was the man to light the fuse. He was a nice guy who would have made a fine Boy Scout leader. He was prone to using "holy kamoly" to exclaim wonder. His enthusiasm was infectious. But his time at Goose Island would become the most difficult era of the brewery's transition to the big time.

Goeler said the right things coming in, even if they were obvious.

"I see Shock Top as very different than Goose," he told the *Chicago Tribune* on the day he was announced as Goose Island's new CEO. "I don't see Goose consumers drinking Shock Top. And Goose is probably too serious for a Shock Top consumer."

Goeler's talent was as a Big Beer guy. Suddenly he was a Small Beer guy—tasked with turning it into Big Beer. The fit was as odd as it might seem. When he professed a fondness for the seasonal Mild Winter, a Goose Island employee mentioned that the beer featured rye in the grain bill, a fairly standard ingredient in a craft brewery.

"I didn't know you could put rye in beer!" Goeler said.

What he lacked in brewing knowledge, he made up for in planning, determination, and a seat at Anheuser-Busch's table. He wasn't impressed with the Goose Island operation when he showed up. He told them they thought small. The brand was a bit confused—especially the brewpub, where they served wine and spirits that distracted from the beer message. But he asked questions and solicited opinions, including John Hall's, which gradually swung John's opinion of his successor. Though few within the brewery immediately realized it, Goeler's appointment to the job signified a commitment from Anheuser-Busch to its wholesalers: Goose Island was a brand to be taken seriously.

Anheuser-Busch was an entirely new universe for Goose Island. There were more resources but also higher expectations and a culture that reflected what it meant to be part of one of the world's ten largest consumer packaged goods companies. That culture was a grind, and Goose Island management was expected to grind along with it. It wasn't odd to find a morning email that had arrived at 2:00 AM. Or to sit through meetings that broke up for dinner, then reconvened so that everyone could work until midnight. One legendary story circulated of a St. Louis executive flying to meetings in Phoenix, Los Angeles, San Francisco, and Portland, Oregon, all in a single day, wrapping up at 10:00 PM.

Goeler was a believer in that culture, and it trickled through Goose Island—especially sales and marketing, the departments he best understood. He underscored the point that planning was required months or even years ahead. The Anheuser-Busch galaxy revolved around SAMCOM, the annual conference where wholesalers gathered under one roof to be fired up and fed marching orders for the coming year. Inside the brewery, those plans needed to be discussed in May so they could be finalized in September, then rolled out at SAMCOM in November. Prior to the sale, Goose Island stitched its existence together by the month, if not the week. Goeler's job was to end that scrappy way of thinking. His expertise wasn't running a craft brewery; it was operating within the vast Anheuser-Busch network—launching a brand impossibly wide, then supporting it. There was no one better.

But the trade-off of seamless entry into the Anheuser-Busch way of doing things was doing things the Anheuser-Busch way. Brewing operations were gradually pushed lower down the ladder. At craft breweries, sales, marketing, and distribution worked to support brewing; at Anheuser-Busch, brewing worked to support sales, marketing, and distribution. Beer didn't start as a recipe at Anheuser-Busch; it began as an idea around a conference table strewn with laptops and spreadsheets. Goeler outwardly championed Goose Island's craft spirit and supported initiatives such as the Fulton & Wood series. But his priority was launching the brewery into a new orbit: Goose Island as national force.

"It's almost like two companies going on here," he told *Beer Business Daily* in 2014. "We're providing great, national craft beers to our system and the consumers around the country. And then we're doing the rare beers, the sour beers, the Bourbon Counties, and we do some things in Chicago."

It was the national half of the equation that proved most challenging on Fulton Street. Just as John Hall and Tony Bowker had predicted before being ushered out of leadership, the national launch of Goose Island's portfolio flopped. It flopped wildly.

The typical Anheuser-Busch launch came with extraordinary support: buy-in from distributors who were able to understand and explain a brand in a sentence ("Budweiser Black Crown is a classier version of Budweiser!") and an endless well of advertising and promotion, including the occasional Super Bowl commercial. Led by 312, Goose Island got little of that. Instead, the portfolio was simply pushed into the Anheuser-Busch wholesaler network, where details of Goose Island's new twenty-four-can sampler pack appeared in the same missive revealing news of the new Bud Light Mardi Gras cans. Thousands of Goose Island kegs headed across the country with little support.

But that didn't stop Anheuser-Busch from trying to make the rollout seem like something it wasn't. A February 2013 press release announcing Goose Island's national distribution said that 312 Urban Wheat Ale, Honker's Ale, IPA, and the seasonal beers would be brewed in Baldwinsville and Ft. Collins "to meet increasing demand from the national launch." It was classic Big Beer: trying to make what it pushed seem like something that consumers were pulling. Production of Goose Island had moved to Anheuser-Busch to enable the launch—not as a result of it. Yet the idea of Anheuser-Busch merely trying to satisfy consumer demand became a common refrain. "Throughout the craft segment, Goose Island's beers are recognized, respected and loved," an Anheuser-Busch vice president told trade magazine *Grocery Headquarters* in mid-2013. "To meet the increasing demand for Goose Island beers, 312 Urban Wheat Ale, Honker's Ale, IPA and the seasonal offerings are now offered nationwide."

Wholesalers were largely left to themselves to figure out how to sell the beer. Those that had seen Sam Adams or Sierra Nevada roll through their warehouses had at least a vague understanding of how to talk about this exotic brand from Chicago. But those getting their first taste of wheat ale or IPA were dumbfounded. The proof was in the sales, which initially were encouraging:

2013			
	Sales	**Growth**	**Percentage growth**
312	$15,678,501	$5,802,809	58.8%
Honker's Ale	$4,204,242	$2,122,272	101.9%
IPA	$4,162,598	$2,662,465	177.4%

A year later, however, the failure was plain: 312 remained nearly flat, Honker's Ale dropped precipitously, and IPA, in a market where the style was on fire, grew unspectacularly:

2014			
	Sales	**Growth**	**Percentage growth**
312	$16,418,117	$739,616	4.7%
Honker's Ale	$3,422,238	–$782,004	–18.6%
IPA	$5,550,476	$1,387,878	33.3%

Thousands of cases of 312 and Honker's were recalled due to a lack of sales. Even with 312 getting the kind of placement that it never could have fathomed from an independent company—arenas, stadiums, and United Airlines flights across the globe—the brand didn't resonate. The quirky name and telephone tap handle that had charmed Chicago confused the rest of the country. It had thrived in Chicago as an easy-drinking beer for an active, urban lifestyle. It was aspirational, reflecting the place where young people went for festivals, concerts, sports, art, nightlife, and a first professional job. That didn't play on grocery store shelves in California. Some people couldn't even figure out how to say it. *Three twelve? Three hundred twelve? Three-one-two?* (The third is correct.) By mid-2014, Goeler acknowledged that they had miscalculated.

"I think the power of 312 is more Midwest," he told *Beer Business Daily*. "It's all over, it's national, but I think people in this Midwest area identify with it, because I think they clearly know that 312 is the Chicago area code."

Goose Island veterans were dismayed. They saw a brand that had failed to connect with a national audience because St. Louis had failed to understand the brand. The intended audience wasn't even clear.

Yet Anheuser-Busch doubled down on the brand with the addition of 312 Urban Pale Ale—a green label beside 312 Urban Wheat's trademark yellow. It only compounded troubles. 312 Pale did a respectable $3.7 million of sales through 2014, but 2015 sales dropped more than 20 percent. Mainstream drinkers were confused by the difference between what they saw as "green 312" and "yellow 312." Seasoned beer drinkers weren't interested; if they were going to drink a pale ale, it was going to be fresh and local, not from the tanks of Anheuser-Busch. A year later, 312 Pale was gone, and so were the plans to turn 312 into a national portfolio of hip, urban brands.

Poor sales were Anheuser-Busch InBev's problem. Andy Goeler's problem. On Fulton Street, brewers and longtime employees had a more basic concern. The character of the brewery was drifting.

Before the sale, brewers experimented until they found something worth scaling up. Now orders were coming from above. That was clearest with the 2013 decision to replace the brewery's longtime seasonal releases—Summertime, Harvest Ale, and Christmas Ale—with a series of seasonal hop-forward beers. The demise of Summertime especially stung. It was a bright, approachable Kölsch that Greg had developed in 1996, one of the earliest beers crafted on Fulton Street. It was a longtime favorite in Chicago and of John Hall himself. With the excommunication of the seasonal beers, John was beginning to believe that Anheuser-Busch failed to appreciate the portfolio it bought. A Goose Island brewer approached Goeler directly to insist that dropping Summertime was a grievous mistake; it was a good beer that if marketed effectively would thrive nationally.

It did no good. In place of Summertime and the other longtime seasonal releases came a series of new hoppy beers to be released every four months: Ten Hills Pale Ale in November 2013, Endless IPA in March 2014, and Rambler IPA in August 2014. It was Goeler's boldest initiative yet, rooted in a bid to appeal to younger drinkers while appeasing wholesalers who complained that no one wanted a beer called Summertime by mid-August or Christmas Ale on December 26. Sales data showed IPAs and pale ales thriving. It seemed a sound gamble to him. "The younger consumer nowadays likes experimentation and variety," he told the *Chicago Tribune*. "This is some easy, low hanging fruit to put some new styles out and get people engaged in what we're doing at Goose Island. It's about continuing the relationship with your consumers and giving them things that they like." Goeler said he thought of Goose Island like a book. John Hall's chapter had come to an end. Now, he was writing a new chapter.

Ten Hills, Endless, and Rambler were all pioneered on Fulton Street, but only for the purpose of being scaled up on Anheuser-Busch's gargantuan system in Baldwinsville. The problem with the beers wasn't that they were bad; it was that they were ordinary. They tasted exactly like what they were: Big Beer imitations of craft beer. "Ended up tasting like caramel tea. Couldn't even finish it," one Ten Hills observation read on a home brewing internet forum. "Reminded me of a hoppy pale that had been sitting on the shelf for months. Drain pour. I'm a Goose Island fan, but I always wonder how breweries can make something like this and say, 'Yep, that's right where we want it. Send it out!'"

The criticism was remarkably shrewd: for the first time, Fulton Street brewers weren't choosing which Goose Island beers to send into the world. When told in a meeting that the seasonal beers would be replaced by a series of hop-forward beers, some brewers were enthused enough to start sharing ideas. They were quickly told to stop; their input wasn't requested. Decisions had already been made. They were simply handed recipes before the first brew, then underwhelmed by what they saw. It was the first time many of them had been called on to simply execute a marketing plan. None of the hop-forward beers sold well, and all were quickly discontinued.

Yet despite any missteps, Goose Island kept growing, fueled mostly by the beer made at Anheuser-Busch breweries:

Year	Barrels	Annual growth
2011 (year of sale to Anheuser-Busch InBev)	150,000	18.7%
2012 (first full year of production at ABI breweries)	210,000	40.2%
2013 (first full year of national distribution)	340,000	61.9%
2014	375,000	10.3%

It was an era of two Anheuser-Busch-sized leaps forward and one little craft step back. Shortly after the sale, for instance, Goose Island made the splashy move of renting a 130,000-square-foot warehouse two miles west of the brewery where it could wildly expand the barrel-aging program, and the Bourbon County family in particular. They'd begun discussing the project following Goeler's arrival, and submitted a proposal—which included massive construction and renovations—in September 2013. St. Louis signed off on it three months later, and by October 2014 Goose Island was moving in. The beer was still made on Fulton Street, then transferred by tanker truck to the warehouse. Goeler championed the move and became instantly smitten with the space; it was unfinished and rough, but the bones—barreled ceilings and wood beams—were an ideal backdrop for a brewery looking to distinguish itself as the home of barrel aging.

Finally, by Black Friday 2014, they could begin to unfurl the growth, with Bourbon County release events in new cities—New York, San Francisco, and Austin, Texas—and at high-volume retailers such as supermarkets, convenience stores, and big-box stores. The problem was that those stores—even in Chicago—had little idea what to do with such unique and costly beer. A Walgreens in Chicago's Wicker Park neighborhood put its cases on sale at midnight on Black Friday—nine hours earlier than intended. Word got out on social media, and the beer nerds descended in the middle of the night, walking away with Bourbon County by the case while others froze in line waiting for far smaller allotments at the usual 9:00 AM Binny's Beverage Depot release across from the brewpub. Word spread of entire cases mistakenly sold at a supermarket for the price of a single bottle—twenty-five dollars. Longtime fans took to social media to vent their rage.

Meanwhile, Chicago bar owners who had supported Goose Island for years were lucky to get even one case of Bourbon County. They wondered why clueless, cookie-cutter chain stores were suddenly getting so much of the precious beer. The answer was that the clueless cookie-cutter chain stores churned through massive sales of 312 Urban Wheat and IPA during the rest of the year. They were being rewarded by a new generation of Goose Island decision makers.

Yet, three years after the sale, Goose Island was finally starting to win the perception wars.

Though it was among the fastest-growing breweries in the nation, Goeler downplayed the leaps in interviews. Getting bigger worked against Anheuser-Busch's preferred image of staying true to Goose Island's roots. Instead, Goeler beat the drum of the brewery as a world-class innovator. Nothing underscored the message quite like the rosy glow of a sprawling new barrel warehouse. Or an idyllic hop farm in northern Idaho, ten miles south of the Canadian border, which Anheuser-Busch essentially handed over to Goose Island after the sale. Goose Island began flying media to the farm for all-expense-paid trips during the summer of 2014 to put its credibility as a world-class *craft* brewer on display. (I visited the farm in 2014 on behalf of the *Chicago Tribune*, though the *Tribune* paid travel expenses.) See, it had its own hop farm! And here, eat this delicious candlelit dinner in a hop field at dusk! Then write about it! (Some writers took the bait more than others. After a media trip to the hop farm in 2016, one blogger wrote, "For a few days, I didn't care who owned whom, what owned what. I only cared about the process of hops traversing the country from Idaho soil to my snifter in Chicago." For Anheuser-Busch, it was mission accomplished.)

Skepticism of the sale, and especially shipping off production to Anheuser-Busch breweries, had mostly faded away, replaced by a steady dose of adulation. In 2013, two years after the sale, a *Crain's Chicago Business* headline declared, "Brewer Holds to Its Craft Beer Roots After Purchase by InBev." A brewer at Solemn Oath, a newly opened suburban Chicago brewery, who had previously dabbled in beer blogging, published a fourteen-hundred-word blog post on the Solemn Oath website titled "Ten Reasons You Should Be Drinking Goose Island Right Now." He praised the fact that 312 Urban Wheat, IPA, Honker's Ale, and the seasonal beers moved to Anheuser-Busch breweries because it turned Fulton Street "into a Bourbon County and Belgian machine with innovation as a core part of its operations" with no drop-off in quality, consistency, or innovation.

"If your final assessment of Goose Island comes down to an ironic scoff at 312 being brewed in different area codes around the country, congratulations on being a smug, holier-than-thou knee-jerker with no appreciation for or understanding of the bigger picture," he wrote.

A month later, advertising and marketing magazine *Ad Age* suggested "the doubters seem to have been proved wrong" about Goose Island's sale. The magazine spun a depiction of how nothing had changed that Goose Island was undoubtedly quite pleased to read:

> As the three-year anniversary of the $38.8 million deal approaches in March, Goose Island has managed to hold on to its street cred. It's stayed true to its roots by avoiding many tactics employed by A-B InBev, such as copy testing, consumer testing or market research. Instead, the brand has relied on grassroots marketing as it puts new beers in the market based on the judgment and creativity of its employees and head brewer.

A month later, a Baltimore beer writer declared that drinking Goose Island was good for craft beer. Immediately after the sale, he had sworn off Goose Island. Beneath the headline "Why I Lifted My Boycott of Goose Island," he declared:

> I am trying to encourage people to reconsider their opinions on Goose Island a little. I have. I want the message to be clear, that I want a good product. If it changes, and becomes a lesser product I will use my capitalist power and move on. But I'm no longer going to abstain solely based on my dislike for the greater corporation. I have actually been impressed that AB-InBev has largely kept Goose Island the same. Letting their brewers experiment, and produce a craft made product. That being said, you won't catch me with a Honkers Ale or Goose Island IPA in my hand any time soon, but if you see me with a glass of Lolita, don't judge.

In February 2014, *USA Today* wrote:

> Goose Island fans may have worried about a watering down of the beloved Chicago brewer's products after its acquisition by AB

InBev, "but two years in, we're not seeing it," says Tom Bobak, editor-in-chief of AmericanCraftBeer.com.

"They acquired Goose Island to get a piece of craft beer's pop cultural energy and its economic energy, of course," Bobak says. "I think they have been careful not to diminish their acquisition. They have left Goose Island to be Goose Island."

Expectations had fallen so precipitously after the sale that anything short of burning the brewery to the ground seemed like victory. On the inside, however, the experiment was at a low point.

A parade of brewers left. John J. Hall, who had written the recipe for 312 Urban Wheat Ale, quit to become brewmaster at Latin-themed Chicago brewery 5 Rabbit Cervecería. Claudia Jendron, who rose to become one of Goose Island's few female brewers after starting as receptionist, took a job at a new suburban brewery. John Laffler, the face of the barrel-aging program, departed to start Off Color Brewing. His boss, Tom Korder, cofounded Penrose Brewing with Goose Island's former sales guru Eric Hobbs.

Several others quit to work for California-based Lagunitas Brewing, which had launched a massive brewery on the edge of Chicago's Douglas Park neighborhood. Amid rumors of Andy Goeler promising to disrupt Lagunitas's Chicago arrival with aggressive sales tactics, Lagunitas founder Tony Magee offered tough words on Twitter. "I said I'd not poach from local breweries to staff Chicago, but I think we could make an exception for Goose folks . . . Call it 'sanctuary' . . ." Magee wrote on January 21, 2013. At least four Goose Island brewers wound up at Lagunitas.

Even more people went to Revolution Brewing, which was started in 2010 by Josh Deth, a former Goose Island brewer who made clear his desire to challenge his former employer for local supremacy. "We've wanted to be Chicago's next hometown beer even before Anheuser-Busch bought Goose Island. Now it gives us even more passion," Deth told the *Chicago Tribune* shortly after Goose Island's sale. Revolution nearly had its pick of Goose Island brewers simply by offering what Goose Island used to be: no low-grade corporate overhaul, no drug testing, and no former Bud Light guy at the helm. Revolution didn't even have to offer raises. It was just a better workplace culture.

Of all Goose Island's departures, however, the most stunning was one that barely registered outside the brewery. Miguel Miguitama was a native of Ecuador who worked for Goose Island almost from the start—first at the brewpub as a bar back, then as assistant brewer, and then as the overnight brewer on Fulton Street. If something bothered him, he didn't go to his boss—he went to Greg. It was how things worked. Everyone knew it. Even more than Goose Island, Miguitama worked for the Halls. He never took sick days or his weekly case of beer allotted to employees. Within the walls of Fulton Street, Miguitama *was* Goose Island. Greg even invoked him in an interview with *Time Out Chicago* during postsale damage control:

> Q: Now what changes?
> A: I hate to say nothing changes. Miguel, a brewer who has worked for us for 20 years, walked into my office and asked the same thing: Is it going to change? And I said "Miguel, when's the last year that nothing changed?" and he said "Things change every year." Exactly. So, we'll continue to evolve by introducing new brands.

But in mid-2013, Miguitama quit to become the overnight brewer at Revolution. If Miguitama could leave, it seemed anything could happen.

A few people saw through the rosy narrative. Addressing a British beer conference two years after the sale, Brooklyn Brewery brewmaster Garrett Oliver drew a comparison to Star Wars. "Once you're involved with something that's all about money, it's no longer going to be about people," he said. "Businesses like that are about money. I loved Goose Island—it was a great brewery. But it's like Anakin Skywalker became Darth Vader and he's not there anymore. Some of the people might still be there, the body might be there, but the spirit isn't. It became something else."

The Andy Goeler years at Goose Island amounted to a professional adolescence—not always comfortable and the direction not always clear, but maturation undoubtedly ahead.

Maturation finally began in early 2014, when Goose Island got what it could have used for the 312 rollout a year earlier: an identity for the twenty-first century. Chicago-based branding and marketing firm VSA Partners crafted an image intended to modernize local perception and create awareness in new markets. First up was a national ad campaign with a pithy, playful tagline just barely on the craft side of Big Beer: "To what's next." Goose Island placed one-minute video ads on food, travel, and music websites, taking viewers inside the Fulton Street brewery amid splashy images of Chicago's elevated train system, skyline, and other iconic scenes. It got full-page and double-page advertisements in *Rolling Stone* and *Travel + Leisure*, beer magazines and alternative weeklies, and became a mainstay on the back covers of publications targeted at millennials, like *Time Out*. Later that year, after toiling for twenty years in anonymity on Fulton Street, the exterior of the brewery was spruced up with black and white stripes and a giant Goose Island logo. It built a gleaming taproom of dark wood and white subway tile and pledged to tap a Bourbon County beer at least once a month. It offered the first-ever public tours of the brewery while the director of consumer experience, Ken Stout, told the *Chicago Tribune* that Goose Island needed to shake off some rust. He compared the brewery to the rock 'n' roll of his college days: "When The Replacements came out, they were underground and sounded great. After a few albums, they got outside of just being played on [alternative rock radio stations] and it was like, 'Oh man, they're not as good as they used to be.' We've got a little of that going on."

Goose Island went after the hip youth, inking its first national sponsorship, for public radio's weekly *Sound Opinions* music talk show. After losing sponsorship rights to Heineken for Chicago's Pitchfork Music Festival—which attracted close to twenty thousand young and impressionable drinkers per day across three days—it bought them back in 2013.

Goose Island also doubled down on Migration Week, a project launched the previous year in which the brewery sent brewers and marketing staff to twenty cities for a series of tastings and tap takeovers. They went after core markets where Goose Island already had a degree of awareness, plus secondary markets where they could seem huge on a relatively small budget. In Charleston or New Orleans, it was easy to grab the attention of local newspapers and bloggers, especially by staging a Bourbon County event. In New York or Los Angeles, it was nearly impossible. In 2013 they visited twenty markets. In 2014 it was up to thirty-two.

Goose Island was winning a series of small battles but had a looming problem: its beer. Honker's Ale was a dead style, and sales proved it. 312 Urban Wheat was adequate but failed to translate to the broader stage. 312 Urban Pale Ale was an outright failure; so was the hop series. To revitalize Anheuser-Busch InBev's investment, it needed a new flagship. The answer was obvious: IPA.

At SAMCOM that fall, on Anheuser-Busch's home St. Louis turf, Goeler paced the stage, energizing his distributors for a new year of selling Goose Island. Matilda and Sofie, which were still brewed in Chicago and maintained their original quality, had been ramped up so that every distributor in the room could order them "every day of the year," Goeler said. He wanted the distributors to think of them as competition for wine—an industry taking a bite out of beer sales. He touted three new seasonal releases that were a tacit acknowledgment of the failure of the hop series: Goose Summer Ale, Goose Autumn Ale, and Goose Winter Ale. He wanted them pushed hard in 2015.

But IPA was key. The beer was up more than 30 percent on its way to $5.5 million in sales, but that was cause for only modest celebration. Even more than sales, Goeler prized growth, and Goose Island IPA wasn't keeping up with the top tier of IPA; Lagunitas IPA was up 66 percent, Bell's Two Hearted had grown 60 percent, and Sam Adams Rebel IPA, in its first full year of distribution, was headed toward $35 million in sales. Goose Island IPA needed a boost.

Tweaks would be made to the packaging to make the brand seem more "urban and impactful," Goeler told his wholesalers. The new six-packs would be rechristened "Goose IPA," a call used by drinkers in New York City, where the beer was a far bigger hit than it ever had been in Chicago. Goose Island IPA had medaled six times at the Great American Beer Festival, making it one of the most honored IPAs in the competition's history. Never mind that it was now a radically different beer and a different recipe on Anheuser-Busch's sprawling machinery—those medals would be prominently featured on the packaging. So, too, would the hop farm in northern Idaho. New television ads would tell IPA's "ingredients story," Goeler said—including the hop farm.

Goeler crossed the stage again and again, whipping his army into frenzy over visions of Goose Island IPA as a national force. For the first time, he said, Goose Island would be among Anheuser-Busch InBev's elite list of "big bets"—the brands wholesalers were told to prioritize. Bud and Bud Light were always on the list. Stella Artois and Michelob Ultra were on it too. Now so was Goose IPA.

"The most disruptive brewery right now is Goose Island," he said to whistles and applause.

And then hops rained from the ceiling. Literally. They landed in clothing and hair as hop dust spun into the air and a dank, piney aroma filled the room. The distributors stood and cheered. They had their marching orders.

24

"A Betrayal of the Spirit in Which We Started the Company"

It's May 2012.

John Hall and Tony Bowker head to Northwestern University, in Evanston, the suburb along Chicago's northern edge. It's fourteen months after Goose Island's sale has been announced and seven months before they will leave the company. (They don't know that yet.) John and Tony are in the midst of fighting a national rollout of Goose Island because they are sure such a rollout will fail. They will lose that battle. (They don't know that yet either.) And the rollout *will* fail.

Today, they are simply sharing their expertise.

In front of John and Tony sit forty casually dressed Anheuser-Busch InBev executives from across the globe. They are spending several days at Northwestern's business school, the Kellogg School of Management, on a professional retreat. John and Tony's hour-long presentation, "Competing in Craft," features an avalanche of buzzwords miles from what these industry titans know of beer. *Innovation. Intimacy. Storytelling. Nuance. Relationships. Relevance. Authenticity. Experience.* But John and Tony are sure to tell the story of craft beer in a language that Big

Beer executives will understand. John and Tony have no idea who these people are. They just know them as global executives for the world's largest beer company. Brazilians and Belgians, mostly. Heavy hitters.

Stretched across forty-four slides, the presentation is intended to give these people a sense of the brewery they bought a year earlier and the world in which it operates. The executives are about brands and marketing and focus groups. For them, beer is a means to an end: Sales. Growth. Shareholder return. Goose Island, John and Tony say, begins with brewers. The second slide makes that clear: "We pride ourselves on being innovators and leaders in the craft of brewing. We create beers that define styles, win awards and capture the hearts, imaginations and palates of beer drinkers."

John and Tony speak of a world where success depends not on point of sale material and Super Bowl ads but on culture, innovation, and life as a community touchstone. The sales staff isn't simply selling a product; it is selling an ethos and a lifestyle. Craft beer, they say, is a transparent relationship between drinker and brewer. The greater the intimacy—and the ability to see, hear, and touch a brewery—the stronger the bond. The stronger the bond, the likelier customers are to stand in line for thirty-six hours in shitty weather on a holiday to buy rare beer. "Bonds are formed by stories that are authentic, relevant to the audience, and told with authority by storytellers who personify the brand," they say.

Who needs Super Bowl commercials?

Each Goose Island employee is the equivalent of a TV or radio ad "playing over and over again with everyone they meet." Don't just sponsor a concert venue or a band, or hang a bunch of banners bearing the name of your product. Influence the band to drink your beer. Then their fans will aspire to do the same. Cultivate the staff at the venue. Get them to recommend your product and to mean it when they do. Expose customers to your culture. Make them want a piece of it. Make them feel ownership.

At the end of the day, everyone in the room, including John and Tony, heads to the Goose Island brewpub for dinner. Course after course rolls out with narration from the chef and two Goose Island brewers. After the dinner, Tony heads to the brewpub's hulking rectangular bar with three of the Anheuser-Busch InBev guys. They spend a couple of hours drinking and talking. It is a rainbow of global leadership: a Belgian, a Brit, and a Brazilian. It is a heartening conversation. Bowker was starting to wonder if these Anheuser-Busch InBev guys got it at all, especially as they bickered over the prospects of Goose Island's national rollout. They were starting to seem like a reactionary bunch of money-grubbers with no vision of the broader picture.

But standing there at the bar, these three guys get it. They are worldly, smart, funny, and curious. If Luiz Edmond is supposed to be the bad cop, he is succeeding. These are the good guys.

Jorn Socquet, the Belgian, is especially impressive. Socquet had been behind the masterful rollout of Stella Artois in the United States. In Bowker's native England, Stella was borderline trash, nicknamed "the wife beater" from its days at 5.2 percent alcohol, which made it the booziest cheap beer in most store coolers. As the thinking went, the slightly higher alcohol content added up over the course of a twelve-pack, leading to arguments and domestic violence. (An urban legend persisted that there was something about the formulation of Stella itself that made people aggressive.)

Yet in the United States, Stella had been positioned as a brand of class and dignity. There had been a large investment in that image, as well as the fact that the original brewery behind Stella dated to 1366 (even though Stella debuted in 1926). The campaign pushed the elegance of Stella's stemmed glassware ("It's a chalice, not a glass," advertising proclaimed) and nine-step ritual pour, beginning with "purification" of the glass and ending with "bestowal" upon the drinker. Stella even got a tasteful Super Bowl commercial in 2011: a handsome actor singing to beautiful women in a dim, smoky European club amid frosty chalices of Stella.

But most important had been the plan for Stella's rollout after the brand had been kicking around the United States for decades as just another import: rather than release the beer in the typical flood, Anheuser-Busch InBev gave Stella to a handful of California wholesalers, which were told only to sell the beer to ten or so high-end accounts at a time. Then, slowly, as Stella's buzz grew, so did the brand's footprint, until Stella was in every grocery store and became beer of the month at Applebee's restaurants in suburban Ohio.

Bowker, in the midst of fighting his own rollout battle, realizes that someone at the company actually gets it. He explains his frustrations to Socquet and asks why he is having such a difficult time. Like in any large operation, Socquet tells him, it's about having the right allies. Goose Island doesn't have them. Not yet. Dispiriting as the thought might be, Bowker finds the exchange of ideas refreshing. He realizes there are some forward-thinking people in the organization. These are the guys he wants to work with.

Fast-forward two years. It's August 2014.

Bowker and John Hall are long gone from running Goose Island's day-to-day operations. But both continue to serve on Anheuser-Busch's "craft advisory board," code for not much in reality. The board meets a few times a year, usually so that Andy Goeler can lay out his upcoming plans for Goose Island—for which he clearly expects nods of agreement from John and Tony—then everyone sips whatever new beers are coming down the Anheuser-Busch pipeline, whether yet another new flavor of Shock Top or one of those awful, bright, sugary Bud Light Lime "Rita" drinks. Then they race to the airport to catch the 7:00 PM flight home.

But the craft advisory board is about to disappear. Anheuser-Busch has announced the formation of an entirely new business unit to show how serious it is about competing in craft. It is none-too-subtly named: the High End. Plucked to lead it is a wiry, bearded Brazilian named Felipe Szpigel, a fifteen-year company veteran. He visits Chicago, where the new High End unit is to be. Bowker is introduced to Szpigel. He sticks out his hand.

"Nice to meet you," Bowker says.

"Tony, don't you remember me?" Szpigel replies.

Northwestern. The brewpub. Two hours talking at the bar with Jorn Socquet. Ah, yes—Tony remembers the new boss.

If the Goose Island sale stunned craft beer, the sale of Blue Point Brewing garnered a collective shrug.

On February 5, 2014, nearly three years after acquiring Goose Island, Anheuser-Busch finally bought its second American craft brewery. John Hall was simultaneously surprised it took so long and surprised it happened at all. When he sold Goose Island, it was plausible that Anheuser-Busch might never buy another American craft brewery. They certainly didn't indicate a broader strategy. As recently as late 2013, Luiz Edmond himself had said that Goose Island might solve all of Anheuser-Busch's craft needs.

But three months later, after nearly a year of covert talks, the Blue Point deal was announced. Founded on Long Island in 1998, Blue Point was the nation's thirty-fourth-largest craft brewery, even though much of its sixty thousand annual barrels of production was contract brewed elsewhere. Its flagship brand, Toasted Lager, was an easy-drinking training ground for new craft drinkers—an ideal entry point when moving beyond Bud and Miller. Just like Sam Adams. And that was the point.

When Blue Point began shopping itself in 2013, mostly as an exercise in figuring out how it could continue to grow, cofounder Mark Burford was pleasantly surprised at the interest of the world's largest beer company. It was frank about the appeal: Toasted Lager was a weapon to battle Sam Adams. Any bar owner who said they could never take one of craft's most iconic beers off tap because it filled such a broad niche could be handed a pour of Toasted Lager. *See? Same easy-drinking, malt-forward accessibility. You don't need Sam Adams. And while we're at it, why don't you try this IPA from Goose Island in Chicago?*

Blue Point announced the sale on its website declaring, "We're not going. We're growing." For a brewery largely unknown beyond the East Coast, and whose most prominent brand was fairly pedestrian, response ranged from a healthy amount of congratulations to jokes about the inevitability of "Toasted Lager Light." The New York State Brewers Association issued a tepid public response: "We're confident that the folks at Blue Point made this deal with the best intentions, they obviously make a quality beer, otherwise this opportunity would never have come to them. It's really the only way big beer can curb the tide." Though the price was never released publicly, it was widely estimated to be about two-thirds of what Goose Island fetched: nearly $24 million.

Beyond New York, the deal barely registered. Even Paul Gatza, director of the craft trade group the Brewers Association, said there was little cause for alarm. "I don't see it as a trend, but some people who started breweries are getting older and evaluating their exit strategies," he told the *St. Louis Post-Dispatch*. "Craft beer is growing so rapidly, a lot of people, the big brewers, are looking at how to take advantage of the market, and others are looking at how to get money out of it." Though Anheuser-Busch buying two breweries in three years didn't quite reek of a strategy, a radical industry shift was indeed underway.

Three years earlier, MillerCoors had formed Tenth and Blake, a division devoted to craft and imports. (Among its earliest initiatives was Dick Leinenkugel's lunch with John Hall.) Tenth and Blake had sent all forty of its employees to trainings about beer history, styles, flavors, and food pairings. Its executives understood that the new division needed to think and talk differently about beer. "In the craft and import business, it is a lot more about education being the new promotion," Tenth and Blake president Tom Cardella told *Ad Age*. "There's a lot of desire for knowledge and learning and training in regards to how beer is made, how beer is looked at in regard to the sensory experience as it pairs with food." All Anheuser-Busch had done was buy a couple of breweries. There was no hint of a broader offensive.

But a plan was brewing.

Six months after the Blue Point deal came an announcement little noticed outside the beer industry but which was the beginning of a profound shift: the High End. Like Tenth and Blake, Anheuser-Busch's new division was dedicated to boosting its presence in craft and imports. It would be based in Chicago to "[place] us in closer touch with urban consumers, their way of thinking, lifestyle and the accounts they visit," Luiz Edmond said in the memo announcing the move on August 6, 2014. (Four months later, Anheuser-Busch shifted the High End to New York as part of the company's slow transfer of power to that city.) The High End would have its own dedicated resources, including hundreds of people for sales, supply, and finance. Its leader would be Szpigel, who joined the company through the management trainee program and rose to a global role in New York as vice president of trade marketing.

Like his colleagues, Szpigel had been a longtime believer in light lagers. Slowly, as he rose through the industry, he developed a taste for Stella Artois and Hoegaarden, two brands the Brazilians acquired with the creation of InBev. Then he heard John Hall and Tony Bowker speak at Northwestern. It was a transformative experience, reinforced by the three-hour dinner at Goose Island's brewpub. With each course of food and beer, brewers stood at the head of the room and told the story of how those beers came to be. They weren't *selling* beer, as Szpigel and his colleagues had been trained to do—they were *telling the story of beer*. Szpigel would equate the day to the birth of his daughter (named Stella, of course). Stella was the brick dropped on his head in his personal life. A night at Goose Island was the professional brick. The idea of getting beer into influential accounts to be consumed by influential people, fueled by romance and storytelling—it all made sense. For decades, Big Beer had thought of craft as an aberration, something to resist. Something to mock. All at once, for any executive in that room paying attention, it was clear that craft beer and the way it was sold wasn't the enemy. It was the future.

When Anheuser-Busch announced the creation of a high-end division, Szpigel raised his hand to lead it. He was all in. The earliest days of Anheuser-Busch InBev had aped the old days of Anheuser-Busch: craft existed only to defend the core of Bud and Bud Light. But with the inception of the High End and the ascension of Szpigel, the thinking had evolved. They couldn't stop change. They would embrace it.

If craft beer had a homecoming king, it would have been Dick Cantwell.

He wasn't the industry's best-known face to the people who bought craft beer—that would have been Ken Grossman or Jim Koch. Maybe even the gentlemanly Fritz Maytag. But within the industry, it was Cantwell.

As cofounder and brewmaster of Seattle's Elysian Brewing, Cantwell was a fixture at major industry events, sitting on judging panels, handing out awards, and frequently public speaking. He became one of craft beer's most revered voices, writing for industry magazines and a pair of books, one of which became a standard for anyone wading into the business: *The Brewers Association's Guide to Starting Your Own Brewery.* He was also half of the industry's most intriguing power couple; his girlfriend was Kim Jordan, cofounder of New Belgium Brewing. The homecoming king had a homecoming queen.

Cantwell founded Elysian in 1996 with Joe Bisacca, a former banker, and David Buhler, an old hippie and German lit major who took on sales and marketing duties. The brewery quickly became a Seattle icon, known for its experimentation and embrace of fresh, piney Pacific Northwest hops. The three partners never imagined that their brewery would get big. They planned simply to run a brewpub. That grew into a second brewpub, and then a third, plus a production brewery and, ultimately, one of the industry's most sterling reputations. Elysian was named Large Brewpub of the Year at the Great American Beer Festival in 1999, 2003, and 2004. Outwardly, all was well. In reality, the three partners began to fray almost as soon as Elysian was born. They were in a fluctuating state of two-against-one, though the one on his heels depended on the day. The biggest problem, Cantwell would eventually conclude, was that the partners had failed to articulate a clear mission for themselves—or an exit strategy.

In the spring of 2014, Cantwell did what he did every spring: he traveled to the Craft Brewers Conference, which that year was in Denver, and sat on a judging panel for the every-other-year World Beer Cup competition. Outside the judges' reception, George Reisch, a longtime acquaintance who was Anheuser-Busch's brewmaster and a company veteran of thirty-five years, approached. He pulled Cantwell to the most private spot he could find—beside a towering pole in the broad convention center lobby—and told Cantwell he was free to walk away and no one would ever know about the conversation about to unfold. But would it be OK to have someone from Anheuser-Busch call Cantwell for a chat? Goose Island had come on board three years earlier, and the Blue Point deal was recently announced. St. Louis was still looking around, kicking tires. It was missing out on craft and wanted to keep growing.

Sure, Cantwell said. He figured he had a fiduciary responsibility to his fellow shareholders to at least listen. He also figured there was almost no chance of such a deal happening. His partners would never go for it.

Reisch thanked him, walked away, and immediately called Michael Taylor.

In casual circles, Michael Taylor referred to himself as an Anheuser-Busch "finance guy." His more formal title was vice president of mergers and acquisition. Armed with an MBA from the University of Missouri–St. Louis, Taylor spent six years with oil giant Premcor before joining Anheuser-Busch in 2004. Taylor did the sorts of things that had nothing to do with beer but everything to do with keeping a $50 billion company humming: accounting, capital planning, investor relations, and property management. By the time of the InBev takeover, he had a particularly important job: vice president of corporate real estate. As part of the company's strategy for furiously paying down debt, it shed many large extraneous assets, such as Kingsmill Resort and Spa, a Virginia property with four hundred rooms, three golf courses, fifteen tennis courts, and six restaurants, sold in 2010 for nearly $24 million. Taylor managed the sale.

By the time he got Cantwell on the phone, Taylor's job had taken on the even weightier role of executing the company's burgeoning M&A craft strategy. He had worked on the Goose Island and Blue Point deals. Now he was casting about for more. He was legendary in the company, a nice guy moving as imperceptibly as possible. His photo was nearly nonexistent on the internet; he needed to be anonymous when showing up at a brewery he might want to buy. But if someone at Goose Island got a note from him—"Your pricing at Ralphs in Los Angeles is wrong"—the rumor mill churned. *What's Michael Taylor doing in Los Angeles?* His call with Cantwell was genial, though vague. He said he would be in Oregon on business and asked if he could swing up to Seattle for a chat. Cantwell agreed but kept to himself how opposed he felt to a sale to the world's largest beer company.

In early summer, Taylor visited. He had short brown hair, blue eyes, and a ruddy, friendly face. He looked far more like a money guy than a beer guy. Which he was. But people liked him. He was enthusiastic and friendly. He could take a joke—a necessity as the first point of contact with craft brewers from big, bad Anheuser-Busch. Taylor laid out the usual talking points about what a sale would mean. Increased access to raw materials. The nation's most powerful distribution network. A well of resources most craft breweries could only dream of. Almost limitless growth. And continued commitment to great beer. Just look at Goose Island, Taylor said. It had grown wildly, but the beer was still good. It was Taylor's most potent argument: *Just look at Goose Island.* On that point, Cantwell believed him. Three years after its sale, Goose Island clearly hadn't been ruined.

Cantwell remained skeptical, but his partners were intrigued. Gleeful, even. And why not? A sale to Anheuser-Busch would make them millionaires.

All the evidence Cantwell needed of the fallout ahead sat 330 miles south. In November 2014, as Elysian's negotiations with Anheuser-Busch were concluding, a small brewery in Bend, Oregon, became the third American craft brewery to sell to the global beer giant. In 2007 brothers Chris and Jeremy Cox and their partner Garrett Wales had launched a brewpub called Wildfire Brewing. Rechristening their venture 10 Barrel Brewing Co., the trio showed aptitude for growth, opening additional brewpubs in Boise and Portland, plus a small production brewery in Bend. They also made good beer: 10 Barrel won three medals at the 2014 Great American Beer Festival.

Buying 10 Barrel was a stunningly nuanced move. The brewery made sixteen thousand barrels of beer the previous year, a healthy number for a small brewery but infinitesimal in the big scheme. (Goose Island produced 340,000 barrels that same year.) How did Anheuser-Busch find *them*? If the Goose Island deal was stunning but perhaps not quite portending an industry shift, and Blue Point's sale worth little more than a shrug, the 10 Barrel deal signaled that something profound was underway. Goliath had stomped into craft beer's backyard. Everything was in play.

The deal was sparked by 10 Barrel's interest in finding money—and, ideally, experience—to continue growing the company. Its Portland distributor, which was aligned with Anheuser-Busch, helped arrange an introductory phone call in March 2014. Three days later, Michael Taylor was in Bend, talking with the Cox brothers and quietly poking around. 10 Barrel offered to sell a 25 percent stake. Taylor responded that Anheuser-Busch wanted the whole thing. The formal offer came in late July. (Chris Cox told the local *Bulletin* newspaper it was "one of the most amazing days of our lives.") The brothers thought they might have sunk the deal a day later, when a bottle of 10 Barrel sour fruit beer called Swill exploded in Idaho. Anheuser-Busch wasn't happy, of course, but if anything, it proved 10 Barrel's need to partner with the world's largest beer company; quality control was one of the things Anheuser-Busch did best. The deal was announced in early November, followed by a quick trip for 10 Barrel staff to Chicago to tour Goose Island. As would become customary, neither company released terms of the deal.

Reaction was swift and fierce. The most optimistic onlookers argued that a savvy Anheuser-Busch, which actually understood craft beer culture and its nuances, was a victory; just as John Hall had told his employees three years earlier, craft beer had won. Anheuser-Busch had no other choice but to step into the ring.

Others forecast an apocalypse and peppered 10 Barrel's Facebook page with one-star reviews and cries of sellout. Most searing was a blog post by Steve Body, a longtime industry observer who wrote as the Pour Fool for both his own blog and the *Seattle Post-Intelligencer*. Beneath the headline "The Short Life and Ugly Death of 10 Barrel Brewing," Body was apoplectic, replete with italics, bolded words, and comparing the deal to a death in the family:

> Folks, it really ***IS*** this effin' simple and don't fall for ***anyone*** with a quick chuckle and a shake of the head who says, "*Hey, it's just business. 10 Barrel will just reach a lot more people, now.*" AB/InBev, the Belgian/Brazilian mega-corporation who just bought

> 10 Barrel for what was probably about what their Board tips for a big lunch, ***is the sworn enemy of craft beer***. I used to have the utmost respect for John Hall, former owner of Goose Island Brewing of Chicago but John Hall decided to get out of his daily grind with Goose Island and sold it to AB/InBev. John Hall—who helped ***create*** the American Craft Beer community—aided and abetted the very corporate monster that's trying, on dozens of fronts all over the US, to hinder or obstruct the growth and business practices of the thousands of small, independent brewers for whom AB has consistently expressed their disdain. As one of their VP's told me in an email, back in 2011, "*Actually, the term 'craft brewing' that you people toss around is wrong. What we do at Anheuser Busch is craft brewing because it involves the craft of brewing. What those weird little breweries do is actually 'amateur brewing,' and the sooner you all figure that out, the better.*" One of their VPs said last year, at the first company convention after their take-over of Goose Island, in speaking of the conflict between Bud and craft brewing, "*We cannot allow the paradigm to change.*"
>
> This is the mind-set that now owns 10 Barrel Brewing. . . .
>
> I'm going to make this as short and unsweet as I can, because I am ***mortally pissed off*** . . . **If you care about craft brewing**—about the community of **people**, not corporations and not abstract legions of faceless laborers—**then you do *NOT*, under any circumstances and for *any* amount of money, sell your craft brewery to a company whose stated objective is to bring about the ruin of that community.**

On the day of the sale, the *Portland Business Journal* posted an online poll that invoked 10 Barrel's flagship beer: "Now that Budweiser owns 10 Barrel, will you still drink that Apocalypse IPA?" The options were, "Yes, it's the same delicious beer," and "No, I'll choose something locally owned instead." Of 731 respondents, 75 percent said they were done with 10 Barrel.

If the Elysian deal went through, Cantwell knew he faced a similar fate. And it was barreling toward the finish line.

Cantwell nursed hope that his partners might consent to a last-minute sale to New Belgium, which had grown into one of the nation's largest craft brewers and become employee-owned the previous year. But the other board members were united that Anheuser-Busch was the best option. It was the offer in hand. Discussions with New Belgium hadn't reached an offer yet, and if they waited around, Anheuser-Busch's interest could disappear. A sale was unlikely to go through without Cantwell's consent—Anheuser-Busch insisted he be part of the deal—but he preferred to make a final appeal rather than threats. In January 2015, he banged out what he dubbed "a manifesto"—1,656 words decrying the sale he had set in motion nearly a year earlier. He sent it to Elysian's board of directors.

> To be sure, we've come a long way down the path of exploring a possible sale to ABI, but that doesn't compel us to conclude it. History would vindicate us if after a good hard look and a lot of consideration we backed away, regrouped and found a better way. I also believe that many of our shareholders—the people who made this possible—would be more comfortable with this outcome. As it is, I believe our story will be considered one of the tragedies of our industry. I know you don't all agree with me on this, and I'm frankly very surprised that discussion of legacy has played so little part in the meetings and conversations we've had over the past several months. I had honestly thought this was something we cared about. It would certainly have meant something to the three partners in 1996 who opened Elysian Brewing Company. Nor do I believe that fiduciary responsibility compels this sale; we are allowed to determine the future course of our company without having to take the first offer that comes along. . . .
>
> I know we've left the days of being happy in our business long behind us, but I truly believe this anticipated action is more than just a personal disappointment for me, it is a betrayal of the spirit in which we started the company.

During the late 1990s, after talks of a sale to local competitor Pyramid Brewing fizzled without an offer, Cantwell felt aligned with Buhler. They were both content to focus on their cozy little pub. Then, when Elysian became more ambitious and started brewing at New Belgium in Ft. Collins, Cantwell aligned with Bisacca, who championed the growth. This time it was Cantwell's turn to be on the outside. In response to Cantwell's letter, Bisacca accused him of having worked more in the interest of the Brewers Association and New Belgium than Elysian in recent years.

Elysian's sale to Anheuser-Busch InBev was announced January 23, 2015, a Friday morning, at the first-ever company-wide meeting at the Seattle production brewery.

Rumors of a sale had swirled so intensely that Cantwell had to leave the company's holiday party a few weeks earlier. He couldn't stand to play dumb. When the day of the announcement finally came, the plan was for him, Buhler, Bisacca, and Andy Goeler to break the news from a deck overlooking the brewing floor. Cantwell had already decided that he wasn't going to do any talking.

He drove down early and strolled through the brewery before any of his partners, or Goeler, arrived. He wanted a little quiet time. Employees filed in, about 120 of them. The last thing Cantwell did before his partners began to speak was share the news with local writers who had championed his brewery and his beer for nearly twenty years; he didn't want them to feel scooped when national writers scored the first interviews with Elysian's founders and Anheuser-Busch executives. At the last moment, Cantwell didn't join his partners on the brew deck; he stayed on the floor with his employees.

For the next several hours, text messages flowed in. They expressed shock, support, concern, and congratulations. Among the messages, at 10:07 AM, was one from Greg Hall:

> Hey, congrats on news. Welcome to the club. They will do a great job with beers and brands.

Cantwell had known Greg for years. They would meet for a beer when Greg was in Seattle, and not even talk about the industry; they talked about family. When Cantwell's daughter, Lucy, moved to Chicago, Greg made sure she was hired at the Clybourn brewpub; she waited tables there for two years. Cantwell considered Greg a friend. Two hours later, he replied:

> We will talk! Thanks. You know more than anyone how tough this is.

That night, Greg was back in touch with some advice. Don't use the pat line "nothing will change," he said. Instead, say, "When was the last year when nothing changed? We brew new beers and retire old ones every year. Change is what makes the beer business exciting for all of us. Here's to change!" It was a line Greg had used many times himself when soothing anxieties about the Goose Island sale: *When was the last year that nothing changed?* Plus, Greg said, Elysian would jump to the front of the global line for hops. "All those who say they will never drink Elysian again are silly," Greg wrote. "You will keep making great beer and many more will drink it. Congrats to you Dave and everyone at Elysian."

Publicly, Cantwell wavered between continuing defiance and vague optimism. "I was hoping for a different outcome, but I can recognize something positive for the future in this," he told the *Chicago Tribune*. He told the *Puget Sound Business Journal* that he would "still represent crafts. That's been understood throughout this deal." Alas—he was encouraged, and agreed, to step down as president of the Washington Brewers Guild.

The oddest turn came ten days after the sale was announced, during, of all things, the Super Bowl. During the second half of TV's biggest event of the year—and the most watched television event in US history to that point—Anheuser-Busch spun out one minute of Big Beer bravado and craft beer mockery. Behind an arena-ready thumping rock anthem, Budweiser's "Brewed the Hard Way" ad portrayed craft beer as painfully earnest and effete, embodied by walking clichés: men with curly mustaches who wore flannel shirts and blocky glasses and dared to sniff or think critically about their beer. Across the screen flashed the words:

> Budweiser
> Proudly a macro beer
> It's not brewed to be fussed over
> It's brewed for a crisp smooth finish
> This is the only beer beechwood aged since 1876
> There's only one Budweiser
> It's brewed for drinking
> Not dissecting
> The people who drink our beer
> Are people who like to drink beer
> Brewed the hard way
> Let them sip their pumpkin peach ale
> We'll be brewing us some golden suds
> This is the famous Budweiser beer

Cantwell first saw the commercial with the rest of the world, while watching the game; Elysian staff had gathered at the home of a brewer (who would soon leave to start his own brewery) to cheer on the hometown Seattle Seahawks. At the conclusion of the commercial, the room was silent. There was, in fact, a brewery that made the very pumpkin peach ale mocked in the commercial: Elysian. Gourdia on My Mind had debuted the previous fall at the brewery's annual pumpkin beer festival.

So, it had come to this. Anheuser-Busch was at once buying craft breweries *and* mocking them.

Budweiser's head of marketing in the United States, Brian Perkins, offered tepid amends in a follow up interview with *Ad Age*, insisting that the commercial was "not an attack on craft beer . . . not an attack on competition." But he also acknowledged a bit of contempt: "Occasionally we do have a little bit of fun with some of the overwrought pretentiousness that exists in some small corners of the beer landscape that is around beer snobbery. That is the antithesis of what Budweiser is all about."

Cantwell was already fairly sure he couldn't work with these people. It wasn't that they were bad guys. Shortly before the deal was announced, he sat through a dinner with Anheuser-Busch InBev's big guns—CEO Carlos Brito, North American zone president João Castro Neves (who had taken over for Luiz Edmond), and Felipe Szpigel. They were in town to meet with Starbucks executives and arranged a dinner with the Elysian partners to push the deal along; Cantwell found himself sitting between Castro Neves and Szpigel, and across from Brito. He was impressed by them all. They were exactly the kind of people you'd want to work with: attentive, respectful, interested, and interesting. Szpigel in particular seemed well suited to his role leading the High End. He was a drummer and a triathlete and truly seemed to understand the revolution sparked all those years ago by Anchor and Sierra Nevada: Quality. Culture. Stories. Romance. He was humble and patient and listened to other points of view. He was known in the company to be attuned to people's ambitions and frustrations and to work hard to reconcile the two. He wasn't above criticizing the company but remained a staunch defender of its principles. As a boss, you could do far worse.

But Cantwell couldn't fathom it. He worried for the brewery's reputation. He worried for his own reputation. He worried for what they had built. And the Super Bowl commercial reinforced that Big Beer was and always would be Big Beer. The negativity. The disrespect. At first he thought of the commercial as a public relations debacle. Then he realized Bud drinkers probably loved class warfare.

Elysian's sale became final on April 1, 2015. Cantwell spent the next week doing the kinds of things that happen as part of Anheuser-Busch InBev: He toured Argentina with John Hall to help plan a new brewpub near Patagonia. He and John stayed a few extra days to explore Buenos Aires, walking endlessly, visiting bars, and checking out sights. While they were there, Cantwell told John he was going to resign.

The day after he flew home, on April 13, he did just that. The informal agreement was that he and his partners would stick around for two years. But his contract said he could leave with thirty days of notice. Andy Goeler said he was devastated; Cantwell told him he had to have seen it coming. And just like that, Cantwell was an industry folk hero once more. He had stood up to the biggest beer company in the world—albeit after being paid handsomely.

That day, another text message arrived from Greg Hall:

> Dick—saw your news. Congrats to you, I know it's weighed very heavy on you for the last few months.

Cantwell next saw Greg that spring in Portland, Oregon, at the Craft Brewers Conference, the same event where his saga had begun a year earlier.

"Well," Greg said. "If it isn't Saint Dick."

25

"I Was the Creative Hall —the Ambitious Hall"

Throughout John Hall's negotiation to sell Goose Island to Anheuser-Busch, everyone assumed Greg Hall was part of the deal.

John thought so. Dave Peacock did too. But Greg was torn. He'd spent twenty years contributing to the new way of eating and drinking in Chicago, and in a constellation of chefs, farmers, and bar owners, he'd found his place in the revolution: he was the alternative to Big Beer. That prestige would be gone.

But the stability and prosperity offered by the biggest beer company in the world was alluring. So was the chance to be a global tastemaker with endless resources. He could forever be known as one of the industry's great innovators *and* the person who took it to new heights. He could make a marriage work that no one thought could work.

Finally, a month before the sale was announced, Greg decided he was out. Mostly. He would draw an annual six-figure salary from Anheuser-Busch to consult for the High End on Goose Island strategy. But he would otherwise apply his modest windfall from the sale toward launching a cider company.

Greg had been long intrigued by cider and had even pushed for Goose Island to start making it a decade earlier. No, John said. Goose Island needed to make more beer. It shouldn't be sidetracked. Through two decades of working together, it was a quintessential father-son argument: Greg's attention was pulled to a new idea with little thought for the bigger picture. John insisted they stay focused. But now, with a check on his way out the door for his 7 percent stake in the brewery, it was Greg's time. And, as he saw it, cider was ready to take off. A typical liquor store sold five thousand wines, one thousand beers, four hundred vodkas, two hundred whiskeys—and five ciders. It didn't make sense. He believed that if people were shown a new path, they would follow. It had been true with beer. Now he would make it true with cider.

John told Greg he was crazy to walk away from an opportunity with the world's largest beer company to gamble on cider.

"That's exactly what your father told you when you started the brewery," Greg replied.

It was true.

John never argued the point again.

A week before the sale was announced, Dave Peacock made a final appeal for Greg to stay. Anheuser-Busch's chief executive officer was at the beach with his family for spring break, but convincing Greg to stay was worth his time. Peacock sensed that Greg was upset about the sale and that John was disappointed in Greg's apprehension. Peacock wasn't sure it was his place to smooth relations between father and son, but it was imperative he do what was best for Anheuser-Busch's imminent acquisition. He wanted the Goose Island masterminds working together—father and son or not.

But Greg told Peacock he was done. He was forty-five and had made his mark on beer. Now he would get ahead of the next big thing. As he later told *Time Out Chicago*, the deal came at an opportune time: "Think about it—if Goose Island was my Mt. Everest, climbing Mt. McKinley would be boring. I've already done the beer stuff. I've created a new style in bourbon stout, I've brought wild fermentation beers to a food community and the masses, and there's got to be at least a dozen Goose brewers working as head brewers around the country and I'm terrifically proud of that. Now it's time for something else."

Peacock said he understood. He suggested that Greg might want to fold his cider venture in with Anheuser-Busch at some point. Who knew? Craft cider might be an interesting space for the world's largest beer company to join.

Most industry observers had assumed that Goose Island would eventually land in Greg's hands. Like at Sierra Nevada or Bell's, where plans were underway for those iconic breweries to pass to the next generation, Goose Island seemed likely to transfer from father to son. (Or, in the case of Bell's, father to daughter.)

That belief was particularly strong within the halls of Goose Island. Most employees, even the veterans who had been privy to the not-uncommon father-son blowup, figured it would happen. In reality, it was never much of an option.

John had been a different kind of brewery founder from the start. Ken Grossman and Larry Bell were beer guys—young, scruffy home brewers who got into the business for a love of brewing. John Hall was a business guy who got into beer because he saw a hole in the market. He loved beer, sure, but he was thinking big from the start. As soon as the Fulton Street brewery whirred to life, he envisioned an exit strategy involving Heineken or some other foreign brand whose business he planned to take. Goose Island wasn't a family business so much as it was something to grow as large as possible. In most other industries, companies were built to sell or go public. Why not craft beer? He believed growth was the only option; if you weren't growing, you were going backward. Your competitors were passing you by.

But to grow, Goose Island needed money. To get to five hundred thousand barrels of production per year—still miles behind Sierra Nevada and New Belgium and just a quarter of Boston Beer's annual output—the brewery needed between $50 and $75 million. Were bank loans possible? Probably. But John was approaching seventy years old; he didn't want that debt. Greg was a brilliant tastemaker. But was he a businessman who could make good on a $75 million loan? Two decades of sporadic bickering between father and son had uncovered a recurring theme: financial discipline. If Greg wasn't afraid to expense $4,000 meals at New York City's finest restaurants or let his marketing director go $400,000 over budget during the short time he ran sales and marketing, could he be a guardian of Goose Island for the next generation? Running a brewery was more than the next great idea—it was the discipline to know which ideas to pursue and, more importantly, which not to pursue. Greg knew that taking over Goose Island might not be the best thing for him, or for the brewery. "A lot of people made the assumption it would be passed down," he told the *Chicago Tribune* in 2012. "My father never made me that promise or said that to investors."

The day the sale was announced, Greg said he would leave to start a new venture, but he didn't share details; he wanted the focus on Goose Island. A few months later, photos of Greg walking through apple orchards in England and France began to appear on social media. A month after that, he announced that his new venture would be called Virtue Cider, a name that had first appeared in Goose Island LLC filings five years earlier. Rosy images followed of Greg's first apple pressing and the forty-eight-acre farm he bought in southwest Michigan. *Esquire* magazine called Virtue Cider one of the "things we're looking forward to" in 2012, just after a forthcoming James Bond movie.

Beer had taught Greg the power of story, and he teed up a good one for Virtue. He told media he first learned of cider by accident, years earlier, while touring breweries in England with six Goose Island brewers. One day they wandered into a pub with forty casks of cider on tap for a tasting. They didn't think much of it, but ordered seven different ciders between them and passed the glasses around the table. They were amazed at the variety. Some were sweet. Some were dry. Some were refreshing. Some were funky. They stayed for another round, then went back to try more the next night.

But outward enthusiasm for his new venture belied a quiet reality, which was apparent to the people who knew Greg best: He was devastated about Goose Island's sale. It wasn't that he was angry. He was sad.

He had long dreamed of steering the business into the next generation, watching craft beer ascend even higher in the public consciousness, then passing Goose Island to his kids (both of whom had a beer named in their honor—King Henry, a barrel-aged barleywine, and Sofie, a saison). But he understood: Growing the company would have been much more difficult, if not impossible, at least at first. As part of Anheuser-Busch InBev, growth was guaranteed.

His PR guru, Ellen Malloy, whom Greg had brought in to help manage the messaging around the sale, wrote on her blog in January 2012:

> [The sale] was great news for the company, [Greg] knew that. And he wasn't one to stand in the way of or criticize what was best for the company. But it wasn't necessarily where he was going in life. It wasn't, you could imagine, great news for him personally.
>
> In fact, during the months between the handshake and the deal, Greg teetered. A lot.
>
> He is a team player and understood his role with the company, so it wasn't likely that anyone outside of maybe four people knew that teetering was going on. But I can assure you, it was.
>
> Should he stay with the company? Should he go? What would he do with his life without Goose Island? How could he stay if he didn't want what the future was seeming to offer? What would happen to his reputation, built up over 20 years, once the sale went through?
>
> After all, to the outside world, Greg Hall ***was*** Goose Island—the beloved public face of a beloved Chicago company. He just couldn't see himself as the beloved local face of a conglomerate.
>
> It is really hard to watch, at point-blank range, the spinning vortex of a friend and colleague's life spiraling out of control. He was in near tears a lot during that time. In tears more than once.

Urinating in beer glasses at Bangers & Lace on a Friday night three weeks after the sale complicated matters, Malloy wrote, as did the incident becoming public when it appeared in the *Chicago Tribune* the following Monday.

And what of that brazen, baffling incident? Malloy didn't weigh in, but industry observers wondered. He was drunk, yes. But was it a cry for help? A brazen *fuck off* to the industry he helped build? Raw emotion in a time of stress? Or just dumb bullshit? Some of his oldest friends swore it was meaningless drunkenness; Greg had threatened to pull such a stunt for years.

"Of course, I regretted doing it," he told the *Tribune* a year later. "This is not an excuse, but, look, I have been out to bars 5,000 nights; one time I do something that stupid—it's not so terrible an average."

And now, Malloy concluded in her blog post, Greg was ascendant once more.

> He understands that it isn't blind faith that gets you through, it is focused attention and follow through.
>
> And so, nine months or so since, Greg formed a company, worked with amazing graphic designers to develop a brand identity, navigated through partnerships and relationships, is sealing the deal on a first round of funding, put up a sign on his Chicago office, and pressed his first batch of apples.
>
> And is already starting on phase two of Virtue (which you'll have to wait to hear about cause I am not giving anything away).
>
> "Dreamers who just dream don't get anywhere," he said to me this morning. "You have to dream and then do something. You have to shoot the puck."

By the middle of 2012, Greg Hall was shooting the puck.

Operating out of a small studio on Chicago's north side, Greg and a team of four—a business partner, an assistant, a cider maker, and a former Goose Island confidant to handle sales and marketing—began preaching the merits of English-, French-, and Spanish-style ciders that paired well with food. The first batch was made under contract at a winery in southwest Michigan, twenty thousand gallons of what would become Virtue's flagship, called RedStreak. It was bone dry with a robustly fruity nose and crisp effervescence. Greg hosted tastings at bars, in restaurants, and at upscale supermarkets, aiming for the drinkers who also valued art and music and a good meal and didn't mind paying more for a quality product. He was looking for the next generation of early adopters, the same sort of people he'd won over during the early days at Goose Island. He became fond of describing his new livelihood in a way that was instantly familiar but also perplexing: "Wine is like cider made from grapes." He preferred it to more obvious reverse phrasing. Made people think.

Within months RedStreak was on draft at more than three dozen of the trendiest restaurants and bars in Chicago. The fact that Greg Hall was attached to the project sealed many of the initial sales. "One thing I've gotten great at is creating buzz, influencing influencers," he told the *Chicago Tribune*. From most people, it would be unconscionable bragging. From Greg, it was bragging laced with truth; people *were* interested in what he thought and what he did. And things were good for the young company. Until they weren't.

The first batch of RedStreak, the one that came out of the winery, was universally lauded. The first version from Virtue's own press was a mess: off flavors that resulted from a lack of proper equipment, quality control, and understanding of the cider-making process. Whatever goodwill Greg had generated quickly vanished. When the third batch reeked of sulfur, Virtue's reputation was officially in tatters. Some of the early accounts, even the places where he'd held release parties, dropped the cider for competing local brands. Greg needed RedStreak to be a viable bedrock. It wasn't. It looked, smelled, and tasted different with every batch. Yet rather than dial in practices, Greg kept growing the company. With one eight-thousand-square-foot cider house built, he embarked on a second before it was needed. He launched in vanity markets—New York and Portland, Oregon—before winning his home market, where a competing Michigan cider, Vander Mill, was dominating. He hired one of Chicago's top beverage directors to represent Virtue in New York but soon couldn't afford to keep him. Even as distribution grew to twenty states, Virtue fell behind on paying employees and suppliers. Finally, in April 2015, the US Department of Agriculture halted Virtue's ability to buy produce following a complaint from a New Hampshire apple grower who said Virtue owed it nearly $110,000. Virtue failed to respond to the complaint, leading the USDA to rule in favor of the grower.

When launching, Greg said he had done so with about $2 million, which he used to buy his forty-eight-acre farm, build the first cider house, and fill it with equipment. However, he admitted to the *Grand Rapids Business Journal*, "as a startup, we were somewhat undercapitalized." To those initially baffled by Goose Island's sale, the fact that Greg hadn't taken over began to make sense. Greg was an idea guy. Not a business guy. He later implied as much in the *Chicago Tribune*: "My father was the disciplined Hall, and I was the creative Hall—the ambitious Hall. I wanted to keep doing more stuff, and he rightly said at the time, 'Let's do more beer.' But I never lost my itch for making great European-style farmhouse cider." Greg said that Virtue intended to pay its outstanding balances with 18 percent annual interest by "bringing more capital into the business"—though he declined to say how.

Enter Anheuser-Busch InBev. Again.

In September 2015, a deal that had been months in the works was announced: the world's largest beer company would acquire 51 percent of Virtue Cider for an undisclosed sum—a sum that was, in fact, zero. No money traded hands; Anheuser-Busch simply guaranteed $7 million in debt for Virtue. The deal was framed as an acquisition by Goose Island, and sure enough, Virtue's cider was trucked to Chicago for packaging and distribution. But, in reality, it was Anheuser-Busch's play, folding Virtue into the burgeoning High End as its craft cider. It was an easy match. Greg had been on the Anheuser-Busch payroll the entire time as a High End consultant. Without an infusion of cash, Virtue would have folded. And for Anheuser-Busch, an inexpensive gamble on cider protected the company in case the segment took off. (The High End followed by buying SpikedSeltzer, an alcoholic seltzer company, as a hedge against that segment blowing up too.)

"This is where the path had led us," Greg told the *Chicago Tribune*. "This was not the original intent in 2011. But I was on the record, at the time, saying that the best thing for Goose Island was partnering with a (larger) brewery for all the same reasons: resources, expertise and a sales force."

Of course, social media had its predictable field day. Greg was a sellout. Twice over. And two years later, Anheuser-Busch would acquire the rest of Virtue.

“I don’t know who’s gonna catch up to me and sell two companies to AB,” Greg told the Good Beer Hunting website shortly after the sale. “I’m the leader in the clubhouse of hate mail, I think, and I’m okay with that.”

26

"We Are Very Happy with Our Future as a Family Owned Company and Not Looking at Any Partnerships"

On a Sunday morning in July 2015, Larry Bell found something shocking, flattering, and inevitable in his email. It was a mere seven sentences below the subject line "Brewery tour and discussion":

> Larry,
>
> I am planning a trip to Michigan and was interested in finding an opportunity to come out to see your brewery and introduce myself. I work closely with Greg Hall as it pertains to Goose Island strategy and thought it would be interesting to tell you a little bit about what we have been doing in the US and have a conversation about Bell's operations, future plans and potentially partnership opportunities. By way of reference, I am in charge of Business Development for Anheuser Busch in North America. I led the acquisitions of Goose Island, Blue Point, 10 Barrel and Elysian.
>
> Are you going to be around the week of 8/3 or 8/10?

> I look forward to speaking with you. If you have any questions feel free to shoot me an email or call my cell phone.

Big Beer had come sniffing before. Ten years earlier, about the time Anheuser-Busch inked its minority stake deal in Goose Island, it made similar inquiries with Bell's. More recently, at an industry conference, a MillerCoors executive tucked a business card in Bell's shirt pocket and said, "If you're selling, I'm buying!" This time it was a simple Sunday morning email signed with best regards from Michael Taylor. Bell had never heard of him.

Bell was fifty-seven at the time, a thickset man with narrow eyes and a trim goatee who spoke with the blunt midwestern syllables native to his suburban Chicago upbringing. He had survived prostate cancer in his late forties and delayed the surgery long enough to watch his beloved Chicago Cubs in the playoffs. If John Hall was a business guy, Bell was the ultimate beer guy: a hard-charging, hard-drinking backslapper. He'd launched Bell's in 1985 beside the railroad tracks in downtown Kalamazoo, in the home brew shop he opened after graduating from Western Michigan University. In a state long dominated by Detroit's Stroh Brewery, Bell's was Michigan's first craft brewer. Bell made fewer than three hundred kegs during his first full year in business, delivering them in a rickety van that was broken just as often as it ran. He expanded distribution to Chicago and slowly built a company that became one of the nation's ten biggest craft breweries, churning out more than three hundred thousand barrels per year—light-years from Anheuser-Busch but significantly larger than, say, Goose Island. Bell didn't do anything audacious; he just made beer that people wanted to drink, in a state where people cared about the idea of drinking fresh and local. He built an enviable portfolio that any brewery would be proud to call its own: accessible beer (Amber Ale), audacious beer (Expedition Stout), inventive beer (Hopslam Ale, a double IPA with honey), seasonal beer (Bell's Winter White Ale), and one of the nation's most revered IPAs (Two Hearted).

John Hall always seemed like an industry outsider to Bell—a business guy, not a beer guy on board for the revolution—but the relationship was always cordial. When his van broke down during a delivery in Chicago during the early 1990s, Bell called Greg Hall for a couch to sleep on. The breweries battled heartily for tap handles; 312 Urban Wheat was a clear attempt to cut into the dominance of Bell's summer wheat ale, Oberon. And it worked. It set Bell's back ever so slightly in one of its most crucial markets. But that was business.

And here was business again, in the form of a Sunday morning email from the M&A guy at the world's largest beer company. Didn't these people rest? Or were they that eager to destroy craft beer? Because that's how Bell saw it: Anheuser-Busch was buying breweries to crush everyone else. He read Taylor's email a couple more times. The interest half scared him. Saying no meant they would come after him.

In the unpredictable realm of brewery ownership, Bell had already almost lost his business. In 2012 he became embroiled in a showdown with eleven investors, publicly stating it was him or them; if they didn't sell their holdings, he would sell the brewery. "I don't want to sell, but it's a great time to sell if I had to," he told a Michigan website that year. "There are many willing buyers." (Dick Leinenkugel called to pitch him on joining Tenth and Blake, but the discussion didn't get far; in reality, Bell had no desire to sell.) In a bid to make investors blink, Bell froze a $52 million expansion. They blinked. He kept ownership with his daughter, Laura, and son, David, to whom Larry transferred a bit more of the company each year. At the age of thirty-one, Laura became Bell's CEO. A sale to Anheuser-Busch would not be happening.

Bell weighed how to write back to Taylor, simply and blandly. Three days later, he replied:

> Michael:
>
> While I am flattered that you would like to meet, I feel that it would be an unfruitful visit for the both of us. We are very happy with our future as a family owned company and not looking at any partnerships.
>
> Larry Bell

Taylor replied within hours:

> Thank you Larry for your candor and reply. Best of luck to you for the remainder of the summer!
>
> Regards,
>
> Michael

And that was that.

A week later, Taylor sent a similar email to Jim Scussel.

Scussel was a founding partner of Four Peaks Brewing in Tempe, Arizona, a college town blending seamlessly into the greater Phoenix morass of desert and concrete. Four Peaks was launched during the first craft beer boom, in 1996, in a cavernous hundred-year-old former icehouse that had taken turns as a creamery and a recording studio. Led by its approachable, malt-forward Kilt Lifter Scottish-Style Ale, Four Peaks had grown to become the state's largest brewery, producing seventy thousand barrels by 2014—double what it made three years earlier. Even more important, it practiced the first rule of smart beer growth: conquer the home market. Every drop of those seventy thousand barrels was sold in Arizona.

The brewery in Tempe was followed by another brewpub in Scottsdale, a tony suburb of Phoenix; a production brewery, where Four Peaks beer was packaged for distribution; and a bar at Phoenix's Sky Harbor International Airport, where Felipe Szpigel and Andy Goeler sat during a layover in 2014 and thought the beer was good enough to merit a chat with the Four Peaks founders.

It was a chance encounter but a classic example of how things got done as mergers and acquisitions consumed craft beer following the Goose Island sale. Tenth and Blake was led to Texas's Revolver Brewing after Dick Leinenkugel tried a pint of Revolver's flagship Blood & Honey, an unfiltered wheat ale made with blood orange zest and Texas honey, at a hotel bar in Frisco, Texas. He passed the tip to colleagues. A year later, MillerCoors bought Revolver. For all the bankers and lawyers fueling a complicated new era of craft beer, many deals were hatched simply by someone sitting at a bar, tasting a beer for the first time, and thinking, *That's good.*

And so it was for Szpigel and Goeler, who urged Michael Taylor to reach out to Four Peaks. Taylor followed up with an email to Scussel, a lifelong entrepreneur whose first breakthrough happened at Grateful Dead concerts. As he followed the band up the West Coast, he saw parking lots reliably filled with merchants selling grilled cheese to the ravenous postshow crowds. He had a thought: *What if I add garlic to the butter?* Garlic grilled cheese! It was a small change, but it made Scussel a parking lot sensation. Each night, he would leave just before the encore to set up that evening's kitchen, then clear $500.

Now he was at the helm of Arizona's largest brewery and elated to hear from Taylor. Just a few months earlier, during one of their weekly Thursday morning meetings in Scussel's office, the Four Peaks partners had agreed to investigate possible next steps for the business. Their skills were tapped out. They were tired. They were small-business guys whose brewery was becoming a big business. The next leap—to regional brewery distributing in multiple states—seemed to require a level of expertise they didn't have. They'd been at it for nearly twenty years, and the landscape was clearly shifting in their favor. Money was flooding into the industry. Anheuser-Busch had bought four breweries. Kansas City's Boulevard Brewing was acquired by Belgian company Duvel Moortgat. Private equity firm Fireman Capital Partners bought Colorado's Oskar Blues, which in turn gobbled up Michigan's Perrin Brewing. One of the most well-known figures in craft beer, Rich Doyle, the former head of Boston's Harpoon Brewery, announced the creation of Enjoy Beer, another private equity–backed consortium intending to build a portfolio of top one hundred craft breweries; its first acquisition was Louisiana's Abita Brewing. The Four Peaks founders decided to find out what they were worth.

They hired First Beverage Group, a Los Angeles–based broker and advisor founded in 2005, which was taking on an increasingly powerful role in a consolidating craft beer industry. First Beverage had helped shepherd the sales of 10 Barrel and Boulevard. Scussel told Michael Taylor he was pleased to hear of the interest, but First Beverage would speak on their behalf.

First Beverage explained three options to Scussel and his partners. There was private equity, which was equivalent to selling to financial investors who would likely flip the brewery in five or ten years for a profit. There was a "strategic" sale to a bigger beer company like Anheuser-Busch or MillerCoors. And there was the emerging hybrid model of private equity money flowing through beer people (like the arrangement hatched by Oskar Blues and Fireman Capital). Just as Goose Island had done five years earlier, Four Peaks and its advisors let the world know that they were open for business. The world was interested.

Four Peaks was an immensely attractive target. It dominated its home state, made quality beer with a dozen Great American Beer Festival medals in its back pocket, and, most importantly, was primed for growth to forty-nine other states. It had interest from all three segments.

But no one could compete with Anheuser-Busch. Michael Taylor was an impressive guy. So was Felipe Szpigel. They articulated a strategy already becoming evident. The High End, formed less than a year earlier, was building a team of American craft breweries. It was regionally varied and had already reached the Midwest, Pacific Northwest, Northeast, and, most recently, Southern California: in September 2015 it struck a deal with Golden Road, a Los Angeles brewery known for slick branding and hoppy beers. (Many observers decried Golden Road as a brewery built only to be sold, though the founders rejected the idea.) Four Peaks would be the Southwest addition. Szpigel liked the fact that Four Peaks had successful brewpubs; the High End had come to recognize them as the ultimate marketing vehicle, the equivalent of fifty salespeople on the street. He even floated the idea of a Four Peaks brewpub in Las Vegas. Or maybe Dallas. Build power within the region.

The High End's craft roster would be closed at some point, and sooner rather than later, Szpigel said. Somewhere around ten breweries, they'd probably be done buying. Then they would focus on growing their acquisitions. Each brewery would have a lead brand, Szpigel said, and for Four Peaks, it would be Kilt Lifter. Within five or so years, Four Peaks could realistically be distributed in most of the nation. Just as Goose Island production had been exported to Anheuser-Busch breweries, so would beers from each acquisition—including Four Peaks—but far more methodically. The truth, Szpigel said, was that they hadn't handled the rollout of Goose Island well. They went too deep, too far, too quickly. Szpigel swore that Goose Island had been a lesson to *slowly* build a stable of successful regional breweries. His words sold Scussel and his partners. So did a valuation of more than $100 million. (The exact terms were not released.)

The deal was announced December 18, 2015. Anheuser-Busch had already been down the path six times (counting Virtue) and guided Scussel and his partners through a clockwork day of phone interviews with national media every half hour followed by visits from local media. At the end of an exhausting day, Michael Taylor shook Scussel's hand and said he had to go. He had a plane to catch.

"Where are you going?" Scussel asked.

"I can't tell you," Taylor said.

That was on a Friday.

The following Tuesday, just before 9:00 AM, Scussel's phone rang. It was Taylor.

"I'm at Breckenridge," he said. "We're about to announce."

Breckenridge Brewery, founded in its namesake mountain town in 1990, had grown to seventy thousand barrels of production and distribution in thirty-five states. Its sale was launched months earlier when Breckenridge owner Todd Usry walked into his office on a Monday morning and found Michael Taylor's business card on his desk. Taylor had taken a brewery tour over the weekend, just like any other customer.

Four Peaks had the privilege of being Anheuser-Busch's newest American craft acquisition for all of four days.

For two frenzied years, this is how it went.

Michael Taylor traveled the country, dropping business cards on desks and emailing beer industry titans on Sunday mornings. After decades of growth and struggle, then more growth and more struggle, craft brewery owners were waking up to interest from unfathomably large and wealthy companies—most notably the largest beer company in the world. Valuations went haywire, including the $1 billion acquisition of San Diego's Ballast Point Brewery by Constellation Brands, manufacturer of Corona and Modelo Especial for the United States. The Ballast Point sale, announced one month before Four Peaks' deal, baffled most industry onlookers. Sure, it was a quality brewery with a solid roster of beers. But how was it worth a billion dollars? (Indeed, it would prove to be an outlier valuation, and Constellation would tacitly admit it was an overzealous move.)

But no one upended craft beer quite like the world's largest beer company. Once it settled on its favored route into the craft arena—buying the kinds of breweries it couldn't create itself—Anheuser-Busch went on a spending spree. In two years, the company snapped up seven American craft breweries. It repeatedly swore no regional strategy was at work, but that was plainly untrue. With the Midwest (Goose Island) and Northeast (Blue Point) spoken for, Anheuser-Busch chomped its way across the map between November 5, 2014, and November 3, 2016: Pacific Northwest (10 Barrel and Elysian), Southern California (Golden Road), Southwest (Four Peaks), Rocky Mountains (Breckenridge), Texas (Houston's Karbach Brewing), and Mid-Atlantic (Devils Backbone Brewing, in central Virginia).

Early on, observers wondered how many sales there would be. A handful? A dozen? Dozens? Szpigel assured founders of the acquired breweries that the group would eventually close. The founders hoped it would; they didn't want to be competing for resources.

Working off a set of thresholds the company used for any acquisition, each deal wound its way up the Anheuser-Busch InBev chain: Taylor was often the first point of contact, followed by Szpigel, who would bring in the head of the North American operation, João Castro Neves, who sometimes, but not always, became directly involved. Once they were unified behind a target, the plan headed up to Anheuser-Busch InBev CEO Carlos Brito, and then the board of directors, a global crew of mostly Belgians and Brazilians that included the company's core of billionaire founders: Jorge Paulo Lemann, Marcel Herrmann Telles, and Carlos Alberto Sicupira. There was little if any pushback from the top on the craft acquisitions. The board craved progress on that front.

Approval was therefore typically a nonissue. The biggest challenge was usually assuaging concerns of their potential acquisitions about what it would mean to be part of the world's largest beer company.

For the first year after the Goose Island sale, Taylor ran into plenty of doubters. But once it was clear that Goose Island hadn't been ruined, and Anheuser-Busch leadership could articulate the lessons it learned from the deal, audiences became increasingly receptive. Some brewery owners decried each sale as a betrayal to the industry; others began to envision their own paydays and endless wells of resources. Some managed to do both.

Less than a year before his brewery's sale to Anheuser-Busch, Breckenridge founder Todd Usry was among the detractors. Beneath a provocative *Denver Post* headline—"Could a Colorado Craft Brewery Sell Out to Big Beer?"—Usry championed independence:

> "The big thing to me is, the craft beer industry was built on individuals and their stories," Usry said.
>
> When craft breweries sell out, "I think there is some serious authenticity that is lost, and that the brand loses," he said. "We're not corporate. We are entrepreneurial and individual."
>
> Usry, like others, is concerned about the business ramifications of big-beer buyouts. "It's going to be harder and harder to get our voices heard at the wholesale level," he said. "It's hard enough for craft beer in general to get meetings with big chain buyers. Now, AB can go in and pitch Elysian."

Ten months later, Anheuser-Busch could also pitch Breckenridge.

The first reply to Breckenridge's announcement of the sale on its website was that passage from the *Post*, thrown back in Usry's face, followed by a comment: "Todd you sure misled a lot of people. Quite the change since Feb of 2015 when you said you wouldn't be a sell out. You are a sell out and a disappointment."

But that's where craft beer had landed: one day a champion for independence, the next day facing unfathomable wealth and resources.

By 2015, the interest for Anheuser-Busch wasn't just going out; it was coming in, mostly from investment bankers hired by brewery owners to shop their businesses. Some of the brewery owners—like those at

Goose Island, Blue Point, and Four Peaks—were at intersections in their lives and careers and sought strategies that would guarantee growth and secure paydays for themselves. Others, like Breckenridge, swore they had no intention to sell but couldn't say no to teaming up with the world's largest beer company in a quickly changing industry. As Meg Gill, cofounder of Golden Road Brewing, said when announcing her sale, "We want to be with the winning horse."

Only about half the deals that went beyond a cursory conversation were consummated. The purchase of Cigar City Brewing, for instance, would have been a coup for Anheuser-Busch and arguably the sexiest name it had acquired to date. In early 2015, two weeks after the Elysian sale, word leaked of talks between the breweries. It was an obvious target. Founded in Tampa in 2009 and fueled by its Jai Alai IPA and Hunahpu's Imperial Stout, Cigar City had become one of the nation's ascendant brands. Founder Joey Redner confirmed for his local newspaper that, yes, Anheuser-Busch had reached out. What he didn't tell the newspaper was that the idea of a sale was pitched. Redner declined.

A year later, the rumors of a sale to Anheuser-Busch resurfaced. This time, Redner didn't deny that he might be inching toward a deal. "There's nothing to announce," he told the Brewbound website. "I've always taken meetings when asked and I'll continue to take meetings moving forward. It's how you learn more about your business, its value and the industry."

A month later, Cigar City did sell, but not to Anheuser-Busch.

Redner reached a deal with one of those new models of industry consolidation: a hybrid, financed by private equity firm Fireman Capital Partners and fronted by Colorado's Oskar Blues. However, there was a twist: Redner acknowledged that he had nearly completed a deal with Anheuser-Busch.

Interest in buying Cigar City had persisted since the brewery's earliest days. By the time Redner was ready to listen, more than a dozen interested parties made themselves known. His initial plan was for both he and his partner—who was his father—to each sell a small piece of ownership to grow the business while reaping a modest payout. However, his father was adamant: He wouldn't bring anyone else into the business. If Redner insisted, his father said he wanted out.

Redner adjusted his plan to find a partner who would acquire a majority of the company while he stayed on with a minority stake to run day-to-day operations. His father, wanting to extract as much money as he could, reached out to the High End. It made an offer. A good offer.

But Redner was only vaguely comfortable with the prospect of a deal. He wanted his father to be happy. He wanted to find a deep-pocketed partner. He signed a letter of intent that included an exclusive negotiating window for Anheuser-Busch. He took a half-hour call from John Hall, who lobbied on his bosses' behalf. "You won't convince everybody," John told him. "But you'll convince most people and you'll have more customers in the end." John thought he had convinced Redner.

It just didn't feel right. The Anheuser-Busch team was more reasonable and down to earth than Redner had expected. But they were corporate warriors. They were not the people he envisioned as partners. Redner liked to operate as an underdog, amid controlled chaos. It was how he built Cigar City into one of the most buzzed-about breweries in the nation. Anheuser-Busch was anything but controlled chaos. It was steady. It was methodical. It was reams of documents. Corporate jargon. Shareholder return. Redner figured that the beer wouldn't suffer. But other parts of Cigar City's culture might.

As talks dragged on, Redner checked with his attorneys to see if exclusivity had lapsed. It had. He went with Oskar Blues, and for less money.

It was a public setback for Anheuser-Busch, though other deals had fallen apart too—just more quietly. Sometimes Anheuser-Busch backed away. Maybe there wasn't a cultural fit. Or the parties disagreed on valuation. Other times it was the target that pulled out; it just couldn't make peace with being part of the world's largest beer company.

Some breweries listened out of courtesy but with no intention to sell. Left Hand Brewing, of Longmont, Colorado, took the meeting. Cofounder Eric Wallace was one of the fiercest critics of breweries that sold, and he turned particularly salty when his longtime ally, Breckenridge Brewery, was among them. "It's a sad day when someone like that, who has been fighting the fight for more than 20 years, sells out," Wallace told *Westword* weekly. "For me, it is inconceivable. How do you sell out to those guys? They are the ones who caused the scorched earth that (craft brewers) have repopulated and re-inhabited." Yet Wallace gave Michael Taylor a tour of the brewery and chatted with him on the patio outside his taproom. He wanted to learn what he could about the Anheuser-Busch plan. Then he said he wasn't interested.

Some of the deals that fell through were particularly disappointing and left Szpigel and Castro Neves wondering what could have been. Firestone Walker hurt. Both Szpigel and Castro Neves were wowed by the central California brewery and the prospect of what they might achieve with the brand. They thought they were inching toward a deal. It didn't happen.

Firestone Walker was one of the industry's touchstones when it hired a banker in 2012 to help navigate its need for growth. It was courted by a handful of large beer companies, including Anheuser-Busch. But Big Beer's muscle and promise of easy dominance couldn't overcome David Walker's concerns about the future of his brewery.

Walker feared that the things he valued most—the people, the brewery, its culture—would be lost. It might take ten years. It might take twenty. But ultimately, any large beer company only needed the brand. Like Larry Bell, Walker figured that saying no to Anheuser-Busch was the more difficult path; the High End's developing regional strategy would mean hurdles for Firestone Walker for decades to come.

But he and partner Adam Firestone opted to sell to Duvel Moortgat for a price estimated in media reports at $250 million. Duvel was a privately held Belgian company that already owned Brewery Ommegang in upstate New York and Boulevard Brewing in Kansas City. CEO Michel Moortgat outlined a multigenerational plan that included a strong and independent Firestone Walker for years to come. It was a more compelling pitch than what publicly traded Big Beer could muster.

Two months later, Anheuser-Busch snapped up a consolation prize: Los Angeles–based Golden Road Brewing, two hundred miles south. Missing out on Firestone Walker was a rare blow. But it was OK. Every failed deal was an opportunity to learn. And for the biggest beer company in the world there were always more deals to be made.

27

Corporate Beer Still Sucks

On an early Saturday evening in October 2015, Kraig Seltzer and Jeanne Reschan walked into a legendary Seattle music venue called the Showbox.

A thrash metal band from New Jersey was playing, and the front bar was packed. Seltzer and Reschan grabbed a table in back. A waitress arrived. The couple asked about available beers. The waitress mentioned several options, including a black ale from a brewery called 10 Barrel. It was from just down the road, in Oregon, she said. Reschan ordered it. Seltzer ordered a ginger ale and mozzarella sticks. Eventually the pair moved to the front bar, where the beer menu was scrawled on a chalkboard above the bar. They scrutinized.

A Goose Island beer was on tap. So was the 10 Barrel black ale. There was Elysian's Loser pale ale, whose tagline had turned acutely ironic since that brewery's sale to Anheuser-Busch earlier in the year: "Corporate beer still sucks." There were Bud and Bud Light, of course. And Stella. And Widmer. The bottle list included Michelob, Rolling Rock, Johnny Appleseed cider, and Montejo, a Mexican import.

Every beer on the menu was affiliated with Anheuser-Busch InBev.

Seltzer and Reschan? They were undercover agents from the Washington State Liquor and Cannabis Board.

Five days later, they visited Showbox SoDo, a sister property of the Showbox, posing as event organizers looking to host a "military gathering." Showbox SoDo's event manager led them through the venue, to a second-floor lounge where a large Budweiser neon sign hung on a wall and seven of the eight taps were Anheuser-Busch beers. Among them, again, were three of its craft beer acquisitions: Goose Island, 10 Barrel, and Elysian. The agents asked if they could secure a keg of Coors Light for their event. The manager shook her head and said the venue maintained an "exclusive" agreement with Anheuser-Busch. If they insisted on pouring non-Anheuser-Busch brands, they would need to pay extra.

It was an illegal arrangement—just like the all-Anheuser-Busch tap list at the Showbox.

After a six-month investigation, the Washington State Liquor and Cannabis Board concluded that Anheuser-Busch had exercised "undue influence" over the Showbox venues, guaranteeing exclusivity for its brands for more than a year. Most customers would have little reason to notice or care that Anheuser-Busch was dominating the menu; it was in the process of building a portfolio that presented the appearance of choice—imports, craft beer from around the country, cheap domestic brands, and, of course, Bud and Bud Light. Few people would recognize a draft list of Goose Island, Elysian, 10 Barrel, Widmer, Stella, and Bud and Bud Light as the absence of choice. Yet, quietly, that's what it was. It was a modern version of a tied house—one of the very things that the three-tier system was intended to prevent. The following May, Anheuser-Busch was fined $150,000 and slapped with a three-day suspension. (However, it was also given the option of paying an extra $1,000 to forgo the suspension.)

In a statement, Anheuser-Busch said it did "not agree with the allegations in the notice." If it wasn't quite a forceful denunciation, it also wasn't an aberration. Anheuser-Busch and its parent company were in the midst of a string of sales and marketing practices attracting the attention of regulators.

- A $300,000 settlement in March 2016 with the Alcohol and Tobacco Tax and Trade Bureau for an agreement to buy back unsold cases of Shock Top Lemon Shandy and Shock Top Pumpkin Wheat Ale.

Nearly 541,000 cases were sold to wholesalers based on the promise of what the industry called "buy back"—a violation of law prohibiting the privilege of returning unsold beer. In a statement, Felipe Szpigel, president of the High End, said Anheuser-Busch believed the program was legal, but "we've decided to move forward in the spirit of partnership and settle the matter."

- A $6 million settlement in September 2016 with the US Securities and Exchange Commission after being accused of bribing Indian government officials to increase sales and production in that country, a violation of the Foreign Corrupt Practices Act. Anheuser-Busch InBev was also accused of threatening a former employee who planned to reveal the arrangement.
- A $400,000 settlement in March 2017 after the California Department of Alcoholic Beverage Control concluded that an Anheuser-Busch wholesaler was furnishing accounts with coolers, televisions, and draft systems across Southern California. It was one of the largest penalties levied in the agency's history.
- An accusation in May 2017 from the Commonwealth of Massachusetts Alcoholic Beverages Control Commission that an Anheuser-Busch-owned distributor curried favor with local bars via nearly $1 million of free equipment: seventy Budweiser-branded draught towers worth as much as $3,500, plus hundreds of coolers ranging in value from $500 to $5,700.

After the Massachusetts fine was announced, Chris Lohring, founder of Notch Brewing, a craft brewery in Salem, Massachusetts, told the Brewbound website that it was just one more instance of the beer industry's unbalanced landscape.

"In all this what concerns me is that Anheuser Busch—and I've lost count of how many craft brands that they've purchased—but this just shows the power of AB to control the marketplace and makes it harder for smaller brands to gain access to distribution channels," Lohring said. "And this is one example of it."

Anheuser-Busch InBev was far from the only beer company deploying illegal sales tactics, but no one exerted greater influence while doing it. It was the industry giant; even its hiccup was a roar. And its legal tactics—some of which barely skirted inside the law—could roil the industry. Whether allegations of pay to play, questionable distribution practices, co-opting media, or gripes about transparency, Anheuser-Busch's push into craft beer raised stakes in all directions.

Like during the reign of August Busch III, the Brazilians realized they could exert much of their power in the place where they maintained a disproportionate advantage against craft competition: Anheuser-Busch's national network of more than five hundred distributors. Deschutes Brewery discovered as much in December 2015. The nation's eighth-largest craft brewery, situated in the high desert town of Bend, Oregon, got a letter from its St. Louis distributor, Grey Eagle Distributors, that was to the point: after more than four years, Grey Eagle would terminate its agreement to sell Deschutes in St. Louis. To anyone remotely paying attention, the move reeked of favoritism: Grey Eagle's president and CEO was David Stokes, a former Anheuser-Busch vice president; his father, Pat, was the company's CEO between August III and August IV.

Deschutes founder Gary Fish was stunned. He had built one of the most lauded craft breweries in the nation, with a bedrock portfolio and the constant hum of innovation. Now he would be frozen out of a large chunk of one of the nation's major cities. Fish was disgusted, but after twenty-seven years in the business, he understood how things were done. Anheuser-Busch had an advantage. It was using it. It was business. Smart, ruthless business. It was Win Together.

Win Together was an updated version of Anheuser-Busch's long-running Voluntary Anheuser-Busch Incentive for Performance program—VAIP for short. The new program was developed through twelve meetings across eight months between Anheuser-Busch InBev and an advisory panel of wholesalers. Until Win Together, the Brazilians' relationship with distributors had soured. August Busch III had treated his distributors like royalty; the Brazilians simply expected them to get on board. They didn't. After all, other than the handful owned directly by Anheuser-Busch InBev, they were independent business and could act independently when they cared to.

Win Together was intended to fix that. Under the old VAIP, the average wholesaler benefit stood at a paltry $30,000 per year. Under Win Together, the figure would be bumped to $200,000. Only 38 percent of distributors had participated in the old program, down from 61 percent just three years earlier. The problem had been craft: the industry was reaching every corner of the nation, and distributors needed small and local brands. The result was less and less exclusivity for Anheuser-Busch. To qualify for rebates under the old VAIP, distributors needed their portfolios to be at least 97 percent Anheuser-Busch products. Maximum payout came at 100 percent alignment.

The updated VAIP—Win Together, announced at a St. Louis wholesaler meeting in November 2015—set more realistic goals. Anheuser-Busch InBev dispensed with the idea of complete exclusivity; maximum payouts could be had for 98 percent alignment. Distributors could sell as much craft beer as they wanted from non-Anheuser-Busch breweries, but with a rub: The breweries had to make fewer than fifteen thousand barrels or sell beer only in one state. Anything larger counted against the threshold. It was a detail that betrayed a long-held belief: Small, local craft breweries with tiny distribution footprints raised awareness for Anheuser-Busch's craft brands. Big craft breweries, like Deschutes, were the enemy. Anheuser-Busch InBev's North American president João Castro Neves declared the program "a new beginning" in the relationship between Anheuser-Busch and its distributors.

In reality, Win Together was one of many ongoing attempts to manipulate the all-important distribution tier. There was the Ambassadors of Excellence program, which rewarded distributors whose management, operations, human resources, technology, and sales cultures aligned with St. Louis. Anheuser-Busch sent teams to interview employees and grade wholesalers on thousand-point scales. Winners were showered with incentives and prizes (a commemorative "Clydesdale trophy" delivered by the iconic Clydesdales themselves) and awarded championship-style rings. When InBev took over, the program was tweaked to focus on how efficiently beer moved through the system. The Brazilians didn't care about human resources; they cared about sales.

Wholly owned distributors, called WODs for short, were the wholesalers owned by Anheuser-Busch through a quirk that allowed breweries to also own distributors in a handful of states. As part of Anheuser-Busch, WODs carried higher profit margins and generated better sales volumes than independently owned wholesalers. WODs were known to reliably carry nothing but Anheuser-Busch beer. By 2017, Anheuser-Busch owned eighteen distributors in ten states, which resulted in a subtle oddity: the nation's largest brewery was also the nation's largest distributor.

In 2015, after Anheuser-Busch went on a spending spree to buy five distributors in three months, the US Department of Justice launched an investigation into potential anticompetitive practices. The question: Was craft beer's access to market being curbed? An anonymous craft executive told Reuters that Anheuser-Busch had recently bought one of its distributors and was "slowly, but surely divesting itself of everything that is not ABI. And we're one of the last ones. We're at the mercy of a lot of big players."

It took a little time for the Brazilians to understand the three-tier system, but once they did, the power of their distribution network was plain. As Edmond told investors in 2013, the company would consider adding more WODs as opportunities arose: "Our number one priority with our wholesalers is to create the best route-to-market system and beat competition in every corner of this country through superior execution." By owning wholesalers, the Brazilians were able to understand how they operated and identify the most efficient practices.

But arguably most important to Anheuser-Busch's control of the wholesaler tier was a strategy introduced in 2011: the creation of anchor wholesalers. Edmond once described them as "the ones with the best performance, financial capabilities, people bench-strength to grow and who are aligned with us."

Anchor wholesalers were not owned by Anheuser-Busch. But they were such loyal soldiers that they might as well have been. The distribution tier had been consolidating for twenty years, and Anheuser-Busch was pushing for more; it wanted anchor wholesalers to grow larger and stronger. The company even crafted a forty-three-page Wholesaler

Consolidation Guide that it sent to its five hundred plus distributors. In its equity agreements, Anheuser-Busch guaranteed itself the right to approve any sales or mergers, and used the right to funnel wholesaler ownership as it wished. In 2016 it intervened in a sale of one Mississippi wholesaler to another, diverting it to a third wholesaler that it preferred. The deal raised alarm at the Brewers Association; though it lent the appearance of Anheuser-Busch owning no more distributorships than it had previously, arranging the sale that it found most favorable was arguably de facto ownership.

"This exercise of the right to meet the terms of the negotiated deal and immediately flip the rights to a friendly distributor increased ABI's control over its distribution network without increasing ABI's percentage ownership of that network, but the harm is similar," the Brewers Association wrote of the deal to the Justice Department.

Anchor wholesalers were among the stealthiest threats to an equitable landscape. WODs were an obvious problem that could easily be regulated. Anchor wholesalers, however, were a gray area that Anheuser-Busch used to its advantage. As David Almeida, Anheuser-Busch's vice president of sales, told a group of investors in 2013, the company had seen twenty-five wholesaler transactions during the previous two years, most of which included the growth of an anchor wholesaler. The company, he said, had used "very clear criteria" to identify "anchor wholesalers who we would like to see grow. We have encouraged those wholesalers to pursue opportunities to acquire other wholesalers."

There was a simple motivation, Almeida said: "Upon completing these acquisitions, our anchor wholesalers have in general increased their investment behind our brands."

Asked during a question and answer session about whether Anheuser-Busch needed to expand its number of wholly owned distributors or anchor wholesalers, Almeida said the company ultimately had no worries when it came to the distribution tier.

"We're not going to be 100 percent aligned and there's always friction, that's part of the relationship," Almeida said. "But the bottom line is that they execute what we ask them to execute."

Few things could be less interesting to most beer drinkers than the politics of distribution. That played to Anheuser-Busch's advantage. But it was an ever-hotter flash-point issue for brewers. In early 2015 Ninkasi Brewing Co., in Eugene, Oregon, left two of its distributors that had been independently owned, then sold to Anheuser-Busch. Sales had plummeted and goals grew incompatible, Ninkasi cofounder Nikos Ridge said when announcing the move: "We are committed to being an independent and locally-owned craft brewery, and feel we will be better aligned long term with independent and locally owned wholesalers."

The 10 Barrel deal two months earlier had led Ridge to the decision. A week later came the Elysian deal.

While Ridge acknowledged that Anheuser-Busch was just practicing "good business from their end," that good business also depressed competition—and he was the competition. "It does kind of disrupt our position within their portfolio when those things happen," Ridge told *Beverage Dynamics.*

Anheuser-Busch had one other means of disruption that its craft competitors did not: pricing. When it descended upon St. Louis in 2008, Anheuser-Busch InBev found that pricing decisions at its new American subsidiary had been largely decentralized—the opposite of how the company operated in other markets. They quickly centralized pricing, creating guidelines and a national revenue team in St. Louis that David Almeida told investors was "closely involved in and approves most pricing decisions."

With its scope and scale, Anheuser-Busch was able to offer consumers extraordinary savings whenever it felt its dominance threatened: four-for-three deals—or even two-for-one deals—on six-packs at grocery stores. "It can selectively do promos like this in [a] way that's really disruptive to its craft competition," beer journalist Harry Schuhmacher wrote in *Beer Business Daily.*

During the initial fevered reaction after the Goose Island deal, Canadian writer Alan McLeod asked a prophetic question on his blog, *A Good Beer Blog*: "What If InBev Keeps Everything but Lowers the Price?"

> Ten days or so ago I asked "What's the Difference Between Cheap and Good Beer?" and suggested it would be nice to know what it would take to add a few more quality ingredients to move a beer that is not the greatest into the conversation. Today, I ask the opposite. What happens if AB-InBev keeps Goose Island beers at the same quality but lowers the price? Would they be any less craft if that were to happen?

When it was necessary, Anheuser-Busch did exactly that. It was a tactic employed by Big Beer for generations that smaller producers could not match—slashing prices. Reports bubbled out of the Pacific Northwest of Goose Island IPA kegs penetrating the market for as little as $56—down from an already-alarmingly low price of about $110. Most smaller competitors sold IPA for about $170 per keg.

Anheuser-Busch wholesalers were handing bars irresistible profits at that impossibly low cost that the consumer never saw. Anheuser-Busch gained countless Goose Island tap handles with those discounts, some of which were lost when price cuts ended, but some of which remained—or went to other products in the Anheuser-Busch portfolio. The pricing shocked even Goose Island veterans back in Chicago. What were these St. Louis people doing with their brand?

Pressed on the cheap kegs, Andy Goeler told *Beer Business Daily* that it wasn't part of a broader effort driven out of St. Louis: "Every wholesaler kind of has their ability to do whatever they need to do to get distribution or to help support brands and so forth. I mean, there is no national Goose Island pricing strategy, I guess is the way to answer that." Though some things may "bubble up locally," the priority was always staying competitive, he said.

Yet, back in 2013, Luiz Edmond had told a room of investors the obvious: the smaller players *had* to charge more for their beer.

"The craft producers, they don't have enough margin to bring the price down," Edmond said. "The profitability level of the craft beer business is very low and with that I believe they don't have a lot of room to bring prices down to compete. That's the reason why they price up—they could not make any money. And by pricing it up, which is why we call them 'high end,' they develop different beers and the prices of these beers are much higher. But the fact is that they could not charge a lower price because simply the profitability is not there because the scale is not there."

While noting that the company was committed to higher prices for craft—profits were juicer—he also said the company could be aggressive with pricing when necessary: "We are always looking at the gaps versus our other competitors, and seeing if we are losing share, then we will have to manage the price point."

Its craft strategy allowed just that. By brewing an IPA in the same tanks and volumes as Bud Light, cost was driven down and prices could become as competitive as needed.

The issue was particularly acute in Seattle. By 2015, Matt Lincoln, the former Goose Island brewer who created the oak-aged blackberry beer Juliet, would walk into bars where Goose Island IPA tap handles suddenly proliferated. It was infuriating. He was making beer for local Fremont Brewing, a midsized brewery trying to grow. Here was his former employer—and an experience he recalled fondly—being deployed against him. For a moment, it tainted what Goose Island meant to him. But then he was able to parse the present from the past. Goose Island wasn't the same company anymore.

Anheuser-Busch had the breweries. It had the distribution. And it had the remarkably aggressive—and occasionally illegal—sales network. What was left? The message.

In 2017 the High End launched a website called The Beer Necessities, which its founder wrote "began with a simple question: is it possible to create a platform that celebrates beer, helps to unify the industry and appeals to everyone from new beer lovers to even the most discerning of beer nerds?" Elsewhere, The Beer Necessities' editor declared, "We seem to be living in a post-craft world: great beer is great beer. And I believe we should celebrate all of it."

Anheuser-Busch had become deeply invested in such sentiments. "Unifying the industry" was code for making peace with the company's increasing dominance. The ideas that "great beer is great beer" and "we should celebrate all of it" meant the world's largest beer company could be camouflaged on taps and store shelves; the sooner distinctions were dropped, the better.

The Beer Necessities was part of a broader effort from Anheuser-Busch to infiltrate the discussion about craft beer without making clear to its audience who was leading the discussion. Simply reading the blogs, magazines, and ratings sites wasn't enough. It needed to *be* the blogs, magazines, and ratings sites.

The effort was shared between the High End and a division launched in 2015, ZX Ventures, which Anheuser-Busch called its "global disruptive growth group." It was housed one floor below the High End, in the same Manhattan building. Anheuser-Busch's version of disruptive growth was minute compared to what the financial services and tech industries deployed. But it sought to apply a similar playbook. Among the efforts was a stake in popular beer rating website RateBeer in October 2016 (never mind that five years earlier, RateBeer founder Joe Tucker had called Anheuser-Busch "a bully in the marketplace that's been antagonizing toward craft brewers"). It also invested in the online beer magazine *October* in combination with the Condé Nast media empire and the semi-journalistic, semi–industry consulting Good Beer Hunting website. (Neither Anheuser-Busch nor RateBeer revealed their deal; it was outed eight months later, oddly enough, by Good Beer Hunting as a journalistic scoop.)

The Beer Necessities was a wholly different undertaking—as an initiative of the High End, it was less about disruption and more of a means to stealthily project its message how it pleased. Simply touting its own brands would, of course, smack of one big advertisement. So, The Beer Necessities was built as a quasi-journalistic enterprise invested in covering the scope of the industry while just so happening to toss out the occasional photo of a 10 Barrel twelve-pack alongside an article titled "Lagers Are Good (and Why You Should Drink 'Em)." Or profiling Golden Road cofounder Meg Gill ("a unique, unfiltered star"). Or an article exploring Goose Island's Bourbon County lineup a few days before the beers went on sale. The Beer Necessities managed to recruit an array of experienced beer journalists to fill its pages despite the blatant grounding in public relations. "There's tons of great beer out there," the website declared. "Some of it's ours, and some of it's not. We'd like to celebrate all of it."

It didn't all want to be celebrated. In May 2017, Gabe Gordon, owner and cofounder of Beachwood BBQ, one of Southern California's most renowned breweries, wrote on Facebook that he had been contacted several months earlier by what he understood to be a freelance journalist wanting to profile Beachwood for a new blog.

"The blog wasn't live yet, so we were unable to check its validity, but we are a small business who supports other small businesses so we agreed to the interview," Gordon wrote. After the eighteen-hundred-word article was published on The Beer Necessities, Gordon discovered the website's affiliation with the High End.

Anheuser-Busch arguably should have known better than to target Gordon. A couple of years earlier, he had pledged to never again pour Big Beer at his bars after hosting a Bourbon County tap takeover. Gordon initially justified the 2014 Goose Island event to himself as serving good beer. Then he realized that that was exactly what Anheuser-Busch wanted people to think: all that mattered was what was in the glass. In reality, Gordon thought, Big Beer was marketing in a glass. It was lobbyists and shareholders. Unconscionable tactics. Obfuscation. If Big Beer was becoming craft beer, Gordon thought, there was no such thing as craft beer anymore. Big Beer had won. But he wasn't quite ready to surrender.

Gordon subsequently donated all proceeds from a leftover keg of Bourbon County Vanilla Rye Stout to the California Craft Brewers Association. In a statement posted to Beachwood's Facebook page, he said he erred by hosting the event for Goose Island:

> Big Beer has always used questionable practices from pay to play, to lobbying the government, to distributor incentives to keep craft brewers and beers from taking market share from them. Every dollar that we spend on Big Beer-owned "craft" brands contributes to their ability to harm craft brewers. I made a mistake by buying this beer. I would like to make amends. So all the money we collect from this keg will go to the CCBA. They do an amazing job advocating for the actual craft brewers.

Now, three years later, Gordon was calling out Anheuser-Busch InBev again. After The Beer Necessities piece was posted, he took to Facebook once more:

> As an independent brewery that has fought hard against the predatory business practices of macro beer for almost a decade, we wholly reject this free promotion and all that it stands for. We don't want it. We don't need it. And if we knew that it would be used, in our opinion, to help AB-InBev in their intensifying quest to dilute the definition of "craft," we certainly would have refused participation. . . .
>
> We also never in a million years would have thought that a multi-national corporation such as AB-InBev would be entering the blogging business. The fact that they have shows the lengths that big beer is willing to go to fool you, the consumer, into thinking that their acquired "craft" brands are truly craft beer and that they (AB-InBev) have somehow come to share the values of independent breweries.

The article about Beachwood had appeared beneath a headline touting the merits of brewpubs: "Yes, You Can Have a Thriving Brewpub in 2017; Brewpubs Are Anything but Dead. Beachwood Brewing, in Particular, Is Leading the Pack, Thanks to Some Fantastic Beers."

Gordon saw it as an obvious effort to use his success to pump up Anheuser-Busch's own interests: The High End was in the process of launching taprooms and brewpubs for Goose Island in Philadelphia and Toronto, Golden Road in Oakland and Sacramento, and 10 Barrel in Denver and San Diego. Gordon's wasn't an unreasonable thought; Anheuser-Busch had long considered smaller breweries legitimizing forces for its own craft efforts: have a pint of IPA at the local spot down the street, then buy a twelve-pack of Goose Island—or Golden Road or 10 Barrel—IPA at the grocery store. By boosting a brewery like Beachwood, it was in reality riding its coattails.

"Some of you may write this off as conspiracy theory talk," Gordon wrote on his Facebook page,

> but we are entering a whole new battle for the hearts and minds of the consumer. When The High End now has media arms that are actively supporting us in order to make the correlation to consumers that we're all the same, they are most certainly trying to move us into a "post-craft" era. However, we reject this completely. In our opinion, AB-InBev has not embraced "craft" brands and quality beer because they share the values of independence and creativity that have fueled the craft beer revolution; they do so because it furthers their only real interest—the endless pursuit of profits.

And that pursuit trickled all the way down to its piece of the information channel. However, at Gordon's request, The Beer Necessities did remove the article about Beachwood from its website. Seven months later, the High End quietly shut down The Beer Necessities, deciding it was wiser for the company to support one craft beer–focused website—its high-profile collaboration with Condé Nast, *October*—instead of two.

28

"If People Do the Work to Find Out That We Own These Craft Brands, God Bless 'Em"

On April 1, 2016, the *Growler*, a Twin Cities–based magazine devoted to local eating and drinking, posted a shocking headline on its website: "Dangerous Man Brewing Sells Majority Stake to AB InBev."

Dangerous Man was just three years old and tiny; it didn't even distribute outside of its northeast Minneapolis taproom. But brewery founder Rob Miller said in the article that he dreamed of the day "when our Peanut Butter Porter can be found on shelves and tap lines across the country."

"We were hesitant at first," Miller was quoted. "But over the last few years, we've seen [Anheuser-Busch InBev] make a serious commitment to supporting craft beer all over the country. Breckenridge, Four Peaks, and Elysian are all world-class brewers, and we're excited to join them."

For anyone too stunned to take note of the date, by midday the article was appended with a disclaimer:

> UPDATE [12:00pm, 4/1/2016]: Editor's Note: Clearly this post was bullshit. Happy April Fools' Day from The Growler and Dangerous Man Brewing.

Selling to Anheuser-Busch had literally become a joke.

By 2016, selling to the world's largest beer company wasn't only a joke—it was the root of an industry tearing at itself. Anheuser-Busch had bought nine breweries in five years. In a regional strategy similar to its chief rival, MillerCoors was up to four—including three acquired during the summer of 2016. Lagunitas, founded in Northern California in 1993, sold half of itself to Heineken for a reported $500 million in September 2015. A mere two years earlier, Lagunitas founder Tony Magee had said on Twitter that he believed Anheuser-Busch was interested in buying his company, but that he wouldn't sell: "Selling one's brewery is selling all of one's best friend's careers, their hearts, the portion of their lives they spent working for you." But now the race for growth was on; it was Magee who initiated the deal with Heineken. Less than two years later, he would also sell the other half to Heineken.

The simmering conflict no longer amounted to cries of sellout after each sale. A full-on introspection had begun. What had been created? What had been co-opted? Who had won? Who had lost? John Hall insisted that craft beer had won; it had forced Big Beer to change. Gabe Gordon, of Beachwood BBQ, swore Big Beer won. It was making so-called craft beer in the same tanks as Bud Light.

Craft beer was dead. Long live craft beer.

Every additional brewery sale to Anheuser-Busch inched the narrative forward with a fresh round of backlash and spite. For Devils Backbone, it came in the form of being kicked out of its own beer festival, the Virginia Craft Brewers Fest, which Devils Backbone had hosted every year since its founding in 2012. After announcing its sale, in April 2016, Devils Backbone was told it would no longer be able to host the festival or enter its competition.

The previous July, 10 Barrel Brewing had been similarly excommunicated from the Oregon Brewers Festival in Portland. 10 Barrel's founders responded with a social media hashtag (#bannedsoweparty) and a black SUV Hummer stretch limousine, emblazoned with the brewery's logo, to shepherd beer drinkers between the festival and 10 Barrel's taproom.

When Golden Road announced plans to open a taproom in Oakland, locals accused the brewery of both gentrification and hiding its corporate roots. A headline in the alternative weekly *East Bay Express* read "Corporate Beer Overlords AB InBev to Open Golden Road 'Craft' Beer Garden in North Oakland." Brewery cofounder Meg Gill told the newspaper, "Anheuser-Busch reads the articles, and they're like, 'What the hell's going on in Oakland?'" (A similar plan in Sacramento generated far less consternation.)

10 Barrel was targeted again in 2017 after opening a taproom in San Diego, where Robert Esparza, a restaurant industry marketer, launched an online campaign to fly a banner behind an airplane reading 10 BARREL IS NOT CRAFT BEER on the day of 10 Barrel's inaugural block party.

"Not going to explain why I'm doing this," Esparza wrote on his fundraising website. "You either get it, or you don't."

Esparza reached his goal of $900 in four hours. After ten days, the total swelled to $2,220. Two weeks later, it was up to $4,840, thanks in part to a $2,500 donation from an anonymously donating brewery owner from the other side of the country.

With his unexpected windfall, Esparza decided to fly the plane twice.

There wasn't a single moment when the chummy, jovial craft beer industry became a battlefield of "us versus them." It happened slowly. And then, seemingly, all at once.

The match was lit largely out of public view, in 2006, when the Brewers Association first created a definition for a *craft brewer*. Until then the term had been little more than a hazy concept first articulated in the mid-1980s and little understood beyond being the opposite of Big Beer. Craft beer was the underdog. It was flavor. It was creativity. It was peace, love, and collaboration. Everyone was included—except for Big Beer. There were no wrong answers.

But when there are no wrong answers, there are no right answers, and the Brewers Association sought to correct that, settling on that definition of *small* (manufacturing fewer than two million barrels per year), *independent* (less than 25 percent could be owned by a company that itself was not a craft brewer), and *traditional* (beers could be made only by traditional brewing methods with adjuncts that enhanced rather than lightened flavor).

Craft beer's second "us versus them" moment was also courtesy of the Brewers Association, and this time it was glaringly public. It came in 2012, when craft beer was ascendant once more. Nearly twenty-five hundred breweries operated as sales grew wildly—up to 6.5 percent of the industry; less than ten years earlier, craft beer's share of the market was still struggling to eclipse 3 percent. The definition of a *craft brewer*, hatched six years earlier, remained, but the production ceiling had been raised to six million barrels per year to avoid penalizing the rapid growth of Samuel Adams.

Since the establishment of the definition, Goose Island had been wholly absorbed by Anheuser-Busch InBev. Blue Moon was on fire. And Shock Top was gaining ground. So on a Thursday in mid-December 2012, the Brewers Association issued a 480-word statement differentiating craft beer from what it called "crafty" beer:

> Witnessing both the tremendous success and growth of craft brewers and the fact that many beer lovers are turning away from mass-produced light lagers, the large brewers have been seeking entry into the craft beer marketplace. Many started producing their own craft-imitating beers, while some purchased (or are attempting to purchase) large or full stakes in small and independent breweries.
>
> While this is certainly a nod to the innovation and ingenuity of today's small and independent brewers, it's important to remember that if a large brewer has a controlling share of a smaller producing brewery, the brewer is, by definition, not craft.
>
> However, many non-standard, non-light "crafty" beers found in the marketplace today are not labeled as products of large breweries. So when someone is drinking a Blue Moon Belgian Wheat Beer, they often believe that it's from a craft brewer, since there is no clear indication that it's made by SABMiller. The same goes for Shock Top, a brand that is 100 percent owned by Anheuser-Bush [*sic*] InBev, and several others that are owned by a multinational brewing and beverage company.

> The large, multinational brewers appear to be deliberately attempting to blur the lines between their crafty, craft-like beers and true craft beers from today's small and independent brewers. We call for transparency in brand ownership and for information to be clearly presented in a way that allows beer drinkers to make an informed choice about who brewed the beer they are drinking.
>
> And for those passionate beer lovers out there, we ask that you take the time to familiarize yourself with who is brewing the beer you are drinking. Is it a product of a small and independent brewer? Or is it from a crafty large brewer, seeking to capitalize on the mounting success of small and independent craft brewers?

The statement was accompanied by a list of thirty-four "domestic non-craft brewers," paired with the reasons that each failed to qualify as craft. The statement was affirmed the next day with a shot fired in Anheuser-Busch's backyard—the opinion pages of the *St. Louis Post-Dispatch*. Beneath the headline "Craft or Crafty? Consumers Deserve to Know the Truth," Charlie Papazian and Bob Pease of the Brewers Association, along with Dan Kopman of Saint Louis Brewery, published an essay invoking the Founding Fathers, craft beer's rapid ascent into a $9 billion industry, and the "faux-craft beer" made by "large international conglomerates." The article echoed the previous day's press release, arguing, "If you think craft breweries are a good force in America, take the time to familiarize yourself with who is brewing the beer you are drinking."

The most fevered response to "craft versus crafty" didn't initially come from Anheuser-Busch InBev or MillerCoors—it came from Minnesota's August Schell Brewing. Schell had landed on the "crafty" list because like the macrobrewers, it employed corn in its brew, an adjunct ingredient not intended to enhance a beer's flavor. Corn was generally seen as a means to make brewing cheaper, but Schell responded with a lengthy online post explaining its use of corn as traditional: When August Schell began brewing in 1860, he used corn because Minnesota didn't have access to the same high quality barley that he'd used in Germany. By the time higher-quality barley was available, Schell's customers were accustomed to a recipe that included corn, and it stayed in the recipe. "Shame on you," the brewery's sixth-generation owner wrote to the Brewers Association.

The Brewers Association heard the criticism and relented. It not only removed the list of "crafty" breweries from its website but also adjusted its definition of *traditional* in 2014 to include breweries that used adjuncts such as corn or rice; Schell and Pennsylvania's Yuengling were brought into the craft beer fold.

But the Brewers Association refused to retreat on one wrinkle of the definition: ownership.

The Brewers Association didn't see corn or rice as out to destroy craft beer. But Big Beer—Anheuser-Busch InBev in particular—seemed intent on the matter. It was equally determined to obscure its role in craft beer, hence the Brewers Association's unwillingness to compromise on the issue of Big Beer ownership.

Eventually, Big Beer bit back.

In response to the "craft versus crafty" statement, Glenn Knippenberg, president and cofounder of AC Golden Brewing Co., a subsidiary of MillerCoors, told a local newspaper that craft beer had nothing to do with ownership.

"Basing the definition on ownership completely dismisses what all of the industry's talented, hard-working brewers are creating every day," he told Boulder's *Daily Camera*. "It also insults craft-beer drinkers as status seekers or beer snobs versus true beer lovers. They don't choose a craft beer because of who owns the brewery; they choose a craft beer in appreciation of its diversity of style, quality and artistry."

Troy Casey, a brewer at AC Golden, said a definition focusing on ownership was "petty and makes the BA look childish."

The Brewers Association and its advocates stressed that they weren't telling people what decisions to make and weren't questioning the quality of Big Beer's craft efforts. They were simply trying to draw attention to the differences between smaller businesses and global conglomerates.

"What craft means to me is you're putting more love into your product," the marketing director of craft stalwart Avery Brewing said in the same *Daily Camera* article. "For us, it's about the beer first and sales second—we want to make the best possible product with the highest quality ingredients out there."

On it went, back and forth, each side claiming to be inside the mind of the craft beer consumer. A week after the "craft versus crafty" statement, MillerCoors CEO Tom Long crafted a fairly reasonable argument on CNN's website. Both Miller and Coors, which fused in 2008, had long been innovative, he said—at least as compared to the lumbering Anheuser-Busch. Coors had created the bestselling craft beer in the nation—Blue Moon—while Miller had had the foresight to buy a depressed Leinenkugel Brewing in 1988 and use it as a hub of innovation that produced the wildly successful lemonade-beer hybrid Summer Shandy.

> As a large brewer, we do not view the emergence of craft beer as a threat, because we know that innovation is essential to the American beer industry. In fact, we appreciate the vital role craft beers play within our industry. And we believe it's good for beer that there are more breweries and more brands available to American beer drinkers than at any other time in U.S. history.
>
> We're determined to continue to play a leading role in that innovation. And whatever style beer you might prefer, all we ask is that you judge us by the quality of the beer in the glass.

It was Big Beer's most critical argument as the "us versus them" fault line grew: *only think about what's in the glass.* As long as drinkers bought in to the sentiment—and didn't think about the strong-armed tactics that might have funneled that beer into their glass—they could be had by marketing and outsized influence they couldn't recognize. Sure, beer drinkers would need to *think* they chose what they drank. But there were a thousand quiet ways to help them reach that conclusion. As long as drinkers believed the only thing that mattered was what was in their glass, they could be had. Beer drinkers were being socialized to believe that they should be buying exactly what Big Beer was selling—just as Big Beer had done for generations.

Bob Pease didn't believe the gentle pleas emanating from Big Beer.

We just want to take part.

We just want to bring these brands to our customers.

We just want to compete.

The moment Anheuser-Busch—or to a lesser degree, MillerCoors—competed in craft beer, the competition was over. Nearly twenty-five years at the Brewers Association led Pease to conclude the obvious: Big Beer wanted to dominate.

Pease started with the Brewers Association as its customer service manager in 1993, back when it was still the Association of Brewers. He stood on the front lines for the early glory days and witnessed the late '90s collapse. By the time he became chief executive officer of craft beer's most powerful advocate, in 2014, the second surge was underway. Nearly four thousand breweries were operating from coast to coast; back in the '90s, the figure never eclipsed sixteen hundred. The other key difference: the creation of Anheuser-Busch InBev. Its formation in 2008 had forever tilted the landscape. Stubborn old Anheuser-Busch had been transformed to something nimble and aggressive.

While the Busch family seemed mostly invested in the legacies of their name and their company, the Brazilians were clearly out to make as much money as possible—and they were very good at it. Anheuser-Busch InBev was applying the Big Beer playbook to craft and changing its basic dynamic in the marketplace: from consumer pull to corporate push. How relentlessly had Americans been beaten over the head with Bud and Bud Light? Or the idea that colder beer was better? Or that "light" beer was the standard? This was just the updated version. Now it was being applied to IPA.

When Pease took the helm at the Brewers Association, the world's largest beer company owned just two American craft breweries: Goose Island and Blue Point. The High End had been formed one month earlier. Then came the 10 Barrel deal and the *holy shit* moment: the Elysian deal. If Dick Cantwell was selling—if Anheuser-Busch was able to buy *that* brewery—something profound was clearly underway.

Silly as it was, the "Brewed the Hard Way" Super Bowl commercial, which Pease watched at home in real time, underscored what he saw as the war at hand. How tone-deaf were these guys? How oblivious? How arrogant? Forget a definition of *craft beer* or the idea that some beer was merely *crafty*. This was the ultimate in "us versus them." He wasn't much of a social media user, but Pease couldn't resist. As soon as the ad aired, he grabbed his phone and typed into Twitter, "Wow—King of Beers? Not! You know the craft sector has arrived when the King of Beers takes a shot at you during a Super Bowl ad!"

He'd always suspected Anheuser-Busch's claims of advancing the interests of the entire industry were hollow. Now he was sure. Its combination of distribution muscle and financial resources upended any semblance of a level playing field. Pease had read *Dream Big*, the book about the partners who grew Brazil's second-largest beer company into a global juggernaut. He understood their playbook.

Buy. Grow. More.

How was there anything approaching a level playing field? With eight or ten or twelve of the kinds of breweries it could never create itself, Anheuser-Busch could scale up beers from them all—just as it had done with Goose Island—and shoot them into national distribution at affordable Big Beer prices. Its distributors could walk into any bar, chain restaurant, supermarket, or convenience store as a one-stop shop: A low-alcohol IPA from Los Angeles! A robust IPA from Seattle! A vanilla porter from Colorado! A stout aged in bourbon barrels from Chicago! An easy-drinking lager from Virginia! And don't forget good ol' Bud and Bud Light! No one ever had to be the wiser that much of the beer was brewed in the same tanks.

The issue, Pease believed, amounted to disclosure—the issue that "craft versus crafty" was intending to raise. If Big Beer wouldn't be clear about its role in craft, then the Brewers Association would do it for Big Beer. None of the packaging for any of Anheuser-Busch InBev's craft acquisitions included the words ANHEUSER-BUSCH INBEV. Not on the bottle. Not on the can. Not on the cardboard twelve-pack. Not anywhere. The closest hint came in the tiny horizontal print on the sides of its bottles and cans. As beer from its craft acquisitions was increasingly off-loaded to Anheuser-Busch breweries, a pattern emerged: the "home" market—where the acquired brewery was physically located—was listed first, followed by the location of the Anheuser-Busch breweries where the beer was actually made:

> Goose Island Beer Co.
> Chicago, IL, Baldwinsville, NY & Fort Collins, CO
>
> Golden Road Brewing
> Los Angeles, CA & Fairfield CA
>
> Brewed and bottled by Elysian Brewing Co., Inc.
> Seattle, WA & Fairfield CA
>
> Blue Point Brewing Company
> Patchogue, NY and Merrimack, NH
>
> Breckenridge Brewery, LLC
> Littleton, CO and Fort Collins, CO

Still, the cans of Golden Road's Wolf Pup Session IPA made at Anheuser-Busch's brewery in Fairfield, California—nearly four hundred miles north of the actual Golden Road brewery in L.A.—declared LOS ANGELES on an electric blue background featuring an image of a palm tree. Bottles of Blue Point made in Merrimack, New Hampshire, prominently featured EST. LONG ISLAND on their front labels. The back label on a Goose Island beer made in upstate New York implied a direct relationship to the Chicago brewery seven hundred miles away: STOP BY AND SAY HELLO. GOOSE ISLAND TAPROOM: AT THE CORNER OF FULTON AND WOOD IN CHICAGO. The label for Breckenridge's Vanilla Porter—boasting a motto of FINE COLORADO ALES—seemed to indicate the beer was made by the brewery whose name appeared on the bottle. In fact, it was made by Anheuser-Busch in Ft. Collins.

Critics such as Pease argued that Anheuser-Busch InBev was taking control of the craft beer industry not only through acquisitions but also with a lack of transparency. The company claimed to be proud of its growing role in craft but did little to make that role clear at the places consumers bought beer, or even in the most basic messaging. Evidence of Anheuser-Busch InBev ownership was scant on the websites of High End acquisitions, and its PR agency would pitch products to media with an origin story—SpikedSeltzer "was founded in a Connecticut garage"—but nary a mention of the current owner or manufacturer.

Big Beer didn't deny its opacity at first. Anheuser-Busch's chief marketing officer, Paul Chibe, told *Adweek* in 2013 that the craft brands needed "separate identities in order to fulfill what the brand promise means to consumers."

"If people do the work to find out that we own these craft brands, God bless 'em," Chibe said. "We have nothing to hide."

Except, of course, who was making the beer. (Or seltzer.)

In 2014, Felipe Szpigel, president of the High End, shifted tactics, telling MarketWatch that the question of transparency amounted to needless bluster. "Consumer feedback tells us beer drinkers care about taste, quality and experiences," he said. "They are not concerned about labels. That criticism is coming from other brewers."

The Brewers Association didn't necessarily dispute as much. Julia Herz, director of the association's craft beer program, told the Boulder *Daily Camera* that brewers *were* distressed: "It became apparent from our membership emanating this sentiment that it was time to insert our voice into the conversation. The lines are becoming blurred, and it's harder to tell on the beer lovers' side who owns certain brands."

For Anheuser-Busch InBev, transparency was a festering matter. In 2015 the company reached a $20 million settlement with Beck's beer consumers, who filed a class action lawsuit after discovering that their "German" lager was in fact made in St. Louis. The label trumpeted the beer's "German Quality," its origins in Bremen, Germany, and the fact that it was made under the "German Purity Law of 1516." Most crucially, it wasn't priced as a beer made in St. Louis; it was priced as an import. Production of Beck's for the US market had shifted to St.

Louis in 2012 in a cost-cutting move. None other than future Goose Island boss Andy Goeler explained the move to *Ad Age* when he was still head of Anheuser-Busch's craft and import wing: "We made this decision after talking extensively with our consumers, who tell us they aren't concerned about where the beer is produced as much as how it's produced."

Earlier that year, Anheuser-Busch InBev had agreed to a nearly identical settlement with customers who claimed they were suckered into believing Kirin Lager was made in Japan. It was made at Anheuser-Busch breweries in Los Angeles and Williamsburg, Virginia.

The Brewers Association began to push back in earnest against Anheuser-Busch InBev in 2012. A definition and fiery rhetoric helped raise awareness, but it was time to push for change where it mattered most: behind the closed doors of Washington, DC.

The spark was Anheuser-Busch InBev's intention to wholly acquire Mexico's largest brewer, Grupo Modelo, maker of Corona and Modelo Especial. They were two of America's most ascendant imported brands and would allow the world's largest beer company to dominate the imports segment, just as it aimed to dominate nearly every other segment—including craft. Adding Corona and Modelo Especial would up Anheuser-Busch InBev's stranglehold on the US market from eight of the nation's top fifteen brands to ten. (Anheuser-Busch InBev already owned half of Grupo Modelo thanks to a deal executed by Anheuser-Busch long before the 2008 takeover. Now it wanted the rest and was prepared to pay $20 billion for it.)

The day the prospective deal was announced, Carlos Brito, Anheuser-Busch InBev's chief executive officer, played the role of Big Beer boy scout: "We believe this transaction brings no change to the U.S. market," he said on a call with analysts.

Investors, however, were agog at the thought of the deal. Fitch Ratings declared "achievement of full control of Grupo Modelo by Anheuser Busch InBev . . . makes good strategic and economic sense. The move would enhance the value of ABI's existing 50 percent stake in Grupo Modelo by providing scope for integration into ABI's organization."

The truth was that allowing Anheuser-Busch InBev to own the two biggest Mexican import brands would have upended the US beer market. Antitrust advocates worked furiously to get the attention of Congress and federal regulators. It worked. On January 31, 2013, the Justice Department announced an antitrust lawsuit to stop the merger, its biggest intervention since suing to stop AT&T's $39 billion takeover of T-Mobile US two years earlier. It was among the most notable roadblocks during the Brazilians' decade-plus run of global consolidation.

"The department is taking this action to stop a merger between major beer brewers because it would result in less competition and higher beer prices for American consumers," Bill Baer, assistant attorney general in charge of the Justice Department's Antitrust Division, said in a statement. "If ABI fully owned and controlled Modelo, ABI would be able to increase beer prices to American consumers. This lawsuit seeks to prevent ABI from eliminating Modelo as an important competitive force in the beer industry."

Two weeks later, Anheuser-Busch InBev came back with a significant tweak to the deal: in the US market, it would spin off the Grupo Modelo portfolio to Constellation Brands, one of the world's largest wine companies, for $2.9 billion. (Constellation had already been in a decades-long joint venture to import and market the Modelo brands in the United States.) On April 13, the Justice Department announced a settlement allowing the deal to go through; Modelo brands would indeed go to Constellation in the United States. "If this settlement makes just a one percent difference in prices, U.S. consumers will save almost $1 billion a year," Baer said.

Lurking in the background were Pease and the Brewers Association. For the first time, the organization had waded forcefully into politics, hiring Washington law firm Jones Day to represent its interests on the merger. Pease found the Justice Department fairly unknowledgeable about beer industry machinations but willing to learn. It didn't even grasp the basics of the three-tier system or the franchise laws that bound breweries to their distributors (but not vice versa). As early as 2009, the Brewers Association first became serious about exercising power as a lobbying body, working for federal excise tax legislation. It never passed, but the effort was invaluable experience, giving an organization known mostly for staging the Great American Beer Festival an anchor to become more politically active. Fruit finally started to bear with the Modelo deal.

Keeping the two most powerful brands in Mexican beer out of the hands of Anheuser-Busch InBev, at least in the United States, was a victory. But it was also only a warm-up. On November 11, 2015, word came of a bigger deal. *The biggest deal.* The world's largest beer company was about to become the world's largest beer company twice over: Anheuser-Busch InBev had agreed to buy the world's second-largest beer company, SABMiller.

Like Anheuser-Busch InBev, SABMiller was also the product of decades of mergers and acquisitions. The core company was born in 1895, serving a growing population of miners and prospectors in and around Johannesburg. Just like what would become Anheuser-Busch InBev, South African Breweries began to take shape as a global conglomerate during the 1990s with a series of acquisitions. In 2002 it acquired America's second-biggest brewery, Miller Brewing. (In the United States, Miller was merged with Coors in 2008 to create MillerCoors, a joint venture between SABMiller and Molson Coors.) Now, Anheuser-Busch InBev stood poised to own it all.

In reality, it was unlikely from the start that regulators would allow Anheuser-Busch InBev to keep the Miller portfolio in the United States. If it had been forced to spin off Corona and Modelo, it would almost certainly need to divest the Miller brands; Anheuser-Busch and Miller accounted for a combined 72 percent of the market. Even so, the combination of the world's two largest brewers was an ideal opportunity for the Brewers Association and others to bring attention to not only the beer industry's rapid consolidation but also how Anheuser-Busch InBev used its growing arsenal of craft brands and network of distributors to reinvent the US beer market.

Just as it had for Anheuser-Busch InBev's Modelo deal, the Brewers Association hired a high-powered law firm—McDermott Will & Emery, based in Chicago, with expertise in antitrust matters—to represent its interests. They delved into the nuances of the three-tier system and explained how state laws allowed Anheuser-Busch InBev to own distributors in fifteen states. They teed up the story of Deschutes losing distribution in St. Louis. And in December 2015, Bob Pease joined a panel of five industry executives to testify about the merger before Congress. He used his remarks not to oppose the merger but to highlight how Anheuser-Busch InBev used its might and distribution network to employ "disruptive and harmful tactics." As a condition of approving the merger between the world's two largest beer companies, he asked Congress to force Anheuser-Busch InBev to divest not only the Miller and Coors brands but also its company-owned distributors *and* its ability to incentivize the network with programs such as 100 Percent Share of Mind and Win Together.

"Left unchecked, these practices will further restrict competition," Pease said. "Alternatives, such as government oversight, supervision and enforcement would take years of effort. The immediate damage to competition that we have already seen in ABI's recent tactics cannot be remedied by relief provided years after competition is destroyed."

To his right sat Carlos Brito, speaking on behalf of the acquisition he so dearly wanted to complete. As with the Modelo deal, Brito did his best to undersell the impact that the merger would have on US beer drinkers.

"Put simply, the purpose of this transaction is to enhance our ability to serve new markets, particularly in Africa, Asia and Central and South America," Brito said. "It is about bringing more choices to more consumers around the world, including extending the reach of iconic American brands such as Budweiser to new markets."

Seven months later, in July 2016, the Justice Department issued a list of proposed conditions for the merger to be approved: Anheuser-Busch InBev would spin off its 58 percent stake in MillerCoors to Molson Coors (though the American Antitrust Institute argued that divestiture to "smaller, more disruptive players in the relevant market" would have been a healthier outcome for the industry). Distributor incentive programs such as 100 Percent Share of Mind or

Win Together were no longer allowed. And a maximum of 10 percent of Anheuser-Busch InBev beer could be sold through the company's eighteen wholly owned distributors.

Interested parties had the opportunity to respond with written comments, and they arrived in the form of tens of thousands of words across 135 pages from twelve corners of the industry.

Two breweries spoke up: Ninkasi, the small, well-regarded Oregon brewery that had struggled with its Anheuser-Busch wholesalers, and Yuengling, one of the nation's few remaining large independent breweries, whose flagship lager routinely took a bite out of Budweiser in each new market it entered. Comments were also submitted by wholesalers from Oklahoma and Virginia, wholesaler trade groups, the International Brotherhood of Teamsters, consumer advocates, a professor specializing in antitrust law, and the Brewers Association. They all struck a theme: the walls were closing in on American beer, with Anheuser-Busch at the center. With SABMiller in the fold, it would only grow larger and more powerful.

The American Beverage Licensees, a trade group working on behalf of both on- and off-premise retailers (bars and stores, respectively) worried about the erosion of the three-tier system as Anheuser-Busch InBev created more "tied houses" in the form of taprooms and brewpubs. (The same was happening throughout craft beer, though to smaller breweries, taprooms were less about marketing, more a means to survive thanks to strong profit margins.)

The Beer Distributors of Oklahoma was opposed to Anheuser-Busch InBev retaining an outsized stake in the distribution tier, which included branches in that state's two largest cities, Oklahoma City and Tulsa. Oklahoma, the association said, was "marked by a clear lack of craft presence. ABI's ownership of distributors is a significant contributing factor in the lack of craft availability for Oklahoma consumers." It also complained that the decree would be difficult to enforce; the 10 percent cap was nearly impossible to track, due in part to "substantial confusion over how this number is calculated." Ideally, it said, Anheuser-Busch InBev should be forced to divest all of its eighteen distributors except for one—the same number owned by MillerCoors.

The Brewers Association, of course, went further still. Anheuser-Busch InBev, it said, should divest its distributorships. It should be prohibited from acquiring more craft breweries. And it should divest all the US craft breweries it had bought to date. The Brewers Association knew the requests were far more than would be granted by the Justice Department. But its strategy had changed. And that was because Anheuser-Busch InBev's strategy had changed.

A war was on for the hearts and minds of American beer drinkers.

The Justice Department approved the deal in July 2016. It closed that October.

Onlookers declared the accompanying consent decree a win for craft beer. The government was standing up to big, bad Anheuser-Busch InBev. Finally, it was reeled in! Based on that premise, *Men's Journal* ran an article beneath the headline "Why Anheuser-Busch InBev Buying SABMiller Is a Win for Craft Beer."

However, Stephen Calkins disagreed. A former Federal Trade Commission lawyer, he reached out to the Justice Department more than two months after the proposed remedies were issued and acknowledged his letter probably wouldn't have any impact. However, he argued, the "future of American craft beer may depend" on the outcome of the merger. While noting "there would be nothing wrong (and everything right) with AB InBev winning this war by making better beer and offering it at lower prices," he insisted that the world's largest beer company was in the midst of a "campaign to disrupt the craft beer movement."

The Justice Department's remedies were "a noble aspiration," he wrote. But, "given the way ABI and MillerCoors have been aggressively buying up craft beers and then using their distribution clout to push those beers into stores and onto taps, I fear it has only a limited chance of being realized." Despite the agency's best efforts, Calkins said, he worried the decree was so toothless that it would be something for Anheuser-Busch InBev to hide behind while continuing to manipulate the industry unabated.

Bob Pease never said it publicly, but he agreed. A win would have been a return to a true three-tier system that forced Anheuser-Busch InBev to divest its distributorships. Why was the world's largest brewer allowed to be the nation's largest distributor? Why was it able to continue buying breweries en route to becoming the nation's largest manufacturer of craft beer?

"Craft brewer acquisitions that may appear competitively innocuous at first blush can have severe ramifications on the industry at the expense of consumers and competition, and any ABI acquisition should be carefully reviewed and considered as part of an overall strategy rather than in isolation," Pease wrote to the Justice Department.

He had heard rumors that a cap might actually be set on future craft acquisitions for Anheuser-Busch InBev. It was a fleetingly exciting thought, though not so disappointing when it proved to be false. It had never seemed likely in the first place.

Anheuser-Busch InBev remained free to continue buying breweries, while keeping the nine it had. Optimism briefly flickered when the Justice Department opened an investigation into the acquisition of Devils Backbone, but that turned out to be mere timing: the sale was announced while the DOJ was ironing out the consent decree. Shortly after the decree was announced, the DOJ dropped its investigation into the Devils Backbone sale, declaring, "Competitive implications of ABI's acquisition of Devils Backbone are too uncertain at this time to warrant further investigation."

Restrictions had been put on Anheuser-Busch InBev, but Pease was certain loopholes remained. There were always new and creative ways to exact the same old results. The consent decree was nowhere near a win for craft beer. Pease, however, was sure that Anheuser-Busch InBev was pleased to see that narrative to unspool.

29

"Buttery, Tart End, Undeniably Infected. Sad."

THE ALARM SOUNDED ON DECEMBER 5, 2015. Quietly at first.

It was a week and a day since Goose Island's annual day-after-Thanksgiving release of Bourbon County Stout, and it had been the brewery's biggest since the beer was first tapped twenty years earlier.

As part of Anheuser-Busch's commitment to Goose Island's growth, the global giant had given its little Chicago outpost a hulking new warehouse to cram with bourbon and wine barrels. Four years after the sale, it was time to unfurl the vision.

Big Beer talked often of consumer "occasions," and a scaled-up barrel-aging program offered countless occasions at relatively high price points. Dinner parties. Bottle shares. Savoring beside the fire on a cold winter evening. Grooms were known to break out their rarest bottles of Bourbon County Stout on their wedding days, to share with groomsmen. An expanded barrel-aging program was an attractive investment to a company that talked endlessly of getting consumers to "trade up"—to spend *more* money on something like Bourbon County Stout (typically fifty-nine cents per ounce to consumers) rather than less on a thirty-pack of Busch Light (four cents per ounce). Even the more accessible barrel-aged beers, priced below Bourbon County Stout, had potential for trading up. The bright, fruity saison Sofie (twenty-three cents an ounce) could be ideal beside brunch. Or at a picnic. Or even dinner. In the Brazilians' vision of perfection, that bright, fruity twenty-three-cents-an-ounce saison might become an everyday occasion—just like the white wine someone pulls from the fridge to accompany dinner.

But Bourbon County Stout would always be the lynchpin. In 2011, the year of the sale, Goose Island made its smallest amount of Bourbon County in years. Amid the pressure of trying to grow in a finite space, there wasn't room in the tanks for a luxury project like Bourbon County Stout. Now, with production of 312, Honker's Ale, and IPA exported to Anheuser-Busch breweries, and with a handsome, sprawling warehouse at its disposal, 2015 was the year to unspool Bourbon County Stout as a national force. Black Friday events were held in tastemaking bars and shops in twenty major cities.

Then came the alarm.

It happened on the BeerAdvocate message board, one of the go-to spots for online beer chatter and an essential forum for one of the most passionate audiences in consumer packaged goods. A drinker in Virginia started a new thread:

> Bourbon County Coffee 2015—Gusher?

Gusher was beer speak for a bottle foaming over upon opening, a trail of tan bubbles rhythmically, relentlessly cascading from the bottle. The author said that his bottle of Bourbon County Coffee Stout had foamed earlier in the day in "a moderate gush." The beer was passable, but only barely: "The coffee qualities would be difficult to differentiate from any possible infection flavors." He wondered if anyone else encountered similar issues.

A handful of replies ranged from affirmation ("Yes. A friend had this happen as well.") to those only satisfied ("Nothing but sweet BCBCS nectar within."). Then the thread went cold as people went on with their lives and stashed their precious Bourbon County beers until the holidays.

On Christmas Day, the thread reignited.

"Off fruity tartness on the back end . . ."
"Not a big fan . . . had a cherry tart/tang at the end . . ."
"Had definite off flavors and [carbonation]. . . buttery, tart end, undeniably infected. Sad."

The same questions soon emerged about Bourbon County Barleywine.

Word trickled back to Goose Island slowly, through a variety of channels. One brewer got an urgent, confused text message from a friend. Another was drinking at Sheffield's, one of the city's premier beer bars, during the week between Christmas and New Year's when a friend offhandedly said that the new batch of Bourbon County tasted odd.

"Oh?" the brewer said. "How so?"

"Well," the friend replied, "Bourbon County Coffee tastes like peppers and Barleywine tastes like garbage."

The words stung like a slap.

At work the next day, the brewer emailed the person who ran social media, who seemed to have the pulse of all things at all times. Don't say a word, he was told. An announcement was coming.

Word spread through the brewery, leaving employees dazed and heads shaking. What had happened? What were they dealing with? Would they survive it? They had battled through cries of sellout. Now this.

The announcement came just before 5:00 PM on a Friday—a classic tactic for burying bad news—in the form of a letter posted to the Goose Island website. It was attributed to brewmaster Jared Jankoski, though in reality it was a team effort written by brewery power brokers from operations, brewing, marketing, and the executive team. Beneath a photo of Jankoski, who wore a bushy beard and baseball cap and held a half-empty pint glass, the letter read:

To our loyal fans,

Each year you stand in long lines in the cold to get your hands on Bourbon County Stout and the special variants. This is beer that we hope is shared on special occasions, or maybe even makes the occasion special. Beer that we truly hope helps strengthen bonds and makes lasting memories.

I want you to know that the entire team at Goose Island puts our heart and soul into making Bourbon County, and we understand and appreciate your high expectations for them. It is always our intention to put forth the best beer we can craft. When we don't meet those expectations we take it personally, and we want to make it right.

It has come to our attention that since bottling the 2015 Bourbon County Coffee and Bourbon County Barleywine, they have developed flavors that are not consistent with our expectation of how these beers should taste. That's not to say the beer doesn't taste good, in fact some drinkers may enjoy it very much. However, it doesn't meet our standards for the taste profile of these beers.

All of our beer goes through a very thorough quality oversight process including sensory and microbiology programs. This by no means is a guarantee of success especially with barrel aged beers. Both of these beers have drifted out of their target character thus leading us to provide refunds for anyone who is unsatisfied with them. Anyone who would like a refund for 2015 Bourbon County Coffee or 2015 Bourbon County Barleywine, please contact us at 1-800-Goose-Me.

In spite of the risks inherent with barrel aging, our quest to grow these beers and our barrel aging program will persevere. I hope you continue to join us in this adventure.

Very Truly,

Jared Jankoski

The letter was the conclusion of ten frantic days of tastings, meetings, and an inescapable conclusion: they had a problem, but no idea why. Goose Island's lab had tried to grow whatever yeast or bacteria overtook the Bourbon County beers, but without success. A mystery remained, but so did a need to make things right with an agitated fan base lighting up message boards and social media. They labored over intentionally vague language—"flavors that are not consistent with our expectation of how these beers should taste"—because they didn't want to say something was *wrong* with the beer. It was just different. However, the hopeful addendum—"That's not to say the beer doesn't taste good, in fact some drinkers may enjoy it very much"—was the pinnacle of wishful thinking. The beers were undrinkable and growing worse by the day.

The letter was also intentionally vague about the refund process, mostly because it was so generous. Faced with the brewery's biggest crisis since the sale, Goose Island's new general manager, Ken Stout, felt an urgency to make things right as quickly as possible. He was a former Heineken guy who came on as Goose Island's Illinois sales director in 2010, shortly before the acquisition. Before Heineken he ran sales for James Page Brewing, a small brewery in Minneapolis that won gold and bronze at the Great American Beer Festival in 1999. Stout was the brewery's only representative on hand, which left him hobnobbing with craft beer's elite with two medals around his neck. He understood craft beer. He understood Big Beer. Now he had a foot in both and needed to guide his hometown brewery out of a crisis.

The thinking around Goose Island—and Stout was a subscriber—was that Bourbon County was more than a family of beers. It was even more than a brand. It was one of the few beers to have its own day. Black Friday. Everyone knew. And the people who still lined up for it were the ones who stuck with Goose Island. They needed to trust the brewery. Trust the beer. Stout therefore endorsed refunds of up to $100 with no proof of purchase; all someone had to do was call the toll-free number that John Hall established decades earlier (800-GOOSE-ME, which now forwarded to Anheuser-Busch offices in St. Louis). Anyone requesting a refund of more than $100 would need to furnish a receipt. But $100 could be had simply by picking up the phone. Drinkers would even get Bourbon County T-shirts for their troubles. Customers could also exchange bottles of Bourbon County Coffee and Barleywine at Goose Island's Fulton Street taproom in a one-for-one swap for regular Bourbon County Stout; they had until February 29—nearly two months—to redeem the offer.

It took only a few weeks for the strangest thing to happen: Goose Island was refunding more money than it had sold in the two tainted beers. Based on sales to that point, the brewery had budgeted less than $100,000 for refunds. By the time it was finished, it had doled out close to $500,000.

Stout had insisted that craft beer drinkers, and Bourbon County fans in particular, would do the right thing. They would be directed by some internal compass, some relationship to an industry built on experimentation and collaboration. Some were. Many weren't. A common tactic was calling the 800-number for a $100 refund, then exchanging the tainted bottles—whether sealed or empty—at the taproom. They were being paid twice—once in cash and once in beer. Stout seethed as he watched the numbers grow. There was nothing he could do about it.

It took three months and four laboratories to figure out what was wrong with the beer.

Lactobacillus acetotolerans.

It was a strain of the bacteria identified in 1986, in the *International Journal of Systematic and Evolutionary Microbiology*. Other strains of *Lactobacillus* were commonly used to sour some of the world's most esteemed beers, including several at Goose Island. But the *L. acetotolerans* strain was only first understood as a threat to beer in 2004, when it ruined a batch at a Bavarian brewery. It was virtually unknown in the United States and no obvious foe for Bourbon County Stout. Most bourbon barrels already carried a degree of *Lactobacillus*—that was understood. But so far as anyone knew, it couldn't survive in beer any boozier than roughly 9 percent alcohol; Bourbon County entered barrels at 11 percent. It came out at 14 percent. *Lactobacillus*, traditionally, had been unable to survive. *L. acetotolerans* turned out to be immune.

By the time a lab in Seattle identified the culprit, drinkers were complaining of off flavors in two more Bourbon County beers: the original and Proprietor's, a version made in tiny amounts and distributed only in Chicago. (It was introduced in 2013 partly to maintain Goose Island's local and craft credibility and to maintain a degree of rarity for the brand.) By July, the brewery issued a second round of recalls for nine bottling dates of Bourbon County Stout and one bottling date of Proprietor's Bourbon County Stout. Having learned its lesson from the first recall, this time it required proof of purchase—neck labels and photos of the back labels bearing a time stamp.

The second round of infections plunged the brewery into fresh crisis. It reignited a story line on beer blogs and message boards that would continue for nearly a year. The most burning question seemed unanswerable: Was this profound lapse tied to the sale to Anheuser-Busch? The answer was likely yes—just not in the way that most people presumed.

Most concerns resulting from the sale were rooted in fears of cost cutting and tanking best practices. But a different tenet of Big Beer helped doom Bourbon County in 2015: growth. Anheuser-Busch was rooted in volume and scale. Goose Island had pushed into that world. Goose Island was filling about thirty-five hundred bourbon barrels at the time of the sale; the plan was to grow as much as two thousand barrels per year—from thirty-five hundred to five thousand to sixty-five hundred to eight thousand to ten thousand and onward. By 2015, it was clear that they had moved too fast. Unfettered Anheuser-Busch-fueled growth had its downside.

Practices had been locked in from a decade of making Bourbon County at the Fulton Street brewery, but the new barrel warehouse presented a wilderness of unfamiliar variables that hadn't been fully understood. Was the problem the warehouse? The tanker truck that transported the liquid between the brewery and the warehouse? The fact that the barrels had been moved so frequently during the move into the warehouse?

They never quite knew. The likeliest culprit was the barrels. To support a fast-growing barrel-aging program, Goose Island needed ever-more barrels. When it came time to fill a massive new warehouse, it was taking barrels from anywhere it could get them—seven different distilleries—with little ability to control the quality of the wood. The issue was compounded by competition for barrels that had grown increasingly fierce, crossed with the plummeting quality of available barrels. In the old days, barrels arrived wet, sloshing with enough bourbon to pour off for the brewers to sip and share. Now distilleries were taking the barrels apart, squeezing every last drop from the wood, and putting them back together. Such dry wood was an ideal desert for bacterial growth—especially *L. acetotolerans*, a largely unknown and particularly hardy strain. Goose Island had wandered into the boozy black version of a perfect storm.

All they could do was change practices. The brewery developed a test for identifying *L. acetotolerans* and tightened protocols for acquiring bourbon barrels—only fresh barrels, and from a single source. They would begin flash pasteurizing Bourbon County Stout—exposing the beer to a brief, intense temperature spike, then rapidly cooling it—to kill any bacteria that might have slipped through.

Still, it was a stomach-turning episode. Goose Island's credibility took a hit, and Ken Stout wondered if he might be the fall guy. He wasn't. No one lost a job over it. Felipe Szpigel, head of the High End, prioritized solving the problem. Everyone told themselves that the episode would make Goose Island a better brewery.

Brewers couldn't help monitoring the message boards. Many drinkers were merciless in their mockery. But the handful of people defending Goose Island—*breweries make mistakes, it's not an uncommon issue in the industry, they're doing their best to make it right*—helped.

John Hall stayed abreast of the Bourbon County infections with periodic updates from the brewery. At seventy-four, he was far removed from the daily decision making but kept in the discussion out of respect. Some people had taken to calling him Goose Island's "grandfather in chief."

It was no fun watching the thing that he had built struggle. But the concern didn't sit in him like a weight. Ten years earlier, fears of infected Bourbon County literally kept him awake at night. It was a disaster that could crush a small, independently owned brewery.

Now that Goose Island wasn't small or owned by him, he still hated to see it happen, of course. But he carried an almost bemused air about the matter—not about the infection itself but at how quickly things could go sideways. One day you're king. The next, you're begging forgiveness. He was bothered, but he had other things to be concerned about.

Pat. His children. His grandchildren. The family's annual spring trip to Tobago. Everyone would be together for the first time in years.

Anyway, it was Anheuser-Busch's problem.

The Bourbon County refunds took a bite out of the budget, but as part of the world's largest beer company, Goose Island still had a banner year for the bottom line.

The year of the sale, the brewery did $17.6 million in sales. As it wedged deeper into the Anheuser-Busch system, Goose Island did what its new owner intended for it to do. It grew.

Year	**Sales**	**Change**
2011	$17.6 million	—
2012	$20.6 million	17%
2013	$35.7 million	74%
2014	$41.9 million	17%
2015	$57.6 million	37%
2016	$72.7 million	26%
2017	$75.7 million	4%

Even with the massive Bourbon County lapse, Goose Island's growth was relentless. Just a few years earlier, Anheuser-Busch had viewed its craft strategy through the lens of two drinkers: the "accessible" drinker, who was happy with the simplest brands, and the "discovery" drinker, always looking for that next great beer. Goose Island had initially been a tool to appeal to the discovery audience.

But now part of a robust craft portfolio, Goose Island was slotted into Big Beer's more familiar world of occasion-driven drinking. In a playbook distributed to High End salespeople, Goose Island's primary consumer target was identified as "experience maximizers"—drinkers between the ages of twenty-one and thirty-five whose "beer selection is driven by the occasion, rather than careful study or analysis . . . [who] use a 'search and enjoy' mentality, believing there is always room for another great beer in their arsenal." More serious beer drinkers—"authentic explorers" who "crave authenticity and meaning in all facets of their lives" and are "actively exploring the beer category"—became a secondary audience.

The company's engine became a lowest common denominator that Andy Goeler had trotted out at SAMCOM the previous fall: IPA. The beer was a shell of its old award-winning self, but in the Anheuser-Busch system, Goose IPA became locked and loaded, showing up at stadiums, airports, and hotel bars across the nation. Distributors in every region had their orders: Goose IPA was a priority on par with Bud and Bud Light, and enough of a priority that the price for a keg should be slashed every other week from $158 to $110—barely more expensive than a standard-priced keg of Budweiser (which also got an every-other-week price cut, from $106 to $80).

In 2012, the first full year under Anheuser-Busch control, Goose IPA was the nation's thirty-fifth-biggest-selling IPA. It lagged behind breweries that an Anheuser-Busch-owned operation had no business trailing: Shiner, Full Sail, Widmer Brothers, plus two brands each from Pyramid, BridgePort, and Samuel Adams. After a jump to number twenty-two, it actually *lost* share among IPAs as the new boss focused on 312 Urban Wheat.

Then came the growth for Goose IPA that few other companies could muster:

Year	IPA Rank (national sales)
2011	26
2012	35
2013	20
2014	22
2015	9
2016	3
2017	4

The battle for supremacy had amounted to a duel with two California breweries—Lagunitas, the clear leader, and Sierra Nevada. By 2017, Felipe Szpigel flaunted a goal of doubling Goose Island's production by 2020—which would send it past one million barrels of annual production—and vaulting Goose IPA into the position of the nation's top-selling IPA. The founder of Lagunitas, Tony Magee, figured that if Anheuser-Busch wanted the crown, it could take it. It was the biggest beer company in the world. It had the most powerful distribution network in the nation. It could do as it pleased.

Things settled down at the Fulton Street brewery.

The exodus of brewers stopped. Employees finally seemed glad to be there. Prideful, even. OK, so they were part of Anheuser-Busch InBev. Who cared? They worked for Goose Island, and Goose Island had proved the doubters wrong. It was still in Chicago. It still made some damn fine beer; Matilda, Lolita, Madame Rose, and Sofie were among the most revered brands in the nation. Even after the setback of Bourbon County in 2015, drinkers continued to line up for the beer hours ahead of its release every year on the day after Thanksgiving. (It remained so popular that the High End tied distributor allocation to how effectively it sold the rest of the Goose Island portfolio throughout the year.)

Unburdened by the high-volume brands, Goose Island made far less beer in Chicago than before the sale, and that was a relief. In 2010, Goose Island pumped out 126,000 barrels from Fulton Street. Five years later, production had dropped by more than half.

Of the fifty-five thousand barrels produced in 2016, five thousand were Bourbon County Stout. After years of wedging in Bourbon County production as it could, the brewery now faithfully made the beer twice a week. It was Goose Island's least efficient beer—each batch commandeered the brew house for thirty straight hours—but that was the luxury of being owned by Anheuser-Busch. Peak efficiency was still key, but it was of a different sort; instead of sheer volume, the goal was to wring as much as possible from production. The brewery had nearly $5 million of new equipment to do the job.

Goose Island also finally settled in to its portfolio as a national brand. After tinkering with its seasonal beers—dumping the original lineup for the ill-fated hop series, then employing a short-lived beer called Summer Ale—the brewery returned to Summertime, the old classic. They had axed Summertime, much to John's consternation, in a bid to be more modern. The old way of doing things turned out to work just fine after all.

Two more year-round beers were also added to the portfolio: Green Line, which lost its Chicago- and draft-only status to become Goose Island's national pale ale (replacing the failed 312 Urban Pale Ale), and Goose Four Star Pils, introduced during the summer of 2015, to climb aboard the slow-growing bandwagon of craft pilsner. Honker's Ale was phased out as an Anheuser-Busch beer, and production for that fading brand, which had jump-started the brewery twenty years earlier, returned to Chicago.

Now that Anheuser-Busch finally got it—that is, actually came to understand the craft landscape—Fulton Street, like every other craft acquisition, was urged to keep pushing for the next big thing. Tastes were changing so quickly—pilsners, low-alcohol IPAs, and sour ales had all surged—that innovation was prized. It was demanded. Four Star Pils was born on Fulton Street as a beer called Blue Line; at first it was available only on draft and in Chicago during the spring of 2015. Once enthusiasm was affirmed—brewers were proud of it, bar owners liked it, and it sold well—the beer was scaled up for national production in Baldwinsville. It was further evidence of how the parent company had learned. Since the earliest days after the sale, Goose Island had pushed to release a pilsner. The old way of thinking in St. Louis said no way—that would cannibalize Bud and Bud Light. Finally, they understood.

The sentiment on Fulton Street was less enthusiastic for another beer traveling a similar path. The idea of a "session sour"—a low-alcohol sour beer—had long been kicked around. Anheuser-Busch wanted it. No one owned the space yet. Not Sierra Nevada, not Dogfish Head, not Lagunitas—though each had dabbled. In late 2016, Goose Island released its attempt at a session sour called Caution Tape. It was roundly reviled within the brewery—an utter miss. It was too sweet amid the sour, showed too much malt character; it was a classic reflection of Big Beer: built toward what marketing minds thought consumers would buy rather than what brewers thought was best. In the old days, what didn't work went down the drain. Not this time.

Because it was penciled in to the Anheuser-Busch production schedule, Caution Tape was released in late 2016 with the intention of scaling up in Baldwinsville by the next year's SAMCOM—just in case it took off with consumers. It was the first beer—and the first time since the sale—that the bulk of Goose Island employees knew was a dud. They were right. The beer tanked. Never to return.

Goose Island reached a unique place in the American craft beer industry.

It was a rare hybrid, serving local, national, and international audiences. It made beer for Chicago, it made beer for stadiums and airport bars, and it was a brand to be exported to Europe and China, Australia and South America. After all the scaling and tweaks, Goose IPA was essentially Anheuser-Busch IPA. 312 was Anheuser-Busch Wheat Ale. Green Line was Anheuser-Busch Pale Ale. All became tepid Big Beer reinventions of what they had been when made in Chicago.

Yet it wasn't uncommon to see a post on social media about how right it felt to be drinking a 312 Urban Wheat or Goose IPA while in Chicago. After all, it was Chicago's beer. Whether those people knew that the beer had been trucked to Chicago from an Anheuser-Busch brewery in Baldwinsville, New York, or Ft. Collins, Colorado, was anyone's guess.

30

"You Sold Out to Big Beer —Again"

In the spring of 2017, six months to the day after announcing its ninth American craft brewery acquisition—Houston's Karbach Brewing—Anheuser-Busch announced its tenth American craft brewery acquisition.

The Karbach sale had caused only a minor stir. Houston was a relatively undeveloped craft beer market, and though popular locally, Karbach had little broader resonance. The world seemingly had made peace with Anheuser-Busch's push into craft beer. It was what it was. And it was apparently just about finished. Leadership insisted that it was time to stop buying, time to start executing.

"There's a limit to how many people I can actually manage and collaborate with," Felipe Szpigel, president of the High End, told Beer Marketer's Insights that January. "I'm not saying that we're not going to have any deal, but we're pretty much good."

Four months later, Wicked Weed Brewing happened.

Launched barely four years earlier in the craft beer hotbed of Asheville, North Carolina, Wicked Weed embraced two of the industry's sizzling trends: robust IPAs and tart, funky wild ales. Two handsome blond brothers, Walt and Luke Dickinson, started the brewery with family friend Ryan Guthy and Guthy's parents, who had made a fortune selling skin care products via infomercial. The Dickinson brothers were the face of the company, but the Guthys were reported to be majority owners, which allowed Wicked Weed to open with a craft beer bang: seven thousand square feet and seventeen draft handles in the heart of downtown Asheville, next to the coolest rock club in town. It was such a slick start-up that some locals presumed it was part of an existing chain. In less than four years, Wicked Weed opened three more spaces—a taproom dedicated to sour beers, a barrel-aging facility, and a fifty-barrel production brewery. By 2017, it was on pace to produce forty thousand barrels of beer—a whopping 471 percent growth from just two years earlier.

Named for a legendary (and possibly misattributed) quote from King Henry VIII—the hop plant is a "wicked and pernicious weed"—Wicked Weed was equal parts outstanding beer and outstanding branding. The Dickinsons looked the part, they had national buzz, and they collaborated with the industry's most credible brewers. People liked Wicked Weed because Wicked Weed had the unique ability to make people *care*—in the beer, in the brand, and in the ethos. And that made its sale to Anheuser-Busch an exacting punch to the gut. It was Goose Island and Elysian all over again. It was a reminder that Big Beer would never stop. It forever had the ability to thrust itself into the heart of craft beer.

Texas's Jester King Brewery—which specialized in the same sort of sour and wild ales as Wicked Weed—spoke for a stunned industry when it issued a statement hours after the announcement:

> This has been a difficult day for us. The news that our great friend Wicked Weed Brewing was acquired by AB In-Bev came as quite a shock. As you might guess, we've been getting a lot of e-mails, media inquiries, and online questions about what we think and what it means for Jester King.
>
> It's no secret that Wicked Weed has been one of our closest friends in the beer industry. Regardless of what has transpired, we'll always consider the people of Wicked Weed friends, and want the best for them and their families.
>
> With that said, we have some core principles that define who we are as a brewery, and those principles must not be compromised. One of our core principles is that we do not sell beer from

> AB In-Bev or its affiliates. We've chosen this stance, not because of the quality of the beer, but because a portion of the money made off of selling it is used to oppose the interests of craft brewers. In Texas, large brewers (and their distributors) routinely oppose law changes that would help small, independent brewers. We choose not to support these large brewers because of their political stances, and in some cases, their economic practices as well.
>
> Because of this core principle, it pains us to say that we won't be carrying Wicked Weed anymore at Jester King. We think Wicked Weed beer is some of the best in the world. Their talent, techniques, and patience produces some of the most beautiful beer we've ever tasted. That, combined with their great friendship, is what makes this decision so tough for us. But like we said, our core values must be paramount at the end of the day.
>
> We wish Wicked Weed the best, will deeply miss having their beer at Jester King and working with them on collaborations, and expect them to continue to make fantastic beer. Like we mentioned, they'll always have our friendship and we look forward to the next time we can share a beer together.

The founder of Denver's Black Project Spontaneous & Wild Ales, James Howat, followed by saying on his brewery's website that he was "shocked" by the sale. "We truly believe that ABInBev intends to systematically destroy American craft beer as we know it," he wrote.

Howat had two collaboration beers with Wicked Weed in process—one at his brewery and one aging in Asheville. He announced that he would no longer lend his brewery's name to the beer at Wicked Weed, and the one in Denver would be blended into existing beers. Also, Howat said, he would not participate in Wicked Weed's annual sour and wild beer festival, the Wicked Weed Funkatorium Invitational, scheduled in Asheville two months later.

And on it went. The North Carolina Craft Brewers Guild announced that it was "disheartened to hear of the sale." A former Wicked Weed employee bought the URL www.wickedweedsoldout.com to post a nine-hundred-word screed in which he called Wicked Weed's founders sell-outs three separate times. Bars and beer stores said they were done with the brewery, including several in Denver, where Wicked Weed had begun distributing to marked excitement just nine months earlier. A dozen bars said they would tap their remaining kegs and then be done, just as they had already cut ties with the rest of Anheuser-Busch's craft portfolio. Even a bar owner in Switzerland aired his disgust, discounting his remaining Wicked Weed bottles to a dollar each. "Although we are taking a loss, we can absolutely no longer stand behind your products, and therefore we look forward to when the bad ghost is finally expelled from our refrigerators," he wrote, in German, on Facebook.

With its rapid growth and extraordinarily deep financing, Wicked Weed did not need to sell, the Dickinson brothers insisted after the sale. But they were ambitious. And while growing into a dominant regional brand seemed attainable—especially after expanding to eight states and forty thousand barrels of production—Anheuser-Busch offered limitless opportunity. Seeds of the sale were planted at the Great American Beer Festival in 2013, when Felipe Szpigel stopped by Wicked Weed's table. He liked what he tasted. He traveled to Asheville to look around and to chat with the founders. When the Dickinsons and Guthys began considering a sale in late 2016 to finance growth while reducing their own risk, they already knew Szpigel. Within weeks, the sides were doing due diligence.

For Anheuser-Busch, Wicked Weed was a seamless fit both geographically (finally—a craft presence in the Southeast) and within its portfolio; after buying IPAs, stouts, and lagers, now it had sour and wild ales. The turning point for the Dickinson brothers was a visit to Goose Island the previous fall. They wanted to see life at an Anheuser-Busch acquisition, and the High End urged them to visit Chicago. The Dickinsons spent a day at the brewery, the barrel warehouse, and the taproom. They liked the beer. They liked the culture. They were impressed by the Fulton Street taproom; it seemed more authentically "craft" than taprooms they'd visited from actual independently owned breweries. They liked that it was built *after* Anheuser-Busch bought the company. The world's largest beer company wasn't afraid to invest in its acquisitions.

The day the sale was announced, as scorn rained down, Szpigel told media that Wicked Weed was "redefining what sophistication in beer can mean," and that sour ales would be key to the next phase of the

High End's development. The Dickinson brothers, meanwhile, handled their repudiation with relative class—and the hope that none of it would eventually matter.

"I in no way have any issue with the statements they put out," Walt Dickinson said of Jester King and Black Project, a day after the sale was announced. "They were very respectful and all they did was distance themselves from us from a professional standpoint because of the partner we decided to align with. They have done absolutely nothing wrong and I fully support those statements and understand their reasoning for them. In the end, I hope one day we can break down some of these barriers and we can get back to just looking at beer for what it is, and look at quality instead of who is the subsidiary of who."

Yet in the coming days, almost every brewery planning to pour beer at the Funkatorium Invitational withdrew. Some did so quite gladly: "They've always rubbed me the wrong way, particularly Walt, because he introduces himself to me every time and says, every time, 'Pleasure to meet you, I'm a big fan of your beers,'" Brad Clark, the founder of one Jackie O's Pub & Brewery in Athens, Ohio, told the Good Beer Hunting website. "A total lack of relevance and compassion and being present."

The day after the sale was announced, Wicked Weed announced that the festival would go on as planned. But a week later, after 80 percent of scheduled breweries dropped out, it had no choice but to cancel the Funkatorium Invitational. It pledged to stage a new event two months later that never happened.

Again and again, the Dickinsons offered up the standard Anheuser-Busch defense: *It's just beer! Can't we all just get along?* The sooner everyone started thinking about the beer in the glass—rather than how it got in the glass—the better. The world's largest beer company was counting on it.

A 2003 documentary film, *The Corporation*, came up with a stunning term to describe corporations. Using the *Diagnostic and Statistical Manual of Mental Disorders*, the Canadian filmmakers concluded that if corporations were people, they would be psychopaths: disregard for the feelings and safety of others, incapable of maintaining enduring relationships, an inability to experience guilt, failure to operate within the bounds of the law, and repeatedly lying for profit.

Greg Koch, the founder of San Diego's Stone Brewing, thought of Big Beer a bit differently. Anheuser-Busch InBev, he became fond of saying, was the Borg—a reference to the insatiable alien collective on *Star Trek* that grew only by devouring its way across the galaxy. Its tagline: "Resistance is futile."

Koch saw the beer industry's Borg as something similar. It didn't have feelings. It didn't have emotion. It wasn't determined to destroy craft; that's just what it did. It existed to grow. To keep devouring. Don't be angry at the Borg, Koch said. The Borg was the Borg. All that mattered was resistance. Don't want to feed the Borg? Don't buy its beer. Koch lamented what he called "the illusion of choice"—twelve beers across tap handles that seemed to come from twelve different breweries but in fact all led to the same company. The same brewing equipment. It was how the Borg wanted it. And as the Borg grew hungrier across six years, it kept eating.

US Craft Brewery Sales to Anheuser-Busch InBev

March 28, 2011: Goose Island Beer Co. (Chicago)
February 5, 2014: Blue Point Brewing (Patchogue, New York)
November 5, 2014: 10 Barrel Brewing (Bend, Oregon)
January 23, 2015: Elysian Brewing (Seattle)
September 23, 2015: Golden Road Brewing (Los Angeles)
December 18, 2015: Four Peaks Brewing (Tempe, Arizona)
December 22, 2015: Breckenridge Brewery (Littleton, Colorado)
April 12, 2016: Devils Backbone Brewing (Roseland, Virginia)
November 3, 2016: Karbach Brewing (Houston)
May 3, 2017: Wicked Weed Brewing (Asheville, North Carolina)

Presumably to obscure its calculating nature, Anheuser-Busch had long denied its shopping spree was fueled by a regional strategy. But one look at a map made that strategy clear. The other obvious trend—obvious in retrospect—were the audiences it was buying; with the exception of Devils Backbone, each acquisition was situated in or near one of the nation's five largest cities (New York, Los Angeles, Chicago, Houston, and Phoenix) or an extraordinarily progressive beer market (Bend, Seattle, Denver, and Asheville). The Borg was savvy. And then the Borg went global: Anheuser-Busch InBev bought craft breweries in the United Kingdom, China, Italy, Colombia, Brazil, Canada, Mexico, Spain, Australia, and Belgium, mostly the same sort of scrappy young upstarts the company itself could never have created.

Shortly after the Goose Island sale, Dave Peacock told *Supermarket News* something that no one wanted to believe: "Our recent acquisition of Goose Island allows us to explore and learn more about how to play more effectively in the high-end segment." Explore? Learn? Never, said the skeptics. But Anheuser-Busch did.

As much as it bungled the Goose Island rollout in the haze of thinking like old Anheuser-Busch, the new company actually came to understand the nuances of craft beer. Story. Experience. Flavor. Variety. Choice. Authenticity. It didn't flood the High End with Anheuser-Busch people; it promoted savvy and experienced craft people who had been acquired along with its breweries. Two Goose Island veterans took on marketing strategy for all of the High End. Longtime Goose Island operations manager Mark Kamarauskas was promoted to run Golden Road. A 10 Barrel founder became the High End's point person on every new brewpub, regardless of brand. The High End had acquired talent. It was using it.

Anheuser-Busch learned to become a good steward of its craft acquisitions, but it had no other choice. The cost cutting and streamlining that followed much of the Brazilians' march across the globe—such as the estimated fifty-five hundred layoffs following the SABMiller takeover—wouldn't work in craft. Stripping away the inefficiencies, the quality, and the people would have proved the skeptics right. Craft beer was immune to the Brazilians' way of doing things—at least at first.

Instead of layoffs, each deal was followed by endless meetings as the new bosses sized up what they had and calculated where it could go. (Too many meetings became the common *har-har* gripe when newly minted millionaire brewery founders were asked what had changed under Anheuser-Busch ownership.) The Brazilians didn't know much about American craft beer, and they knew that. That was one of their strengths: they knew what they didn't know. They were willing to learn. They bought their education.

And as they did, their craft breweries didn't shrink—they grew. Though a three-hundred-person national High End sales force was created and then eliminated three years later, the breweries themselves hired more people. Resources increased. Standards were raised. Safety became a priority. They continued to innovate. They made some outstanding beer. They were the opposite of Rolling Rock, the Pennsylvania brand acquired by old Anheuser-Busch a decade earlier and driven into a ditch. These breweries were thriving. They were thriving on behalf of the world's largest beer company, and the world's largest beer company sorely needed them: Anheuser-Busch was still losing share in the United States, and global profits were down. In the spring of 2017, after the company fell short of analysts' earnings estimates for a seventh consecutive quarter, CEO Carlos Brito missed out on his lofty bonus for the first time since 2008. Much of the company's sluggishness was due to an earnings drop in its core market of Brazil. But a bright spot, Brito told reporters, was the United States. Budweiser was still losing share, but there were signs it was stabilizing. Michelob Ultra and Stella Artois were growing. And so was craft—it was up more than 30 percent from the previous year. Brito said the company had assembled a "winning portfolio" in the United States. (By late 2017, rumors swirled that Anheuser-Busch might exercise an option to buy out the Craft Brew Alliance. It was less interested in Widmer and Redhook than it was intrigued by Kona as a challenge to Corona and Modelo as a "lifestyle brand.")

By 2017, Anheuser-Busch, a company that had no credible craft brands six years earlier, was the nation's second-largest producer of craft beer. Beer Marketer's Insights estimated Anheuser-Busch's cumulative annual craft production for the previous year at 1.2 million barrels, which left it behind only Boston Beer in terms of volume. Quietly, there had been a changing of the guard for second place: Anheuser-Busch surpassed the iconic Sierra Nevada. Half of Anheuser-Busch craft production was Goose Island, and the great majority of that beer was made at Anheuser-Busch's Baldwinsville and Ft. Collins breweries. That led to a subtle but astonishing fact: much of the beer from the nation's second-largest craft beer company was coming from the same tanks as Bud Light.

It was a trend that would continue. By the summer of 2017, twenty-five brands from six of Anheuser-Busch's craft acquisitions—Goose Island, Blue Point, Elysian, Golden Road, 10 Barrel, and Four Peaks—were being made at Anheuser-Busch breweries in New York, New Hampshire, California, and Colorado. Goose Island, with eight Anheuser-Busch-made beers, accounted for the most for any one acquisition, a relic of the fast rollout that it was forced to endure. Now Anheuser-Busch was moving slower. It *had* to move slower, partly because of the lessons learned from Goose Island. With the exception of IPA—priced aggressively and handpicked as a distributor priority—Goose Island sales were struggling by the end of 2017: 312 Urban Wheat Ale, Four Star Pils, and Green Line Pale Ale were all markedly down from a year earlier. It turned out you couldn't force beer on craft drinkers after all. You couldn't blast craft beer into the national consciousness and assume success. Deliberation was required.

"It's not a one size fits all approach," Szpigel told Beer Marketer's Insights while describing future national rollouts. "Some might take longer, some are more mature."

Craft beer won: it forced the biggest beer company in the world to change.

Craft beer lost: it had been commandeered by the biggest beer company in the world.

By 2018, or 2019 at the latest, that company would be the biggest producer of craft beer in the United States. Was Anheuser-Busch simply taking its share or attempting to grow the category? It pledged the latter. But as a publicly traded company, all that mattered was the former. American beer consumption had fallen since the 1980s. Wine and spirits had grown since the late 1990s. The High End tried to position itself as vanguard of *all* craft beer—while simultaneously trying to dominate it.

It did little to tout its growing scope or the fact that it was in the process of eclipsing Boston Beer, Sierra Nevada, and New Belgium at the head of the table. It touted itself as "beer positive" and swore it was celebrating all craft beer. It insisted it wasn't engaged in a war; it was simply giving customers what they wanted.

"The concept of big versus small in craft is both old and unrealistic," Felipe Szpigel told *U.S. News & World Report* in 2016. "There have never been so many beer options available to consumers, and that's great. Consumers, just like retailers and wholesalers, have options. From our perspective, our focus is on celebrating, and amplifying, the beers, brands and cultures we have in our craft portfolio to provide great options to enjoy. We welcome all the brewers and cider makers that are focused on consumers and sharing amazing beers, ciders and experiences, as we are."

Meanwhile, shareholders heard a different story. In its annual letter in 2016, the company touted the fact that it continued to build its global craft beer portfolio while "working to leverage the scale of our organization to introduce these special beers to a broader audience."

Leverage the scale of our organization.

Was that beer positive?

Each of Anheuser-Busch's ten US craft brewery acquisitions was followed by a fresh round of questions. What did it mean for the industry? For competitiveness? For consumer choice? They were the right questions but in the wrong context. The issue wasn't the present day or even the next five years—it was the next twenty years. The next fifty years. After initially investing in its craft acquisitions, would they all stay robust and healthy, or would they be torn down to nothing but the brands? Would some be sold off? Were the early positive optics just an illusion? For a company grounded not in beer but in profit, there was no way to know.

What was clear was that Anheuser-Busch InBev was setting itself up for generations to come. It was cultivating a landscape where Big Beer and craft beer would be indistinguishable, where thousands of small breweries were allowed to grow only so large amid a handful of dominant players. And, as always, it would be the most dominant player of all.

In late June 2017, two months after the Wicked Weed sale, the Brewers Association took another swipe at Big Beer's growing dominance. The initiative had been a year in the making: a logo differentiating what it considered "independence." Any brewery that qualified under the Brewers Association's definition of "craft"—small, traditional, and independent—was free to use the logo, whether on bottles, cans, posters, or simply as a sticker on the front door of a brewery's taproom. The design was an upside-down twenty-two-ounce bottle, a reference to how craft beer had upended the industry. Inside the bottle it read:

INDE
PEN
DENT
CRAFT

The hope was that consumers cared enough about who was Big Beer and who was not that a visual would help inform shopping choices.

Three days later, the High End responded with a video featuring five of its craft brewery founders, plus Felipe Szpigel, arguing against the upside bottle logo. They insisted "consumers don't necessarily care about independence." They said craft beer needed to band together to fight the growth of wine and spirits. They employed shame ("To be truly punk, you don't use the logo—you do your own thing and you follow your own rules"). They even got ornery: "The problem is that the BA continues to refuse to let the consumer make up their own mind and try to make it up for them," said Garrett Wales, the 10 Barrel cofounder who became the High End's vice president of brewpubs. "They have a little bottle that someone told me 'That's what I have to buy,' because there is a bottle on the six-packs—but that doesn't mean shit to me."

The video was widely mocked as tone-deaf and defensive.

Four months later, the Brewers Association launched the next phase of its campaign, a mock $213 billion crowdsourced fundraiser to acquire the king of all acquirers, Anheuser-Busch InBev. With the rallying cry of "Take Craft Back," the Brewers Association allowed donors to pledge up to $1,000 while sharing nothing more than an email address. In exchange, the Brewers Association would send a "Take Craft Back" cap, sticker, koozie, or T-shirt. The Brewers Association had no intention of raising anywhere close to enough money; as it pointed out on the "Take Craft Back" website, it would need $28.78 from every person on earth to reach $213 billion (which was likely an underestimation of the company's market value anyway).

In reality, the Brewers Association aimed to raise awareness about the acquisition spree that had realigned American craft beer. If Anheuser-Busch InBev would obscure its role in the industry, the Brewers Association would speak loudly and clearly on its behalf—albeit in a mocking and jovial tone. But a funny thing happened: this time, a significant chunk of public sentiment turned against the Brewers Association. In the echo chamber of social media, many argued that such an elaborate effort to mock Anheuser-Busch InBev was overwrought negativity. This time, the High End stayed quiet. The silence worked to its advantage as it instead fell back on its old trope of staying "beer positive."

Goose Island never saw any of it coming.

Back in 2011, there was no grand strategy. There was no war for the hearts and minds of craft beer drinkers. No indication that Anheuser-Busch would ever buy another craft brewery. Anheuser-Busch had a need. Goose Island had a need. They solved each other's needs. Then Anheuser-Busch tinkered, made mistakes, and learned. Then it kept buying.

The old Anheuser-Busch was a proud and stubborn company that believed in nothing more than its own greatness; whatever needed to be done, it could do. Craft beer was but a hiccup in the universe, a speed bump on a highway paved with Budweiser. Anheuser-Busch InBev was a brilliant and ruthless company that knew the only way to be all things to all people was to acquire what it wasn't. And then acquire some more.

It was how Brazil's second-largest brewery became the world's largest beer company. There hadn't been a lightbulb moment for its American craft strategy. It emerged as if on a dimmer switch, with the realization that a shift was underway. People were drinking less beer. They were drinking less of the same old brands. The industry was fragmenting. Anheuser-Busch was woefully underrepresented in the directions it was headed.

With ten breweries in the High End portfolio, Goose Island had evolved from crown jewel to a jewel in the crown. Sure, it was a little disappointing. And yes, John's final year at the company had been one aggravation after another; he'd wondered more than once if the whole thing was a mistake. And OK, Michael Roper, proprietor of Chicago's iconic Hopleaf bar, an early defender of the sale, declared on Facebook in late 2017 that his optimism had been misplaced, that "the company culture of Goose Island has gone through a slow but steady change toward the worse . . . swallowed up by a company [whose] goal is to conquer all."

But look at how things turned out. By virtue of being first in the fold, and a strong brand from a city that resonated around the world, Goose Island led Anheuser-Busch InBev's global craft strategy. The breweries that hadn't sensed a coming industry transformation faltered, including the one that inspired John's entry into the business all the way back in 1986, on that unmoving airplane: Hopland Brewery, which became Mendocino Brewing, abruptly shuttered in early 2018 amid a correction following years of unbridled craft beer growth. Meanwhile Goose Island was launching pubs in London, Toronto, Shanghai, Seoul, São Paulo, and Monterrey, Mexico, plus a new division—Goose Island International, headed by Ken Stout—to manage it all. (Greg Hall's childhood friend Todd Ahsmann took the helm at Goose Island domestically.)

Anheuser-Busch InBev went after those global markets aggressively, employing similar tactics used for years in the United States. *Fortune* magazine reported that beginning in 2016, Anheuser-Busch InBev had "inundated" Beijing and Shanghai with Goose Island in a weak regulatory climate, pressuring distributors not to carry other craft beers, incentivizing bars to promote Goose Island at the expense of rivals, and digging into its pockets to hire away the best local brewing talent. "A-B InBev wants to be a craft beer brewer," Gao Yan, owner of Master Gao brewery in Nanjing, told the magazine. "But they want to act like a big brewer."

What John Hall saw, however, was his dream going global.

On January 8, 2017, after twenty-eight years, seven months, and twenty-six days, John Hall's brewpub served its last pints of beer.

A week earlier, Goose Island had announced a gut job that would drag on for ten months to reinvent the space for a contemporary audience. John's original vision had been "a very comfy pair of blue jeans we've had for 30 years," Ken Stout told the *Chicago Tribune*. Privately, Greg Hall had been saying for years that the Clybourn brewpub needed to close or be remodeled; it was a museum for another era in American craft beer. The original intention was to keep the bottom half of John's iconic bar in the center of the room while ripping out the top half of dark wood moldings and curlicues. Then the decision was made to rip out the whole thing and start fresh. The result would be shockingly new: sleek, bright, and modern. John was given periodic updates, but he learned most of the plans in the newspaper. He couldn't believe they would touch his original bar. But that was fine. It wasn't his company anymore.

John showed up for the last day of service at 4:30 PM, on a cold, clear Sunday in Chicago. He was stunned to find the barroom already packed. He walked in through the original door—the one that led to Willow Street, below the sign hanging off the corner of the building that flashed BREWERY/PUB—and got a standing ovation. John wore a blue pullover sweatshirt bearing the pub's original logo: a fluffy white goose trotting a grassy patch, looking backward, neck outstretched beside the words GOOSE ISLAND.

Former employees showed up to take one last turn behind the bar. Much of the beer was given away, free, in three- or four-ounce pours. There was no beer menu; bartenders just drained whatever kegs were in the basement. It all had to go. One longtime patron pointed to the spot at the bar where he'd decided to ask his wife to marry him. A former bartender got drunk and told anyone who would listen that it was "a love-filled room." A baby girl wore a pink Goose Island onesie. John posed for photo after photo with customers who whipped out their phones to commemorate the evening. Drinking beer in that room was once defiance. It was variety and quality and flavor. John's little idea born on an airplane thirty years earlier was right—people *did* want choice in their beer. He gave it to them. Then the world's largest beer company came knocking.

Greg was in Michigan tending to Virtue Cider. He told his dad he would try to be there for the final night, just as he'd been there for the pub's last big party, its twenty-fifth anniversary, on May 13, 2013. This time, though, he didn't make it.

John had announced the sale of the brewpub a year earlier, almost five years to the day after announcing the sale of Goose Island's production brewery.

For the second time, Goose Island staff was summoned for a meeting and a major announcement. Except this time, there wasn't the weight of months of preparation. This was an inevitability. John stood beside the bar where it all began and announced what many people already suspected: he was selling the brewpub to Anheuser-Busch too. Unlike five years earlier, there was no shock; word had slowly spread as John told managers.

It was John who first broached the sale, at a High End meeting in Bend, Oregon, the previous year. He asked Michael Taylor, the mergers and acquisitions guy, if he was ready to buy Goose Island's brewpub.

"Yeah," Taylor said. "We'd probably be interested in that."

Two phone calls later, it was agreed. Just John and Taylor. No lawyers, no executives, no flying in the big guns from New York. Just two phone calls. Anheuser-Busch would buy the rest of Goose Island.

None of the staff was terribly upset when John made the announcement that Friday morning. It all made sense.

The next day, John showed up at the brewpub as usual. He wanted to show his face and let people know he was still involved. He still cared. He sat at the bar and drank beer, just as he had for the last twenty-eight years. He slapped backs. He made small talk. Customers were supportive. They were appreciative.

Except for one guy. His name was Geoff, and he had been a regular for years. John knew him well. He had even done a little design work for Goose Island years back. John was walking out. Geoff was walking in.

"You son of a bitch," Geoff said. "You sold out to big beer—again."

There was no smile. No ribbing.

Five years of naysayers and second-guessers swelled to a geyser. John had changed how people drank beer in Chicago. He had built something good. Now it was being shared with the world. Couldn't people see that?

"Fuck you," John said.

And he walked to his car and drove home.

John regretted how angry he became. He didn't regret the sale, though.

Acknowledgments

I'VE NEVER BEEN SURE—do the most important people get the first line or the last? First gives them primacy. Last gives them power. I'll go with first. Thank you to the two most important people in my life, Lauren and Evan. Every day is a joy in its way, and I'm so thankful for you both. Lauren, without your support and understanding, this book would have been half finished forever.

Deep gratitude to many family members, friends, colleagues, and sources.

Thank you to a supportive and loving family: Stacie Geller and Jonathan Frenzen; Howard and Rhoda Noel; Gabriel Noel and Kaleena Bajo; Aunt Carla; Marsha Stern, Bob Shen, and the Shen family; Peter, Gloria, Leon, and Lewis; Sima, Keith, Alit, Dan, Maya, and Ricki; the Rubenzik-Brodsky-Rosenfeld clan of Arizona and San Diego; the Mittman family; and the Atkin family of London.

Several people made this book better by reading some or all of it along the way. Thank you, John Lavelle, Andy Crouch, Steve Johnson, Louise Kiernan, Heather Schroering, Lauren Stern, and Brett Nolan, whose influence is impossible to overstate. Brett slogged through the first draft of the first chapter, diagnosed its strengths and weaknesses, and made the suggestions that eventually turned into this book. He was the first person to read the book in its entirety—while still in an unenviable state—and made patient, painstaking suggestions. If you want to write a book, my suggestion: find yourself a Brett Nolan. Thank you, Brett; I owe you a thousand rounds of nonlight beer.

Thanks to the people behind the scenes who helped make this book possible: my agent, Alice Speilburg, and my (very patient) editors at Chicago Review Press, Yuval Taylor and Ellen Hornor.

I've been fortunate to learn from so many colleagues, mentors, and friends, past and present: Ira Berkow, Ross Werland, Lori Rackl, Colin McMahon, Amy Carr, Peter Kendall, Cindy Dampier, Jeff Carlson, Curt Eysink, Fred Kalmbach, Greg Trotter, and Alison Bowen ("write short sentences!"). Special thanks to Joe Gray, who started me writing about beer at the *Chicago Tribune* in 2009 and has been endlessly supportive ever since.

Many people were generous with time, thoughts, expertise, and archives during the reporting of this book: Randy Mosher; Ray Daniels; Kevin Masi at Torque; Benj, Eric, Chris, and David at Beer Marketer's Insights; Harry Schuhmacher at *Beer Business Daily*; Dan Wandel and his former team at IRI; Don Russell (a.k.a. Joe Sixpack); Julia Herz, Bart Watson, and Barbara Fusco at the Brewers Association; my business guru Peter Stern; Josh Deth, of Revolution Brewing; Rebecca Wolcott; Julissa Schindler; Jon Larson; Ashley Brandt, for his legal expertise; Brett Nolan (again), for his legal expertise; Kate Bernot; Jonathan Frenzen, for delving into online libraries; and Adam Warrington, Megan Lagesse, and Lisa Derus at Anheuser-Busch InBev for answering questions and facilitating interviews. Special thanks to people most responsible for making Goose Island what it became, and for sharing voluminous insights with me: John Hall, Greg Hall, and Tony Bowker. And deep thanks to the countless Goose Island employees past and present who took time to share insights, context, memories, and stories. Some of you are named in this book and some are not; you were all essential to assembling this narrative, whether with an on-the-record interview, a covert three-hour chat over several pints, or a quick question by text message. Thank you all for your thoughtfulness, your candor, and your beer.

What's life without friends? Thank you, Joe and Leslie Connell; Henry and Sherri Brean; Derrick and Megan Nunnally; Kerry Maloney (and Sam and Dan); Ryan Goudelocke; Scott and Amanda Brothers;

Melissa Arne and Jeff Klein; the Hottles; Tony Olivo; Caryl and Linda; Susan Harris and Dave Rogers; Julie Wernau; Brendan McCarthy; Mike Hawthorne and Paula Tordella; Brett Nolan and Gillian Flynn; Emily Stone and David MacLean; Lauren and Adam Nevens; Alexia Elejalde-Ruiz and Rahul Pasarnikar; Alison and Nate Gonner; Rob Mitchum and Laura Zimmermann; Andy Howard and Debbie Stulberg; Dan and Amie Larkin; Tim and Kendra Murray; the Kling family of Durango; and Shelia and Brian Seyfried.

Thanks to all the people in Chicago and across the nation I've had the pleasure of meeting who have made craft beer such a vibrant, fascinating, and wonderful industry: brewery founders, brewers, sales and marketing folks, bar owners, shop owners, salespeople, podcasters, and especially my fellow journalists. Keep telling the story. It's only just begun.

And—since they're so vitally important, they get the last line too—immense love and gratitude to Lauren, Evan, and Evan's sister, who will join the world just about the same time as this book. I can't wait to meet you.

Selected Bibliography

Original Interviews

Todd Ahsmann
Glenn Allen
Eddie Anderson
Jeff Baker
Larry Bell
Joe Bisacca
Laura Blasingame
Tony Bowker
Ashley Brandt
Matt Brynildson
Mark Burford
Nolan Burke
Sam Calagione
Dick Cantwell
João Castro Neves
Jim Cibak
Bob Collins
Pat Conway
Jessica Coughlin
Steve Crandall
Jonathan Cutler
Ray Daniels
Josh Deth
Paul DeVries
Luke Dickinson
Walt Dickinson
Victor Ecimovich III
Andy Ellis
Robert Esparza
Gary Fish
Michelle Foik
Calvin Frederickson
Jesse Friedman
Dave Fronczek
John Glick
Andy Goeler
Gabe Gordon
Teri Goudie
Ken Grossman
Greg Hall
John Hall
John J. Hall
Patricia Hall
Steve Hamburg
Mark Hegedus
John Hickenlooper
Eric Hobbs
Hilary Hodge
Tracy Hurst
Jared Jankoski
Claudia Jendron
Mark Kamarauskas
Bob Kenney
Karen King
Greg Koch
Florian Kuplent
John Laffler
Bruce Lange
Pat Lawling
Dick Leinenkugel
Chris Lennert
Matt Lincoln
Tony Magee
Kevin Masi
Mark McDonnell
Terry Michaelson
Randy Mosher
Marty Nachel
Jason Neton
Dave Peacock
Bob Pease
Mary Pellettieri
Jeff Peterson
Brett Porter
Chris Quinn
Joey Redner
George Reisch
Nikos Ridge
Michael Roper
Jared Rouben
Tim Schoen
Harry Schuhmacher
Jim Scussel
Mark Sellers
Jacob Sembrano
Christopher Shepard
Eric Shepard
Tony Short

Steve Sobel
Jeff Sparrow
Mitch Steele
Benj Steinman
David Steinman
Ken Stout
Chris Swersey
Felipe Szpigel
Brian Taylor
Rob Tod
Ryan Tucker
Terry Usry
Todd Usry
Adam Vavrick
Jim Vorel
David Walker
Eric Wallace
Suzanne Wolcott
Phil Wymore
Percy Young

Note: Additional interview subjects are not listed due to a promise of anonymity.

Books

Acitelli, Tom. *The Audacity of Hops: The History of America's Craft Beer Revolution*. Chicago: Chicago Review Press, 2013.

Cantwell, Dick, and Peter Bouckaert. *Wood & Beer: A Brewer's Guide*. Boulder, CO: Brewers Publications, 2016.

Cuadros, Alex. *Brazillionaires: Wealth, Power, Decadence, and Hope in an American Country*. New York: Spiegel & Grau, 2016.

Daniels, Ray. *Designing Great Beers: The Ultimate Guide to Brewing Classic Beer Styles*. Boulder, CO: Brewers Publications, 2000.

Grossman, Ken. *Beyond the Pale: The Story of Sierra Nevada Brewing Co*. Hoboken, NJ: John Wiley & Sons, 2013.

Hieronymus, Stan. *For the Love of Hops: The Practical Guide to Aroma, Bitterness and the Culture of Hops*. Boulder, CO: Brewers Publications, 2012.

Hindy, Steve. *The Craft Beer Revolution: How a Band of Microbrewers Is Transforming the World's Favorite Drink*. New York: Palgrave MacMillan, 2015.

Knoedelseder, William. *Bitter Brew: The Rise and Fall of Anheuser-Busch and America's Kings of Beer*. New York: Harper Business, 2012.

Macintosh, Julie. *Dethroning the King: The Hostile Takeover of Anheuser-Busch, an American Icon*. Hoboken, NJ: John Wiley & Sons, 2011.

Magee, Tony. *So You Want to Start a Brewery? The Lagunitas Story*. Chicago: Chicago Review Press, 2014.

Mosher, Randy. *Radical Brewing: Recipes, Tales and World-Altering Meditations in a Glass*. Boulder, CO: Brewers Publications, 2004.

———. *Tasting Beer: An Insider's Guide to the World's Greatest Drink*. North Adams, MA: Storey, 2009.

Neu, Denese. *Chicago by the Pint: A Craft Beer History of the Windy City*. Charleston, SC: History Press, 2011.

Ogle, Maureen. *Ambitious Brew: The Story of American Beer*. Orlando: Harcourt, 2006.

Oliver, Garrett, ed. *The Oxford Companion to Beer*. New York: Oxford University Press, 2012.

Skilnik, Bob. *Beer: A History of Brewing in Chicago*. Fort Lee, NJ: Barricade Books, 2006.

Steele, Mitch. *IPA: Brewing Techniques, Recipes and the Evolution of India Pale Ale*. Boulder, CO: Brewers Publications, 2012.

Tonsmeire, Michael. *American Sour Beers: Innovative Techniques for Mixed Fermentations*. Boulder, CO: Brewers Publications, 2014.

Tremblay, Victor J., and Carol Horton Tremblay. *The U.S. Brewing Industry: Data and Economic Analysis*. Cambridge, MA: MIT Press, 2009.

Verstl, Ina, and Ernst Faltermeier. *The Beer Monopoly: How Brewers Bought and Built for World Domination*. Nuremberg, Germany: Brauwelt International, 2016.

Newspaper and Wire Service Articles

Appel, Ted. "Lagunitas Dragged into Beer Brouhaha." *Santa Rosa (CA) Press Democrat*, October 13, 2000.

Andel, Mark. "Strange Brews: With Intense Flavors and Higher Alcohol Content, Trendy New 'Extreme' Beers Pack a Punch." *RedEye* (Chicago), June 17, 2003.

Baker, Jeff. "Craft Beer Versus Crafty Beer." *Burlington (VT) Free Press*, May 17, 2013.

Barr, Diana. "A-B InBev CEO Brito to Forgo Bonus After Earnings Drop." *St. Louis Business Journal*, March 2, 2017.

Bartz, Diane. "U.S. Probes Allegations AB InBev Seeking to Curb Craft Beer Distribution." Reuters, October 12, 2015.

Bergman, Rhonda. "The Clash on Clybourn Avenue: Along Chicago's 'Gaza Strip,' Manufacturers Are Trying to Face Down Developers and Yuppies Who Want to Gentrify the City's Industrial Sector. The Question: Can Steel Mills and Gourmet Groceries Coexist?" *Los Angeles Times*, October 19, 1988.

Bomkamp, Samantha. "United Airlines to Serve Goose Island's 312 Urban Wheat." *Chicago Tribune*, June 27, 2014.

Borrelli, Christopher. "Against the Grain: Former Goose Island Brewmaster Greg Hall Wants You to Try His New Cider. Yes, Cider." *Chicago Tribune*, May 24, 2012.

Brown, Lisa. "A-B Adding New Johnny Appleseed Hard Cider." *St. Louis Post-Dispatch*, March 22, 2014.

———. "A-B Adds NY Office, Shrinking St. Louis Role in Sales and Marketing." *St. Louis Post-Dispatch*, December 9, 2014.

———. "A-B Buying New York's Blue Point Brewing. Brewer Hopes to Replicate Its Success with Goose Island." *St. Louis Post-Dispatch*, February 6, 2014.

Cancelada, Gregory. "A-B Takes Another Gander at the Microbrew Market; Goose Island Gains Distribution Clout; Anheuser-Busch Boosts Exposure to Craft Beer." *St. Louis Post-Dispatch*, June 8, 2006.

———. "A-B Wants a Taste of Microbrews; Brewer Is Reportedly Close to Acquiring a Minority Stake in Goose Island Beer Co." *St. Louis Post-Dispatch*, May 23, 2006.

———. "Raz-Matazz: A-B Adds to Its Bacardi Silver Line." *St. Louis Post-Dispatch*, August 26, 2003.

Cazentre, Don. "Bud's New Brew Is Coming to Baldwinsville." *Syracuse (NY) Post-Standard*, June 28, 2015.

Connole, Jon. "Pabst Brewing Veterans Now Think Small: Brewing Systems Brings Love of Beer to Microbrewery Consulting Business." *Milwaukee Business Journal*, May 18, 1987.

DaParma, Ron. "Anheuser-Busch Might Add Rolling Rock to Stable." *Pittsburgh Tribune-Review*, May 5, 2006.

Desloge, Rick. "Report Card: A-B Grading Distributors on Loyalty." *St. Louis Business Journal*, November 17, 1996.

DiNunzio, Miriam. "A Rhapsody in Brew: Micropubs Are a Beer Lover's Delight." *Chicago Sun-Times*, November 1, 1996.

Ditzler, Joseph. "10 Barrel Partners: No Apologies for Sale." *Bend (OR) Bulletin*, January 24, 2015.

Dorsch, Jim. "Midwestern Brewers Display a Knack, Even a Love, for Experiments." *Chicago Tribune*, July 19, 2000.

———. "Mugs Overflow at the Great American Beer Festival." *Chicago Tribune*, October 25, 1995.

———. "Not so Micro: Success of Small Breweries Attracts Competitors." *Chicago Tribune*, January 8, 1997.

Drummond, Bob, Greg Stohr, and Lisa Pemberton-Butler. "Anheuser-Busch Distributor Rewards Eyed in U.S. Probe." *Seattle Times*, October 3, 1997.

Eastes, Beau. "10 Barrel: Looking Back a Year After the Sale." *Bend (OR) Bulletin*, November 12, 2015.

Evans, Pat. "Feds Impose Sanction on Hard Cider Maker." *Grand Rapids Business Journal*, May 1, 2015.

Fields-White, Monée. "Sam's Wines Succumbs to Rival Binny's." *Crain's Chicago Business*, October 9, 2009.

Freisler, Eduard. "Satisfaction, at Last." *New York Times*, August 17, 2010.

Gallagher, Jim. "Anheuser-Busch Fined $1 Million in NY Dumping." *St. Louis Post-Dispatch*, September 16, 1989.

Gasparro, Annie, and Ezequiel Minaya. "Kraft Heinz Management Shake-up Illustrates 3G Capital Partners' Strategy." *Wall Street Journal*, September 17, 2017.

Gazeta Mercantil (São Paulo). "Brahma Grows 73 Percent in 1995." March 11, 1996.

Gorski, Eric. "Could a Colorado Craft Brewery Sell Out to Big Beer?" *Denver Post*, February 15, 2015.

Groves, Martha. "'Davids' Sue Beer Goliath." *Los Angeles Times*, July 30, 1997.

Hahn, Fritz. "Amid Deal with Anheuser-Busch, Craft Brewery Gets Kicked out of its Own Festival." *Washington Post*, August 13, 2016.

Hamilton, Martha M. "Putting Its Brand on Beer Distribution." *Washington Post*, October 3, 1997.

Hart, Hugh. "Grin and Beer It—and This Local Brewery Will Show You How." *Chicago Tribune*, September 9, 1992.

Hassell, Greg. "Changing Their Strategy: Big Beer Makers Copy Microbreweries." *Houston Chronicle*, May 25, 1995.

Hayes, Charles. "Industrial-Strength Shopping Mall Being Developed on the North Side." *Chicago Tribune*, November 16, 1986.

Hendricks, Mike. "Anheuser-Busch Buys Schlitz Brewery." Associated Press, February 1, 1980.

Herhold, Scott. "Microbreweries over a Barrel." *San Jose Mercury News*, March 15, 1998.

Hill, Andrew, and Scheherazade Daneshkhu. "AB InBev's Hard-Nosed Kings of Beer." *Financial Times*, June 15, 2015.

Hughlett, Mike. "Craft Beers Brewing up Success Story in Down Market; Goose Island, Others Offer a Bright Spot as Recession Wallops Flagship Brands." *Chicago Tribune*, September 8, 2009.

Jackson, Cheryl V. "Goose Island's Golden Egg." *Chicago Sun-Times*, June 4, 2007.

Kesmodel, David. "Anheuser Explores Sale of Struggling Rolling Rock." *Wall Street Journal*, April 13, 2009.

———. "Beer Distributors Want More than One Best Bud." *Wall Street Journal*, February 6, 2008.

Kesmodel, David, and Annie Gasparro. "Kraft-Heinz Deal Shows Brazilian Buyout Firm's Cost-Cutting Recipe." *Wall Street Journal*, March 25, 2015.

Kirk, Jim. "Dominick's Labor Issues Won't Go Away, So Sale Remains on Shelf." *Chicago Tribune*, August 8, 2004.

———. "Goose Island Taps Growth." *Chicago Sun-Times*, April 16, 1996.

———. "Macro-Squeeze for Microbrewers: Tougher Competition from Every Quarter Puts New Pressure on Craft Beer Makers." *Chicago Tribune*, October 8, 1997.

Knoblauch, Mark. "At Goose Island Brewing Co., Go for the Beer." *Chicago Tribune*, July 15, 1988.

Kiss, Tony. "Swiss Beer Drinkers Protest Wicked Weed Sale." *Asheville (NC) Mountain Xpress*, May 18, 2017.

Lazarus, George. "'Chicago' Microbrew Hits Street." *Chicago Tribune*, September 26, 1995.

———. "More Small Breweries over a Barrel." *Chicago Tribune*, August 26, 1997.

Lerman, Rachel. "Elysian Founders Defend Decision to Sell to Anheuser-Busch, Promise Beer Won't Change." *Puget Sound Business Journal*, January 27, 2015.

Logan, Tim. "Big Payday Coming to Top A-B InBev Execs." *St. Louis Post-Dispatch*, March 10, 2012.

———. "Brewery's Last Top Executive Holdover Leaves A-B InBev." *St. Louis Post-Dispatch*, January 24, 2012.

———. "Dave Peacock's Farewell the Latest Change at Anheuser-Busch InBev." *St. Louis Post-Dispatch*, January 24, 2012.

Lovering, Daniel. "Rolling Rock Sale Clouds Pa. Town's Future." Associated Press, May 19, 2006.

Manor, Robert. "Brewer Drops Upscale Beer; Critics Liked A-B Product." *St. Louis Post-Dispatch*, March 22, 1991.

McGuire, Matt. "Roll out the Barrel—Beer Aged in Bourbon Barrels Gains Flavor as Well as Converts." *Chicago Tribune*, December 20, 2006.

Michael, Tom. "Microbreweries Are Still a Curiosity in the Midwest." *Chicago Tribune*, November 4, 1993.

Miller, Nick. "Corporate Beer Overlords AB InBev to Open Golden Road 'Craft' Beer Garden in North Oakland." *Oakland (CA) East Bay Express*, March 24, 2017.

Miller, Sabrina L., and E. A. Torriero. "Jackson Contacts Cultivated Beer Deal; Dad Indirectly Helped Two Sons Through a Friend." *Chicago Tribune*, April 8, 2001.

Newsday. "Beer Dispute Coming to a Head." October 3, 1997.

Noel, Josh. "$45 per Bottle for Bourbon County Stout." *Chicago Tribune*, November 23, 2010.

———. "Bar Incident Leaves Goose Island's Greg Hall Contrite." *Chicago Tribune*, April 11, 2011.

———. "Bourbon County Stout Is a Legend, but Probably Not as Old as We Think." *Chicago Tribune*, October 31, 2016.

———. "Craft Brewery Co-Founder Not Happy with Super Bowl Ad Snark." *Chicago Tribune*, February 2, 2015.

———. "Goose Island Gets New CEO: Andy Goeler, the Man Behind the Mohawk at Shock Top, Will Be the New CEO of Goose Island." *Chicago Tribune*, November 16, 2012.

———. "Goose Island Identifies Bacteria That Caused Tainted Beer, but Not Source." *Chicago Tribune*, May 26, 2016.

———. "Goose Island Offers More Bourbon County Refunds." *Chicago Tribune*, July 15, 2016.

———. "Goose Island Offers Refunds: Off Flavors in Some Bourbon County Beer." *Chicago Tribune*, January 8, 2016.

———. "Goose Island to Open Taproom, Begin Tours at Fulton Street Brewery." *Chicago Tribune*, October 2, 2014.

———. "Goose Island's Clybourn Brewpub Closing for 5-Month Renovation." *Chicago Tribune*, January 4, 2017.

———. "Goose Island's John Hall Promises Commitment to Creativity Won't Change." *Chicago Tribune*, March 28, 2011.

———. "Hop Farm Harmony: Goose Island, Anheuser-Busch Find Common Ground at Hops Farm." *Chicago Tribune*, August 26, 2014.

———. "In Anheuser-Busch Hands, Goose Island Solid." *Chicago Tribune*, March 30, 2016.

———. "Revolution Will Bottle and Can Its Beers." *Chicago Tribune*, March 30, 2011.

———. "Virtue Cider Selling Majority Stake to Anheuser-Busch." *Chicago Tribune*, September 4, 2015.

Noland, Claire. "Karl Strauss, 94: Master Brewer for Pabst Helped Pioneer Microbrew Trend." *Los Angeles Times*, December 27, 2006.

Olewnick, Tiana. "When Life Gives You a Sour Batch of Matilda, Make Dominique." *Newcity* (Chicago), February 21, 2011.

Papazian, Charlie, Bob Pease, and Dan Kopman. "Craft or Crafty? Consumers Deserve to Know the Truth." *St. Louis Post-Dispatch*, December 13, 2012.

Parsons, Dan. "Kingsmill Sold to Colorado-Based Company; Sale Announced by Busch Properties Monday Afternoon." *Newport News (VA) Daily Press*, July 12, 2010.

Pistor, Nicholas J. C. "August Busch IV Settles Wrongful-Death Suit over Girlfriend for $1.75 Million." *St. Louis Post-Dispatch*, October 30, 2012.

Portland Business Journal. "Now That Budweiser Owns 10 Barrel, Will You Still Drink That Apocalypse IPA?" (poll). November 5, 2014.

Pridmore, Jay. "Clybourn Boom Likely to Be Boon For 18-Year-Old Edith's." *Chicago Tribune*, September 4, 1987.

Queary, Paul. "Popularity of Microbrews Rattles the Beer Giants." Associated Press, July 15, 1993.

Rice, William. "A Craft on Draft: America's Small Brewers Do Their Part to Satisfy a Thirst for Big Flavors." *Chicago Tribune*, October 13, 1994.

———. "What's Brewing? A Pub Crawl to Rate Chicago Beers." *Chicago Tribune*, August 12, 1988.

Romero, Simon. "Brazilian Regulators Approve the Merger of 2 Big Brewers." *New York Times*, March 31, 2000.

———. "Brazilians to Acquire a Stake in Argentine Brewery." *New York Times*, May 3, 2002.

Rosica, James L. "Anheuser-Busch Interested in Buying Tampa's Cigar City Brewing." *Tampa Bay Times*, February 8, 2015.

Rowe, Peter. "Bavarian First to Tap Microbrew in San Diego." *San Diego Union-Tribune*, December 22, 2006.

———. "What's Next for the Craft Beer Industry?" *San Diego Union-Tribune*, May 2, 2012.

Russell, Don. "Craft Brewers Bothered by Anheuser-Busch Invasion." *Philadelphia Daily News*, June 16, 2006.

Saxon, Wolfgang. "Bert Grant, 73, a Beer Maker Who Developed Microbreweries." *New York Times*, August 6, 2001.

Schmeltzer, John. "Bear Market Stirs Brewers: As Hard Liquor and Wines Continue to Eat Away at Market Share, Companies Like Anheuser-Busch Are

Testing New Products with a Somewhat Different Flavor." *Chicago Tribune*, March 9, 2006.

———. "Brewer Takes Stake in Goose Island Beer; Bud Distributors Will Deliver the Local Brew." *Chicago Tribune*, June 8, 2006.

Shikes, Jonathan. "Breckenridge Brewery's Todd Usry Explains the Sale to Anheuser-Busch InBev." *Westword* (Denver), December 23, 2015.

———. "Craft Beer Bars Cutting Off Wicked Weed, Other AB InBev-Owned Breweries." *Westword* (Denver), May 4, 2017.

Singer, Drew. "Budweiser Trademarks '215,' Plans Challenge to Local Brews." *Philadelphia Inquirer*, July 16, 2011.

Skube, Michael. "Anheuser-Busch Product Gets Crafty." *Atlanta Journal-Constitution*, May 29, 1997.

Sloan, Gene. "Tapping Micros' Success: Beer Buyers Raise Toast to New Brews." *USA Today*, October 21, 1994.

Smith, Tony. "A Bet on a Brazilian Brewery Pays Off for 3 Investors." *New York Times*, March 4, 2004.

Snider, Mike. "Goose Island Drafts New Promotions and New Beers." *USA Today*, February 8, 2014.

Stambor, Zak. "Craft Brewers Inspired by Belgian-Style Sour Beers." *Chicago Tribune*, April 8, 2009.

Stamborski, Al. "A-B Makes a Big Move in a Small Market." *St. Louis Post-Dispatch*, March 22, 1998.

———. "A-B Offers Tequila-Lime Beer." *St. Louis Post-Dispatch*, February 5, 1999.

Stroud, Jerri. "Old Is New: A-B Goes into Past for Its Latest Brew." *St. Louis Post-Dispatch*, September 29, 1995.

Syracuse (NY) Post-Standard. "Business Certificates Filing at the Onondaga County Clerk's Office." July 24, 2011.

Tarrazi, Alexis. "Celebrate National Beer Day with 10 Refreshing Spring Brews." *Woodland Park (NJ) Record*, April 7, 2012.

Thompson, John. "Why I Lifted My Boycott of Goose Island." *Baltimore Post-Examiner*, January 24, 2014.

United Press International. "Busch to Push Ahead with Low-Alcohol Beer." May 14, 1984.

USA Today. "A Stroh for All Seasons." May 20, 1993.

Van Zandt, Emily. "Meet the New Guy: Goose Goes In-House to Pick Its New Brewmaster." *RedEye* (Chicago), March 29, 2011.

Vettel, Phil. "Fresh and Proud of It: Microbreweries Offer Star-Quality Beers and Solid, Complementary Food." *Chicago Tribune*, September 29, 1996.

Volkmann, Kelsey. "Peacock: 'Stars Aligned' for Goose Island Acquisition." *St. Louis Business Journal*, March 28, 2011.

Walzer, Philip, and Carolyn Shapiro. "Raising the Bar." *Virginian-Pilot*, May 8, 2011.

Washburn, David. "Spreading the Word: Strauss Led the Way for County's Brewers." *San Diego Union-Tribune*, May 3, 2005.

Waterloo (IA) Daily Courier. "Two Traffic Deaths in Waterloo Probed." June 25, 1962.

Wax, Alan J. "Beer's Big Boys Tapping into Microbreweries." *Newsday*, May 7, 1995.

Wilmes, Tom. "Craft Brewers Call for Greater Transparency in Brewing." *Boulder (CO) Daily Camera*, December 20, 2012.

Worthington, Rogers. "Giant Miller to Take a Swig out of Leinenkugel's Stein." *Chicago Tribune*, December 14, 1987.

Yue, Lorene. "How Goose Island Held on to Its Craft Beer Cred." *Crain's Chicago Business*, May 4, 2013.

Magazine and Journal Articles

Allen, James. "The Beliefs That Built a Global Brewer." *Harvard Business Review*, April 27, 2012.

Allyn, Matt. "Why Anheuser-Busch InBev Buying SABMiller Is a Win for Craft Beer." *Men's Journal*, no date available.

Angrisani, Carol. "David Peacock." *Supermarket News*, July 18, 2011.

Arthur, Tomme. "The Bourbon Standard." *All About Beer*, January 1, 2013.

Cendrowski, Scott. "China's New Craft-Beer Bully." *Fortune*, March 16, 2017.

Edgar, David. "The Industry in Review." *New Brewer*, May–June 1999.

Entani, Etsuzo, Hiroshi Masai, and Ken-Ichiro Suzuki. "*Lactobacillus acetotolerans*, a New Species from Fermented Vinegar Broth." *International Journal of Systematic and Evolutionary Microbiology* 36 (October 1, 1986): 544–549. doi:10.1099/00207713-36-4-544.

Hendershot, Steve. "It Will Take a Stoner Savant to Lead the Craft Beer Revolution." *Chicago Magazine*, September 12, 2013.

Hochstein, Mort. "Goose Island Brewing Co. Is on the Expansion Trail." *Nation's Restaurant News*, June 19, 1995.

Johnson, Julie. "How the American Beer Landscape Is Changing." *Beverage Dynamics*, October 10, 2016.

———. "Pull Up a Stool with Greg Hall." *All About Beer*, September 1, 2010.

Leonard, Devin. "The Plot to Destroy America's Beer." *Bloomberg*, October 26, 2012.

Lenderman, Maxim. "Mind Games: Anheuser-Busch Wants Its Wholesalers' Whole Attention." *Beverage World*, September 1, 1996.

Mcdowell, Bill. "A-B Campaign Chastises Boston Beer Marketing; Radio, Print Ads Urge Sam Adams Brewer to Clarify Where Product Is Produced." *AdAge*, October 28, 1996.

Modern Brewery Age. "A-B Red Wolf Launched in Southeast." October 10, 1994.

———. "Brewer's Association Position Paper on Miller Contract." January 11, 1999.

———. "Craft Beer Volume Grew 11.3% in 2010, BA Reports." March 28, 2011.

———. "Craft Brewing Greats Headline Annual Craft Brewers Conference in San Francisco." March 28, 2011.

———. "Goose Island Forms Affiance with United States Beverage." April 10, 2000.

———. "Goose Island to produce 312 wheat at A-B." July 29, 2011.

———. "Miller Wants 'Fair Share' from Wholesalers." November 23, 1998.

O'Brien, Maria. "The Killer Instinct." *LatinFinance*, April 2004.

Papazian, Charlie. "Losing Sight of the Good Fight." *New Brewer*, May–June 1999.

Prince, Greg W., Larry Jabbonsky, and Eric Sfiligoj. "Miller This Time." *Beverage World*, July 1, 1995.

Raddatz, Anna. "Something Wicked This Way Comes." *Capital at Play*, October 2014.

Schultz, E. J. "A-B InBev Establishes Chicago Foothold with New High-End Unit; Brewer Wants to Get Closer to Urban Consumers." *AdAge*, August 6, 2014.

———. "A-B InBev Proves a Good Home for Goose Island as Big Brewer Helps Cult Craft Rise; Brand Readies First Ad Campaign After Three Successful Years Under Wing of Beer Giant." *AdAge*, December 16, 2013.

———. "Bud Is Proudly 'Macro' Amid Micro-Brews in Swagger-Filled Super Bowl Ad." *AdAge*, February 1, 2015.

———. "Does Heritage Trump Origin in Beer Brands?" *AdAge*, November 14, 2011.

———. “Inside MillerCoors’ Craft Brewery, Tenth and Blake.” *AdAge*, November 22, 2010.

Sellers, Patricia. “Bud-Weis-Heir August Busch IV Is Rebellious, Risk-Taking and (Nearly) Ready to Rule the World’s Largest Brewer.” *Fortune*, January 13, 1997.

Sellers, Patricia, and Barbara C. Loos. “How Busch Wins in a Doggy Market.” *Fortune*, June 22, 1987.

Soat, Molly. “Crafting a National Identity: Goose Island Beer Co. Is Hoping That Its Deep Roots in Beer-Savvy Chicago Will Preserve Its Handmade Identity as the Craft Brand Goes Corporate.” *Marketing News*, November 30, 2012.

Soergel, Andrew. “Crafting a Future.” *U.S. News and World Report*, April 7, 2016.

Steinriede, Kent. “Distribution Is a Rocky Road for Craft Brewers.” *Beverage Industry*, October 1997.

Turcsik, Richard. (No headline.) *Grocery Headquarters*, June 1, 2013.

Voight, Joan. “Big Beer Brands Are Fooling Us with Their Crafty Looks; Indie Brewers Want Transparency.” *Adweek*, March 31, 2013.

Video

Achbar, Mark, and Jennifer Abbott, dirs. *The Corporation*. 2003; New York: Zeitgeist Films, 2004. www.youtube.com/watch?v=KMNZXV7jOG0.

“Brewed the Hard Way.” Anheuser-Busch commercial, 2015. www.youtube.com/watch?v=2uJKhkwTG64.

“Six View Points from the High End.” Vimeo video. 4:12. Posted by “The High End.” July 2017. https://vimeo.com/223773287.

Skala, Mark, dir. *Festival of Wood and Barrel Aged Beer 2012 (FOBAB)* documentary. Skalawag Productions, BeerFX, and Chicago Beer Geeks. https://vimeo.com/57575049.

Original Internet Journalism

Alworth, Jeff. “The Goose Island Deal.” *Beervana: The Blog*. March 30, 2011. www.beervanablog.com/beervana/2011/03/goose-island-deal.html.

Anand, Priya. “10 Things the Beer Industry Won’t Tell You.” MarketWatch. December 13, 2014. www.marketwatch.com/story/10-things-the-beer-industry-wont-tell-you-2014-11-28.

BBM! (Belgian Beer Me!) “Honk If You Like Goose Island/AB InBev.” March 30, 2011. www.belgianbeerme.com/good-beer-santa/2011/03/honk-if-you-like-goose-islandab-inbev.html.

Beaumont, Stephen. "Michael (Hopleaf) Roper's Take on the Goose Island Deal." *Beaumont Drinks* (blog). http://beaumontdrinks.com/micheal-hopleaf-ropers-take-on-the-goose-island-deal.

Beer Marketer's Insights. "AB Acquired Craft Over 1.2 Mil Bbls, We Estimate; 'Betting Even Bigger' in 2017; 'Pretty Much Good' With # of Partners." Email newsletter, January 27, 2017.

———. "AB Prexy Dave Peacock on 'Alignment,' 'Anchor Wholesaler' Consolidation Guide, SOTs." Email newsletter, November 8, 2011.

———. "AB Unveils 3 Yr 'Win Together' Plan Developed with Distribs; A 'Turning Point,' Sez João." Email newsletter, November 19, 2015.

Body, Steve. "The Short Life and Ugly Death of 10 Barrel Brewing." *The Pour Fool* (blog). November 5, 2014. https://thepourfool.com/2014/11/05/the-short-life-and-ugly-death-of-10-barrel-brewing.

Brooks, Jay. "Fowl Ball? Widmer Buys a Piece of Goose Island." *Brookston Beer Bulletin* (blog). June 8, 2006. http://brookstonbeerbulletin.com/fowl-ball-widmer-buys-a-piece-of-goose-island.

———. "Fritz Maytag & Ken Grossman Give Keynote at CBC 2011." *Brookston Beer Bulletin* (blog). March 24, 2011. http://brookstonbeerbulletin.com/fritz-maytag-ken-grossman-give-keynote-at-cbc-2011.

Chan, Tristan. "Growing List of National Breweries Rescind RSVP to Wicked Weed Funkatorium Invitational." PorchDrinking.com. May 4, 2017. www.porchdrinking.com/articles/2017/05/04/growing-list-of-national-breweries-rescind-rsvp-to-wicked-weed-funkatorium-invitational.

Crouch, Andy. "Why the Anheuser Busch InBev-Goose Island Deal Is Good for Craft Beer." *Beer Scribe* (blog). March 28, 2011. www.beerscribe.com/2011/03/28/why-the-ab-inbev-deal-is-good-for-craft-beer.

Dunlop, Pete. "Anheuser-Busch's Latest Counteroffensive: Pricing." *Beervana Buzz* (blog). April 14, 2014. www.beervanabuzz.com/2014/04/anheuser-buschs-latest-counteroffensive.html.

Eisenberg, David, and Chris Furnari. "Ninkasi Realigns Wholesale Network in Pacific Northwest, Expands in Southern California." Brewbound. January 15, 2015. www.brewbound.com/news/ninkasi-realigns-wholesale-network-pacific-northwest-expands-southern-california.

Eisenberg, David, and Michael Kiser. "From the Gutters to the High End—How Wicked Weed Grew Like One." Good Beer Hunting. May 3, 2017. http://goodbeerhunting.com/sightlines/2017/5/3/anheuser-busch-acquires-wicked-weed.

Furnari, Chris. "Cigar City Founder Calls Buyout Rumor 'Speculation.'" Brewbound. February 10, 2016. www.brewbound.com/news/cigar-city-founder-calls-buyout-rumor-speculation.

———. "Elysian's Dick Cantwell Resigns from A-B InBev." Brewbound. April 13, 2015. www.brewbound.com/news/elysians-dick-cantwell-resigns-from-a-b-inbev.

———. "Fireman Capital to Purchase Cigar City." Brewbound. March 14, 2016. www.brewbound.com/news/fireman-capital-to-purchase-cigar-city.

———. "TTB Accepts $300,000 Settlement from Anheuser-Busch InBev." Brewbound. March 4, 2016. www.brewbound.com/news/ttb-accepts-300000-settlement-from-anheuser-busch-inbev.

Hagerman, Pat. "Widmer, Goose Island Strike Deal." ProBrewer.com. June 7, 2006. www.probrewer.com/widmer-goose-island-strike-deal.

Hieronymus, Stan. "Craft Beer: The 1986 Definition." *Appellation Beer* (blog). July 13, 2010. https://appellationbeer.com/blog/craft-beer-the-1986-definition.

———. "Perspective." *Appellation Beer* (blog). March 28, 2011. https://appellationbeer.com/blog/perspective-2.

———. "The Class of '88." *Appellation Beer* (blog). February 1998. https://appellationbeer.com/blog/the-class-of-88.

———. "What Is Craft Beer?" *Appellation Beer* (blog). February 21, 2007. https://appellationbeer.com/blog/what-is-craft-beer.

Jackson, Michael. "How Bert Grant Saved the World." Beer Hunter. August 3, 2001. www.beerhunter.com/documents/19133-001575.html.

John. "Anheuser-Busch Buys Goose Island." *The Pint Glass* (blog). March 28, 2011. https://thepintglass.wordpress.com/2011/03/28/anheuser-busch-buys-goose-island.

Kendall, Justin. "Anheuser-Busch Accused of Inducing Massachusetts Retailers." Brewbound. May 9, 2017. www.brewbound.com/news/anheuser-busch-accused-inducing-massachusetts-retailers.

Kiser, Michael. "Critical Drinking—Greg Hall of Virtue Cider." Good Beer Hunting. September 14, 2015. http://goodbeerhunting.com/blog/2015/9/12/critical-drinking-greg-hall-of-virtue-cider.

Liberty, John. "Bell's Brewery Inc. to Be Sold? Larry Bell Says It's Possible." M Live. April 29, 2012. www.mlive.com/news/kalamazoo/index.ssf/2012/04/bells_brewery_inc_to_be_sold_l.html.

Long, Tom. "Judge Brewers by Their Beer." CNN.com. December 21, 2012. www.cnn.com/2012/12/21/opinion/long-beer-brewers/index.html.

Malloy, Ellen. "Motivation Monday: Shoot the Puck." January 9, 2012. ellenmalloy.com (content removed).

Morton, Andy. "Just the Answer—Brooklyn Brewery Brewmaster Garrett Oliver." just-drinks. March 18, 2013. www.just-drinks.com/interview/just-the-answer-brooklyn-brewery-brewmaster-garrett-oliver_id109821.aspx.

Myers, Erik Lars. "The Terrifying Future of the New Anheuser-Goose." *Top Fermented* (blog). March 28, 2011. www.topfermented.com/2011/03/28/the-terrifying-future-of-the-new-anheuser-goose.

Ogle, Maureen. "AB InBev and Its Golden, Um, Goose." Maureen Ogle's blog *Observation Post*. March 29, 2011. www.maureenogle.com/maureen-ogle/2011/03/29/ab-inbev-and-its-golden-um-goose.

Powers, Matthew. "Elk Mountain Farms: A Lesson in Hops, a Lesson in Beer." *Chicago Now: A Pint of Chicago* (blog). August 29, 2016. www.chicagonow.com/pint-chicago/2016/08/elk-mountain-farms.

Schneider, Paul. "Ten Reasons You Should Be Drinking Goose Island Right Now." Solemn Oath Brewery. November 22, 2013. http://solemnoathbrewery.com/sob-stories/ten-reasons-you-should-be-drinking-goose-island-right-now.

Schuhmacher, Harry. "Andy on the State of the Goose." Beer Business Daily. June 17, 2014. www.beernet.com/publications_daily.php?id=3216.

———. "SAMCOM Day 2: The High End, and Wholesaler Concerns." Beer Business Daily. November 4, 2014. www.beernet.com/publications_daily.php?id=3325.

———. "Sting Operation Reveals Alleged A-B Pay-to-Play Activities." Beer Business Daily. May 13, 2016. www.beernet.com/publications_daily.php?id=3775.

Shouse, Heather. "Greg Hall Talks About Goose Island and Anheuser-Busch." TimeOut Chicago. May 27, 2011. www.timeout.com/chicago/food-drink/greg-hall-talks-about-goose-island-and-anheuser-busch.

Thunderfoot, Jeremiah. "What Is a Craft Brewery? Part II." What's Brewing. September 10 2015. www.whatsbrewing.ca/2015/09/what-is-a-craft-brewery-part-ii.

Vorel, Jim [Kid Carboy Jr., pseud.]. "Goose Island Is Cooked by Anheuser-Busch." *Aleheads* (blog). March 28, 2011. https://aleheads.com/2011/03/28/goose-island-is-cooked-by-anheuser-busch.

Wilmore, James. "Will Blue Point Buy Be First of Many for Anheuser-Busch InBev?" just-drinks, February 9, 2014. www.just-drinks.com/comment

/comment-will-blue-point-buy-be-first-of-many-for-anheuser-busch-inbev_id112764.aspx.

Zoller, Mike. "Former Goose Island Brewmaster Behind Virtue Cider." Porch Drinking.com. November 28, 2016. www.porchdrinking.com/articles/2016/11/28/former-goose-island-brewmaster-behind-virtue-cider.

Miscellaneous

@Goose_Island_PR Twitter account. https://twitter.com/goose_island_pr.

"10 Barrel Is Not Craft Beer." www.gofundme.com/10-barrel-is-not-craft-beer.

"ABC Fines Two Large Beer & Wine Wholesalers and Numerous Retailers for Unfair Business Practices." California Department of Alcoholic Beverage Control press release. www.abc.ca.gov/press/PR2017/PR17-13.pdf.

Anheuser-Busch InBev annual reports (various). www.ab-inbev.com/investors/reports-and-filings.html.

Anheuser-Busch InBev presentations (various). www.ab-inbev.com/investors/presentations.html.

Anheuser-Busch InBev SEC filings (various). www.sec.gov.

"Anheuser-Busch Offers Northern Californians a Native Brew; Pacific Ridge Pale Ale Was Created by California Brewmasters for California Beer Drinkers." Anheuser-Busch press release. November 11, 1996.

Anheuser-Busch SEC filings (various).

"Anheuser-Busch to Introduce American Originals Family of Beers." Anheuser-Busch press release. September 28. 1995.

"Award Winners." World Beer Cup website. www.worldbeercup.org/winners/award-winners.

"Bourbon County Coffee 2015—Gusher?" BeerAdvocate forum thread started by "siege06nd." December 5, 2015. www.beeradvocate.com/community/threads/bourbon-county-coffee-2015-gusher.361997.

Brewery production rankings. *New Brewer*, various years.

Craft Brew Alliance SEC filings (various).

"Elephant Red Beer from Specialty Brewing Group of Anheuser-Busch, Inc. Thunders into National Distribution." Anheuser-Busch press release. May 15, 1995.

"Elk Mountain Amber Ale and Elk Mountain Red Lager to go National Dec. 12." Anheuser-Busch press release. December 8, 1994.

Festival of Wood and Barrel Aged Beer, 2012 program.

"Fobab 2012 Results." BeerDownload.com. Posted by matt@beerdownload.com. November 17, 2012. www.beerdownload.com/wordpress/2012/11/17/fobab-results.

"From Chicago, Goose Island Migrates Across America; In a Phased National Launch, Four Goose Island Beers Are Now Available on Draught, with Bottles Coming to Consumers Nationally This Spring." Anheuser-Busch press release. February 7, 2013.

"GABF Winners." Great American Beer Festival website. www.greatamericanbeerfestival.com/the-competition/winners.

Goose Island newsletter. *The Honker*, vol. 3. 1998.

"Goose Island Ten Hills." Homebrew Talk forum thread started by "tagz." December 7, 2013. www.homebrewtalk.com/forum/threads/goose-island-ten-hills.446656.

Hack, Jonathan. "About Us." The Beer Necessities website. https://thebeernecessities.com/about-us.

"Historical U.S. Brewery Count." Brewers Association website. www.brewersassociation.org/statistics/number-of-breweries.

"History of the Group." Smurfit Kappa website. www.smurfitkappa.com/vHome/com/AboutUs/Pages/History.aspx.

Holmes, Jed S. "An Open Letter to Wicked Weed." www.wickedweedsoldout.com.

Howat, James, and Sarah Howat. "Thoughts on the Wicked Weed Acquisition." Black Project Spontaneous & Wild Ales website. May 3, 2017. www.blackprojectbeer.com/report/thoughts-on-the-wicked-weed-acquisition.

"Justice Department Files Antitrust Lawsuit Challenging Anheuser-Busch InBev's Proposed Acquisition of Grupo Modelo." US Department of Justice press release. January 31, 2013. www.justice.gov/opa/pr/justice-department-files-antitrust-lawsuit-challenging-anheuser-busch-inbev-s-proposed.

"Justice Department Reaches Settlement with Anheuser-Busch InBev and Grupo Modelo in Beer Case." US Justice Department press release. April 19, 2013. www.justice.gov/opa/pr/justice-department-reaches-settlement-anheuser-busch-inbev-and-grupo-modelo-beer-case.

"Lactobacillus Acetotolerans—A New Beer Spoiler?" PIKA Weihenstephan website. http://pika-weihenstephan.de/en/the-challenge-lactobacillus-acetotolerans.

"The Long View," Beer Marketer's Insights, 2015.

Metzger, Margot Knight. "Statement on the Sale of Wicked Weed Brewing." North Carolina Craft Brewers Guild. May 3, 2017. https://ncbeer.org/2017/statement-sale-wicked-weed-brewing.

"Ninkasi Brewing Company Announces New, Independent Wholesale Partners in Downstate Oregon and Western Washington." Company press release. January 13, 2015.

"Our Company History." Mendocino Brewing Co. website. www.mendobrew.com/aboutus/history.html.

Plachy, Jim. *Goose Island Meltdown* (Tumblr blog). http://gooseislandmeltdown-blog-blog.tumblr.com.

"The President's News Conference with Prime Minister David Cameron of the United Kingdom." July 20, 2010. www.presidency.ucsb.edu/ws/index.php?pid=88212.

"SEC Charges Anheuser-Busch InBev with Violating FCPA and Whistleblower Protection Laws." US Securities and Exchange Commission press release. September 28, 2016. www.sec.gov/news/pressrelease/2016-196.html.

Stuffings, Jeffrey. "On the Wicked Weed Brewing Purchase." Jester King Brewery website. May 3, 2017. http://jesterkingbrewery.com/on-wicked-weed-brewing.

"Union Beverage Company Sells Distribution Rights for Goose Island and Grolsch for $9.1 Million." Glazer's Distributors of Illinois press release. June 15, 2006.

"U.S V. Anehuser-Busch InBev SA/NV and SABMiller PLC" (various). US Department of Justice. Updated September 15, 2017. www.justice.gov/atr/case/us-v-anheuser-busch-inbev-sanv-and-sabmiller-plc.

Usry, J. Todd. "A Letter from Your Friends at Breckenridge Brewery." Breckinridge Brewery website. December 22, 2015. www.breckbrew.com/blog/a-letter-from-your-friends-at-breckenridge-brewery.

"Wicked Weed Brewing Brings Flavor and Funk to The High End." Anheuser-Busch press release. May 3, 2017.

Note: Goose Island sales data sourced from Beer Marketer's Insights and IRI, which surveys grocery, convenience, big box, and drugstores; if draft beer and liquor store sales were included, Goose Island sales—and in some cases, sales rank—would be higher. Production figures supplied by John Hall and Beer Marketer's Insights.

Index